Theory of Language

Theory of Language

Steven E. Weisler ■ **Slavko Milekic**

A Bradford Book

The MIT Press

Cambridge, Massachusetts

London, England

This book was designed and set into type by Ellen Rooney, and printed and bound in the United States of America.

Library of Congress Cataloging-in-Publication Data

Weisler, Steven.
    Theory of language / Steven Weisler, Slavko Milekić.
        p.   cm.
    "A Bradford Book."
    Includes bibliographical references (p.   ) and index.
    ISBN 0-262-73125-8 (pbk. : alk. paper)
    1. Linguistics. 2. Language and languages. I. Milekić, Slavoljub P., 1955– .
II. Title.
P121.W427   1999
410'.1 — dc21   99-44297
Second printing, 2001   CIP

Contents

List of Authors xi
Preface xiii
Note to the Teacher xv

Chapter 1: Introduction

1.1 The Pervasiveness of Language 1

1.2 The Central Role of Language 2

1.3 Homo Loquens 2

1.4 Language and Thought 3

1.5 Language and Society 4

1.6 Dialects and Status 7

1.7 The Power of Language 9

1.8 Expressiveness 9

1.9 The Longest Sentence 9

1.10 Novelty 10

1.11 How Many Sentences Are There? 10

1.12 The Specialness of Linguistic Knowledge 10

1.13 The Poverty of the Stimulus 11

1.14 Errors in the Data 11

1.15 Language Learning and Imitation 13

1.16 Learning without Evidence 13

1.17 Tacit Knowledge 15

1.18 Summary 16

Chapter 2: Sounds

2.1 The Representation of Sounds 17

2.2 More on Aspiration 19

2.3 Articulatory Phonetics 20

2.4 Voiced Sounds   22

2.5 Bilabials   24

2.6 Alveolars   26

2.7 Velars   26

2.8 Fricatives   27

2.9 Inter-dentals   28

2.10 Alveolar Fricatives   28

2.11 Alveo-palatal Fricatives   28

2.12 Other Alveolar Sounds   29

2.13 Glides   29

2.14 English Vowels   31

2.15 Front Vowels   31

2.16 Back Vowels   32

2.17 Diphthongs   33

2.18 The Vowel Triangle   33

2.19 The Consonant Chart   34

2.20 The Phonetic Alphabet   35

2.21 Beyond Phonetics   35

2.22 Aspiration Revisited   37

2.23 The Aspiration Rule   41

2.24 Prefixes and Aspiration   45

2.25 Vowel Lengthening   51

2.26 Rule Ordering   52

2.27 Morphemes and Lengthening   53

2.28 The Schwa   55

Chapter 3: Words

3.1 Lexical Knowledge   61

3.2 Do Words Exist?   62

3.3 Lexical Access   65

3.4 Lexical Decision   65

3.5 Lexical Entries   66

3.6 The Size of the Lexicon   68

3.7 Lexical Productivity   71

3.8 Morphological Processes   72

3.9 Derivational Morphology   79

3.10 Productivity   80

3.11 Some Complications   81

3.12 Rule Interactions   83

3.13 Inflectional Morphology   86

3.14 Inflection and Derivation   88

3.15 Compounds   89

3.16 Identifying Compounds   90

3.17 Lexical Meaning   92

3.18 Thematic Roles   94

3.19 Feature Representation   96

3.20 Lexical Items   97

3.21 Morpho-phonemics   99

3.22 More Past Forms   103

3.23 The Plural Revisited   108

3.24 A Third Plural   110

3.25 Morpho-syntax   111

3.26 Lexical Features   112

3.27 Lexical Dependencies   114

3.28 Number Agreement   115

3.29 Pronouns and Case   116

3.30 Morphological Gender   118

3.31 Person, Number, and Pronouns   121

Chapter 4: Sentences

4.1 From Word to Sentence   125

4.2 The Case of *That*   130

4.3 Syntactic Representation   133

4.4 Parts of Speech   136

4.5 Categories and Rules   139

4.6 Constituents   142

4.7 Tests for Constituency   146

4.8 From Rule to Tree   151

4.9 Binary Branching   153

4.10 Syntactic Ambiguity   157

4.11 Subordination   160

4.12 Subcategorization   165

4.13 Modifiers   166

4.14 More Modifiers   172

4.15 Specifiers   174

4.16 Case   180

4.17 Theta Checking   184

4.18 Displacement   188

4.19 Generalizing the Problem   190

4.20 Approaches to Displacement   193

4.21 Lexicalism and A'-displacement   197

4.22 Transformations and A'-displacement   200

4.23 Bounding Theory   204

4.24 Binding Theory   208

4.25 Ellipsis   213

4.26 Universal Grammar   214

4.27 Principles and Parameters   220

Chapter 5: Meaning

5.1 Language and Meaning   227

5.2 The Nature of Meaning   229

5.3 Extending the Model   231

5.4 Conjunction and Disjunction   235

5.5 Complex Sentences and Ambiguity   238

5.6 Tense and Possible Worlds   241

5.7 Names and Descriptions   243

5.8 Meaning and Reference   245

5.9 Names and Substitutivity   246

5.10 Sense   249

5.11 Sense and Substitutivity   252

5.12 Sense and Possible Worlds   253

5.13 Quantification   257

5.14 Quantification in English   258

5.15 Quantifier Scope   260

5.16 Analyzing Scope   261

5.17 English Scope Ambiguity   266

5.18 Restrictions on Scope   268

5.19 Wh-quantifiers   270

5.20 Summary   271

Chapter 6: Brain and Language

6.1 What Is Neurolinguistics?   273

6.2 Neural Structures Supporting Language Functions   276

6.3 Neurolinguistic Methods of Study   280

6.4 Brain and Language   280

6.5 Broca's Discovery   282

6.6 Wernicke's Model   283

6.7 Learning from Brain Damage   287

6.8 Modern Techniques   287

6.9 Lateralization of Function   295

6.10 Unit of Localization   296

6.11 Early Classifications   296

6.12 Clinical Classifications   297

6.13 Luria's Model   300

6.14 Neurology and Linguistics   301

6.15 Summary   303

Glossary   *305*
Bibliography   *331*
Index   *339*

List of Authors

Steven E. Weisler

M.A. in Speech Communication (Case Western Reserve University) and Ph.D. in Linguistics (Stanford University). Director of Cognitive Science, Professor of Linguistics, and Director of the Innovative Instruction Laboratory in the School of Cognitive Science, Hampshire College. Research and publications in syntax and semantics. Coorganizer of the 1993 national workshop on undergraduate cognitive science, funded by the National Science Foundation. Editor of *Theory of Language* and primary author of chapters 1, 2, 3, 4, and 5.

Slavko Milekic

Slavko Milekic holds both a medical degree (Belgrade School of Medicine) and a Ph.D. in Psychology (University of Connecticut). Associate Professor of Cognitive Science & Digital Interface Design at The University of the Arts. Among other activities, he taught neurolinguistics and the psychology of human/computer interaction in the School of Cognitive Science at Hampshire College. Dr. Milekic is currently engaged in the design of computer-based neuropsychological tests and building digital interfaces for very young children. Primary author of chapter 6 and designer of the interface for *Theory of Language: CD-ROM Edition*.

Preface

Theory of Language was originally conceived as a CD-ROM-based introduction to linguistic theory with the aim of providing students with a "digital learning environment" in which to investigate linguistic theory. Our goal was to develop an application that encouraged exploration, hypothesis testing, argumentation, and lively discussion; critical ingredients in an inquiry-based approach to teaching science. We also shared the conviction that presenting real data, demonstrating actual results, and challenging students to build their own analyses would be facilitated by the tools available in the multimedia repertoire, helping to make more apparent what it is that fascinates linguists about language and theory.

As this project developed, we engaged many of the fundamental questions that all textbook authors consider: How should the material be organized? What level of difficulty should we seek? How do we present analyses that seem to change in the time it takes to write about them? Because we were working in a computational environment, novel solutions to familiar problems sometimes emerged, and many of these ideas suggested new ways to approach the design of a conventional textbook as well. For example, the availability of hypertext in multimedia applications encouraged us to write the text on several levels, with historical context, conflicting analyses, and in-depth discussions running parallel to the "main" discussion. The desire to promote interaction between the student and the program led us to make broad use of questions based on linguistic data; to provide a rich, easily accessed glossary; and to alter the rhetorical style of the text so that it did less telling and more showing.

The book you hold in your hand is the result of incorporating the materials and pedagogical strategies developed for *Theory of Language: CD-ROM Edition* into a (somewhat unconventional) textbook. The book is designed to be used either on its own, or in conjunction with the electronic version. Both contain the complete text, along with questions, and a glossary (although digital edition adds expert interviews, a tree building and analysis module, a transcription tutorial, and other electronic features). The text is designed for beginning- and intermediate-level undergraduate classes in linguistic theory, but with a judicious selection of the more advanced materials presented in the "In Detail" commentaries, the level of presentation can be adjusted in either direction to a considerable degree.

1. Introduction

1.1 The Pervasiveness of Language

How many social activities can you think of that do not involve language in any way? It is difficult to think of many examples, because language is a part of virtually every aspect of human interaction. Whether we are reading the newspaper, giving a speech, conversing, listening to the lyrics of a song, or muttering to ourselves, we use language. Some researchers have even suggested that our thoughts are cast in terms of the language we speak (Whorf 1956; Bloom 1981; see also Fodor 1975:56).

Precisely because language is pervasive, it seems an unlikely candidate for scholarly inquiry. We tend to take our linguistic ability for granted, scarcely noticing its nature or use. However, as cognitive scientists have discovered, the investigation of an organism's most basic abilities and skills often lends the greatest insights into its nature (Chomsky 1968:24). In this spirit, we note that normal bodily functions such as respiration, digestion, and circulation are central topics for biologists.

The study of language is also motivated by an even more compelling consideration: Language may distinguish humans from all other organisms (Chomsky 1968:6). Consequently, by studying language we hope to uncover some of the fundamental properties of human nature. One of our goals in this inquiry is to determine the most fruitful theoretical perspectives and best analytic methods to advance our investigation.

What would you consider to be some other "basic" properties of human beings? Are any of these so important that an organism lacking them would not count as human?

How many academic disciplines that you are familiar with are concerned with the study of language? Can you list some of these for which matters of language are particularly important?

IN DETAIL 1.1

People often report that they think in the language that they speak. But the concept of thinking itself needs clarification before we can evaluate this claim. Thinking crucially involves unconscious operations. Consequently, we do not have introspective access to our thought processes. We should not expect to be any more aware of the essential nature of our cognition than of our internal digestive processes. Perhaps thoughts are merely translated into a linguistic form as they make their way into consciousness. Thus, the so-called "language of thought" may be *nonisomorphic* to linguistic representation (see Fodor 1975).

In this view, thoughts, which may be initially represented quite differently from language, are given linguistic form; for example, when they are expressed. This analysis leaves open the question of whether, and to what extent, people who speak different languages think differently, a position sometimes known as the Whorfian Hypothesis (see Caroll 1956; Bloom 1981). ■

Early twentieth-century linguists and psychologists frequently championed the position that thought and language are intertwined. For example, Edward Sapir argued that thoughts require language in order to be thinkable (Sapir 1921:15); and Ferdinand de Saussure, claimed that thought without language is inchoate (de Saussure 1959:113). Perhaps the most well-known linguist to propound the view that the language we speak influences our thinking was B.L. Whorf (see Caroll 1956). Whorf argued that different languages provide their speakers with radically different sets of conceptual categories *(linguistic relativity),* and that the character of one's experience of the world depends on the nature of these interpretive categories *(linguistic determinism).*

Whorf believed that languages like English, French, and German (which he counted among the "S(tandard) A(verage) E(uropean)" languages) were structurally similar enough to one another that they did not entail different conceptual schemes. But his study of American Indian languages like Hopi, Apache, Navajo, and Nootka persuaded him that these languages offered their speakers very different conceptual systems than did any of the SAE languages. Most linguists of the two decades following Whorf's writings ultimately failed to be persuaded by his arguments. Questions about methodology, argumentation, and data analysis were raised that seriously undermined his conclusions. In addition, more and more researchers became convinced that the extent to which languages differed from one another had been exaggerated by previous work (Whorf's included), and that a more fruitful basis for the study of language would be established by searching for universal linguistic properties rather than for distinguishing characteristics.

Nevertheless, Whorf's work continues to be very controversial to this day (Pullum 1991; Gumperz and Levinson 1996), and students of linguistics continue to be drawn to the questions Whorf considered with great enthusiasm. ■

1.5 Language and Society

What do people's speech styles tell you about their schooling? About their credibility, or about the likelihood that you will become close friends? About their trustworthiness? We frequently make important judgments about other people on the basis of their speech style, rendering instant and far reaching decisions about a speaker's linguistic competence, social class, education level, and intellect. Many of us presume that we can judge correct speech (even though we believe that we, ourselves, fall short of "perfect" English).

But does the idea of a proper English withstand closer scrutiny? Which of the following examples strike you as correct English?

1. Just between you and I, Jim won.
2. Just between you and me, Jim won.
3. Who are you talking to?
4. Whom are you talking to?
5. To whom are you talking?
6. Whom shall I say is calling?
7. I was like, Oh my god!
8. I do no diligence to shewe craft, but o sentence.

Do you have an accent? Are there any speakers who do not have an accent?

Judgments about linguistic style often turn on rather subtle features of language; the vocabulary, sentence structure, and pronunciation all play a role in the evaluation. Here, for example, is a piece of a transcript taken from an interview with a middle-aged, working-class male from Western Massachusetts:

Yeah, come right out of school and went into plumbing…

This sentence lacks a subject in a declarative sentence (*I* is understood), something not possible in many dialects of English. Although so-called *pro-drop* languages, for example, Hebrew and Spanish, generally employ subjectless declaratives, many dialects of English generally require subjects in such cases.

Ahavti yalda (Hebrew)
liked   girl
I liked a girl.

Vimos a Juan (Spanish)
saw to Juan
We saw Juan.

Finally, the verb *come,* although ostensibly in the past tense, is uninflected for tense. In many dialects of English, only *came* would be possible in this construction.

These sorts of variations often lead us to categorize people in terms of race, class, and socioeconomic status. Some of these linguistic features have taken on a stigmatized status, the *come/came* substitution being a case in point. ■

The key question is, of course, What counts as correct speech? We can complicate the question by asking who is speaking or being spoken to (that is, "correct" in which *speech community?*), in what circumstances the speech is taking place (you do not speak to parents the same way you speak to friends), when the speech took place (is Shakespearean English correct today?), what the purpose of the speech is, and whether it is being uttered or written down. For example, some English-speakers raised in Boston pronounce *forties* as "fawties," whereas speakers who grew up in Cleveland tend to pronounce their rs in most words. Students of the English of the 10th century must treat it as a foreign language, while Chaucer looks much more familiar, and Shakespeare, writing in the middle of the sixteenth century, seems mostly accessible:

Faeder ure thu the eart on heofonum, si thin nama gehalgod. (First line of the Lord's prayer, West Saxon Gospel of St. Matthew, about 1000 AD.)

Pardee, hit oghte thee to lyke; for hard langage and hard matere is encombrous for to here at ones… (Geoffrey Chaucer, *House of Fame,* late 1300's AD.)

Now pile your dust upon the quick and the dead, til of this a flat mountain you have made… (Shakespeare, *Hamlet,* late 16th Century)

In short, the question of linguistic correctness turns out to be a thorny one. The literature is full of commentary and advice from those who see themselves as upholding linguistic standards *(prescriptive linguists).* However, many modern linguists ignore these issues claiming that English, like any natural language, is a dynamic, variegated system with no one standard form. These so-called *descriptive linguists* tend to pursue a set of questions more deeply rooted in the connections between language and learning.

PRO 1.5

Why does language keep changing? Because it is a living thing, people will tell you. Something that you cannot press forever, like a dead flower, between the pages of a dictionary. Rather, it is a living organism that, like a live plant, sprouts new leaves and flowers. Alas, this lovely albeit trite image is — as I have said before and wish now to say with even greater emphasis — largely nonsense. Language, for the most part, changes out of ignorance. Certainly new words can become needed, and a happy invention or slang can sometimes supply useful, though thoroughly perishable, synonyms. But by and large, linguistic changes are caused by the ignorance of speakers and writers, and in the last few centuries — given our schools, dictionaries, and books on grammar — such ignorance could have been, like the live nettle or poison ivy it is, uprooted. (Simon 1976)

Linguistic change is first manifest in small degrees of variation that may eventually lead to wholesale changes in pronunciation, word meaning, and sentence structure. Can this change be controlled? Can we understand its causes and predict its direction? And, perhaps most importantly, is the change for the better or the worse? John Simon claims that most linguistic changes derive from ignorance, and to the extent that such change moves us further from correct English, it should be prevented. ∎

CON 1.5

How can we determine the correctness of language? Is there some independent measure of expressiveness or communicative efficiency (or any other function of language) that we can use to evaluate different speech styles? Can we identify a standard against which speech can be measured? Many critics fall back on an accepted form of the language that is taken to be the norm — Standard English, in the case of English. And by "Standard English" is meant some version of middle-class English, more or less as codified in dictionaries and grammar books. However, the linguist William Labov (1972) offers a less charitable evaluation of middle-class English:

The highest proportion of well-formed sentences are found in casual speech, and working-class speakers use more well-formed sentences than middle-class speakers…It is true that technical and scientific books are written in a style which is markedly 'middle-class'. But unfortunately, we often fail to achieve the explicitness and precision which we look for in such writing; and the speech of many middle-class people departs maximally from this target. All too often, 'standard English' is represented by a style that is simultaneously over-particular and vague. The accumulating flow of words buries rather than strikes the target. It is this verbosity which is most easily taught and most easily learned, so that words take the place of thought, and nothing can be found behind them.

Furthermore, mere dialect differences are often mistaken for incorrect usage. For instance, some speakers from the Boston area pronounce words like *Saturday* without sounding an *r* in the second syllable. Is this a mistaken pronunciation? Notice, for example, that such speakers do pronounce some *r*s (i.e., at the beginnings of words, as in *rationing*). Moreover, the pronunciation of *r* in such dialects is far from haphazard, although it may follow a different pattern than that followed in most standard dialects.

There is, finally, no evidence that dialect differences impede communication or limit expressiveness within a single dialect group. Ultimately, "standard" English is a social construction determined by what is deemed prestigious, reflecting class and power structures rather than any linguistic truth. ∎

There is a long history of scholars and literary figures worrying about the degeneration of language. For example, Johnathan Swift was known to fret that English was turning into a dialect of French (at the same time that the French Academy feared that French was becoming too much like English). More recently, journalist Edwin Newman and playwright Jean Stafford have lamented the direction of linguistic change, Stafford, in particular, arguing that English was turning into "anthropoidese." It is clear, however, that English has been changing continuously since its beginnings in the seventh century; now Modern English speakers can scarcely make out a word of the English of Beowulf, so great are the changes in vocabulary, sentence structure, and pronunciation.

It is thus difficult to imagine how a single snapshot of English can be justifiably claimed to represent "correct" English. When critics say that the language is deteriorating, their complaint can be best understood to register their distress that some of the language they hear is different from what they expect to hear. Although this kind of intergenerational linguistic change often draws notice, there is no evidence that it produces any deterioration. ■

Selection from *Beowulf*.

**Da com of more under mist-hleoþum
Grendel gogan, Godes yrre baer;
mynte se man-scaða manna cynnes
sumne besyrwan in sele þam hean
Wod under wolcum to þaes þeh win-reced,
gold-sele gumena, gearwost wisse,
fættum fahne.**

Translation:

Then up from the marsh, under misty cliffs, Grendel came walking; he bore God's wrath. The evil thief had planned to trap some human, one of man's kind, in the towering hall. Under dark skies he came till he saw the shining wine-hall, house of gold-giving, a joy to men, plated high with gold. (Chickering 1989:88-91)

1.6 Dialects and Status

One way to appreciate the subtleties involved in making judgments of linguistic correctness is to consider the status of *African-American English* (*AAE* — sometimes referred to as *Black English Vernacular*). One of the often noted features of AAE is the frequent absence of the verb *to be*. The following examples from Labov 1972 illustrate this phenomenon.

1. We on tape
2. He gon' try to get up
3. They not caught

Do these examples reveal a "primitive notion of the structure of the language" and "a badly connected series of words and phrases" as some prescriptive grammarians have claimed (Bereiter et al. 1966); or is AAE a *dialect* (or a group of dialects) of English?

The first thing to notice is that many attested dialects of English

What is acceptable in a language changes over time. Can you list some of the linguistic innovations of the last few years in your speech group that you think may "make it" into the language? Try to think of some examples that concern aspects of language other than vocabulary.

allow the *contraction* of the verb *to be* in the same set of circumstances in which a speaker of AAE might omit it:

4. We're on tape.
5. He's gon' try to get up.
6. They're not caught.

Furthermore, in constructions such as those illustrated in (7) and (8) in which contraction is not permitted, speakers of AAE will not omit *to be* (see examples (9–10)). An asterisk before an example means it is not well formed. (Examples are from Labov 1972.)

7. Here I am. ≠ *Here I'm.
8. What is it? ≠ *What's it?
9. *Here I.
10. *What it?

How do we know when it is possible to contract and when it is not? We will maintain that speakers learn a set of rules and principles that guide their linguistic behavior. Consequently, there must be a rule that determines when contraction is possible. Similarly, speakers of AAE follow a rule that governs where the verb *to be* may be absent that seems to apply in the same types of sentences as contraction does. As linguists, we are interested in describing the patterns of language, and in this particular case, the interesting pattern of the comings and goings of the verb *to be*. So when we present a rule — the rule for contraction in your dialect of English, for example — it is not promoted as a rule you should follow, but rather as a rule you <u>do</u> follow.

We view the language a person speaks as a naturally occurring phenomenon to be understood, rather than as a condition to be remediated. The incorrect underestimation of AAE stems from the mistake of judging a speaker's linguistic behavior by the rules of a different dialect. As linguists, if we find a group of speakers who don't follow a certain linguistic rule, we change the rule to improve our description, rather than attempt to

---

IN DETAIL 1.6

The process of contraction fuses certain sequences of words into a single word, with the omission of some of the sounds in the input. In the English spelling system, contractions are typically marked with an apostrophe. Although most English contractions involve two input words, examples such as *I'dve* (as in *I'dve tried harder if I could have*) start with three inputs — *I, would,* and *have.* There are several different kinds of contraction phenomena in English, as the following examples illustrate:

1. I'm   (= I am)
2. I'll   (= I will)
3. Bill's   (= Bill is)
4. you'd   (= you would)
5. you're   (= you are)
6. didn't   (= did not)
7. can't   (= cannot)
8. wanna   (= want to)

Examples (1) through (5) involve auxiliary contraction, (6) through (7) are cases of negative contraction, and (8) shows an instance of so-called *wanna*-contraction.

Although each example involves some omitted material, there are important differences among them. For example, auxiliary contraction is generally blocked at the ends of sentences, whereas negative and *wanna*-contractions are not:

9. You are not happy but I am (*I'm).
10. I ate the cabbages but you did not (didn't).
11. I did the dishes even though I didn't want to (wanna).

Contraction is best thought of as a kind of linguistic rule with some fairly subtle complexities, rather than a haphazard process of casually leaving something out. ■

change speakers' behavior. In this regard, a linguistic rule is like any other scientific principle.

1.7 The Power of Language

As anyone who has tried to learn a foreign language knows, languages are simultaneously organized on many levels. To learn a second language, you must learn the sounds, the vocabulary (including how to pronounce words both in isolation and in sentences), and how to form sentences. Even short sentences require considerable analysis.

One frequently hears the homily that sloppy speech makes for sloppy thought. How would you evaluate this conjecture in the light of the present discussion?

1.8 Expressiveness

Language is an amazingly flexible tool that allows us a vast range of expressiveness. We can talk about what might have been the case, what is false, what we would have done if things had been different, and even about what we do not understand. Some psychologists argue that this powerful capacity for linguistic categorization underlies our ability to think abstractly (for example, Vygotsky 1962:51). In contrast, other organism's *communication systems* are more limited. For most animals, the content of their signals is restricted by what seems to be true, by the here and now, and by a stereotypical repertoire.

Can you think of some animal communication systems that illustrate these systematic restrictions? Can you think of any systems that seem to be as unrestricted as human language (in the relevant ways)?

1.9 The Longest Sentence

One of the properties of language that underlies this expressiveness and power is its unboundedness. Consider how long the longest English sentence can be. We all know that there are unremarkable sentences that span many clauses, but is there an absolute limit — a point beyond which a string of words ceases to be English simply because it is too long?

One way to pursue this question is to start with a sentence like *I know that 1 isn't the largest number and I know that 2 isn't the largest number (...)* and to consider how long you could continue in this vein. Apparently, there is no longest English sentence! Notice, for example, that the sentence below can be repeatedly extended by adding more phrases to the end of it. The result may be clumsy or redundant, but still, arguably, a sentence of English:

> Our backs were to the wall, and you were next, and the results would soon be clear, and Mary knew that we gave it our all, and...

It may be protested that strings so long that they could not be produced or understood in a lifetime cannot be considered part of a language, since they are not part of the ability of any real speaker of the language. Discuss this objection.

1.10 Novelty

In order for the unbounded character of language to be fully exploited, speakers must be able to readily produce and interpret original utterances. Notice that you have no difficulty understanding a rather lengthy sentence even though you may have never heard it before. In fact, the vast majority of sentences you hear and produce each day are novel utterances — utterances that have never been uttered in exactly the same way in your experience.

1.11 How Many Sentences Are There?

We have discovered that there is no longest English sentence, and that any fluent English speaker is capable of producing and comprehending entirely novel utterances.

The ability to speak English is a *creative* process of great power and range. In fact, it follows from our observations that English has an infinite number of sentences, and that perfectly average speakers of English have an infinite linguistic capacity. How do we represent the rules and principles that allow us to engage in the infinity of language? How do we learn an infinitely large language in a finite length of time? These are two of the central questions addressed by the study of linguistics.

At the heart of the analysis of linguistic creativity is the notion that speakers make infinite use of finite means, and that "new" utterances can be constructed out of familiar parts. Does this take on creativity explain other creative processes (like art or music)? Why or why not?

1.12 The Specialness of Linguistic Knowledge

How many tasks can you think of that are easier for a young child to accomplish than for you? Although you are the better bet for most tasks, children between the ages of six months and puberty have a special ability to learn language in ways which are not fully available to adults. In the normal course of development, children are called upon to determine the rules and structures of their native language on the basis of exposure to a linguistic environment called the *primary linguistic data.* Included in this input typically are the utterances of parents, siblings, and other members of the speech community. The child's mission is to extrapolate the knowledge of his or her language from this experience. We are particularly interested in determining to what extent language learning depends on the richness of the input and to what extent the resulting knowledge of language depends on the ability of the child to learn in this domain.

One approach is to look carefully at some of the characteristics of the information that is available to the child as a way of determin-

It is sometimes contended that children have an easier time with language than adults because their minds are freer, or less "full." Does this seem persuasive? Can this hypothesis explain why language learning (but not, say, long division) falls within a young child's competence?

ing just how rich the language-learning environment is. The three-part argument from the *poverty of the stimulus* (the stimulus is the information on the basis of which the child learns language) suggests that there are important shortcomings in the primary linguistic data that the child must cope with and ultimately overcome in order to acquire a native language.

1.13 The Poverty of the Stimulus

Although both important ingredients involved in language acquisition — the child's information-processing abilities and information presented to him or her — deserve careful investigation, researchers have taken rather different positions on which of these domains (roughly, *nature* or *nurture*) plays the most interesting role in the process.

HISTORY 1.13

The nature-nurture debate centers on a dispute about the degree to which an organism's development is shaped by the environment, and the degree to which it is a consequence of the organism's essential nature. This debate is at least as old as the writings of Plato: in the *Meno,* he writes of a slave who discovers principles of geometry without the benefit of direct instruction. This kind of knowledge, Plato argues, is grounded in the nature of reason rather than in one's experience in the world. Building on a position developed in the early 1960s, linguists have argued that in the same vein, the ability to learn a native language depends on a mental faculty arising as a consequence of human nature. One of the central tasks of linguistics is to determine the nature of this mental endowment, and to investigate the role that it plays in the course of language acquisition. ■

1.14 Errors in the Data

The first argument from the poverty of the stimulus concerns the quality of the data presented to a language learner. To better understand this issue, imagine a simple experiment: you are watching the trial of a game that you have never played before, the object of which is to move one of your pieces to the far end of the board. Your goal is to try to figure out the rules. Suppose further that some small but significant percentage of the time, the players make illegal moves (say, because they aren't paying close enough attention). Under these circumstances, imagine how difficult it would be to learn the rules of this game.

Children learning language are faced with the same sort of problem: some of the examples of the language they hear contain (inadvertent) mistakes. Here is an example of a short transcript of running speech that illustrates this point:

> I think that some of my favorite times when I was a kid growing up was the the movies on Saturday afternoon. They always had this matinee — Lash Larue — or somebody. And, um, ah, during World War II, I think we had to collect, ah, we didn't have to actually pay to get in to the movies…What we did was we collected, ah, metal for the war drive, uh, steel hub caps, or something like that…take them down to the movie theater, put them in big piles, as we went, and, um, tsk, and we got to see a free movie.
> [Mistakes are underlined]

Can you conjecture why each of the errors was made in this example? How many different kinds of errors are represented here?

No doubt the current example is not representative of the kind of language we typically use with young children. But there are many mistakes that often find their way into our speech. Wandering attention or failing to find the right word can result in *slips of the tongue* or other *performance errors*. Notice that we do not conclude that a speaker who makes these kinds of errors does not know the language. Indeed, such speakers often notice performance errors even as they produce them (and certainly would label them as errors if called to their attention). It is just that one's *linguistic competence* (language ability) is not always faithfully manifested in *linguistic performance* (language use).

During language acquisition, to the extent that the primary linguistic data include performance errors, the task of learning a language is especially complicated. We can think of the child as a kind of language-acquisition device, and language learning as a procedure that extrapolates linguistic competence on the basis of the available input combined with special principles for analyzing and processing this input. Since the primary linguistic data cannot be taken at face value, these principles must support language learning despite the impoverished nature of the input. In the end, children succeed in learning language in the face of many complicating conditions. For example, even if a child is called upon to learn two or more languages simultaneously, until the circumstance is recognized for what it is, every sentence, word, or sound of one language is at risk for being construed as relevant to the other language. Perhaps surprisingly, children do quite well in this learning environment.

1.15 Language Learning and Imitation

To approach the second argument from the poverty of the stimulus, consider the following examples that illustrate the behavior of a new arithmetic operator, Δ.

See if you can fill in the answer to the following problem. (Hint: the answer is a one-digit number.)

   1 Δ 10 = ?

Notice that you cannot just memorize the right answer (see below); you have to figure it out. Learning involves more than merely committing a set of examples to memory; it involves deducing a rule or principle that allows you to project the proper behavior of Δ beyond the given examples. In this case, the result of applying the Δ operator is calculated in two steps. First, add the two arguments to Δ together, and then add the digits of the sum together:

   A. 1 + 10 = 11
   B. 1 + 1 = 2

So:

   1 Δ 10 = 2

As we shall see, language learning involves the same kind of projection problem, and it requires a similar ability to extrapolate complicated generalizations from limited evidence.

Two simple arguments support this conclusion. First, we have seen that there are an infinite number of sentences in English (or any other natural language). Consequently, although your knowledge of language must take the form of a finite system based on a finite amount of experience, it must provide the resources for an infinite language. Memorization and imitation are not powerful enough to account for a learning task of this magnitude. Second, even at early stages of language development, and continuing on throughout life, language learners produce *novel utterances*. This creative aspect of language cannot be accounted for by imitation or any other model that depends on copying one's verbal repertoire from the primary linguistic data.

1.16 Learning without Evidence

The third argument from the poverty of the stimulus concerns the many details of a language that a child must master during the

Examples:
1 Δ 0 = 1
1 Δ 2 = 3
14 Δ 5 = 10
9 Δ 3 = 3
93 Δ 9 = 3
1 Δ 9 = 1
34 Δ 5 = 12

process of language development. Let's begin by deciding which of the following examples are *grammatical* English sentences:

1. You saw Bill with who(m)?
2. You saw Bill and who(m)?
3. Who did you see Bill with?
4. Who did you see Bill and?
5. The president called Sam up.
6. The president called up Sam.
7. The president called me up.
8. The president called up me.
9. Selma doesn't get around much anymore.
10. Selma gets around much anymore.

IN DETAIL 1.16

Let us consider more carefully some of the data presented in the main discussion. In the following pair of examples

1. You saw Bill with who(m)?
2. You saw Bill and who(m)?

we find a kind of question sometimes called an echo question (the form of the question word, *who* or *whom,* depends on your dialect). These examples are quite similar in meaning, and (1) is also virtually synonymous with (3).

3. Who(m) did you see Bill with?

The puzzle, then, is why, on analogy, is (2) not interchangeable with (4)?

4. *Whom did you see Bill and?

The apparent analogy between (1) and (3) and (2) and (4) breaks down because, despite their similarities in meaning, (1) and (3) are quite different in structure. Questions in

which the question word is inside a prepositional phrase (like *with who[m]*) have very different properties than questions in which the question word is part of a conjunction (like *and who[m]*). English-speakers must categorize these kinds of examples differently, and language learners must not expect that the alternation between (1) and (3) implies that (4) is an alternative to (2). In a similar vein, although (5) and (6) are synonymous, (7) and (8) are not interchangeable:

5. The president called Sam up.
6. The president called up Sam.
7. The president called him up.
8. *The president called up him.

Here, again, the plausible analogy between the two pairs of examples breaks down. It appears that the privileges of occurrence for the particle *up* depend on whether the object is a pronoun — the verb-

phrase-final position is not possible in the pronoun cases (cf. *The president called up me/you/us/her*).

Finally, although most negative sentences are paralleled by affirmative counterparts (for example, *Selma doesn't get around easily/Selma gets around easily*), (9) is not paralleled by (10):

9. Selma doesn't get around much anymore.
10. *Selma gets around much anymore.

In (10), the *negative polarity item much* is not grammatical in a simple affirmative context; and in most dialects, *anymore* is subject to the same restrictions. As in the previous examples, language learners notice and become appropriately sensitive to these syntactic and semantic distinctions in extrapolating the organization of their language's grammar. ■

This is, of course, a fairly straightforward task, since English-speakers can readily distinguish English sentences from *ungrammatical strings* of English words. Furthermore, we manifest this ability even in the face of ungrammatical strings that we have never before encountered. In some of the more interesting of such cases, children learning English must resist quite concrete analogies that threaten to pull them in the wrong direction, potentially leading to false conclusions about what is possible in the language. Moreover, given a large range of ungrammatical strings, children seem to automatically discount the possibility that they are part of English. They learn what is not possible without any direct evidence to support their conclusions.

Taken together, the arguments from the poverty of the stimulus concern the richness of the linguistic environment that the child draws from when learning a language. These considerations point to certain ways in which the quantity and quality of the available information seems incommensurate with the infinite, creative character of linguistic competence. These considerations also suggest that aspects of the language learner's nature — in this case, information-processing principles that support language development — play an important role in the acquisition process. To the extent that the environment fails to systematically provide and organize relevant linguistic data, language learning requires more than imitation or other strategies that are tied too closely to characteristics of the primary linguistic data.

Although we have been at pains to explain some of the ways in which the learner is not dependent on the details of the primary linguistic data, there are many aspects of one's native language that are direct reflections of this input. Can you list and discuss some of these aspects?

1.17 Tacit Knowledge

We have described the linguistic ability manifested by native speakers of a language in terms of linguistic knowledge. It is clear, however, that this knowledge is special in a number of ways. It is, for example, *tacit knowledge*. Indeed, even the most familiar linguistic paradigms tend to involve details that we are scarcely aware of. As a case in point, consider the process of plural formation in English. What are the plural forms for the words in the first column?

How about the words in the second column? Does this seem like the same question? Although in a sense it is, it will probably surprise you to discover that the plural ending sounds quite different in this set of words than it did in the first one. In the first group the plural ending is the *s*-sound, but in the second block it is the *z*-sound.

book	poem
clock	bill
top	dove
pit	emu

It turns out that some words in English take *z*-plurals and some take *s*-plurals. Furthermore, any native speaker of English somehow knows this complication, or else it would not be possible to systematically produce the correct plural. We can test this claim by providing speakers with a choice of possible plural examples and asking them to choose the right one. One might say that they do not know (consciously) what they know (unconsciously). Such is the status of a great deal of linguistic knowledge.

1.18 Summary

The ability to learn a *natural language* distinguishes humans from other animals, and is normally engaged during the first decade of life during the *critical period* for language acquisition. The linguistic system that develops pervades everyday life, providing for an infinite linguistic capacity and for the essential *creativity* of language. The use of language is sensitive to a variety of social and contextual variables and can be analyzed at many different levels of description. Language learning is also complicated by the problem of the poverty of the stimulus. That is, language development is successful despite errors in the linguistic input, finite input, and an unsystematic exposure to the full range of representative primary linguistic data.

There is a third regular plural ending in English that appears in examples like churches *and* judges. *How would you describe the phonetic difference between this plural form and the z-plural?*

2. Sounds

2.1 The Representation of Sounds

Every native speaker must master the sound system of his or her language. In the case of English, this knowledge includes the pronunciations of English sounds and words, information about intonation and stress, and a grasp of how pronunciations are affected by a variety of other linguistic and nonlinguistic factors. You know, for example, that even though the second *c* in *electrical* and in *electricity* are pronounced differently, the word *electric* is part of both words; or that people from different parts of the English-speaking world may pronounce the same words differently. You also know how to make many subtle discriminations in both sound production and perception; for instance that small differences in pronunciation can make a big difference in meaning (consider *false*

PRO 2.1

Although we often use the word "accent" to refer to speech styles that are different from a perceived norm, it is impossible to speak without an accent! Different dialects of a language tend to differ in a number of ways, but most dramatically in the nature of their sound systems. For example, the "same" word may be pronounced with different vowels (e.g., a Canadian pronunciation of *about* compared with a typical American English one). In other cases, the "same" vowel can be pronounced differently in different dialects. Every speaker of a language speaks at least one dialect of that language; there is no way to speak a language without using one of its dialects. While some speech styles may stand out to a greater degree, and others may be deemed more prestigious or regular, they are each no more and no less than conventional pronunciations adopted by a particular speech group. In short, the only kind of verbal behavior that is accent free is silence. ■

CON 2.1

Although it is technically true that anyone who speaks a language must use a speech style of a particular dialect of that language, all speech styles are not equal. When it comes to rendering the complex social judgments that are typically made about people on the basis of their speech style, speakers often are unconsciously (and sometimes consciously) rated as more or less well educated, more or less intelligent, and more or less desirable as employees according to how they sound. We can see this linguistic hierarchy rendered transparent in the case of German, where one distinguishes the case of High German from "the dialects." Of course, one could point out that High German is a dialect, but that obscures the more important point that certain speech styles are systematically marginalized in the minds of many speakers. Consequently, there is an important sense in which some speech styles are marked as accents, whereas other styles are tacitly taken to be the norm from which other styles vary to some degree. ■

and *falls*). You may also render a range of judgments about another speaker that turn on tiny differences in pronunciation.

Linguists interested in the sound system want to understand how you manage to make speech sounds, represent relevant distinctions, and establish these judgments; in short, what your knowledge of the sound system of your native language consists of, and how it is represented and acquired. As we shall see, much of the information you acquire and apply takes the form of tacit knowledge. As a consequence, you will discover many important discriminations and judgments that you have been making consistently for as long as you have been a fluent speaker of English but that will nevertheless come as a surprise to you. We have already considered the case of the polymorphous English plural, so let us briefly examine some other examples to underscore the character of the sound system.

Consider the pronunciations of *bit* and *bid*. Although we think about the *vowels* in both examples as being the same, in fact the vowel in *bid* is about twice as long as the vowel in *bit*, as indicated by these *spectrograms* (a representation of the acoustic signal in terms of frequency [corresponding more or less to pitch] and energy level [corresponding more or less to loudness]).

The difference in vowel length in these cases is not unique. The *i*-sounds in the words in the first column, below, are generally short, like the vowel in *bit*, and those in the second column are long, like that in *bid*.

Short	Long
rip	pig
pick	give
gif	his
pith	rib
hiss	pill

Although English-speakers are quite systematic about vowel length in these cases, few are aware of the variation. There is, furthermore, a large and interesting number of similar phenomena involved in the sound system of any natural language. To take just one more example from English, consider the pronunciation of *pop*. Most English-speakers do not notice any difference between the *p*-sound at the beginning of the word and the one at the end. In fact, the two are quite different, as you can see by looking at the different acoustic signatures the two *p*s have in a spectrogram of *pop*.

Can you think of any pronunciation rules (other than the plural rule) that English speakers follow? Can you think of a pronunciation rule that speakers of a foreign language employ? What about a pronunciation rule used in a particular region of the country?

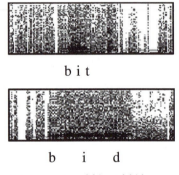

b i t

b   i   d

Spectrograms of *bit* and *bid*.

Can you suggest an explanation for the difference in vowel length between bit *and* bid*? Can you think of any other examples that seem to manifest this contrast?*

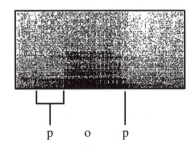

p   o   p

Spectrogram of *pop*.

As with vowel-length differences, the alternation between these two *p*-sounds is not arbitrary. All of the *ps* in the words in the first column sound different from those in the second column.

pirate	slop
pill	unzip
potato	rap
pathetic	equip
prior	remap
protagonist	drip
protest	bop

2.2 More on Aspiration

We can describe the difference between the two *p*-sounds more carefully by concentrating on how they are pronounced. The initial *p* finishes with a puff of air (called *aspiration*) that the final *p* lacks. What about *ps* in the middle of words; for instance, the *p* in *spit*? Can you tell whether this *p* is aspirated or unaspirated? One also wonders if the distinction between aspirated and unaspirated sounds applies to sounds other than *p*. If we study examples like *top*, *stop*, and *pot*, we discover that the initial position has aspiration associated with it, but the others do not. Finally, let's consider two more sets of aspiration data. Which of the underlined sounds in the following examples would you expect to be aspirated?

l̲ip	o̲pen
sl̲ip	so̲ld
pil̲l	als̲o̲

You may have been surprised to find out that *o* and *l* do not aspirate in any of these words (indeed, they never do!). But as an English-speaker, you always behave in such a way that aspiration does not apply to these kinds of sounds. And if we make up a nonsense word say, *calatious* or *grieby*, you automatically know to aspirate the initial sound in the first word, but not the first sound in the second word. Although you may be surprised at the patterns in the emerging data, you are never in any doubt about when to aspirate sounds when you encounter them (even in unfamiliar words). As linguists, we want to uncover the principles that underlie this kind of behavior and to understand the sound patterns of English, and ultimately those of other languages as well. Since this knowledge is generally tacit, we must develop a method of inquiry by which to approach our topic. And, as we begin to enter into the details of linguistic analysis we must recall two central questions which motivate our investigations: What do children learn when they learn language, and how do they learn it? Only by carefully examining the richness of linguistic knowledge will we be able to address these most basic questions about human nature.

At this point you must be curious about the correlation between the position of a sound in a word and whether or not the sound is aspirated. Can you state a generalization that captures the proper relationship?

How do you know where to apply aspiration in nonsense words like calatious? *Since, presumably, you have never heard this word before, you could not have memorized its pronunciation. So how did you figure it out?*

2.3 Articulatory Phonetics

Having preliminarily discussed vowel length and aspiration, let us now consider the sound system of English more systematically. We would like to understand what information about English pronunciation is incorporated in a speaker's knowledge of language — a central question of *phonetics*. First, a related question: What does an English-speaker do to make English sounds? To put this question schematically, it is well and good to ask about when *p* is aspirated and when it is not, but we must also know how to make a *p* in the first place. We can begin this investigation by familiarizing ourselves with the names and functions of the articulators and important regions in the *vocal tract*.

By moving parts of the tract, for example the tongue and lips, we can change the shape of the cavity, thereby altering the acoustic character of speech sounds. Let's examine this process in greater detail.

HISTORY 2.3

Studies of young children learning language have revealed that the place of articulation is a very important factor in determining the order in which sounds are acquired and the nature of sound-substitution errors. This pioneering work was begun by Roman Jakobson, who investigated the early linguistic sound patterns of children learning a wide range of languages, including Swedish, Norwegian, Danish, Russian, Polish, Bulgarian, Zuni, English, and German (Jakobson 1968). Jakobson discovered that, although the rate at which different children acquire the sound system of different languages (and, indeed of the same language) is remarkably variable, the order of "of phonological acquisitions in child language appears to be stable in its fundamental characteristics…"

(Jakobson 1968:46). For example, *a* generally emerges as the first vowel, *p* as the first consonant, and the alternation between *m* and *p* as the first opposition that children take advantage of to build contrasting sound items (like *papa* vs. *mama*).

Jakobson also determined that children learning different languages tend to make similar speech-production errors, substituting the same sounds for each other. Thus, Swedish children say *tata* for *kaka*, German children substitute *topf* for *kopf*, and English-learners produce *tut* in for *cut*. The swapping of *t* for *k* follows from a corollary observation: Children tend to master *t* before mastering *k*.

Although Jakobson's work has proven to be controversial in some regards (see Reich 1986), perhaps its

most important conclusion is the striking generalization that, despite the superficial differences of the world's languages, under careful analysis, significant universal aspects of acquisition emerge. Moreover, Jakobson noticed that linguistic elements acquired relatively early on also seem to be more broadly distributed across the world's languages, while elements acquired relatively late seem to be more rare (Jakobson 1968:57). These correlations between properties of the world's languages and the milestones of language acquisition suggest that children are more easily able to learn aspects of language that have a broad cross-linguistic distribution. We return to discuss the implications of these parallels in the next chapter. ■

We begin with the *consonant* system of English, and in particular, with the *stops*. Stops involve a constriction of the vocal tract so extreme that the column of air making its way through the tract is, for an instant, completely stopped. We call the point at which this closure occurs the *place of articulation*. The various stop consonants of English involve different points of articulation. They sound different as a consequence of the changes in the shape of the vocal tract.

The first stop consonant we examine is the *p*-sound. A *p* is made by expelling air from the lungs, through the *oral* cavity, which is constricted by a closure made by bringing the two lips together. The lips are then moved apart, and the sound is released. Because it is the two lips that come together and pull apart to form the stop release, the *p* is categorized as a *bilabial* (meaning two-lipped) stop consonant.

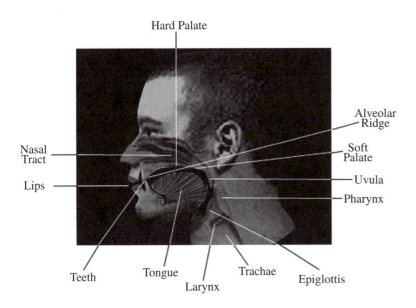

The vocal tract.

Since we notice that swapping *p* for *b* in a word changes its meaning, we might wonder how to characterize the proper relationship between sound and meaning. Although there are admittedly many cases that obscure this fact, the connection between sound and meaning is not always arbitrary! Consider, for example, that certain sets of English words that share aspects of their interpretation also share sound signatures. For instance, *spit, spew, spatter, splatter, spill, splash, splutter, spout, spray, spume, spurt,* and *sputter* all have to do with the discharge of liquid in a more or less haphazard manner. Since each of these words begins with *sp*, this raises a question about the relationship between sounds and meaning: Is there some feature of meaning that is associated with *sp* words as a consequence of the sound character of the words?

Another example involves onomatopoetic words: words that sound like what they mean. For instance, the *z*-sound at the end of *buzz* suggests the sound of buzzing, and the *s*-sound at the end of *hiss* is an example of a hissing sound. Many words for animal sounds fall into this category; *woof* and *cock-a-doodle-do* clearly involve sound symbolism. On the basis of these data, it seems too much to conclude that sound and meaning are only arbitrarily related. In at least some interesting cases, aspects of an expression's meaning may be correlated with certain sounds because of their acoustic character. ■

Sound and meaning are arbitrarily related — the sounds of a language do not convey meaning as a result of their acoustic character. There is nothing about the sounds that make up the word *dog* that is responsible for the fact that *dog* refers to dogs. It is only when sounds are organized into *morphemes* that a sound-meaning correspondence is established. Although much is made about certain sound-meaning correlations that do not appear arbitrary (like the assertion that *fizz* and *zip* both contain segments that sound like what they mean — so-called *onomatopoeia*), these claims are exaggerated. Certainly there are many more words that contain *z*-sounds that lack any trace of sound symbolism (e.g., *plaza, razz, zoo,* and *fez*) raising the likely possibility that the few examples where a case for sound symbolism might be made are merely coincidences of sound and meaning. Furthermore, in most instances of alleged onomatopoeia, it is not so clear that a word sounds very much like what it means at all. Only in cartoons do dogs go *woof.* ■

2.4 Voiced Sounds

Although we have begun to determine the features that distinguish *p* from the other sounds of English, there are other English sounds that also involve bilabial closure, for example, *b*. Although *p* and *b* are quite similar articulatorily, they do not sound alike. Furthermore, by substituting one for the other in a word (consider *pit* and *bit*), we change the meaning of the word. The two words that result from this substitution constitute a *minimal pair,* since they differ in

Evidence presented by Eimas et al. (1971) suggests that children are biologically specialized to identify the contrast between pairs of sounds like *p* and *b* that differ only in the feature of voicing. Children of approximately two months of age show sensitivity to voicing and other distinctive phonetic features indicating that "language learners have relevant information in advance about the inventory of possible phonetic elements" (Gleitman et al. 1988:154). In other words, the ability to detect the voicing feature seems to be an innate capacity of the language learner. Support for this position comes from studies of the ability of very young children to detect phonetic features like voicing that are important in defining the segmental repertoire in many languages. For example, in English, vocal-cord vibration occurring 20 to 30 milliseconds after the release of a consonant (the *voice onset time* or *VOT*) is associated with the consonant, which is consequently perceived as voiced (i.e., as a *b* rather than a *p*).

Eimas et al. (1971) investigated the capacity of very young children to detect this contrast by providing subjects with a nonnutritive nipple that measures an infant's rate of sucking. Children tend to increase the sucking rate in reaction to the presentation of a novel stimulus. When a familiar stimulus is presented repeatedly, habituation takes place, resulting in a decreased sucking rate. Next, a series of synthetic speech stimuli was constructed including *p, b,* and several "in-between" sounds, that each incorporated periods of voicing of progressively longer duration after the consonantal release.

Test subjects were first presented with either a *p* or *b* stimulus, until their sucking reached a habituated rate. The stimulus was then changed to one of the other sounds in the stimulus sequence. Any change in the rate of sucking was then recorded. If the rate remained constant, that suggested that the subject failed to detect the stimulus transition. If the rate changed, this was evidence that the subject detected a novel stimulus.

As you might expect, subjects did systematically detect the transition from *p* to *b* or from *b* to *p*. But it was of considerable interest that subjects did not detect transitions within clusters of sounds with relatively little voicing or within clusters of sounds with relatively more voicing. Rather, subjects split the continua of stimuli into two equivalence classes: relatively voiced sounds and relatively unvoiced sounds; and they only discriminated transitions across these two classes (but not among the members of any one class). This type of *categorical perception* allows children to concentrate on linguistic differences that make a difference. The absolute phonetic difference between two indiscriminable stimuli might be as great as or greater than the difference between two discriminable elements. But children simply dichotomize the continuum of sounds into two categories, reflecting the salience of the voiced/voiceless contrast as compared to other less linguistically useful contrasts that escape their notice.

There may also be other learning-theoretic consequences of categorical perception for voicing. Some languages, Thai and Spanish, for instance, associate preceding consonants with periods of voicing at delays longer than the 20 to 30 millisecond envelope typical in English and many other languages. Experimental studies of Spanish-speaking children suggest that up to the age of about six months, they continue to use the regular categorical boundaries for voicing even though their target language employs different values (Lasky et al. 1975). As Reich (1986) suggests, Spanish-learning children may be somewhat delayed in their ability to discriminate parts of the Spanish sound system. This provides indirect evidence that there is an innate voicing detection mechanism that is at least temporarily frustrated when the language to be learned exhibits an idiosyncratic timing envelope for voicing (see Goodluck 1991 for further discussion). ■

just one sound yet have different meanings. *p* and *b* are both bilabial stop consonants, and they function as different sounds in English. To understand what accounts for the articulatory difference, we must explore in more detail the role that the *larynx* plays in speech production.

The larynx (or "voice box") contains the *vocal cords,* which are movable and flexible. During vocalization, they may stay apart, as, for example, with *p* or they may be brought close together, as is the case with *b*. Since they are flexible, and the airflow passing through them involves considerable turbulence, in this "close" position the vocal cords are set into vibration. The resulting acoustic effect is a buzz known as *voicing.*

2.5 Bilabials

When we add voicing to a bilabial stop consonant we produce a *b*. In other words, *b* is a *voiced* bilabial stop, differing from *p*, the voiceless bilabial stop, in its *manner of articulation.* There is a third English bilabial stop, *m*. The articulation of *m* is quite intriguing, since it not only shares with *p* and *b* a bilabial stop closure, but like *b* it is voiced. Nevertheless, the minimal-pair test (consider *pit* versus *mitt*), not to mention our intuition, quickly convinces us that *m* is a distinctive sound in English. We are therefore left with a puzzle: If *m* shares place of articulation and manner of articulation with *b*, wherein lies the difference? It turns out that in the articulation of the vast majority of English sounds (including *b* and *p*), the *soft palate (velum)* is raised, sealing off the *nasal tract*, with air passing through the *oral tract.* However, it is also possible to lower the soft palate (including the *uvula*), allowing air to escape continuously through the nasal passages. This is what contributes the nasal quality to sounds like *m*.

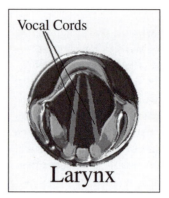

The minimal-pair test can be used to establish which sounds are distinctive in a given language. Identify two different sets of minimal pairs based on the frame _ it.

Try (very gently) making an n-sound while pinching your nose so that air cannot escape through the nasal tract. What do the results of this task tell you about the articulation of nasal sounds?

Even a cursory examination of the sounds of the world's languages reveals that languages differ from one another in their sound inventories. To use French as a point of contrast, French contains nasal vowels (cf. *bon* — 'good'), but English does not. English has a *th*-sound in words like *the,* but French has no such sound, and so it goes. Languages that seem to share the same sounds may nevertheless vary in the exact details of pronunciation. For example, the Chinese *b* does not sound exactly like the English *b* (which may explain the confusion concerning the spelling of the capital of China, which used to be spelled *Peking* and now is spelled *Beijing*). In Chinese, the instant when the vocal cords begin vibrat-ing during the articulation of *b* (the voice onset time, or VOT) is slightly later than it is in English. So, there would seem to be ample evidence that there is no universal sound system (i.e., a sound inventory common to all the languages of the world). But if we approach the question at a higher level of abstraction, we may draw a rather different conclusion.

Although Chinese and English differ in the specifics of the pronunciation of *b,* both languages manifest a voiced/voiceless distinction in their consonant systems. That is, *p* and *b* contrast with one another, can mark minimal pairs, and differ in the feature of voicing in both languages. Indeed, the voiced/voiceless contrast is commonly found across the languages of the world. Similarly, while languages may not agree in their inventories of consonants and vowels, all languages have a contrast between these two types of speech sounds. Our quest for a universal sound system must be construed as a search for an inventory of contrasting properties (like voicing and the consonant/vowel opposition) that may be incorporated into the sound systems of the world's languages. In order to properly understand the sound system of a language, one must provide a detailed account of the universal properties that form the system's core. ■

While there may be some overlaps among the sound inventories of the world's languages, and even some universal contrasts (like the conso-nant/vowel contrast discussed previ-ously), it is important to understand the many dimensions along which the sound systems of languages may vary. We have already discussed variation in consonant/vowel systems across languages, but that is only the tip of the iceberg. Tone languages like Chinese use pitch as a sound feature to distinguish words, so that *ma,* with a rising tone means 'hemp' and *ma* with a falling tone means 'blame' — a minimal pair based on tone. English allows no such contrasts. Languages can also differ in the sequences of sounds that are permitted, even when they share sounds in common. For ex-ample, English allows *st, str, sp, spr,* but not *sr* to begin a word. So, *stop, strap, spot,* and *spray* are English words; but English *phonotactic* con-straints prohibit words like *srot* or *srop.* In contrast, Khmer, the lan-guage of Cambodia, freely allows *sr* sequences — *Srei* is a typical Khmer name.

In general, then, languages may draw from common inventories of sounds and contrasts, but there is still a rich domain of variation that is the hallmark of the sound sys-tems of the world's languages. In order to properly understand a language's sound system, one must provide a detailed account of the particular properties that make that language distinctive. ■

2.6 Alveolars

The other stop consonants of English are produced by making a closure at the *alveolar ridge* or the *velum*. The three English *alveolar* stops *t*, *d*, and *n*, differ along the dimensions of voicing (*t* is voiceless and *d* is voiced) and nasality (*n* is nasal).

2.7 Velars

Sounds produced with velum as the point of articulation are known as *velar* sounds. There are three velar stops in English: one voiceless (*k*), one voiced (*g*) and a nasal velar stop that occurs in words like *wrong* and *sing*. Before considering other English consonants, we should address two further considerations pertaining to the voiced velar nasal. First, there is the matter of how to represent this sound. It is tempting to use the English spelling *ng* to designate it. But this gets confusing, since *ng*, as it appears in the spelling of other English words, is not always pronounced like a voiced velar nasal (for example, in *mongoose*). Since the sound spelled *ng* and the voiced velar nasal are not always the same sound, we need to invent a special

HISTORY 2.7

In 1886, an association of language teachers was formed that took an interest in phonetic theory in general and phonetic transcription in particular. The association published a newsletter, originally called *Dhi Fonètik Tîtcer,* which had the distinction of being the first such document to be printed entirely in phonetic transcription. The group's earliest interests were mainly limited to English phonetics, but there soon arrived a demand for a more universal linguistic phonetic system. During the first two years of the association's activities, there were a number of rival phonetic alphabets used by its members, and it was not unusual to find that different articles employed different notational systems.

The idea of developing a universal phonetic alphabet is attributed to Otto Jespersen in a letter printed in the Association's newsletter in 1886. By 1888, the first version of the IPA was constructed in an attempt to embrace the following principles:

1. There should be a separate letter for each distinctive sound; that is, for each sound which, being used instead of another, in the same language, can change the meaning of the word.

2. When any sound is found in several languages, the same sign should be used in all. This applies also to the very similar shades of sound.

3. The alphabet should consist as much as possible of the ordinary letters of the roman alphabet, as few new letters as possible being used.

4. In assigning values to roman letters, international usage should decide.

5. The new letters should be suggestive of the sounds they represent, by their resemblance to the old ones.

6. Diacritic marks should be avoided, being trying for the eyes and troublesome to write. (from International Phonetic Association 1949) ■

symbol to stand for the latter sound (reserving *ng* for the sound sequence in *mongoose*). The symbol we will adopt is ŋ, one of the symbols in the International Phonetic Alphabet *(IPA)* used to unambiguously designate speech sounds. To indicate IPA symbols, we will put them in brackets for example, [ŋ] for the voiced velar nasal. Since the stop sounds we have studied so far happen to have their usual English characters for their IPA symbols, we can continue to use these characters, now written within brackets (for instance, [b], [p], and [m]) to represent these sounds.

The second matter of interest pertaining to the voiced velar nasal [ŋ] concerns its distribution in English and other languages. Unlike the other English stops, which can appear at beginnings, in middles, and at ends of words, [ŋ] has more limited privileges of occurrence: it seems to be restricted to ends of words, and the rare word with an initial [ŋ] that has been borrowed from another languages seems hard for English-speakers to pronounce. Of course, word-initial [ŋ] is possible in other languages; for example, *Nguyen* is a common Vietnamese name that is pronounced with an initial [ŋ]. The restrictions on the distribution of [ŋ] in English remain to be explained. And there are other similar puzzles (such as why there are no English words that begin with the second consonant in *measure*) that we will need to consider if we want to be systematic in describing of the distribution of English sounds (so-called *phonotactics*).

2.8 Fricatives

Returning to our overview of the consonant system, we next consider consonants that are not stops. Included in this class of sounds are *fricatives* — sounds which are made with a constriction of the oral tract that stops short of complete closure. As in the case of stops, the place of articulation is crucial in determining the acoustic character of each fricative. However, the places at which English fricatives are articulated can differ from the places at which English stops are articulated. We begin with two fricatives made by restricting the flow of air by bringing the lower lip and the upper teeth together. The result of this articulation is [f], the voiceless *labio-dental* fricative, and [v], the voiced labiodental fricative. Because the juxtaposition of the lips and teeth form a leaky seal, air continuously rushes past the place of articulation. The difference between the two labio-dental fricatives is their value for voicing. Just as in the case of the stop consonants, this alternation yields a pair of *homorganic* sounds (sounds with the same place of articulation).

Make up five other sound sequences that could not be well-formed words in English because of their phonotactic properties. What do you think accounts for the impossibility of these items? Would you expect that all such items are also impossible in other languages? Discuss.

We have seen that [ŋ], the velar nasal, is limited in distribution in English. What about [f] and [v]? Can you identify three words that begin with [f] or [v], and three others that end with [f] or [v].

2.9 Inter-dentals

The next two fricatives are rare in the languages of the world. The place of articulation is the *inter-dental* region, into which the tip of the tongue is placed. Both the voiced ([ð]) and the voiceless inter-dental fricative ([θ]) are often spelled with a *th* (consider *thy* and *thigh*, a minimal pair).

2.10 Alveolar Fricatives

There are also four fricatives articulated in the vicinity of the alveolar ridge. The first pair, [s] (*sing*) and [z] (*zing*), are made by bringing the tip of the tongue just below the ridge. As by now you might expect, [s] and [z] differ in voicing ([s] is *unvoiced* and [z] is voiced).

Transcribe the following words using the phonetic symbols introduced in the text (use [æ], the vowel in glass, to represent the vowel sound in each item): ask, adds, as, act, axe, ass, *and* adze.

2.11 Alveo-palatal Fricatives

There are two *alveo-palatal* fricatives made by placing the tip of the tongue just under the area between the alveolar ridge and the *hard palate*. The voiceless version, often spelled *sh* is represented by the phonetic symbol [š]. The voiced version, represented as [ž], appears in *measure* and *azure*.

PRO 2.9

Certain sounds in certain languages are harder to learn than others. The inter-dental fricatives [ð] and [θ] are a case in point. At the time that children are acquiring the majority of the sounds in the consonant system, the nervous system has not yet concluded a stage of development called *myelinization*. During this process, *myelin,* a white fatty substance, forms an insulating sheath around the auditory nerve, thereby improving audition in the higher-frequency range. Prior to myelinization, it is more difficult for children to hear speech sounds that include a substantial amount of high-frequency energy; and sounds that are difficult to hear are quite naturally difficult to learn. The two inter-dental fricatives are sounds with an unusual amount of high-frequency information. As a result of the difficulty in detecting them, it takes children many extra months to acquire these sounds. Thus, perhaps, it is not surprising to find that sounds like [ð] and [θ] are relatively rare across the world's languages. ∎

Have you ever heard children or nonnative speakers of English who cannot produce inter-dental fricatives attempt words that are supposed to contain these sounds? Which sounds have you heard such speakers substitute for the inter-dentals?

Do you know any languages other than English that use inter-dental fricatives? What is an example of a word in one such language?

2.12 Other Alveolar Sounds

There are two other English consonants articulated in the alveo-palatal region. The first pair, [č] and [ǰ], share properties of both stops and fricatives. [č], the voiceless alveo-palatal *affricate*, sounds like a rapid sequence of the stop [t] followed by the fricative [š]. It appears in words like *cherry*. [ǰ], the voiced alveo-palatal affricate, appears in *jump*. Finally, there are two other alveolars that share with the fricatives the property of being *continuants* — they involve a constriction of the oral cavity that stops short of a complete closure. In some dialects of American English, [r] is an alveolar sound with a *retroflex* tongue position, as, for example, in words like *rabbit*. Regarding [l] (as in *lip*), as far as the tongue is concerned, it is identical to [t] in that both sounds require the tip to be brought into contact with the alveolar ridge. The difference lies in the position of the blade of the tongue. In the case of [t], the column of air passes over the tip of the tongue and out the mouth after the stop is released. In contrast, to make an [l], the sides of the tongue are lowered and air escapes continuously, resulting in a *lateral* release.

2.13 Glides

If you examine the articulation of [l] and [r] closely, you notice that they involve less constriction of the vocal tract than any other consonants. Consequently, there is no significant friction during

Transcribe the following words: shack, ash, azure, cash, beige, shame, and sham. The vowel sounds you hear are either [æ] (the vowel in glass) or [e] (the vowel in hay).

Transcribe the following words: badge, batch, chair, age, jail, rage, and h ("aitch"). The vowel sounds you hear are either [æ] (the vowel in glass) or [e] (the vowel in hay).

All normally developing speakers learn the sound system of their dialects completely and perfectly. Although certain speech sounds (like the inter-dental fricatives) may take longer for children to learn, eventually all speech sounds are mastered and all sounds are produced and identified with equal apparent ease. There simply is no such thing as a difficult sound! Just the same, many people have the impression that some sounds in some languages are difficult to make. It is probably best to interpret this to mean that the difficulty is manifest only for speakers of other languages. But native speakers of any given language can use its entire sound system effortlessly. Finally, even though sounds that are acquired by children relatively late in the course of language development are typically rare across the world's languages, such sounds may nevertheless have a very high frequency of occurrence in the languages in which they do occur. Here again, the inter-dental fricatives [ð] and [θ] are a nice example — words like *the, that, these,* and *this* are among the most frequently appearing words in the English language. ■

CON 2.9

PRO 2.12

Children develop their native language on the basis of exposure to primary linguistic data — the sum total of linguistic and nonlinguistic experience that constitutes the input to the language-acquisition process. Thus, children exposed to English learn English, those exposed to French learn French, and so on. The acquisition of linguistic competence by all normally growing children is one of the most marvelous accomplishments of human development, one that we seek to understand more fully. To put the question in a very general form: How do children learn so much in such a short time (on the basis of so little evidence)? One piece of the answer may be the special role that parents and other caretakers play in the early stages of development.

For example, parents and caretakers are responsible for providing examples of linguistic behavior to children, who use this information variously to facilitate their linguistic development. Many of the aspects of the sound system, lexicon, and syntactic systems that children acquire are established in consideration of the positive evidence provided during the course of language acquisition. There is also a special form of primary linguistic data provided by parents and caretakers, called *motherese* that helps to bootstrap the acquisition process. Motherese is a simplified version of a language that involves relatively short utterances, exaggerated intonation patterns, considerable repetitions, and an unusually high proportion of questions and imperatives. This particular input may play a special role in draw-

ing the child's attention to certain important aspects of language, especially when the language in question manifests irregularity or idiosyncrasy (see Newport et al. 1977:145). ▪

the production of these sounds (which are sometimes called *liquids*). There are three other English sounds, [h], [y] and [w], that share certain properties with both consonants and vowels — indeed, they are sometimes classified as *semi-vowels*. [h] (as in *help*) is produced by passing air through the vocal tract in its rest state (with the only constriction in the *glottal* region). The turbulence produced as air passes through the larynx is responsible for the acoustic character of [h]. [y] (as in *yell*) involves raising the tongue blade toward the hard palate; [w] (as in *weigh*) requires *rounding* the lips and moving the tongue blade toward the soft palate (a *labio-velar* sound). The articulation of [h], [y], and [w] is said to "glide" into that of a neighboring vowel, hence the name *glide*.

Transcribe the following words: hay, weigh, yea, yak, ham, yam, *and* wham. *The vowel sounds you hear are either [æ] (the vowel in glass) or [e] (the vowel in hay).*

Children learn their native language on the basis of a limited exposure to primary linguistic data — this much is beyond dispute. But the relative contribution to language development made by the child's linguistic experience as compared to that of the child's language-learning system is a controversial, open question. Furthermore, there is reason to think that the role of that the linguistic environment (and the role of parents, in particular) in the acquisition process is less than one might expect. In the case of the sound system, for example, there is no doubt that parents and caretakers provide a considerable amount of the child's early primary linguistic data. Indeed, it is tempting to conceive of the problem of acquiring the sound system as amounting to little more than the task of the child imitating the sounds provided by primary caregivers. But there are several reasons to think that this view is incorrect.

To begin with, by virtue of the smaller size and different proportions of the child's vocal tract, the child is physically incapable of imitating adult speech sounds; for example, the child's pitch will be much higher than that of the typical adult. It is also hard to see how the child could imitate the articulatory gestures involved in the majority of speech sounds given that these gestures are not visible to the child. The learning task involves much more than imitation: The child has to determine what to do with the articulators to produce a sound that sounds like a given target sound, ignoring the systematic differences between the adult and child's forms like pitch, speech rate, volume, and so forth. Finally, consider a child being raised by parents whose speech differs substantially from the child's larger speech community. Parents who speak a different dialect than that of the speech community, or parents with foreign accents, are typical instances of this incongruity. Suppose, for example, that a girl is raised in Western Massachusetts by a father whose native language is Serbo-Croatian and speaks with a nonnative accent. Would you expect the girl to acquire the foreign accent of her father or to sound like a native of Western Massachusetts? In fact, the girl would display no trace of a nonnative accent. It is clear that she could not learn the sound system of English by imitating her father. To sum up: parents do not teach children to speak! ■

CON 2.12

2.14 English Vowels

Having examined the consonant system of English, we now consider the vowel system. Whereas the consonants are typically distinguished by a point of maximum constriction known as the place of articulation, the vowels are individuated by the orientation of the tongue in the oral cavity. The position of the tongue is categorized along two axes: front to back, and top to bottom.

2.15 Front Vowels

We begin by investigating the *front vowels*. There are five English front vowels. [i] (*beet*) and [ɪ] (*wit*), the two *high* front vowels, involve moving the

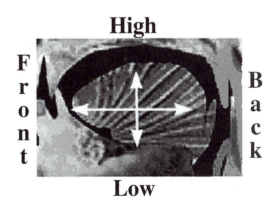

Axes of tongue movement during vowel production.

tongue forward and up relative to its rest position. [e] (*weigh*) and [ɛ] (*pet*) are also front vowels, but the tongue is less high in the oral tract. Finally, [æ] (*glass*) is the low front vowel. Since both [i] and [ɪ] are high front vowels, we need to identify some articulatory difference that distinguishes them. As it turns out, [i] is a bit higher and more forward than [ɪ], a contrast that is referred to as the *tense/lax* distinction. [i] is tense in that the root of the tongue is more advanced than with [ɪ], which is lax; correspondingly, [e] is tense and [ɛ] is lax.

Transcribe the following words: eat, let, play, bit, bat, in, and weight.

2.16 Back Vowels

The English vowel system also has sequence of *back vowels* that differ from each other in terms of height and tenseness. In addition, some of the back vowels of English involve rounding of the lips — a feature that no English front vowel manifests. [u] (*newt*) and [ʊ] (*pudding*), respectively the tense and lax high back vowels, both involve *rounding*. The second pair, [o] (*phone*) and [ɔ] (*mall*) are less high than [u] and [ʊ] but share with them the feature of rounding. [o] is tense and [ɔ] is lax. [a] (*bother*), the low back vowel is unrounded.

In addition to front and back vowels, English has two *central vowels* represented by [ʌ] (*about*) and [ə] (*basket*) that are made with

Transcribe the following words: own, boon, rook, oar, on, plot, and dune.

PRO 2.17

Even a cursory investigation of the vowel systems of different dialects of the same language (let alone the vowel systems of different languages) quickly confirms that these vowel systems are, well, different. Nevertheless, there are still significant universal properties of the vowel system that provide important insights into the nature of language and mind. One of the most striking universal generalizations is the fact that all the vowel systems of all of the world's languages contain the vowels [i], [u], and [a]. Indeed, some languages (like classical Arabic, for example) only have these three vowels.

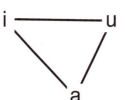

The vowel triangle.

Notice that [i], [u], and [a] form the corners of a vowel triangle, and that these vowels are maximally distant from each other in terms of articulatory space. Their universality may be connected to the relative salience of these vowels, which facilitates the process of sound discrimination. ∎

The English vowel [æ] is quite frequent in distribution in English words, but relatively rare across the world's languages (Jakobson 1968:56). It is also learned relatively late by children (and well after the acquisition of [i], [u], and [a]). Can you explain this correlation?

the vocal tract very close to the rest position. [ʌ] is the tense central vowel, and [ə] is slightly more lax. The lax central vowel is also known as the *schwa*, about which we say more below.

2.17 Diphthongs

We conclude our discussion of phonetics by discussing a special kind of English vowel, the *diphthong*. Diphthongs are composed of a two vowel sequence pronounced in the approximate time frame of a single vowel sound. The American English diphthongs are [ai] (*fry*), [au] (*bough*), and [ɔi] (*annoy*).

2.18 The Vowel Triangle

We can summarize this account of the vowel system by considering the relative position of each vowel in a graphic that abstractly represents its phonetic properties.

Transcribe the following words: bow, coy, eye, lie, out, cow, *and* I.

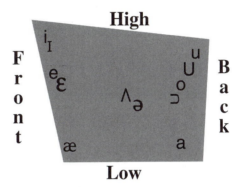

The vowel chart.

One of the richest domains of variation across different languages (and even the different dialects of a single language) is the vowel system. Even across languages with which English shares a common history, the differences abound. French, for example, has a series of nasal vowels that are missing from English entirely. And the distribution of lip rounding is another interesting difference between the two languages. In English, only back vowels can be round (i.e., [u], [ʊ], [o], and [ɔ]). But in French, there is a high front rounded vowel in words like *tu*. Once we notice this difference, we can begin to understand why this vowel is so difficult for English-speakers to make (but now you know the secret — just make an [i] sound while rounding your lips as if you were going to make an [u]).

One final reason that English-speakers have trouble pronouncing French vowels has to do with differences in the uses of diphthongs in the two languages. Although English/French word pairs like *say/c'est, low/l'eau,* and *pea/pis* may seem to be *homonyms,* the vowels in these pairs are actually quite different from one another. The English vowels [e], [o], and [i] tend to diphthongize in many English dialects to [ey], [ow], and [iy], resulting in longer vowels with a different phonetic character. French vowels do not undergo this process. ■

HISTORY 2.18

Although it is well known that languages change over time, precisely what causes linguistic change is one of the less understood parts of the theory of language. Many casual observers believe that language change is for the purposes of maximizing efficiency or to achieve a more simple linguistic state. Others worry that linguistic change is a process of deterioration and decay, citing contemporary colloquial speech or the patterns of "nonstandard" dialects as their chief evidence. One kind of linguistic change that is most difficult to interpret in these ways is phonetic change. As a case in point, consider some of the changes that have taken place in the vowel system of Modern English, which differs markedly from that of earlier forms of the language.

One such change is that Modern English seems to have lost two vowels that originally appeared in Old English. There is evidence that words like *oexen*, 'oxen,' and *cyning*, 'king,' contained the vowels [oe] and [y], respectively. The former is a front rounded vowel and the latter is somewhat higher rounded vowel. In Modern English, all round vowels are back vowels, a generalization that obviously did not hold in Old English. Still, it is difficult to see how this kind of change can be seen as an instance of decline or simplification, especially when it is viewed in the context of other sounds changing and still others being added to English throughout its history. ■

Can you think of any other English sounds that have changed in pronunciation or been added or lost? Are there any such processes that you think may be at work today? Discuss.

2.19 The Consonant Chart

Finally, here is a table that categorizes the consonants and semivowels for American English.

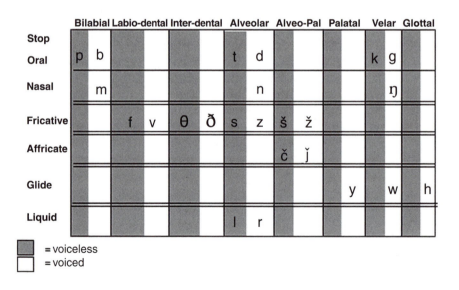

	Bilabial	Labio-dental	Inter-dental	Alveolar	Alveo-Pal	Palatal	Velar	Glottal
Stop Oral	p b			t d			k g	
Nasal	m			n			ŋ	
Fricative		f v	θ ð	s z	š ž			
Affricate					č ǰ			
Glide						y	w	h
Liquid				l r				

▢ = voiceless
▢ = voiced

English consonants and semivowels.

2.20 The Phonetic Alphabet

While investigating some of the articulatory details for the sounds of American English we have simultaneously identified a set of phonetic symbols that uniquely identify each sound. It is this *phonetic alphabet,* rather than the spelling system of any natural language, that we use to describe phonetic events. It is easy to accumulate evidence in favor of this decision. Pronounce the following words to yourself, and consider how good a job the spelling system does of capturing the correct pronunciation:

play	by
car	buy
wrote	bye

In each case, there is quite a discrepancy between the English orthography and the phonetic representation. Notice, in particular, that the same letter (*a* for example) can stand for different sounds in different words; and the same sound can be spelled in several different ways. On the other hand, if we use phonetic representations to describe phonetic events, we can avoid these complications. See if you can determine the English words represented below.

[æks]	[dɔgz]
[æsk]	[pʌzl]
[foni]	[æŋšəs]

Transcribe each word in the following sentence: How much wood would he chuck if he could?

2.21 Beyond Phonetics

Having concluded our survey of the phonetics of American English, we return to our original questions about the nature of a child's linguistic knowledge. Every child who learns English as a first language develops a system of phonetic knowledge that can be abstractly described by the charts representing the consonant and vowel systems of the language. But there is a good deal more to a speaker's linguistic knowledge about the sound system than can be sufficiently characterized in the terms of this sort of database. As we now discover, there are several important considerations indicating that English-speakers know considerably more about the sound system of English than merely its general phonetic characteristics.

To investigate, we begin with a simple hypothesis about how information about the sound system is represented, and then test it against several different kinds of linguistic data. In this view, if

There are many reasons why the English spelling system fails to present an accurate phonetic representation of the words of the language. For one thing, since there are different dialects of English with considerably different pronunciations of even common words, it would be impossible to maintain an accurate orthographic system in the face of this variability. To choose a single example, many speakers pronounce *often* as "offen," while others say "often." Clearly the spelling system cannot be simultaneously faithful to both of these pronunciations.

Another process that undermines the accuracy of the spelling system is that of language change. English spelling was once reasonably in tune with standard pronunciation, but then the pronunciation changed. One sweeping change of this sort concerns the pronunciation of final vowel sounds in unstressed positions. In time of Chaucer, words like *name, stone, wine,* and *dance* were pronounced as two-syllable words with a final vowel sound. But by the time of Shakespeare, the final vowel ceased to be pronounced, resulting in the famous silent *e* in the English spelling system (see Roberts 1994 for discussion).

A second profound change in English pronunciation took place sometime between 1400 and 1600 and was known as the Great Vowel Shift. This sound change affected the vowel system of the language in a highly systematic and profound way. The relatively low front and back vowels raised to the next-highest vowel, and the high vowels turned into diphthongs. For example, *name* used to have the vowel of *father, he* was pronounced like *hay,* and *moon* had the vowel of *moan* (see Roberts 1994).

To the unending disadvantage of the English spelling system, the writing system was codified prior to the Great Vowel Shift. Furthermore, the invention of the printing press by Caxton in 1475 made it difficult for spelling conventions to change, even as the old representations became more and more opaque with respect to the emerging colloquial pronunciations. For these reasons among others, English orthography makes a poor substitute for a phonetic alphabet. The IPA will serve us much better when careful representations of phonetic information are needed. ■

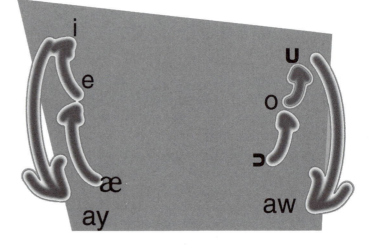

The Great Vowel Shift.

speakers want to say the word *cat* they access [kæt] and then follow a procedure for making each of the sounds in the phonetic representation ([k], [æ], and [t]) in rapid sequence. Understanding an utterance of [kæt], and recognizing it as *cat* involves following a different set of instructions that allows one to map an incoming acoustic signal onto the corresponding vocabulary item.

Hypothesis 1
Native speakers know a list of words of the language, each of which has a phonetic representation coupled with instructions for how to produce and recognize the represented sound sequence.

Let's see if we can develop the assumption that the pronunciation of *lexical items* takes the form of a list of phonetic representations. Consider once again the phenomenon of aspiration. The conclusion we reached was that aspiration has a limited distribution in English. As a preliminary hypothesis, we can describe the distribution by claiming that only word-initial voiceless consonants are aspirated. This explains why the [t] is aspirated in *top*, but not in *stop* or *pot*, and why the initial sounds in *ban*, *lip*, and *open* are unaspirated, as well.

Since speakers can aspirate the appropriate sounds in the appropriate positions, we expect that lexical representations must distinguish sounds that involve aspiration from those that do not. We would also like our analysis to explain why aspiration applies to [p], [t], and [k] but not to many other sounds. [p], [t], and [k] constitute a *natural class* of sounds by virtue of all being members of the same type of sound — the class of voiceless stops. Sounds that can be described in these relatively general ways are more likely to be affected as a group by the rules and principles of a phonological system. So, we would expect that stops, high vowels, or voiceless sounds might pattern together with respect to a certain principle, but [p], [t], and [o] would not participate in the same process.

2.22 Aspiration Revisited

In our account of aspiration we want to somehow capture the fact that this process applies to a natural class of sounds. Let us try to state the relevant generalizations within the parameters of hypothesis 1. Suppose that we introduce a special symbol, [ʰ], to indicate aspiration, using [tʰ] to indicate an aspirated voiceless alveolar stop and [t] to denote an unaspirated voiced alveolar stop.

If we apply this convention, the lexical entries for *top*, *stop*, *pot*, *ban*, *lip*, and *open* will look like this:

top	[tʰap]
stop	[stap]
pot	[pʰat]
ban	[bæn]
lip	[lɪp]
open	[opʰn]

In this view, if a speaker needs to determine whether or not to aspirate a given consonant, a lexical lookup must be performed. In other words, in order to decide to pronounce *pot* as [pʰat] rather than as [pat], you would have to retrieve the correct *phonetic form* from your mental dictionary. There are several objections to this approach to modeling phonetic knowledge. First, suppose that an

PRO 2.22

A native speaker's linguistic competence is only one factor involved in an act of linguistic performance. A speaker who perfectly well knows the sound pattern of a language (or any other aspect of linguistic knowledge for that matter) may nevertheless suffer from wandering attention, an unsuccessful lexical lookup, or a motor error. In any of these cases, the result will be a failure to produce speech that accurately reflects the speaker's underlying linguistic competence. In other words, we all make linguistic mistakes. One way to tell that a mistake has been made is to simply ask speakers producing speech errors if they said what they meant to say. In most cases, the speaker is the first person to notice the error, and to correct it.

A simplified sketch of our model of speech production looks something like this.

There is the potential for error to creep in during the operation of any of the subsystems of the processing module or in the motor processes that produce the final phonetic output. The system is probably not simply linear and may involve a degree of parallel processing. In speech understanding, the speech module provides the input to the system. ■

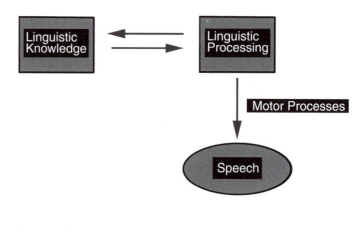

Model of linguistic processing.

English-speaker is presented with an unfamiliar word — one that, by hypothesis, does not occur in that speaker's *lexicon*. We'll use *treacle* as an example. The present account would predict that the speaker would be unable to choose between a pronunciation with an aspirated initial stop ([tʰ]) and an unaspirated initial stop ([t]), since there is no phonetic form that can be looked up to decide the matter. But this is clearly mistaken; even speakers unfamiliar with it know to pronounce *treacle* with an aspirated initial [tʰ].

A second objection concerns a class of speech errors in which sounds are substituted for one another within and across words (sometimes with comical results). These include *spoonerisms;* for example, the spontaneous utterance of *tons of soil* where *sons of toil* is intended. Fromkin and Rodman 1988 discuss other speech errors that bear on our discussion of aspiration in an interesting way. Consider the utterance of *smuck in the tid* in place of *stick in the mud;*

CON 2.22

Suppose a speaker of African-American English says *He tall* in a circumstance in which I would have said *He is tall,* or a working-class speaker pronounces *business* as *bidness.* Aren't these to be considered linguistic errors that should be avoided by a proper speaker of the language? Certainly not! English speakers who produce these forms are simply following the rules and principles of the linguistic system of their dialects. They can only be construed as making mistakes if we judge their speech by the standards of a different dialect (and everyone else's speech would likely fare just as poorly if judged by the standards of a different dialect, as well). While it may be true that certain dialects are accorded higher prestige, there is no linguistic criterion by which any one dialect is superior to any other. Most of the time when speakers are accused of committing a linguistic error they are merely exhibiting a linguistic difference.

In the case of *He tall,* for example, we must compare this form to the perhaps more familiar *He's tall* — a case of contraction that is fully acceptable in most dialects of English (including African-American dialects). If someone were to complain that contracted forms of the verb *to be* were worse than uncontracted forms, the argument would not be taken seriously. We might also point out that all English dialects allow the verb *to be* to be missing in cases like *I consider John tall* (compare: *I consider John to be tall*). So wouldn't it be more logical to argue that if I can consider John tall then I ought to be able to say *John tall?* Furthermore, since many other languages have dialects that omit *to be* in constructions in which it would be present in most English dialects, it simply will not do to argue that *to be* must be expressed to achieve proper speech. In Hebrew, for example, *I am a nice boy* is *Ani yeled tov,* (literally, 'I boy nice'), crucially, omitting *to be.* In this regard, then, Hebrew bears a superficial similarity to African-American English (and also to Russian, Hungarian, and many other languages).

Finally, the argument that letters in the spelling system ought to be pronounced as they are written (as a way of justifying, for example, that *business* ought to be pronounced *business* rather than *bidness*) would also commit us to pronouncing the *i* in *business* (and *knight* and *phlegm* as the way they are spelled). Not likely. ■

here the [t] in [stɪk] has been substituted for the initial [m] in [mʌd]. The resulting forms, [smʌk] and [tʰɪd], are of interest for two reasons. First, since they are nonsense words, their pronunciation cannot be looked up in the lexicon; and second, there is something more interesting than simple sound substitution going on here. The additional change is the introduction of aspiration after the initial [t] of [tʰɪd]. The crucial question is, how does a speaker in the midst of a speech error manage to apply aspiration to the [t] even though, when it occupies the position that it "comes from," the [t] is unaspirated? Given that the speaker cannot find *tid* in the lexicon, it is not clear how our account of aspiration can explain these curious facts.

Each of these last two considerations suggests that speakers do not merely look up lexical entries that indicate how to pronounce each word. A third objection to this approach is a theoretical concern. Listing phonetic forms lexical item by lexical item as a way of accounting for aspiration environments is unsatisfying because it fails to capture the generalization that we started out with — that only word-initial, voiceless consonants are aspirated. Each occurrence of an initial voiceless stop is treated as a separate case, and nowhere is the distributional principle that explains the facts formally registered. Furthermore, this theoretical objection is at the root of the failure of the current approach to explain how we can accommodate new vocabulary items with appropriate aspiration patterns (as well as the speech-error data). In short, we have no way of predicting that all English words follow the same rule for aspiration. Let us consider how we might develop a more successful approach.

In addition to applying to the segments [p], [t], and [k], aspiration also applies to [č], explaining why church *is pronounced [čʰrč]. Can you explain the inclusion of [č] in the set of sounds that aspirates?*

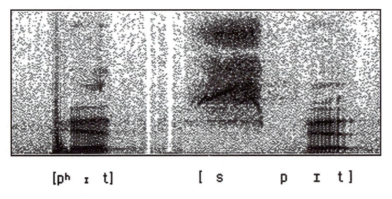

[pʰ ɪ t]   [s   p   ɪ t]

Spectrograms of *pit* **and** *spit*.

2.23 The Aspiration Rule

We have established that aspirated and unaspirated sounds are acoustically distinct (see the spectrogram, opposite) and that they involve different articulatory gestures. We now add the observation that the distribution of aspirated stops is predictable. That is, English aspirated and unaspirated stops occur in a *complementary distribution* that can be described by the following phonological rule:

> *English Aspiration* (version 1)
> Word-initial voiceless stops are aspirated.

While this rule makes no special reference to any particular word in the English lexicon, it affects the pronunciation of lexical items beginning with a word-initial segment that falls within a certain natural class of sounds — the voiceless stops. Since the rule is perfectly general, it will apply to new words that enter the language; and, if we assume that this rule is recruited as part of the process of producing utterances, we can explain why utterances resulting from speech errors follow the same distributional pattern for aspirated sounds.

In this view, sounds may be listed in lexical entries unmarked for aspiration, and an aspiration rule will apply where appropriate. This approach takes the form of a *derivation:*

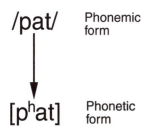

/pat/   Phonemic form

[pʰat]   Phonetic form

Derivation of *pot.*

Since English *p* and *b* are in *contrasting distribution,* it is possible to construct minimal pairs that diverge in meaning while differing phonetically only in that *b* and *p* are intersubstituted (e.g., [bæd]/[pæd]). Therefore, /p/ and /b/ count as two different *phonemes* of English (notice that phonemes are written between slashes rather than brackets). We have seen that pairs of aspirated and unaspirated sounds, [t] and [tʰ], for example, do not play this role in English: There is no possible minimal pair [tap]/[tʰap] where the second word is *top* and the first means something else, because [t] and [tʰ] do not overlap in their distribution. We can predict whether a given sound will be aspirated if we know its position and its phonetic features (for example, if it is in a position that aspirates, and if it is a voiceless stop). Because, [t] and [tʰ] are in *complementary distribution* they count as *allophones* of a single /t/-phoneme.

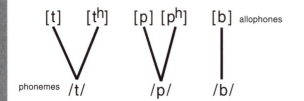

Some examples of allophony.

For English, then, [p] and [b] are different phonemes, and [p] and [pʰ] are not. What about other languages? Do they have the same system of phonemes that we find in English? We can address this question by considering some data on the distribution of aspirated sounds in

Assamese, a language of northeastern India.

| [pat] | 'leaf' | [bat] | 'road' |
| [pʰat] | 'split' | [bʰat] | 'boiled rice' |

Even in this small amount of data, we find two significant differences in the distribution of aspiration in Assamese compared with that in English. First, notice that [b], a voiced sound can be aspirated in Assamese. Even more importantly, the alternation between [p] and [pʰ] and between [b] and [bʰ] can produce minimal pairs in Assamese — these distributions are contrastive in Assamese (while the distribution of [p] and [pʰ] is complementary in English!). This suggests the following picture for Assamese.

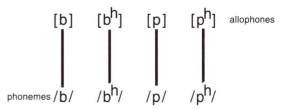

Some allophones and phonemes of Assamese.

Clearly, English and Assamese do not share the same phonemic inventory. More generally, it is common to find differences in the phonemic inventories of the world's languages. At the same time, the inventory of possible phonemes from which a given language's repertoire is drawn is quite limited, there being thousands of languages and fewer than two hundred phonemes from which to choose. ■

The input to the rule, /pat/, is an *underlying form* (also called *phonemic* form) designated by flanking virgules. This is the form in which *pot* is listed in the lexicon. The derived form (the *phonetic form*), written between brackets, indicates how the word is pronounced. The *phonemes* associated with *pot*

HISTORY 2.23

The construct of the phoneme was developed in the Western tradition at the end of the nineteenth century by two Russian linguists, Baudoin de Courtenay and his student Kruszewski (Caroll 1955). This work was developed further by the members of the Prague circle, a group of linguists working in the late 1920s and 1930s whose scholarship led to contemporary work in the generative tradition.

The circle included two linguists, Jakobson and Trubetskoy, whose work on phonemic analysis has directly influenced the modern concept of the phoneme. Indeed, the birth of a more general distinction between the "-emic" and the "-etic" aspects of an analysis can be traced to the work of these Prague linguists. The contrast distinguishes the aspects of analysis that that are special to the case at hand (the "-emic" characteristics) from those that follow from more general, perhaps universal principles (the "-etic" characteristics). These terms of analysis have been found useful in fields other than linguistics, for example in cultural anthropology (see Hymes 1964). ■

(/p/, /a/, and /t/) represent unpredictable aspects of its pronunciation — the phonetic information that cannot be derived by applying phonological rules (like the Aspiration Rule). Since the Aspiration Rule is very general, it applies to every phonemic form entered in the lexicon that begins with a voiceless stop. Furthermore, any entry that begins with something other than a voiceless stop is ignored by the rule, and any noninitial occurrence of any segment also fails to trigger the rule.

Before investigating other phonological rules, we can summarize the approach to phonological derivations with the following diagram:

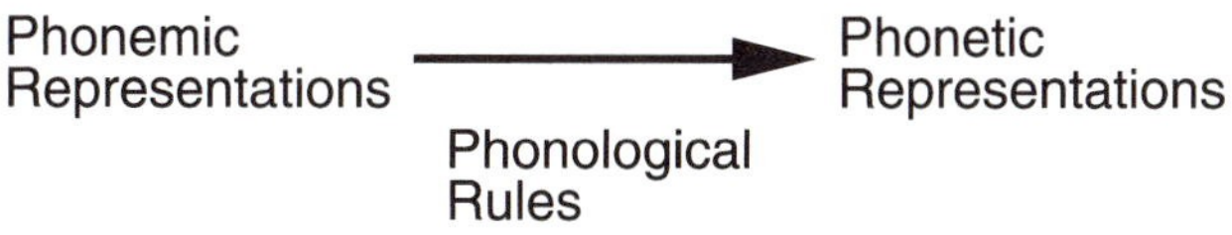

Are rules like the Aspiration Rule descriptive rules or prescriptive rules? Explain the sense in which aspiration can be considered to be a rule.

Phonemic
Representations ⟶ Phonetic
Representations

Phonological
Rules

Phonological derivations.

In adopting this model of phonological derivations we have radically departed from our first assumption about the form in which phonetic information is stored in the mind of a native speaker. In the current hypothesis, lexical entries include a phonemic representation that serves as an input to a phonological rule system.

HISTORY 2.23

Although the modern conception of the phoneme developed from work undertaken at the end of the nineteenth century by the Prague-circle linguists, there was a much older body of research developed over hundreds of years by the great grammarians of India containing a startling number of the insights that ground this more recent history. The linguistic investigations of Panini, the notable Hindu grammarian, can be traced back to approximately the third century BC, and are perhaps the best-known examples of this early work. Although Panini's grammatical analyses were generally ignored by linguists working in the West until the nineteenth century, the exegetical work of Frits Stall has shown that some of the most technical generalizations of contemporary linguistics were anticipated by Panini's work over a millennium ago (see Staal 1988 for discussion). To give the flavor of his interests, Staal discusses Panini's analysis of long and short vowels, assimilation rules, and the distinction between root and suffix. Even a cursory examination of these analyses justifies the high praise for Panini that Staal attributes to the great American linguist Leonard Bloomfield, who described Panini's work as "one of the greatest monuments of human intelligence." ∎

Hypothesis 2
Native speakers know a list of words of the language, each of which has a phonemic representation. These underlying forms are operated on by a set of phonological rules that derive phonetic representations (which are coupled with instructions for how to produce and recognize the represented sound sequence).

We can examine the productive nature of the Aspiration Rule by implementing a *generative* rule that checks the first segment of a phonemic representation and applies aspiration as necessary. The result of applying this rule can be illustrated by the following list of inputs and outputs:

Inputs	Outputs
/pap/	[pʰap]
/tep/	[tʰep]
/pæt/	[pʰæt]
/bæn/	[bæn]
/gæb/	[gæb]
/kag/	[kʰag]

So far, so good. Notice that in each case, the voiceless stops ([t], [p], and [k]) are aspirated. Unfortunately, there are certain phonemic representations for which the current version of the Aspiration Rule is unsatisfactory. Consider, for example, what happens if we apply the rule to *re-try*, *biplane*, and *declaim*.

Inputs	Outputs
/ritrai/	[ritrai]
/baiplen/	[baiplen]
/diklem/	[diklem]

In each case, our rule incorrectly predicts that all the non-word-initial occurrences of voiceless stops will be unaffected by the Aspiration Rule. We purposely excluded such occurrences from the scope of the rule so that the many previous cases in which noninitial voiceless segments are unaspirated would be properly handled. We now discover that not all non-word-initial instances of voiceless stops can be treated equally by the Aspiration Rule.

2.24 Prefixes and Aspiration

Something is wrong with our hypothesis: the clear-cut distinction between initial and noninitial voiceless stops is not the right one for characterizing the distribution of aspiration in English. What we need to figure out is, What distinguishes the word-internal occurrences of voiceless stops in words like *stop* from those in words like *re-try*, *biplane*, and *declaim*? These last three examples are complex words made up of two meaningful parts called *morphemes*. In the case of *re-try*, for example, there is a *prefix*, *re-* and a *root try*. We will say more about *morphology* in the next chapter, but for now we note that for the purposes of the Aspiration Rule, the /t/ in *re-try* triggers aspiration just as if the prefix were not there. More generally, root-initial occurrences of voiceless stops aspirate as, for instance, in examples like *biplane* ([baipʰlen]) and *declaim* ([dikʰlem]).

Suppose we change the Aspiration Rule to reflect these new observations:

English Aspiration (version 2):
Root-initial voiceless stops are aspirated.

To test this hypothesis we need to formally mark the distinction between prefix and root at the level of phonemic representation. Suppose we use the symbol + to indicate the boundary between a prefix and a root. The representation for *re-try*, for example, is /ri+trai/. Since the /t/ is root-initial in this case, the revised Aspiration Rule will apply, and the correct phonetic form, [ri+tʰrai], is derived.

Before moving on to other phonological phenomena, we should reflect on the approach we have adopted. We have discovered that it is important to frame precise generative rules that can be tested

Can you formulate a hypothesis that correctly distinguishes these cases? Can you think of any other data that supports your hypothesis?

IN DETAIL 2.24

Although the original data continue to be correctly handled by the new Aspiration Rule, and examples like *re-try,* that motivated the revision of the Aspiration Rule are correctly accounted for as well, there remain two weaknesses in this version of the rule, one empirical and one methodological. The empirical problem involves cases with prefixes that themselves begin with voiceless aspirated stops such as *trans-, pre-,* or *pro-.* Consider, for example, the result of applying version two of the Aspiration Rule to cases like *telephone, pretest,* or *pro-life.*

In *telephone* we expect the phonetic form to be [tʰɛlʌ+fon]; the output for *pretest* should be [pʰri+tʰɛst], and for *pro-life,* [pʰro+laif]. Unfortunately, since the current version of the rule fails to aspirate the non-root-initial voiceless stops at the beginning of each prefix, the initial aspiration in these examples is not predicted. Apparently, the property of being root-initial is sufficient but not necessary to trigger aspiration. When a condition for a rule is sufficient but not necessary, one possibility is to add further conditions to capture the extra cases. For example, we could entertain a version of the Aspiration Rule that combines the insights of each of its previous versions so that voiceless stops that were either word-initial or root-initial would

aspirate. Call this version 3 of the Aspiration Rule:

English Aspiration (version 3): Root-initial voiceless stops are aspirated and word initial voiceless stops are aspirated.

Of course, we can convince ourselves that this version of the rule accounts for all of our previous data. But this strategy highlights a second problem with the path we have been pursuing — each new set of data seems to require another condition in the Aspiration Rule. Such an analysis is more complicated than we would like and fails to coherently describe the aspiration environment in English. We would prefer an account that explained all of the data with a single generalization. Furthermore, as is often the case with generalization-losing rules, it is not difficult to think up still more problematic cases that would require still more separate conditions.

Can you think of any other kinds of examples that could pose problems for the current version of the Aspiration Rule?

There are, for example, words like *anti-pro-life* — [æntʰipʰro+laif] — that involve multiple prefixes. Notice that even the third version of the Aspiration Rule fails to correctly aspirate the first [p] in this word, since it is neither word-initial nor root-initial. The aspiration of the [t] is even more problematic because it is

contained within the first prefix. Clearly there is something incorrect in the current formulation of the Aspiration Rule. A close examination of these last problematic cases (and, indeed, all previous cases of aspiration) suggests that the distribution of aspiration can be simply described in terms of syllable structure as follows:

Aspirate syllable-initial voiceless stops.

To better understand this proposal, we begin by examining the notion of a syllable more closely:

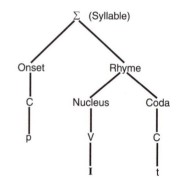

Representation for *pit*.

Syllable structure is a level of organization at which sequences of consonants (C) and vowels (V) are organized. Syllables must contain a *nucleus* (normally a vowel with the exception of words like [mirəkl]

Create syllable representations for the following words: man, weight, transfer, prepare, joking, family, *and* reunion.

IN DETAIL 2.24

[miracle] in which a sonorous consonant — in this case [l] — serves this role). We might call this the *Nucleus Constraint.* The nucleus is preceded by zero, one or two consonants in an *onset* position; and followed by zero, one, or more consonants in a *coda.*

A number of general principles work to define the array of possible syllable structures of a language. One such principle, the *Maximal Onset Principle* (MOP), guarantees (all things being equal — see below) that a consonant is syllabified with the onset of a syllable rather than with a coda. For example, a sequence like *pataka* is syllabified as *pa-ta-ka* rather than *pat-ak-a.* To consider a real case from English, *attack* will be syllabified [ʌ-tæk] rather than [ʌt-æk] (using hyphens to indicate syllable boundaries). Let us look at the syllable structure tree for *attack (above).*

Notice, in particular, that the [t] is attached to the C in the onset position rather than the one in the coda, in accordance with the Maximal Onset Principle.

Build syllable structures for the following words: surprise, winter, *and* resume. *Discuss how the Maximal Onset Principle applies in each case.*

Languages restrict what can constitute a legal sequence of consonants in the onset of a syllable. In English,

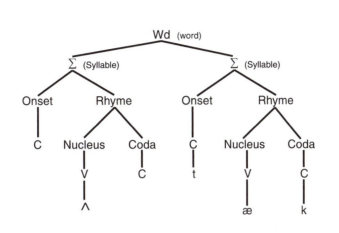

Representation for *attack.*

the onset may consist of as many as three consonants; for instance in the word [spri] *(spree).*

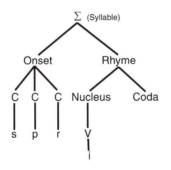

Representation for *spree.*

But onsets such as *psr* or *kpl* are not grammatical. There are parallel limitations on what can appear in a coda. Roughly speaking, legal coda sequences look like legal onset sequences but in the reverse order. So, whereas *pl* and *sk* are acceptable in

Can you explain why many English speakers pronounce the Yiddish loan words knish *and* kvel *with an extra [ə] — [kənɪš] and [kəvɛl], instead of [knɪš] and [kvɛl]?*

onset position (as in *plea,* [pli], and *ski,* [ski]), we find *lp* and *ks* in coda position (in, for example, *help,* [hɛlp], and *ox,* [aks]). We can describe these sequences in terms of the *sonority hierarchy* — a continuum of consonant sounds that grade from least to most constriction of the vocal tract during production. So the stops [p], [t], and [k] are the least sonorous (that is, they are *obstruents*) because the oral tract is completely occluded at the place of articulation. The nasals, [m], [n], and [ŋ] are next on the continuum because they involve closure in the oral tract, while at the same time allowing air to pass unrestricted in the nasal tract. Fricatives, [r] and [l] and glides are progressively more sonorous, since they involve even less overall obstruction than nasals.

Create syllable trees for the following words: string, spore, *and* screw. *Are these words consistent with the sonority hierarchy? Discuss your conclusion.*

In general, onsets allow sequences of consonants in order of decreasing sonority, whereas codas permit sequences of consonants with increasing sonority. Moreover, these conditions on onset and coda sequences are also observed generally across the languages of the world. English also allows sequences of two vowels in the nucleus (so-called diphthongs), but the range of permissible sequences is restricted to [ɔi], [ai], and [au] in most dialects. Words like *annoy, eye,* and *bow* will be represented by trees in which each vowel of the diphthong occupies a separate vowel slot in the nucleus.

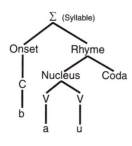

Representation for *bow*.

Create syllable trees for the following words containing diphthongs: bow, coy, eye, lie, out, cow, *and* I.

English has a further restriction (the *Lax Vowel Constraint*) that allows lax vowels (such as [ɪ]) only in *closed syllables* — syllables that do not end in vowels. Consequently, *open syllables* like *[pɪ] are not possible words in English (see above).

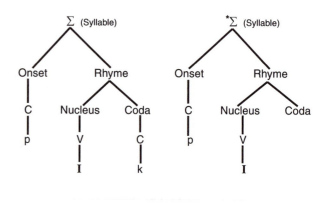

Representations for lax vowels.

Create syllable trees for the following French words: je *('I')*, fait *('fact'), and* deux *('two'). (You may need to find an informant if you do not speak French.) On the basis of this data, determine whether French observes the Lax Vowel Constraint.*

We can now return to the final set of data that hampers our current version of the Aspiration Rule. Recall that certain voiceless stops in non-word-initial position are subject to aspiration, while others are not. For example, we need to distinguish the [t] in *anti-pro-life*, which does aspirate, from the [t] in *stop*, which does not. Here are some other relevant data:

enter	([ɛntʰr])	present	([pʰrəzɛnt])
appear	([ʌpʰir])	unstrap	([ʌn+stræp])
alcove	([ælkʰov])	apt	([æpt])
anchor	([æŋkʰr])	aardvark	([ardvark])

Try to develop a generalization explaining the distribution of aspiration in this data set. It may help to consider the syllable representations of this data. You should also test your hypothesis against the other data discussed in connection with previous forms of the rule.

IN DETAIL 2.24

In each case where aspiration applies, the aspirated segment is a syllable onset. The syllable structure for *appear,* right, gives an illustrative example.

In contrast, in each case where a candidate voiceless stop fails to aspirate, that segment is not in an onset position. The representation for *apt,* below, is a case in point.

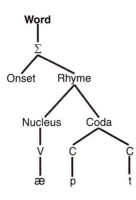

Representation for *apt.*

Suppose we propose a fourth and final hypothesis about English aspiration that captures this relationship between aspiration and syllable structure.

English Aspiration (syllabic version):
Aspirate all syllable-initial voiceless stops.

Notice that this formulation has many virtues: It is simple, it seems to cover the problematic cases under consideration; and, since all word-initial segments are by definition syllable-initial, this rule correctly handles all the foregoing aspiration data!

One final interesting consequence of this analysis of English aspiration stems from an interaction between aspiration and the Maximal Onset Principle. We have seen that this principle ensures that words like *appear* are syllabified as *ʌ-pir* rather than as *ʌp-ir.* As a result, the voiceless stop [p] must end up in the syllable-initial onset

position, and (given the way we have formulated the Aspiration Rule) must undergo aspiration. Indeed, [ʌpʰir] is the correct result. In the case of a word like *happy* ([hæpi]), however, Selkirk (1980) has argued that the [p] is resyllabified into the coda slot of the first syllable (i.e., *hæp-i*), effectively, overriding the Maximal Onset Principle. The result is that the [p] of *happy* is not aspirated because it is not in syllable-initial position — a rather subtle interaction that we can describe with this approach.

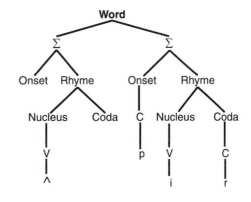

Representation for *appear.*

Create syllable trees for the following words: mental, attic, *and* antipode. *Which segments undergo aspiration in these examples?*

But what distinguishes *happy* from other two-syllable words like *repair,* in which the [p] is in the onset of the second syllable (pursuant to the Maximal Onset Principle) and is (consequently) aspirated? The contrasts can be explained by considering the stress patterns associated with the two different kinds of data. For words like *repair,* which follow the Maximal Onset Principle and associate aspiration with the medial stop, the second syllable bears the primary stress. However, in cases like *happy* and *open,* primary stress is assigned to the first syllable, and here, the stop in the onset of the second syllable is resyllabified into the coda position of the first syllable. We can tentatively call this principle the *Resyllabification Principle.*

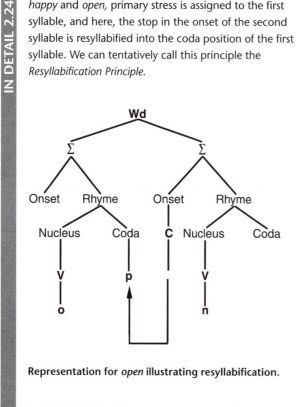

Representation for *open* illustrating resyllabification.

Can you explain the difference between cases like repair *and* happy? *You should also consider* open, retro, *and* attic *(which pattern like* happy *in that they do not involve aspiration on the medial stop) and* attack *and* appear *(which pattern like* repair*).*

Although we cannot formulate the Resyllabification Principle precisely until we have discussed the representation of stress in more detail (below), we can note some general conclusions concerning the interaction of this principle with the Maximal Onset Principle.

In a sense, these two principles conflict with one another: Satisfying one principle comes at the cost of violating the other one! The particular claim about English that we are considering is that the Resyllabification Principle takes precedence over the Maximal Onset Principle (for cases such as *happy* and *open* in which there is first-syllable stress). In such cases, violations of the Maximal Onset Principle do not necessarily rule out a particular representation (in that it may be "saved" by satisfying the Resyllabification Principle). This counts as an extra complication in the phonology of English, which allows us to correctly distinguish the two kinds of cases at hand. ■

against a set of data. Furthermore, the best hypotheses are not always intuitive — if you ask a native English-speaker where they aspirate their voiceless stops, they are unlikely to know the answer (even if you explain the question) unless they have taken a linguistics course; at the same time, they know perfectly well how to apply aspiration when in the throes of linguistic performance. Finally, we have developed some confidence in a general framework of analysis in which lexical items are associated with phonemic forms that are abstract representations. These underlying forms are mapped onto surface, phonetic forms by phonological rules (the English Aspiration Rule being our first detailed example).

2.25 Vowel Lengthening

We now revisit the phenomenon of vowel lengthening in English, and incorporate a new rule into the phonological system we are developing to account for these facts. The basic generalization is that vowels located before voiced sounds are lengthened, explaining the contrast in vowel length between *bit* and *bid*. We can represent this distinction in vowel length at the level of phonetic form by recruiting the symbol : to indicate lengthening. The phonetic forms for *bit* and *bid* are [bɪt] and [bɪːd], respectively. If we posit /bɪt/ and /bɪd/ as the underlying forms, then it remains to formulate a rule that correctly maps these phonemic representations into the correct phonetic forms:

English Vowel Lengthening
Lengthen vowels before voiced consonants

This version of the Vowel Lengthening Rule seems to correctly predict the distribution of vowel length for our data set. Moreover, in combination with the Aspiration Rule, our phonological system is beginning to account for an interesting part of English *phonology*. There is, however, a complication concerning words that manifest both aspiration and lengthening (for example, *cog, tail,* and *comb*). The Aspiration Rule correctly predicts that the initial segment is aspirated, and the lengthening rule correctly lengthens the vowel; but we must also allow these two changes to apply in a single phonetic representation, for example, [kʰaːg]. Our rule system must allow that both rules can apply cumulatively in a single derivation.

How would you revise the current conception of the rule system to be able to derive cases like cog? *Describe the step-by-step derivation of* cog *in your revised approach.*

2.26 Rule Ordering

Assuming that we allow phonological rules to apply in sequence, we can cycle through them using the output of the first rule as the input to the second. For many cases in the data set, at most one phonological rule introduces a structural change. But in *cog, tail,* or *comb* we see a single derivation that involves both rules. Furthermore, such cases are not rare in English. Any word that begins with a voiceless stop and contains a vowel that precedes a voiced consonant will require the application of both rules. We use *cog* as an illustrative example:

Derivation of *cog*.

The discovery that phonological derivations can involve more than one rule leads to interesting further questions; for example, whether the order in which the Aspiration Rule and the Vowel-Lengthening Rules are applied makes any difference. We can determine whether the order of rule application is important by comparing the final phonetic form derived from one ordering with that derived from the alternate ordering (again, using *cog* as an example).

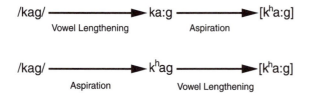

Alternative derivations of *cog*.

On the basis of this data, it appears that rule ordering does not make any difference in the output. (We will, however, return to the question of ordering later in the next chapter.)

2.27 Morphemes and Lengthening

Finally, let's consider examples like *debone* and *re-do* (that involve sequences of vowels and voiced consonants separated by a mor- pheme boundary) to see what our rule system predicts. Notice that the Lengthening Rule does not lengthen the vowels in the prefixes *de-* and *re-*, since they each contain a vowel followed by a voiced consonant, but these are separated by a morpheme boundary + and do not count as adjacent for the purposes of the rule. We can test this conclusion by measuring vowel length. The spectrograms of *read* and *re-do* support our prediction. The [i] in *read* is long since it precedes a [d], a voiced consonant. In contrast, the [i] in *re-do* is not lengthened in spite of preceding an [d] (since, in our account, the latter sound is not strictly adjacent to the [i]).

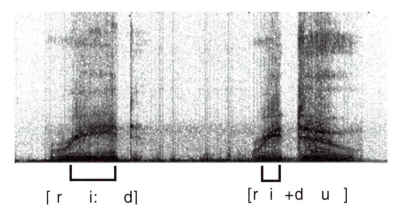

[r   i: d]   [r i +d u]

Spectrograms showing vowel length for *read* and *re-do*.

IN DETAIL 2.27

Let us now consider further data that suggest that syllable boundaries, rather than morpheme boundaries, must be referenced in the best account of vowel lengthening.

drag	([dræ:g])	dragoon	([dræ$gun])
cub	([kʌ:b])	kabob	([kʌ$ba:b])
cam	([kʰæ:m])	Camus	([kʰæ$mu])
rag	([ræ:g])	ragout	([ræ$gu])

In each of the cases in the first column, the voiced segment following the vowel is in the same syllable as the vowel. In the second column, the underlined vowels are separated from following voiced consonants by a syllable boundary ($). The current version of the Vowel-Lengthening Rule fails to distinguish the cases the rule applies to, lengthening indiscriminately in all cases. We can remedy this problem by adopting the same kind of strategy we adopted in our investigation of English Aspiration in the following revision of the Lengthening Rule.

English Vowel-Lengthening (Syllabic version)
Lengthen vowels before a voiced consonant in coda position.

This version of the Lengthening Rule will correctly distinguish the cases in most recent set of data. Let us examine two, *cam* and *Camus*, in detail.

In *cam*, the [æ] lengthens because it is followed by a voiced sound ([m]) in coda position. In the second example, *Camus*, the [æ] does not lengthen because the following coda is empty. Furthermore, since morpheme boundaries always occur at syllable boundaries, all of the original contrasts involving multimorphemic cases in which lengthening is blocked across morpheme boundaries are also correctly handled by the current formulation of Vowel Lengthening. ■

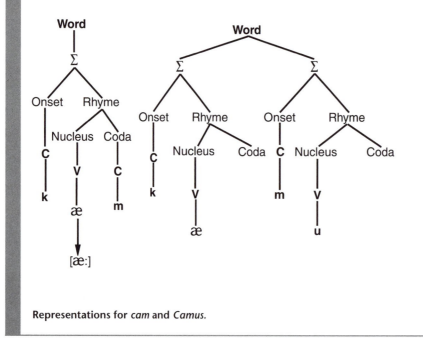

Representations for *cam* and *Camus*.

2.28 The Schwa

We now turn to one final rule of English phonology that concerns the distribution of [ə], the *schwa*. In the approach we have been developing, each lexical item is paired with a phonemic representation. This representation contains all the aspects of the word's pronunciation that are not predictable by the rules of phonology that generate phonetic representations. In particular, the basic sequence of consonants and vowels that are associated with each word must be provided in the lexical entry, since one cannot predict which phonemes a word will consist of based on its meaning or part of speech. One might suppose that this strategy would also extend to the case of schwa. So, the underlying representation for a word that contained a schwa like *basket*, for example, would be /bæskət/. But this approach quickly encounters complications and missed generalizations.

Consider, for example what lexical entry you will provide for a word like man ([mæn]) that contains an [æ] vowel in isolation, but which contains a schwa in words like *woman* ([wʊmən]) and *chairman* ([čærmən]). We would like to explain this variation in pronunciation. Ambiguous words like *present*, also show a kind of variation, having alternative pronunciations in which the schwa may be in either syllable depending on whether we are dealing with the noun or the verb. Again, we would like to understand what conditions this alternation.

To address these concerns, we must determine whether there is a generalization that governs the distribution of schwa. If so, we can account for its privileges of occurrence within our phonological system. The question is, what is the common environment in which schwa appears in words like *basket*, *woman*, and *present*? In each case, the vowel that reduces to schwa is in an unstressed syllable.

We can see this correlation clearly in words like *telepathy* and *telepathic*. The phonetic forms for these words are [tə̆lɛpə̆ði] and [tɛlə̆pæðə̆k], respectively (using the [˘] to indicate a lack of stress). Notice that the stress patterns are different for these two words, and that in each case the schwa's position shifts to the unstressed syllables. We can codify this principle in the following rule:

English Vowel Reduction
Substitute [ə] for vowels in unstressed syllables.

The Vowel-Reduction Rule applies in phonological derivations along with the Aspiration Rule and the Vowel-Lengthening Rule. As with the other two rules, the Reduction Rule plays a role in the mapping from phonemic to phonetic representation; for example, turning /wʊmæn/ into [wʊmən]. An interesting consequence of this analysis is that schwa is not a phoneme of English. That is, unlike the other distinctive sounds of the language, the distribution of schwa is predictable, and hence derived by a reduction rule. In this regard, the status of the English schwa turns out to be rather like that of long vowels in English — there is a length difference in English vowels at the level of phonetic representation, but long vowels are derived rather than posited as phonemes of the language. The English schwa, too, is best treated as generated by a phonological rule.

Notice the prediction that this rule system makes for basket, *specifically with respect to the (non-)aspiration of the [k]. Is this the correct prediction? What assumptions are being made about syllabification?*

IN DETAIL 2.28

Although this approach seems adequate for the data at hand, there are further difficulties to consider (see below). These considerations, combined with studies of stress and meter, have led researchers to develop a new level of representation at which a more fruitful analysis of Vowel Reduction can be developed (see Liberman and Prince 1976; Selkirk 1984; Prince 1983; Hayes 1980, 1982). The first problem has already been alluded to: Many words that contain a schwa do so only when assigned a particular stress pattern. We have already seen examples like *present* which can be pronounced either [prəsɛnt] or [prɛsənt]. It is, of course, possible to account for this variation by assigning two different phonemic representations to *present,* but we would generally like to avoid this multiplicity of underlying forms.

Make a list of as many other words that reveal the alternation in stress patterns observed in the noun present *and the verb* present. *Is there a correlation between the stress pattern and the part of speech in your examples?*

Moreover, there are some alternations in stress patterns (which, in turn determine the distribution of schwa) that cannot be adequately analyzed by positing alternative underlying stress patterns. For example, the root *telepath* must have reduced stress (ultimately resulting in a schwa) in the second syllable ([tɛlĕpæð]), but the stress pattern shifts when we add suffixes like *-ic* or *-y* as in *telepathic* and *telepathy.* In short, we cannot determine the stress pattern for a word beginning with *telepath-* unless we know which (if any) suffixes will be attached.

If we can provide a systematic analysis of stress assignment, and, in particular, of how stress assignment changes when roots combine with other morphemes, then we can better understand the distribution of the schwa in English. One promising approach depends on representing the metrical structure of words and phrases. In a metrical theory, a stressed syllable is represented as "strong" (S) relative to a "weak" (W) syllable with which it is paired. In this view, we do not mark stress directly on a syllable; instead, stress is a matter of relative promi-

nence defined with respect to another element in a representation. For example, a two-syllable word with second syllable stress like *persist* is associated with the following metrical structure (since the top node is not relative to any other element, it is arbitrary whether we consider it strong or weak. Thus, you might think of the top S as standing for "start" rather than "strong"):

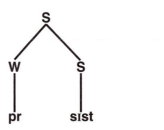

Representation for *persist.*

The structure for the adjective *perfect,* which has first syllable stress, reverses the relative prominence.

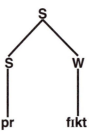

Representation for the adjective *perfect.*

IN DETAIL 2.28

The structure associated with the verb *perfect* (which has second-syllable stress) is the same as that associated with *persist*.

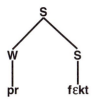

Representation for the verb *perfect*.

Suppose we combine this metrical analysis with our previous work on syllable structure and then reconsider our account of Vowel Reduction. For an example like the noun *present* (with first-syllable stress), a full representation might look like this.

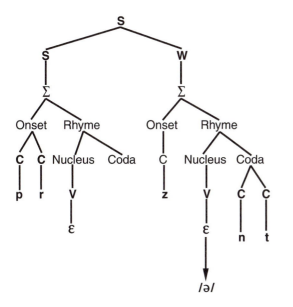

Representation for the noun *present*.

Notice that the second syllable is weak relative to the first syllable, and that this syllable undergoes Vowel Reduction. This suggests a new generalization aimed at capturing the distribution of the English schwa. Suppose we rewrite Vowel Reduction so that it is sensitive to metrical structure as follows:

Vowel Reduction (metrical version)
Reduce vowels in weak syllables.

This version of the rule predicts that the second syllable of the noun *present* is reduced — the correct prediction. Now let's examine the structure for the verb *present,* with second-syllable stress.

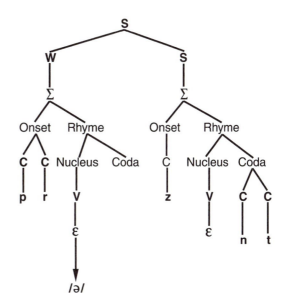

Representation for the verb *present*.

In this case the rule correctly predicts that the first syllable is reduced because it is weak.

Explain the different patterns of vowel reduction in the noun progress *and the verb* progress.

There is one further phonological process at work in these vowel reduction environments that bears consideration. Consider the following data:

telepathic	([tʰɛləpʰæðɪk])	telepathy	([tʰəlɛpəði])
prepare	([pripʰær])	preparation	([prɛpərešn])
recall	([rikʰɔl])	recollection	([rɛkəlɛkšn])

Here is the puzzle: The underlined voiceless stops in the examples in the left column aspirate, but those in the right column do not. How can we explain this difference?

Below is the representation for *telepathy*. The crucial consideration is the constituency of the [p]. As it stands, the [p] constitutes the onset of the third syllable — *te-le-pa-thy*, a result required by the Maximal Onset Principle, predicting that the [p] should aspirate. Never-

theless, the [p] in *telepathy* is not aspirated. If the [p] were located in the coda of the second syllable — *te-lep-a-thy*, we could account for the lack of aspiration, but at the cost of violating the Maximal Onset Principle. This recalls our analysis of the syllabification of *open* and *happy*, discussed above in which we argued that the [p] is located in the coda position of the first syllable, in contradiction to the Maximal Onset Principle. This unexpected syllabification was claimed to be a consequence of the Resyllabification Principle that was triggered by stress patterns associated with such examples.

Suppose we formulate the Resyllabification Principle in the terms of our metrical theory of stress as follows:

Resyllabification Principle
Attach the onset of a weak syllable to a preceding coda slot.

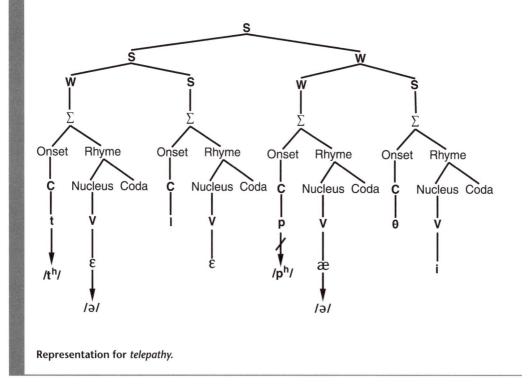

Representation for *telepathy*.

This accounts for the resyllabification in examples like *happy* and *open* since in these cases the second syllable is weak, and the [p] can be reassigned to the coda position of the first syllable.

By the same reasoning, we predict that restructuring will apply in the case of *telepathy*.

Restructuring explains why the medial [p] fails to aspirate (since aspiration is limited to codas and restructuring reassigns the [p] to onset position). Combined with the Maximal Onset Principle and an approach to aspiration that is sensitive to metrical structure, this analysis of restructuring allows us to capture extremely subtle aspects of English phonology. ▪

Unlike the [p] in telepathy, *the [p] in* telepathic *is aspirated. Can you explain why?*

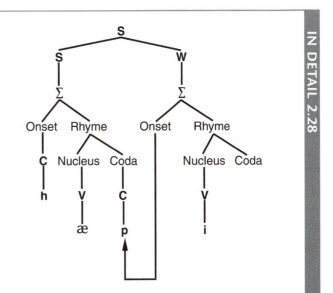

Representation for *happy*.

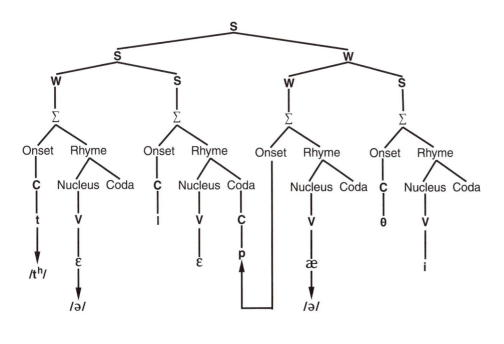

Revised representation for *telepathy*.

3. Words

3.1 Lexical Knowledge

In the previous chapter we examined certain aspects of the sound system — one of the subsystems of a *generative grammar*. Our aim was to explain how a speaker's knowledge of a native language is represented and, ultimately, to understand how it is acquired. More specifically, we have been concerned with how to understand the portion of a speaker's knowledge that pertains to the phonetic and phonological properties of a language. Of course, there is more to linguistic competence than merely having a command of a language's sound system. In this chapter we take up a second aspect of linguistic knowledge that is central to our investigation of linguistic theory: *morphology*, the study of words and their constitutive parts.

As with phonetic and phonological knowledge, most aspects of morphological knowledge turn out to be tacit. That is, we should expect the rules and principles involved in lexical representations to seem just as surprising as those involved in phonetic and phonological analyses (for example, the Aspiration Rule). And our investigation of morphological rules and principles once again requires us to gather and assess linguistic data, measuring our tentative understandings of how lexical information is organized in the mind of native speakers against these sets of facts, and applying the usual principles of scientific investigation. In other words, we propose that there is a complex body of knowledge that supports the common ability to understand and produce words, and that merits our investigation.

Our study of words has several aspects. We begin by discussing the organization of the lexicon, with the aim of understanding what kinds of information must be represented and how they must be organized. We also examine the internal structure of words. We have already discovered that words are composed of sequences of sound segments; but, as we have seen, words are also organized on a second morphological level. Here our interest in word structure focuses on how morphemes may be combined to build complex words out of smaller meaningful parts. We are concerned with the study of *affixes* — prefixes, suffixes, and *infixes* (affixes inserted into words) — but also with other morphological processes that demand our attention. We then move on to discuss the process of lexical interpretation, investigating how word meanings are composed of the meanings of morphological parts, how semantic information is represented, and how lexical knowledge and world knowledge are interconnected.

Finally, we examine interactions between morphology and other components of the grammar. *Morpho-phonemics* concerns aspects of the morphology-phonology interface. Here we discover interesting phonological consequences in many lexical derivations. For example, we have already considered the case of *electric*, which ends in a [k], while the root in *electricity* ends in an [s]. The rule that introduces the [s]-sound is a good example of a *morpho-phonemic* rule (one that operates on the border of phonology and morphology). We study a number of other morpho-phonemic interactions below. We conclude by examining some cases in which the structure of words depends on aspects of the structure of sentences, what we might call *morpho-syntax*.

3.2 Do Words Exist?

How many words does the following sentence contain:

Do words exist?

Obviously, three. This task seems very easy; in fact, almost simple-minded. This is because it is so natural for us to pick out words from a speech signal that we don't even realize what is required to accomplish such a task. To understand this process, let us first look at the speech signal itself:

How many words are there in the following utterances:

a. Jeet yet?

b. D'ja wanna leave?

c. Amena go.

d. Was he supposeda hafta leave?

How can you justify your answers?

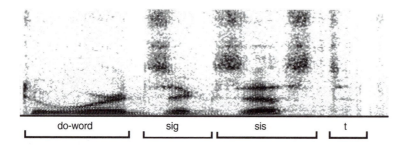

| do-word | sig | sis | t |

Spectrogram of *Do words exist?*

Notice that there is nothing in the speech signal to indicate where one word ends or another begins. Thus, the sentence that we hear as:

There are no spaces between spoken words.

could be represented on the level of the acoustic signal as something like this:

therearenospacesbetweenspokenwords

And in fact, the situation is even worse. The sounds that make up different words are not arranged in an orderly fashion but are in fact spread across perceptual word boundaries. This phenomenon is known as *coarticulation*. If we try to depict the actual situation in

---

HISTORY 3.2

Although it may seem surprising, it has been quite controversial to develop a linguistic procedure for systematically identifying words (say, in an unfamiliar language). But how could there be any question about the number of words we are dealing with in any given case? Beginning students of a language often assume that words are conveniently demarcated by the writing system, and wonder what more evidence for their identification is needed. But we have already seen that the spelling system is misleading as far as the phonetic properties of lexical items are concerned, so there is no reason to take the boundaries imposed by the writing system too seriously, either.

Furthermore, thousands of languages do not have writing systems, and there are many others for which the writing system yields counterintuitive or inconsistent results. For example, consider the following data from Warao, a language of Venezuela (from Osborn 1967, cited in Langacker 1973). How would you go about identifying the words in these examples?

mipumeherepute
'they will want them to see'

kapatameheremoana
'has not yet wanted (him) to cut'

norohupute
'they will sit down individually'

Martinet (1960) suggests approaching these questions by applying linguistic tests rather than relying on the writing system. He discusses French cases like *sac à main* ('purse'), in which the writing system indicates that we find three words, while the principles of French morphology would indicate that it is one word. The evidence that Martinet cites concerns the plural form, which is *sac à mains* rather than **sacs à main.* Since the plural comes at the end of the string of items, Martinet argues, it must collectively constitute a single word. He contrasts the string *carte à jouer* ('playing card') which, in contrast to *sac à main,* may optionally appear with an internal plural *(cartes à jouer).* The form of the plural, Martinet notes, varies across speakers. This suggests the intriguing possibility that *carte à jouer* is one word for some speakers of French and three for others! In English, the point is illustrated by the expression *attorney general.* Although written as two words, many speakers pluralize the form as *attorney generals* (as in *Kennedy and Reno were two attorney generals*) whereas others use the plural form *attorneys general.* For the former group, the expression functions as a single word, and for the latter it functions as two. ∎

writing, the sound information reaching our ears can be represented by the string below.

therære nospacesbetweespokerwords

Everything described so far would already be complex enough if the words we hear were always produced in exactly the same way. But this is not

the case, as many properties of the acoustic signal are influenced by physical characteristics of the vocal tract, which vary from one individual to another (for example, by overall size). So, utterances that are perceived as containing exactly the same sounds vary dramatically in their acoustic properties depending on who produced them. For example, the same utterance articulated by three

---

PRO 3.2

Of course words "really" exist. Even though there is not always a space between words in the speech stream, we can still develop a linguistic criterion for what defines a word. Leonard Bloomfield, an influential linguist writing in the 1930s, defines the word as follows:

A free form that does not consist entirely of lesser free forms is a word. Thus, 'boy,' which admits of no further analysis into meaningful parts, is a word; 'boyish,' although capable of such analysis, is a word, because one of its constituents, the '-ish,' is a bound form; other words, such as 'receive,' 'perceive,' 'remit,' 'permit,' consist entirely of bound forms. (Bloomfield 1933:25)

By applying this morphological test, we are always able to determine which linguistic elements are words and which are not. See if you can apply Bloomfield's procedure to identify the words in the following example:

[tzvɛrizitəkaunðənʌmbrvwrdsnõɪsɛnəns] ■

CON 3.2

Words do not exist...not "really." We have already seen that the English writing system does not help to consistently identify words, and that there is no obvious phonetic information that we can use. It is not clear that there is any other available method of individuation. Martinet (1960) explains that

It would be a vain endeavor to seek to define more closely the concept of 'word' in general linguistics. We might be tempted to do so in the framework of a given language. But even in this case the application of rigorous criteria often leads to analysis which do not accord with the current use of the term.

...It is much less easy to grasp a unit of the same type in languages like English...[compared to Latin]. It is known that the accentual unit of these languages does not coincide with what might be called the word, and this is linked with the difficulty in deciding the number of words contained in utterances like I'll go out...*English presents the additional difficult of the notorious 'genitives' of the type* the King of England's *(pp. 107-108).*

What problems in determining the number of words does Martinet have in mind when he worries about examples like I'll go out *and* the King of England's? *Why is it difficult to identify the number of words in these examples?*

The best we can make of the notion *word* is that it is a theoretical concept that may be replaced by other formal concepts like *morpheme* and *affix* when we want to achieve a scientific analysis of language. ■

different speakers involves three different acoustic signals. However, we still interpret these different physical signals to compose the same words. This continues to be an outstanding problem in the area of computer voice recognition, and not restricted simply to the variation in sound properties among speakers: Even the utterances made by the same individual may vary significantly depending on factors like excitement, tiredness, colds, and alcohol intoxication.

3.3 Lexical Access

In spite of the incredible complexity of the task of identifying the actual words in the speech signal, the skill of an average listener does not end there. For, even if one manages to isolate all the words in certain message, the effort is wasted unless we know what the words mean. Furthermore, recognizing and interpreting a spoken or written word is something we do amazingly quickly. The process is completely automatic and unavoidable. And, given that an average-educated English-speaking adult knows more than 50,000 words, the speed with which we identify words is even more impressive. While it is generally agreed that the words and their meanings have to be stored somehow in our minds, the structure of this mental dictionary is an open scientific question.

The past two decades have been very fruitful in designing experimental procedures for the study of the organization of the lexicon. One of the most popular approaches, still in use today, is to carefully measure the time needed to complete a specific linguistic operation. By designing reaction-time experiments that measure the time required for *lexical access* we hope to determine which kinds of lexical items are easy to retrieve from the lexicon, and which are more difficult.

These types of comparative data help us to develop hypotheses about the internal organization of the lexicon and about the process of lexical access itself. Other reaction-time experiments allow us to explore the structure of the lexicon in greater detail.

3.4 Lexical Decision

A slightly different reaction-time experiment measures how quickly you can identify a string of letters as a word of the language. Like the previous task, a *lexical decision* task involves a lexical look-up, but also requires the subject to determine whether a stimulus is in the lexicon. Try to imagine a procedure for deciding that a sequence of letters — say, *d-r-i-x* — was not in your lexicon How would you

Discuss how differences in the size and shape of the vocal tract might effect the phonetic character of speech sounds across speakers. Can you explain how children learning their first speech sounds might be able to cope with this kind of variation in their primary linguistic data?

go about examining the contents of your mental dictionary to safely conclude that *drix* was missing?

Example of instructions for a lexical decision experiment.

THE PURPOSE OF THE EXPERIMENT

To study lexical decisions.

EXPERIMENT DESCRIPTION:

When you start the experiment, an X will appear in the center of this box. After a brief delay, a string of letters will appear in the location of the X. Look at the X and when the string appears, as quickly as you can, press the Shift-key IF IT IS A WORD, and the Option-key (two keys to the right or left of the space-bar) IF IT IS NOT A WORD. Be sure not to press any keys until the experiment begins. Additional examples will follow after a brief delay.

3.5 Lexical Entries

Suppose we wish to look up a word in a (paper) dictionary. We examine the headings on each page and determine where the word we want falls in the alphabetic order of the dictionary. If we are looking for a word that begins with *p* we don't start with the *a*s and work down. Rather, we enter the dictionary at a point about two-thirds of the way through (since that is where we expect the *p*s to begin). In contrast, the lexicons of native speakers are not organized this way, and speakers' search routines differ from the routine described above. Speakers can search for words with a certain meaning (think of a word that means 'one who fixes cars'), by *rhyme* (what rhymes with *fish?*), and by category (think of a abstract word, or a dirty word). These kinds of searches are not possible in a standard dictionary.

We would also like to know what the entry for a given item in a speaker's lexicon looks like. When we locate a word in a conventional dictionary, we find a transcription indicating its pronunciation; a label showing its part of speech; perhaps a bit about its history (often tracing it back to Latin or Old French); and finally, a definition. Is it reasonable to expect that entries in the lexicon would be organized in the same way? We immediately suspect that this hypothesis about the structure of lexical entries is not plausible. For one thing, speakers do not know the history of most lexical items. We have also seen evidence in the previous chapter that

Try thinking of a word that begins with dis-, *one that ends in* -able, *and one that has* -al- *in the middle. Does the relative degree of difficulty associated with these three tasks seem the same? Can you explain your answer?*

Find a partner and try to find three words that you know that your partner does not, and vice versa. Do your respective lexicons seem mostly the same or pretty different?

Lexical entries evolve in many different ways. The pronunciation of a lexical item is a property that is highly susceptible to change. One type of evidence for this kind of change is the impressive amount of opacity in the English spelling system. That is, many words in Modern English continue to be spelled in a way that more closely reflects their pronunciation at an earlier stage of English. *House, mice,* and *mood* (which were pronounced [husə], [misə], and [mod] respectively in Middle English) are typical examples of phonetic change.

Another interesting case of phonetic change can be observed in the case of the word *ask,* which in earlier periods of English was pronounced "aks." The difference between these two pronunciations is that the *s-k* sequence in Modern English reversed the older *k-s* order thorough a process known as *metathesis.* ■

Many words have acquired new optional pronunciations in your lifetime (totally and cool *are examples in many speech groups). Can you think of three other examples of this kind of linguistic change? Does the phonetic change come with a correlated semantic change in each case?*

In some forms of AAE (African-American English), ask is pronounced [æks]. How would you respond to someone who thought that this was a linguistic error?

Debates about meaning go back at least as far as Plato and Aristotle, who famously disagreed about its nature. Plato analyzed meanings as idealizations that were known by the mind independent of the worldly experience that awakened them. Aristotle, finding himself unable to recognize the transcendental realm in which Platonic meanings reside, rejected this conception of meaning. Throughout the centuries, meaning has been variously analyzed as ideas, images, behaviors, concepts (public and private), procedures, uses, and features, among other things. Some philosophers (for example, J.L. Austin) have even doubted whether there is any such thing as word meaning! We return to this fascinating subject in chapter 5. ■

representations of the pronunciation of a lexical item need not be fully spelled out in a lexical entry. So, while a phonemic representation resembles a dictionary transcription to some degree, it is considerably more abstract, requiring the application of phonological rules to derive the full pronunciation of a given item.

Finally, regarding to the representation of semantic information, dictionaries present definitions that employ (presumably) more familiar words to point to the proper use of a word being looked up. In short, words are defined in terms of other words. But it is clear that when children learn the vocabulary of English they must learn more than which combinations of English words are (more or less) interchangeable — they have to represent the meanings of the words. These meaning representations must escape the domain of language or else the interpretation process can never begin.

One final regard in which a lexical entry differs from a dictionary entry, which we will discuss at some length, concerns the derivational character of morphology. Suppose, for example, we consider the dictionary entry for *smell*. We are told that when it is used as a verb, *smell* has *smelling,* and *smelled* (or *smelt*) as alternative forms. But no mention is made of the third-person singular form *smells* (as in *John smells*) or of the plural noun form *smells* (as in *the smells*). And even though *smelly* is listed, *smellier* and *smelliest* are missing. More fanciful possibilities like *smellaroony* and *smellify* are also omitted. Finally, although some *compounds* like *smelling salts* are listed, many other compounds like *smell detector, smell potential,* and *smell factor* are nowhere to be found.

In general then, the dictionary lists certain unpredictable aspects of a word's morphology, and simply assumes that you know most of the predictable features. However, since our theory of the lexicon aims to describe and explain all the lexical information possessed by a native speaker, we must provide a more systematic account of the basic morphological patterns of the language. It might seem a small matter to add the omitted information to the dictionary by simply adding the missing forms of *smell,* and, similarly, all the missing forms of all the other words in the language. But let us now turn to some evidence that morphological information cannot be systematically represented in the form of a large list, considering the implications for our conception of lexical organization.

3.6 The Size of the Lexicon

We have already estimated that the number of vocabulary items for a typical English-speaker can surpass 50,000. But there is a sense in which our lexical capacity exceeds even this rather impressively large quantity. First, all English-speakers are free to make up new words and to create new uses of existing words at the spur of the moment. These

How many other words can you think of that contain smell *as a part?*

PRO 3.6

There is overwhelming evidence for the existence of a critical period in a child's development during which language may be naturally acquired (Lenneberg 1968). That is, like many other biologically rooted abilities, language acquisition proceeds most efficiently at a particular stage of ontogeny (in this case, roughly between birth and puberty). During this "window of opportunity" for language development, special information-processing abilities that facilitate linguistic development are available to the child. Although it is possible to acquire language outside of the critical period, the process and outcome are strikingly different: All normally developing children learn their languages equally well, whereas post-critical-period language learners exhibit considerably variable abilities, and typically fail to completely master the language.

Perhaps the most striking evidence in favor of the critical-period hypothesis comes from investigations of English learned as a second language by immigrants. Henry Kissinger, the famous politician, arrived in the United States and learned English as a young boy, as did his brother. Although we may assume that their language-learning environments were quite similar, Henry speaks heavily foreign-accented English, while his brother passes for a native speaker. The explanation? Henry was older than his brother, and outside the critical period for language acquisition.

might be words for inventions (like *internet*) novel compounds (like the recently coined *screen saver*), or amusing extensions of the language that press proper names into service as verbs (like *I hope he doesn't Clinton her*). There seems to be no obvious limit to the number of possible additions to the vocabulary.

There are also morphological processes that contribute a kind of unlimited capacity similar to that which we discussed in connection with syntactic capacity in the previous chapter. For some

Identify three words that have been added to your dialect of English in the last few years. How many of these terms would be recognized by your parents or grandparents? Do you think these words will make it into the dictionary soon? Why or why not?

PRO 3.6

The fact that we can easily add new vocabulary words to our lexicons throughout our lifetime (beginning late in the first year of life) stands in striking contrast to the normal diminution of our ability to acquire language. It is clear that vocabulary acquisition does not reflect this time-sensitivity, suggesting that the acquisition process for words may be fundamentally different from that for the rest of language. Perhaps this is because the acquisition of new words involves meaning, whereas most other aspects of language acquisition involve the mastery of structure (that is, sound structure, morpheme structure, and so forth). Meaning is bound up with experience and with conceptual ability in a way that extends well beyond the limits of the linguistic system. This may explain why the acquisition of vocabulary is not time-bound in the same way as are other aspects of linguistic development. ■

CON 3.6

It is clear that language acquisition is time-sensitive — that there are periods in the course of ontogeny during which language acquisition is facilitated by special information-processing abilities of the normally developing child. But it does not follow from this that there is a critical period for language acquisition: Different aspects of the linguistic system emerge at different stages of development. There is no one single ontogenetic stage at which all of language is acquired.

Put another way, there are multiple linguistic critical periods. For example, it appears that the "window of opportunity" for acquiring a foreign-accent-free sound system closes around the age of six or seven, but the ability to fully acquire the syntactic system persists somewhat beyond that point. This explains why Kissinger and his brother both developed the syntactic competence of native speakers despite the discrepancies in their phonetic and phonological competence. The fact that vocabulary acquisition persists throughout life hardly contradicts this analysis. It is clear that word acquisition has an onset (the beginning of a critical period), and it is interesting that it lacks an offset (the terminus of a critical period). In this regard, it is no different than many other biologically based systems. ■

Identify three other biologically based human abilities or other properties that do not diminish throughout the lifespan.

examples, we need to recall that English allows the application of a rich variety of suffixes that can shift the syntactic category of a lexical item with a corresponding effect on its meaning. We are all familiar with the suffix *-ly* which can turn adjectives like *quick* and *sudden* into the adverbs *quickly* and *suddenly*. The suffix *-er* combines with verbs like *jump* and *spell* to derive the nouns *jumper* and *speller*. There are also many prefixes that can attach to lexical items to change meaning in some systematic way (for example, the prefix *un-* negates the meaning of adjectives [e.g., *unhappy* and *unwise*]).

Note that it is possible to have more than one affix attached to a single lexical item. For example, *re-reading* has three morphemes. In this example, the root is the verb *read* to which two affixes, the prefix *re-* and the suffix *-ing,* have been attached. Furthermore, both affixations are quite general; *re-* combines with a very large number of English verbs (e.g., *re-do, remake, re-visit,* etc.), and *-ing* combines with virtually every English verb to derive its *progressive* form.

Of course, we could describe all this detail for each item in the lexicon by listing the right combinations of morphemes in just the right order. Such an approach treats each lexical item as an exceptional case that must be handled separately. It would be far more economical to identify regular morphological rules that capture significant lexical generalizations. Furthermore, it is possible to apply quite a long string of suffixes, as words like *anti-post-representational* illustrate. How many affixes in principle can a single word have? If there is a limit on the number of times an affix can be added to a word to form a new word, then it would still be possible to list all possible combinations of items (although this would be a remarkably uninsightful analysis). However, there are some kinds of derivations that may not have an upper bound on the number of attachments. The simplest such example would be a *recursive* derivation — a derivation in which a given rule can apply to its own output, any arbitrary number of times. Convincing examples of recursive lexical processes are rare, since words complicated beyond a certain point become extremely unwieldy (and of dubious status); but there are a few plausible examples. One case in point trades on the notion that for every kind of missile there is a corresponding weapon whose purpose is to destroy that kind of missile — an "anti" missile, if you will. It would seem any word of the form $anti^n$ $missile^{n+1}$ (where $n \geq 1$) is a word of English (*anti-missile missile, anti-anti-missile missile missile,* and so forth)!

Think of a word that has the largest number of morphemes that you can find. What is the word, and how many morphemes does it have?

3.7 Lexical Productivity

A second kind of evidence that lexical entries cannot be simply listed in the lexicon concerns the productivity of lexical rules. If English-speakers must memorize each individual lexical entry, we would not expect such speakers to be able to generalize their morphological

Throughout our exploration of linguistics, we have concentrated on a *synchronic* approach — one that examines the current state of the language. It is often the case, however, that consideration of *diachronic* factors — those involving change over time — can add considerable depth to the arguments we seek to develop. One of the most interesting ways that languages change is by addition to, deletion from, and modification of the lexicon over time. New words may be added by coining new terms (*dweeb*) creating acronyms (*snafu,* from 'situation normal all fucked up'), clipping (*rad,* from *radical*), creating new combinations of morphemes *(tele+vision),* shifts in part of speech (e.g., turning the noun *cream* into a verb *to cream),* and shifts in meaning (*meat* used to mean 'food').

By examining how lexical entries change over time, we discover more evidence in favor of the idea that lexical knowledge is productive (and, consequently, that it cannot be represented in the form of a list of lexical entries). One strategy for adding lexical items, *backformation,* provides compelling evidence of this sort. Backformation involves (mis-)

analyzing a newly added lexical item into a combination of a root plus affix(es), and then coining new words by applying other existing morphological rules to the falsely identified root form, to derive novel lexical forms. For example, Lehman (1962) points out that the noun *hamburger* was originally analyzed as *hamburg+er* from the German affix *-er* meaning 'of' or 'from' when used with place names. In English, these constructions became associated with meat products (e.g., *wiener* and *frankfurter)* with *hamburger* getting reanalyzed as *ham+burger.*

After reanalysis of *hamburger* into *ham+burger,* the *ham* could be stripped off, and since, by coincidence ham was a kind of meat (yet, curiously, one not used in hamburgers!), it became possible to substitute expressions standing for other foods that can be turned into burgers (*fishburger, tofuburger,* and so forth). In another innovation, we find forms like *cheeseburger* or *chili-burger,* in which the first morpheme names something that goes on a burger rather than something that goes into one.

In short, the addition of one word followed by a reanalysis spawns a

legion of new lexical items. The best account of how these new items enter the language requires that we conceive of morphology in terms of productive rules that operate in language change as well as in our account of linguistic knowledge. Of course, the process of adding and reconceiving new vocabulary items continues to this very day. Among the many words that seem to be in the process of being lost are *thee* and *thou.* But whether these will finally go the way of *maumet* ('idol') and *cere* ('wax'), two previously existing English words that have been lost over time, remains to be seen (see Langacker 1973:185). ■

Children sometimes make amusing lexical mistakes by using words that are not part of the adult language. How would you explain the following such utterances?

a. I have a bru (bruise).

b. Gimme my pant (pants).

Older children sometimes use words like gruntled *and* effable. *What accounts for these forms?*

knowledge to novel lexical items. Suppose, for example, we tell you that *trimp* means to wrap something neatly. Which derived forms of *trimp* seem possible?

Your ability to predict possible words is not explained by assuming that you have listed the acceptable forms in your lexicon, since you have never encountered these forms before. You must be capable of applying morphological rules that creatively derive new output forms based on the input *trimp*. The permissible range of derived forms depends on certain properties of *trimp* (its part of speech, meaning, and pronunciation) combined with knowledge about English morphology (see Matthews 1974:42).

A final example illustrating the productivity of the lexical knowledge concerns a type of affix rare in English — the infix. Infixes are morphemes that can be inserted into another lexical item (rather than at its beginning or end). The infix *frigging* (and its more colorful counterparts) as in *ri-friggin-diculous* is a case in point. But notice that its distribution is limited in quite an interesting way. Try inserting *frigging* into randomly chosen places in a word like *hippopotamus* — *hipp-frigging-popotamus*, *hippopota-frigging-mus*, and so forth. Even though you have probably never performed this task before, if you are a native English-speaker you know the privileges of occurrence for *frigging* to the extent that you can easily predict its distribution (only *hippo-frigging-potamus* is grammatical), but you probably cannot state the rule without considerable reflection. In general, then, morphological knowledge resembles phonological knowledge in the regard that it is tacit, creative, and derivational. As a consequence, in order to understand the nature of morphological competence we must investigate morphological phenomena more carefully, ultimately developing a system of rules and principles similar to those we previously deployed to understand sounds.

3.8 Morphological Processes

Morphemes can be divided into two general classes. *Free* morphemes are those which can stand alone as words of a language, whereas *bound* morphemes must be attached to other morphemes. Most roots in English are free morphemes (for example, *dog, syntax,* and *to*), although there are a few cases of roots, like *-gruntle* (as in *disgruntled*) that must be combined with another bound morpheme in order to surface as an acceptable lexical item. Try to identify whether the underlined morphemes in the list at right are either bound or free.

trimped	trimpster
trimps	trimpification
trimply	trimpist
neo-trimp	trimpest
trimpy	re-trimp

The more colorful alternative to frigging *is a member of the class of taboo words — words that one is supposed to avoid in speech situations where conventional principles of politeness apply. What counts as a taboo word is relative to context, use, age, and education of the speakers involved, and even to the language and culture. Think of three other English taboo words and write them down, if you dare…*

Try to state the rule that captures the distribution of frigging. *Be sure to test your analysis by considering at least five "host" words other than* hippopotamus. *How many other English infixes can you think of? List them, and see if they follow the same pattern of distribution that* frigging *does.*

cran<u>berry</u>	mis<u>take</u>
warm<u>th</u>	out<u>let</u>
<u>length</u>	<u>organ</u>ize
re<u>gurg</u>itate	tur<u>key</u>

HISTORY 3.8

The word *cranberry* entered the language as *craneberry,* so-called because part of the plant resembled a crane (the bird, not the heavy machinery). In time the pronunciation changed, eventually yielding the current form *cranberry.* As a result of the change in pronunciation, a new bound base *cran* has emerged, which cannot be connected to its original history by most living English-speakers. There is, however, another change afoot! *Cran* has begun to take on a life of its own as an emerging free morpheme, appearing in new adjectives like *cranlicious* and *crantastic,* as well as in compounds like *cranapple* and *crangrape* (see Akmajian et al. 1995 for discussion). ■

Young children sometimes pronounce the word butterfly as flutter-by. Which linguistic process is at work?

Free morphemes can be further subdivided into *content words* and *function words*. Content words, as their name suggests, carry most of the content of a sentence. Function words generally perform some kind of grammatical role, carrying little meaning of their own. One circumstance in which the distinction between function words and content words is useful is when one is inclined to keep wordiness to a minimum; for example, when drafting a telegram, where every word costs money. In such a circumstance, one tends to leave out most of the function words (like *to, that, and, there, some,* and *but*), concentrating instead on content words to convey the gist of the message.

Most bound morphemes take the form of affixes (prefixes like *re-,* suffixes like *-ly,* and infixes like *frigging*) or bound roots (*gruntle*), but there are a few other kinds of bound forms that do not fit neatly into any of these categories. One such case is that of contraction (for example, *Bill's here*) in which a part of the verb *is* is fused onto the end of the preceding word. A second type of contraction reduces *to* to [ʌ] when it is preceded by certain verbs like *want* and *going,* as in *Do you wanna dance?* (= 'Do you want to dance?') The final vowel [ʌ] in [wanʌ] counts as a bound morpheme because it cannot stand alone as an instance of *to* (for example, **I love [ʌ] eat ice cream*).

Can you think of any other examples of contractions that involve the word to? Why do you think to is so vulnerable to this process? Can you explain why two *cannot contract to produce *I wanna ice cream cones* from *I want two ice cream cones or why* too *can't contract in* I want too many things *to yield *I wanna many things? How do young children who cannot read sort these cases out?*

In both of these contractions, there are interesting restrictions governing the possibilities of deriving a contracted form. Which of the examples at right seem well formed to you?

In the case of *to be* contraction, there is a curious restriction on the process at the ends of sentences. The examples involving *to* contraction demonstrate that *to* must be an *infinitive* marker, and not a *preposition* in order to participate in contraction.

These conditions on contraction provide interesting clues about the representation of lexical information. In particular, they suggest that contraction involves more than just leaving out linguistic material, and that it does not appear to be simply motivated by a principle of least effort (i.e., to say as little as possible). Instead, contraction is a rich linguistic process subject to a complicated set of morphological and other structural considerations.

1. God is!
2. *God's!
3. I know who is going.
4. I know who's going.
5. I know who isn't going and I know who is.
6. *I know who isn't going and I know who's.
7. I am going to leave.
8. I am gonna leave.
9. I am going to Spain.
10. *I am gonna Spain.

PRO 3.8

Prescriptive linguistic advice is typically not taken to heart by most speakers in their spontaneous colloquial style. But when it comes to writing, a different set of conventions applies. If you want to write to impress your reader (and garner good grades), you would do well to adopt the time-worn principles of good writing. Among these principles is the traditional advice; don't split infinitives. If you pen sentences like *I am going to definitely try an alternative,* many teachers will suggest relocating the adverb *definitely* so that it does not interrupt the infinitive *to try.* No matter how progressive one's linguistic agenda is, there is no getting around the value of this kind of normative rule in preserving narrative style. ▪

CON 3.8

While it is no doubt true that the grammatical rules and principles underlying our ability to speak differ in interesting ways from the canons of good writing, the latter are prescriptive rules nonetheless. Like any other normative linguistic conventions, rules of writing are sometimes followed, and sometimes violated. They are also time-bound, conservative, and only potent if you are worried about making a nice impression (a smart thing to do with a job application). In many cases, there is little actual linguistic motivation for these conventions. Take, for example, the admonition not to split infinitives. This advice is a holdover from languages like French, where the infinitive is but a single word (as in *parler* for 'to speak' or *chanter* for 'to sing'). Splitting an infinitive in these cases would involve interrupting a word, a process that is not freely available in such languages. In English, however, we find instead a sequence of *to* followed by the root form of the verb (e.g., *to speak*). It is, of course, possible to successfully split up word sequences in English; with adverbs, for example (there — we just did it!). In fact, even the most conservative writers are forced to split English infinitives in some cases...even if they don't want <u>to</u>... (split them). ▪

There are still other types of bound morphology in English that raise special issues. The examples at right include cases that are "irregular" in one way or another.

In the first column, the first two pairs (*dog/dogs* and *cat/cats*) show the usual alternation between singular and plural, the latter form involving the

dog/dogs	kick/kicked	ring/rang/rung
cat/cats	jump/jumped	sing/sang/sung
datum/data	stand/stood	run/ran/run
fish/fish	go/went	kick/kicked/kicked

IN DETAIL 3.8-A

We can gain considerable insight into the nature of morphological knowledge by examining the stages that children pass through on their way to attaining the mature state of the lexicon. In particular, linguists have found the acquisition of irregular paradigms (such as *go/went*) especially instructive in understanding lexical organization and morphological processes. It is common to discover that language learners move through many linguistic stages prior to mastering irregular forms. Kuczaj (1978) notes that the acquisition of these patterns often begins with children using the correct irregular form, but at later stages of development they introduce forms like *goed*. Although the frequency of regularized forms like *goed* is relatively small for any given speaker (Marcus et al. 1992), the use rate of such forms remains constant for years before finally discontinuing.

This sequence of development — from a period in which the correct forms are used to one where some incorrect forms are introduced, to a final stage at which the correct forms prevail and the incorrect, regularized forms are given up — is sometimes called "U-shaped development."

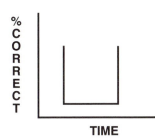

U-shaped development curve.

It is U-shaped because overall performance in deploying irregular verbs seems to start strongly, then decline, then finally improve again. We are left with two central questions: Why does the child invent incorrect forms like *goed,* and why do they persist for so long? The standard explanation is that children begin by imitating irregular forms, and that only at a subsequent point when they learn a more powerful generalization that allows them to predict the past tense form, do they introduce *goed*. Because *goed* fits the generalization they have learned, they posit it as the past-tense form, even though they do not hear it in the discourse of their parents and other caregivers.

This explains why *goed* is invented, but why does it persist for so long? Apparently the principle allowing children to predict past-tense forms is very potent. Indeed, some children continue to use regularized forms like *goed* and *understanded* for five or more years, despite being corrected and even despite knowing, in some sense, that such forms are incorrect. Here, the emergence of a linguistic generalization actually leads the child away from identifying the correct forms of lexical items. But in regular cases the same generalizations constitute a powerful learning device that allows the child to incorporate a large number of correct forms as a single class of phenomena, rather than on a case-by-case basis. So, the persistence of incorrect forms over time provides intriguing evidence that reveals the extent to which the acquisition of lexical knowledge is shaped by linguistic generalizations (see also Rumelhart and McClelland 1986; Pinker and Prince 1988; and Marcus et al. 1992). ■

attachment of a plural suffix. In the third pair, however, the method for marking the distinction between singular and plural is different. *Datum/data* follows an irregular pattern derived from Latin in which both singular and plural involve a suffix (-*um* for the singular and -*a* for the plural). But this raises the question of what to say about the more well-behaved cases like *cat* and *dog*. Since the singular is generally unmarked in English (the odd case of *datum* aside), we are forced to conclude that some aspects of interpretation may lack a phonetic realization (see Matthews 1974:118).

This notion is also useful in explaining the fourth contrast (or lack thereof) in the first column between the singular *fish* and the plural *fish*. Here, there is no overt marking for either singular or plural. In order to maintain the distinction between singular and plural in these last two cases, we posit the abstract feature *NUMBER* with values *[SINGULAR]* and *[PLURAL]* as part of the lexical representation for nouns. (Notice that features like *NUMBER* are capitalized and values for features like *[SINGULAR]* are capitalized and written inside brackets). In cases in which there is a phonetic realization for a feature value, we must ensure that the right suffix gets attached (for example, the plural marker at the end of *dogs* and *cats*). But even in cases like *fish* we can distinguish *fish* NUMBER[SINGULAR] from *fish* NUMBER[PLURAL] despite the fact that neither of the features has a phonetic realization.

IN DETAIL 3.8-B

1. One crab is in the net.
2. *One crab are in the net.
3. *Two crabs is in the net.
4. Two crabs are in the net.
5. One fish is in the net.
6. *One fish are in the net.
7. *Two fish is in the net.
8. Two fish are in the net.

Suppose we try to resist the admittedly abstract claim that nouns that are phonetically unmarked for singular and plural nevertheless bear the lexical features *[SINGULAR]* or *[PLURAL]* (along with nouns that do inflect for plural). The data above show that a singular subject requires *is,* the singular form of the verb *to be,* and that plural nouns require *are,* the plural form. If we assume that *one* introduces nouns that are marked *[SINGULAR]* and that *two* introduces nouns marked *[PLURAL]*, we can provide a systematic account of (1) through (4) (as well as explaining why we can't say *one crabs* or *two crab*).

The second four sentences display the same pattern of distribution, except, of course, for the absence of overt plural marking on the noun *fish.* If we assume that the occurrences of *fish* in (5) and (6) bear the feature value *[SINGULAR]* and that those in (7) and (8) bear the feature value *[PLURAL]*, we can explain these data in analogy to those in (1) through (4). Without positing the abstract features values *[SINGULAR]* and *[PLURAL]*, it is difficult to see how these generalizations could be captured. ■

The first two pairs of examples in the second column (*kick/kicked* and *jump/jumped*) exhibit the usual contrast between present- and past-tense verbs in English, which is marked by a past-tense suffix. But the next two pairs (*stand/stood* and *go/went*) are again irregular. In the first case it is an internal vowel change that marks the present-past contrast, and in the second case there is no obvious phonetic connection at all between the present tense *go* and the *suppletive* past form *went*. The triples *ring/rang/rung* and *sing/sang/sung* in the third column exemplify a three-way alternation among the present, past, and past-*participle* forms of the verb. However, many verbs in English fail to display the full range of forms that we observe in these two examples. The third triple in column three (*run/ran/run*) exemplifies one typical pattern in which the present tense form (*I run*) doubles as the past-participle (*I have run*). The fourth triple (*kick/kicked/kicked*) illustrates a third pattern. In this case the past-tense form (e.g., *I kicked first*) is identical in form to the perfective (*I have kicked first*). These overlapping patterns of form and function contribute to the overall complexity of the system of English morphology.

Finally, we explore one last case of bound morphology, *tones*, which, although central to the sound systems of many languages, are not part of English phonology. In so-called tone languages, words may be distinguished solely by differences in pitch. An example of this phenomenon can be found by examining some data from the African language Etung. In Etung, one-syllable words can be associated with high pitch (H), low pitch (L), rising pitch (R), and falling pitch (F).

How are we to analyze tones such as those found in Etung? It is important to notice that it is not the absolute but the relative pitch at which a word is pronounced that determines the tone category (see Martinet 1960:78). Furthermore, a contrast in tone can mark a minimal pair. Consider the data at right from Lonkundo, a language spoken in central Africa.

Identify three other examples of suppletion in English. Can you think of any examples that are not verbs?

Tone data from Etung.

H		L	
kpa	'fist'	kpe	'even'
F		R	
na	'it is'	no	'how'

Tone data from Lonkundo.

L L L
lokolo 'fruit of a palm tree'

L H H
lokolo 'exorcism'

The segmental information is the same in these two Lonkundo words, the tones constituting the only point of contrast. Goldsmith (1976) has argued that the features of pitch exploited by tone languages are best analyzed as *autosegments* — discrete elements on a separate tier of organization rather than as inherent features of the segments that make up the phonetic form of a lexical entry (e.g., voicing). So, for example, the Etung words *oda* ('platform') and *ekat* ('leg') would be represented like this:

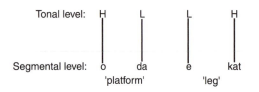

Tone data from Etung.

In the autosegmental view, tones are treated as independent elements of the language, on a par with and parallel to segmental units like [p] and [o]. From the morphological point of view, however, we are interested in a further property of tones: Can they play the role of independent morphemes in a tone language? The following data from Lumasaaba, a Bantu language from East Africa (cited in Matthews 1974) confirm that tones can indeed be bound morphemes:

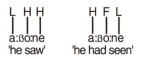

Tone data from Lumasaaba.

In this Lumasaaba data, the segmental information is the same in these two items (the [ß] represents a voiced bilabial fricative also present in the Cuban Spanish pronunciation of [kußʌ] *Cuba*). The only distinction between the two forms marking the difference between the past tense and the perfective (in English, *saw* vs. *had seen*) is the tone sequence LHH as opposed to HFL. The languages of the world apparently incorporate several different ways of conveying morphological information. Furthermore, each morphological process tends to be governed by quite subtle conditions, giving rise to an intricate and highly organized system of linguistic competence. In the next sections, we explore the nature of this system of rules and principles in more detail.

3.9 Derivational Morphology

So far we have divided the class of English bound morphemes into subcategories: roots, prefixes, suffixes, infixes, contractions, internal sound change, and a few other special cases. We now turn to a more functional distinction between *derivational morphology* and *inflectional morphology,* two basic morphological processes available in English that combine morphemes for different purposes and in somewhat different ways.

Derivational morphology builds complex lexical items (for example, by the attachment of affixes to roots) with a concomitant shift in meaning and, often, in syntactic category and phonetic form. We have already seen examples of derivational morphology, for instance the case of the suffix *-ly* that converts the adjective *quick* into the adverb *quickly.* In this quite standard case, the application of derivational morphology has three consequences: The phonetic form of the input is altered (i.e., [li] is added to the end of the form), the syntactic category of the input is shifted (from adjective to adverb), and the meaning of the input is modified (taking on the meaning 'in the manner of'). There are quite a few other instances of derivational morphology that have the same general profile. For example, consider the case of the *-er* suffix that is added to verbs like *paint* to derive *painter.* The resulting item (with the phonetic form *root+er*) is a noun that means 'one who Xs.'

Suppose now we combine the *+ly* rule and the *+er* rule into a single rule system. In particular, notice what happens if the *+ly* rule applies to a verb or if the *+er* rule applies to a noun. The forms that result, like **screamly, *climbly, *suddener,* and so forth, are ungrammatical. We can exclude these output forms by limiting the application of the *+ly* rule to adjectives, and the *+er* rule to verbs. However, if we restrict the rules in this way, we become unable to generate forms like *quicker* because the root, *quick* is not a verb. But there is independent evidence that this omission is proper: *quicker* does not carry the expected meaning ('one who Xs'). We conclude that this form must have another source.

We have discovered that each morphological operation applies only to the members of certain syntactic categories; in the cases above, to the members of a single syntactic category (the *+ly* rule to

Several of the nouns derived by the +er rule can have another meaning in addition to 'one who does X.' Consider the range of meanings for reader, jumper, and speaker. How would you characterize these alternative meanings? Can you think of any other nouns ending in -er that carry these kinds of meanings?

Can you propose a plausible derivation for quicker and warmer? What part of speech do they belong to? What is the suffix? How does the application of this suffix change the meaning of the input? Can you think of other examples of this morphological process?

adjectives and the +*er* rule to verbs). Although this is the normal case, there are a few instances in which an affix may apply to more than one syntactic category. The suffix -*able* is an example (see Akmajian et al. 1995:39); it attaches to verbs like *drink* to derive the adjective *drinkable,* but can also attach to certain nouns, for example, *sale* to form the adjective *salable.* Furthermore, it often contributes the meaning 'able to be...' Just the same, the application of the -*able* suffix is strictly limited to members of these two syntactic categories. Notice, for example, that it is not possible to apply -*able* to adjectives *(*happyable)* or adverbs *(*quicklyable).*

Finally, we should look at a case of derivational morphology that involves a prefix — a bound morpheme attached to the front of a root. As with the derivational suffixes, the attachment of the prefix *un-* to adjectives like *healthy* to derive *unhealthy* affects the phonetic form and the meaning of the input. But in this case (which is typical of English prefixes), the syntactic category of the input is not affected: Both *healthy* and *unhealthy* are adjectives.

3.10 Productivity

We have determined that the application of derivational morphology is restricted only to the members of certain syntactic categories. We now need to determine whether such morphology can apply to *all* the members of an appropriate category. In other words, we want to determine how productive derivational morphology is. There are some cases that come close to full productivity. For example, Matthews (1974:52) discusses the suffix -*less,* which attaches quite freely to nouns to derive other nouns with the meaning 'without *X.*'

clue/clueless	brain/brainless
virtue/virtueless	face/faceless
hope/hopeless	shoe/shoeless
penny/penniless	defense/defenseless

There are, however, many other nouns that yield a much less satisfactory result when -*less* is added.

idea/idealess	nose/noseless
honesty/honestyless	eyelid/eyelidless
belief/beliefless	shoes/shoesless
dollar/dollarless	cleverness/clevernessless

In some, it is difficult to see why the acceptability is reduced — compare *hopeless* and *beliefless,* for example. The difference may be

Can you think of other examples of verbs that combine with -able to form adjectives? How about other examples of nouns that take -able? Which of these kinds of examples is easier to think up?

How do you judge the acceptability of the following cases of un-*prefixation?*

a. *The president did a very un-Clinton thing.*

b. *It was a rather un-Chomsky analysis.*

c. *His clothes were completely un-James Dean.*

Do these cases convince you that un- *can attach to (proper) nouns as well as to adjectives? Why (or why not)?*

that *hopeless* is conventionally lexicalized, whereas *beliefless* has the feel of an invented word. In such cases, acceptability may be improved by considering a context that might occasion using a particular example. Suppose we had just tried out a ray gun that is designed to remove all of Superman's beliefs. In this circumstance, asking *Is he beliefless yet?* seems perhaps not so bad.

Following Matthews, we may categorize rules like the one that attaches morphemes like *-less* as being *semi-productive,* by which we mean that they may be used sporadically to create new lexical items. At first, this is a creative act; we can expect that some new forms will be conventionalized, and that others may not. With this qualification, however, we can continue to treat the rules of derivational morphology as establishing permissible patterns for the lexical items in a language.

3.11 Some Complications

In analyzing a complex lexical item morphologically, we seek to subdivide it into a sequence of morphemes, say, a root combined with its affixes. To determine this structure, we identify the phonetic, syntactic, and semantic consequences of affixation, ultimately establishing a morphological derivation. Certain cases, however, introduce complications that we must be aware of. First, let us consider the operation of the prefix *de-*. The prefix *de-* attaches to verbs and derives new verb forms — *decentralize* and *dehydrate* are illustrative examples — adding the meaning 'to reverse the action of.' The phonetic and semantic effects are easily discernible, and the fact that there is no syntactic category shift is consistent with our expectations for English prefixes. So far, so good.

It is tempting to extend this account to the following examples as well:

deflate	denuclearize	depress
dethrone	deodorize	delouse
defrost		delete

But in each of these cases, there are difficulties that challenge this explanation. Working down the first column, on our analysis, *deflate, dethrone,* and *defrost* would be divided into *de-* followed by *flate, throne,* and *frost.* Obviously *flate* is not a word of English, despite the fact that *de-* seems to be contributing just the sort meaning we would expect it to. One way of reconciling these observations to is analyze *flate* as a bound morpheme which combines with *de-* in the usual way. Some evidence for this claim is provided by

By analyzing morphological rules such as the one that attaches -less *to the ends of nouns as semiproductive rules, we can explain some of the variation in acceptability in the data in the text. But does this explanation account persuasively for all of the data presented there? In particular, how can we explain the status of* shoesless, honestyless *and* clevernessless?

examples like *inflate* and *inflation* which are based on the same root. We might also note that for some speakers, *deinflate* is an available alternative to *deflate*. Of course *throne* and *frost* do exist as free morphemes of English, but they are mostly encountered as nouns (but note the related verb *to frost* as in *That really frosts me!*). Claiming that *throne* and *frost*, like *flate* are bound roots would of course solve our problem; but there is little independent evidence for this analysis.

In the second column, *denuclearize* and *deodorize* present a related difficulty. Once again, we would like to break these forms down to *de-* followed by *nuclearize* and *odorize*, the latter evidently not being English verbs. However, *nuclearize* and *odorize* cannot be analyzed as bound roots, because they are not roots at all. Each allows for further analysis into *nuclear* or *odor* plus *-ize*. Here we must say that *nuclearize* and *odorize* are possible English words that have not been conventionally lexicalized; and at this cost, our current analysis can be preserved.

The cases in the third column, *depress, delouse,* and *delete*, illustrate further difficulties. Although they may seem related to the other cases we have discussed, they probably are not. *Depress* can be divided into *de-* and *press,* but here *de-* certainly doesn't mean 'reverse the action of.' *Delouse* also divides neatly into *de-* and *louse*, but the latter is a noun and the meaning is subtly different (roughly, 'to remove *X*' — *degrease* and *debone* are similar examples). The final example, *delete* seems to have approximately the right meaning to support an analysis into a prefix followed by a root, but the semantic similarity to the other bona fide *de-* cases is accidental. There simply is no independent evidence for a verb *lete*.

These examples illustrate some of the pitfalls of morphological analysis. We frequently encounter gaps in distribution and other symptoms of limited productivity that make it difficult to establish unqualified lexical generalizations. In the worst cases, we have to recognize a residue of exceptions to the rules of derivational morphology that must be handled differently than the regular cases, and listed as separate lexical entries. Despite a degree of irregularity, however, we have seen that it is possible to posit morphological rules with considerable generality and independent motivation. In this spirit, let us conclude our discussion of *de-* by considering one last set of data.

These examples are instances of *negative evidence* — cases in which *de-* has been attached to a verb with an ungrammatical result. We

Can you break down military *even further into constitutive morphemes? (Hint: Consider words like* militant, militate, *and* militia.) *Is the root that you must posit bound or free?*

could, of course, simply brand these cases as exceptions, but we would prefer a more principled account for why verbs like *elapse* or *sit* do not take *de-*. It turns out that each of these verbs is *intransitive* (verbs that do not take *objects*); whereas all the verbs that successfully combine with *de-* — *activate,* and *sensitize,* for example — are *transitive* verbs (verbs that take objects). Furthermore, adding *de-* to a verb always produces a transitive verb:

1. John decoded the message.
2. *John decoded.

It appears, then, that our earlier description of the function of the *de-* prefix is too loose. It is not precise enough to say that *de-* attaches to verbs to derive new verbs; rather, it maps transitive verbs into transitive verbs. This qualification neatly explains the contrast between the ungrammatical and grammatical examples.

3.12 Rule Interactions

Let us now recall two morphological rules, the one that attaches the suffix *-ly* to adjectives, and the one that attaches the suffix *-er* to verbs. In those cases we argued that only one of the two rules could apply to any given input, depending on whether it is an adjective or a verb. Let us consider now how to generate forms like *undrinkable* and *unaffordable,* which require the sequential application of an *un-* rule and an *-able* rule. Of course we could generate these forms by letting the *un-* and *-able* rules apply freely (that is, irrespective of the syntactic category of the input to the rule), but this move would introduce undesirable forms like **undrink* and **readyable,* which we want to avoid. We also want to avoid other ungrammatical forms like **unreadyable* and **unhappyable,* as well. In other words, the *un-* rule must be restricted to adjectives. This accounts for the existence of forms like *unready* but none like **undrink.* But if we block *un-* from attaching to *drink,* how can we derive *undrinkable?*

*de-elapse	*de-rest
*de-sit	*de-stand
*de-die	*de-expire

Even after we eliminate intransitive verbs from the scope of the de- *rule, there remain other examples of verbs to which* de- *cannot freely attach. Can you explain why the following examples are ill formed?*

*a.   *de-know*
*b.   *de-throw*
*c.   *de-touch*

As we have discussed, most of the forms produced by attaching un- *to verbs (for example, *undrink) are ungrammatical. But one such combination,* undo *is well formed. Can you explain this putative exception to the generalization?*

Let's retrace our steps to determine how to best approach this problem. Ignoring infixes for the moment, suppose we adopt the assumption that roots and affixes can combine in either of two ways which can be shown more formally as follows:

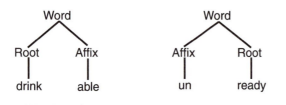

Two representations for affixes.

The leftmost structure accounts for the attachment of suffixes; the rightmost, accounts for the attachment of prefixes. To generate forms like *undrinkable*, we could introduce a third structure that combines these two options. Unfortunately, appealing to this structure also invites examples like **unreadyable*, along with other undesirable results.

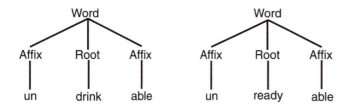

Representations for *undrinkable* and **unreadyable*.

Our assumptions about the structure of **unreadyable* and *undrinkable* are at the root of the problem (pun intended). Suppose we modify our conception of word structure so that each combination of morphological items composes a separate *constituent* (unit of the analysis).

Create word-structure trees for the following:

a. quickly
b. retouch
c. smartest
d. detour

Create word-structure trees for the following:

a. hopeless
b. pre-cooking
c. druggist
d. reformer

We recognize a second kind of root (sometimes called a *derived root*) that is the result of combining a root and affix to produce a derived form and that in turn can combine with another affix to produce a lexical item. Here is the structure for *undrinkable*:

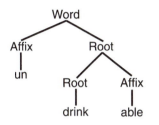

Representation for *undrinkable*.

Create word structure trees for the following:

a. refinisher
b. decoding
c. unreadable

Do refinisher *and* unreadable *have the same analysis tree (ignoring the sound segments)? Explain.*

As we discussed above, the application of the *un-* rule must be restricted to adjectives. This accounts for the existence of forms like *unready* but none like **undrink*. Notice that to build this structure, the *-able* rule applies to *drink* to yield the derived root *drinkable;* and since *drinkable* is an adjective, the *un-* rule can apply, yielding *undrinkable*.

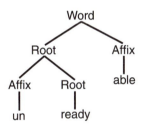

Representation for **unreadyable*.

The word unzippable *has two meanings: (1) 'unable to be zipped' and (2) 'able to be unzipped.' Draw two different word-structure trees for* unzippable *corresponding to the two different interpretations. Explain which reading goes with which analysis tree.*

The structure for the ungrammatical form **unreadyable* is a bit different. Here, *un-* can combine with the adjective *ready* to produce the derived root *unready*. However, since the derived root is (still) an adjective, the *-able* rule cannot apply. This more highly structured approach to morphological derivations allows us distinguish these cases in a principled manner. In particular, by conceiving of the attachment of affixes in terms of *binary branching* representations, we can account for how the effects of category-changing morphological rules interact with the application of other rules in a single derivation.

3.13 Inflectional Morphology

Derivational morphology, in its canonical instances, has three manifestations: a change in soundshape (typically involving the addition of a prefix or suffix), a change in syntactic category, and a change in meaning. The rules of this system, we have argued, are productive (or semi-productive), generative rules that allow speakers to derive new lexical items from a basic set of roots. The application of these rules is capable of adding new words to the language; and as a result, the rules of derivational morphology underlie part of the creative character of linguistic competence.

Typical cases of English inflectional morphology also involve attaching prefixes and suffixes to roots and, like the rules of derivational morphology, inflectional rules involve modifying the meaning of the items they apply to. As we shall see, applying inflectional rules produces an extremely regular semantic effect by modulating certain grammatical aspects of meaning; for example, *person, number,* and *tense.* We will also discover that inflectional morphology is more productive than its derivational counterpart and, finally, that inflectional rules never change the syntactic category of a linguistic item they apply to.

A prototypical example of inflectional morphology is the English plural. To form a plural noun, we start with a root noun, say *dog,* and add the plural morpheme as a suffix — *dogs.* Consequently, *dogs* consists of two morphemes, *dog*+PLURAL, derived by the applying a rule of inflectional morphology (the Plural Rule) to the root *dog.* Although the English plural rule is quite general, there are several classes of exceptions that deserve to be noted. We have already discussed cases in which the phonetic manifestation of the plural rule is either null (for example, *fish/fish*) or takes the form of an irregular suffix (*datum/data*). There are also instances in which an internal vowel change marks the plural morpheme, as in *foot/feet, mouse/mice,* and *woman/women.* In addition to these irregular examples, there is a very large class of English nouns that does not have a plural form at all. Examine the following nouns and deter-

Which suffix seems more productive, -less or -y? Give five examples of words that incorporate each suffix and three examples each of unacceptable words that seem to be consistent with the general pattern of distribution of the suffix. Can you explain the unacceptability?

Create analysis trees for the following:

a. rats

b. cats

c. giraffes

IN DETAIL 3.13-A

Children learn the rudiments of the plural system quite early in the course of language development, often before the age of two-and-a-half. A classic experiment used to document this accomplishment, devised by Jean Berko Gleason (Berko 1958), is known as the "wug" test. Children are taught the name of a made-up fantasy creature (a "wug"), and are then asked what one would call two such creatures. How is it that young children can successfully identify the plural, "wugs"? If they were merely memorizing the plural forms for familiar nouns, they would be unable to determine the correct one for "wug," having never encountered either it or its plural before. Instead, we must conclude that they have learned a generalization that allows them to predict the plural form for novel lexical items. By conceiving of morphological relationships as productive patterns that children can creatively apply to extrapolate new lexical forms, we can begin to explain how children master such a rich body of lexical knowledge on the basis of relatively little triggering data. ▪

mine which take a plural form and which do not. Then, try to figure out what distinguishes the two classes of nouns from each other.

    veal
    hotdog
    memory (as in computer memory)
    memory (in the sense of a recollection)
    space (as in outer-space)
    space (as in an empty space)
    bliss
    hope
    creativity
    creation

For most speakers, words like *veal* and *bliss* do not take a plural. These words are sometimes called *mass* nouns because they name a mass of material. In contrast, *count* nouns, which name individuated objects of certain kinds, typically inflect for plurality. Many English nouns do double duty, possessing both a mass and a count sense. For example, *hamburger* is a count noun when it picks out the sandwich served at fast-food restaurants, but a mass noun when it stands for the material that this comestible is made of. So we say (redundantly) *Those three hamburgers were made out of hamburger* but not **Those three hamburgers were made out of hamburgers*. In short, the distinction between mass and count nouns allows us to treat an apparent exception to the English plural rule as a qualification: The plural rule applies to singular count nouns to yield plural count nouns.

IN DETAIL 3.13-B

Although the ability to take a plural form is one of the most easily identified differences between mass nouns and count nouns, they also differ in other important ways. One difference is the complicated dependency between a determiner and the noun it introduces. Mass nouns permit but do not require a determiner; so, with slightly different interpretations, we can say either *I found evidence in your room* or *I found the evidence in your room*. Plural count nouns behave the same way: *I found animals in your room* and *I found the animals in your room* are, again, both grammatical. In contrast, singular count nouns must be introduced with a determiner. So, while *I found the iguana in your room is* grammatical, **I found iguana in your room* is not. ■

A second example of English inflectional morphology is the so-called *progressive* (or *-ing*) form of the verb (e.g., *kicking*). The progressive is invariantly marked by the suffix [ɪŋ], spelled *ing,* and contributes the meaning 'in the process of.' Although this is a highly productive rule of English morphology, even here there are apparent exceptions in the form of certain verbs that do not undergo the rule. For example, many English-speakers note reduced acceptability in examples like **I am knowing the answer, *John was mistrusting Bill,* and **Mary is wanting to eat.* Verbs like *know, mistrust, and want* are called *stative* verbs. Statives seem to signify states of mind rather than actions or processes, and therefore seem awkward in combination with *-ing.* Verbs like *seem* and *appear* are also incompatible with the progressive in some of their uses (consider **It was seeming late* vs. *It seemed late* and **It is appearing to be time to leave* vs. *It appears to be time to leave*).

Here the problem has to do with the unusual character of the dummy subject *it* which has no real meaning of its own and does not stand for anything that could be in a process. As with our refinement of the *-able* rule to limit its application to transitive verbs, semantic restrictions on the application of the *-ing* rule are not so much exceptions to it as they are qualifications. In any event, despite the relatively productive character of the rules of inflectional morphology, there are interesting and subtle considerations that bear on their applicability.

Create analysis trees for the following:

a. winking
b. restoring
c. unthinking

3.14 Inflection and Derivation

Having introduced and considered some examples of inflectional morphology, we now examine some of the interactions between the two kinds of morphological rules. First we try to build some more complicated examples that combine inflection and derivation.

Using the following list of items and applying them to the root *create,* try freely forming complex strings of morphemes:

post	ive
re	ist
ly	ing
ion	s
anti	ed
pro	ity
al	er

There are many combinations of prefixes and suffixes that result in words of English, and still others that yield possible words that have not been conventionalized. However, notice what happens if you build a word in which an inflectional ending (like *-s* or *-ed* appears before a derivational suffix like *-ive* or *-ion.* Can you construct a well-formed item of this type? It seems that there are no words like **creat-ing-ive* or **creat-ed-ion* where derivation follows inflection. Furthermore, words like *creations* that do combine derivational and inflectional morphemes do not tolerate having their affixes in the opposite order (e.g., **create-s-ion*). In short, there are no successful combinations of suffixes in which an inflection appears "inside" a derivational affix.

This interesting observation deepens our conviction that the derivational and inflectional systems are two independent sub-systems of English morphology. But having noticed this condition on clusters of suffixes, it remains to find a way to explain this distribution in our theory of morphology. One way to account for the restriction is to allow all of our derivational rules to apply before applying of any inflectional rules. By ordering the application of the rules in this way, we guarantee that all inflectional endings will appear at the ends of lexical items. Of course, more research is needed to sufficiently justify this analysis, but it illustrates at least one way to cope with the interactions between derivational and inflectional affixes.

3.15 Compounds

Up to this point, we have mostly concentrated on morphological processes that involve attaching bound morphemes to roots or derived roots. It is also possible to combine two (or more) free morphemes to form a compound. For example, *police* and *man* can combine to form the compound *policeman,* and *fire, engine,* and *red*

Consider the following Aztec data (Langacker 1973):

a. tlamatini 'knower' (one who knows something)

b. Nitetlazotla 'I love someone'

c. tlamati 'to know something'

d. tlazotlani 'lover' (one who loves someone)

Describe the process that changes an verb into a noun with the meaning 'one who Xs.' Which morpheme of English plays the same role?

all appear in the compound *fire-engine red*. Compounding is an extremely productive process in English. There are many compounds that are conventionally recognized as part of the language, and an apparently indefinite number of spontaneously created compound forms that speakers produce freely in a variety of situations. To better appreciate this point, try combining the following roots to form as many compounds as you can:

program	time
driver	monitoring
safety	universal
first	device
stress	over
active	factor

Notice that many compounds belong to the category of nouns (for example, *time-monitoring principle* and *safety factor*) but that compound adjectives like *over-active* and compound verbs like *over-stress* are also derivable.

One interesting complication in the analysis of compounds is the matter of how to distinguish them from ordinary sequences of words; for instance, we want to conclude that *policeman* is a compound but that *nice picture* is not. It may seem tempting to fall back on English orthography to resolve such questions, but we hope that you have come to be wary of relying on spelling conventions to inform linguistic analyses; and sure enough, where compounds are concerned, English spelling is (once again) inconsistent. For example, although *policeman* is spelled as one word, many other two-word compounds are spelled with a space between items. A quick examination of some compounds based on *post* confirms this impression:

postmaster	post office
postmark	post route
postscript	post card

There are also some compounds like *pushbutton* that have alternative spellings with spaces between the free morphemes (*push button*). In other cases, compounds are marked by hyphens, but this identifying characteristic is also unpredictably distributed; for example, we find *lip-read,* but also *lipreader, lipreading,* and *lip service* (not to mention *lipstick*).

3.16 Identifying Compounds

Since we find ourselves in a circumstance in which *ice cream, ice-cream,* and *ice-cream cone* are all recognized as compounds, we need to appeal to factors other than *orthographic* conventions to ground our analysis. Three general properties of compounds that help us identify them are certain aspects of their interpretation, their resistance to taking internal modification, and their stress patterns. We consider these in turn.

In many compounds, the interpretation of the whole is not a simple function of the interpretations of the parts. For example, *ice cream* is not literally ice and cream, and may sometimes involve neither of these substances. How can this observation about the meaning of compounds help to identify them? We can develop this semantic property into a helpful heuristic by examining minimal pairs like *blackboard* and *black board*. *Blackboard* is a compound that refers to a flat surface that can be written on with chalk. It need not be made out of a board (plastic will do), and the color could be gray or dark brown. In contrast, *black board,* which is not a compound, refers to a board that is black in color (in typical circumstances). A gray, plastic object simply will not do. Although not all compounds feature this sort of loose interpretation, we can use the type of contrast in interpretation between *blackboard* and *black board* to help identify them.

A second factor helping to identify compounds concerns their "modifiability." Continuing with *blackboard* and *black board,* notice that the compound doesn't permit modification of *black* (**an extremely blackboard*) but *black board* does (*an extremely black board*). Try using this test to identify which of the following are compounds:

the (mostly) white house
the (*mostly) White House.
a (*very) blackbird
a (very) black bird.
a (*certifiably) legal eagle (= a lawyer)
a (certifiably) legal eagle (= a bird)
a(n) (extremely) hot dog (= animal)
a(n) (*extremely) hot dog (= food)
a young lady killer (= young woman who kills)
a young lady killer (= youth liked by ladies) (? liked by young ladies)

A final feature that can distinguish compounds from non-compounds is their characteristic stress pattern. In the noncompound interpretation of *black board,* *black* and *board* are two separate words, each of which receives word-level stress (with additional phrasal stress on *board*). In its compound interpretation, *blackboard* receives compound stress, resulting in the primary stress shifting to *black*. Although some compounds do not exhibit compound stress (*Fifth Avenue,* for example), it is usually a reliable way of identifying them.

You should now be able to identify compounds by using the above guidelines. Examine the following transcript, and try to determine how many compounds the speaker uses.

I grew up in Boston in the Forties and that was World War II time and I remember being a little kid and participating in the war effort. The war effort meant you collected kapok for life jackets, you collected metal for scrap metal drives, in fact the local movie theater would let you in if you brought so many pounds of metal.

Discuss the structure of scrap metal drives. *Be specific: Identify the morphemes and indicate how they combine to build the phrase. Justify your answer.*

We have seen that compound nouns like *blackboard* have a special stress contour compared to noncompound sequences of lexical items. We can account for *compound stress* by assigning different *metrical* analyses to compound and noncompound items. The metrical tree for the sequence *black board* appears below.

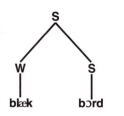

Representation for *black board*.

Notice that the main stress is on *board*, consistent with the normal principles of phrasal stress assignment in English. In the case of the compound *blackboard*, the *Compound Stress Rule* reverses the relative prominence.

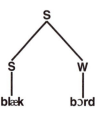

Representation for *blackboard*.

We can also apply this analysis to more complicated examples like *light blue dress*. In this case, *light blue* is a compound adjective but the whole phrase is not a compound. Consequently, *dress* receives primary stress and *light blue*, secondary stress. However, within the compound *light blue*, the compound stress rule applies, resulting in the assignment of stronger stress to *light*.

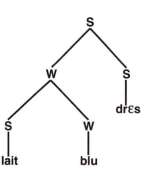

Representation for *light blue dress*.

Finally, consider the case of the compound ice-cream cone that contains the compound *ice cream* as a part. Here, the compound stress rule requires that *ice* be strong with respect to *cream* and that *ice cream* be strong with respect to *cone*. ■

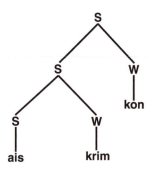

Representation for *ice cream cone*.

Create metrical trees for the following:

a. *grease monkey*
b. *hip hop*
c. *blackboard jungle*

3.17 Lexical Meaning

Our examination of morphological processes has thus far concentrated on morphological structure and lexical rules. It is now time to consider the interpretation of lexical items. Most linguists agree that an entry for a lexical item must include information about the item's meaning. Indeed, it may seem reasonable to suppose that in this regard, at least, a standard dictionary definition is close to what we have in mind. Unfortunately, there are a number of flaws in this approach; and we once again use the dictionary as a foil to help develop our own ideas about meaning.

Our first worry is that dictionary definitions are often much more detailed than speakers' meanings. Consider, for example, the case of *beech* and *elm,* two names for trees. Do you know these words? Most people (botanists and serious gardeners aside) recognize that these are English words that stand for different kinds of trees, but they cannot tell a beech from an elm. Dictionary definitions, on the other hand, can be quite specific. For example, our dictionary defines *beech* as "any of a number of related trees with smooth, gray bark, hard wood, dark-green leaves, and edible three-cornered nuts." Clearly, this is a poor account of what a typical speaker of English takes to be the meaning of *beech.*

A second concern, paradoxically, is that there also a sense in which dictionary entries represent far less than what a native speaker knows about the interpretation of a lexical item. There is a vast amount of information that speakers associate with many lexical items that is far too general to make it into any dictionary. Suppose, for example, that you tell someone that you propose to paint a house white. It is clear that you mean that the outside of the house will be painted. Similarly, if you describe a house as white, you mean a house that is white on the outside. On the other hand, if you complain of a dirty house, you mean a house that is dirty inside; whereas when you speak of an expensive house, it seems to involve the whole house as an aggregate. There is reason to think that this kind of semantic information may not be simply gleaned from experience with houses, but that it derives, in part, from the basic assumptions we associate with what we might call "container" words (that is, words for things that have insides, outsides, and capacity). White cars, white boxes, white vases, and white cups are also white on the outside. This suggests that certain properties of container words ought to be captured in our theory of the lexicon. Furthermore, it is easy to show that this type of lexical knowledge is productive: If we introduce a new container term say, a *drix,* you automatically know that a white drix is one that has a white exterior.

A third complication with the idea that lexical meanings are like dictionary definitions concerns the distinction between content words and function words. It just is not clear that function words have meanings in the usual sense of the word. For example, the

Do the meanings of the words beech *and* elm *seem more elusive than those of other kinds of things? Would you have done better if we had asked you to define (exactly)* robin, Texas, *or* impeachment? *Discuss.*

entry for *to* in our dictionary treats the *to* of *I want to leave* as "a sign of the infinitive..." and has no entry at all for the *to* of *I gave the car to Mary.* Clearly, we need to provide a more systematic account of the lexical information associated with function words.

A fourth consideration is redundancy. The dictionary treats items that are obviously related as if they were independent of one another. We are told that a *baker* is "one who bakes," and that a *singer* is "one who sings," missing the generalization that the *-er* suffix typically contributes the meaning 'one who Xs.' A more general manifestation of the tendency of dictionaries to treat related words as unrelated is their failure to capture other kinds of meaning-relations among lexical items. For example, English-speakers know that *dogs* and *presidents* stand for animate objects, *veal* and *bliss* are mass terms, and the meaning of *leg* is related to the meaning of *arm* in that both are inalienable body parts. We must record this type of lexical knowledge in each lexical entry.

The fifth objection pertains to the productive character of morphological processes. We have already noted the fact that many morphological rules can be applied creatively to a large range of input forms. Compounds, in particular, can be freely formed by speakers "on the fly." Suppose we invent the compound *elephant icebox* to describe an invention. Although native speakers are able to interpret this item without difficulty, they cannot look up the word in their lexicon, since it has been newly created. Speakers can calculate the meaning of a compound on the basis of the meanings of its free morphemes. This meaning is compositional, and speakers can compose the interpretations of compounds in a way that is not explained by adopting static, dictionary-type entries for lexical meanings.

Finally, we must remind ourselves of a thorny methodological problem: the dictionary defines words in terms of other words, but meanings must ultimately be something other than words. This is a problem we return to in Chapter 5.

3.18 Thematic Roles

Although there are many open questions about exactly what lexical representations of meaning look like, one kind of semantic information that must be represented is *thematic roles*. Thematic

One of the ways that the lexicon of a language adds new items is through the processes of lexical borrowing — the incorporation of lexical items from another language. In English, for example, only about 14 percent of the contemporary vocabulary is native Anglo-Saxon (Roberts 1994). English borrowed lexical items from Norse (*sky, law, leg,* and *thrust*) and Latin (*cheese, butter, bishop,* and *kettle*) in its early stages of development. After the Norman conquest in 1066, there was a tremendous infusion of new lexical stock from French: words for food (*veal, bacon, peach*), household terms (*blanket, chair, towel*), and colors (*blue, scarlet, vermilion*), among many other lexical categories.

When lexical items are borrowed from one language into another, there may be interesting discrepancies between the original and the copy. Very often the sound systems of the two languages are incompatible, resulting in sound substitution for certain "unpronounceable" sounds. For example, English *dance* derives from French *danse,* but the latter contains a nasal vowel, a category that is lacking from English. The English vowel [æ] was substituted, which is ironic in that [æ] is missing from the French vowel system! Lexical items borrowed into a language can also involve a shift in meaning. English borrowed *gentle* from the French *gentil,* 'nice,' demonstrating how the meanings of the two terms have drifted apart over time. ∎

roles are best conceived of as an abstract set of relations that indicate who (or what) is doing what to whom. For instance, in one type of simple English sentence, the subject of the sentence is assigned the thematic role of *agent* — roughly, the executor of the action. So, in *Mary snored*, the subject, *Mary*, is interpreted to have undertaken the action of snoring. Consider next a sentence with a transitive verb, e.g., *Mary tripped John*. *Mary* is again the agent, and *John* the *theme* (the receiver of the action). Other sentences, however, provide different thematic profiles.

1. The window opened.
2. Seymour feels inadequate.
3. Sue seemed hesitant.
4. John touched the dog.
5. The dog was touched by John.

In the first example, the subject *the window* is clearly not an agent inasmuch as someone or something (unmentioned) must be responsible for applying the force that caused the window to open. *The window* is a theme, even though it is in subject position because *open* assigns its thematic roles differently than *snored*, a fact that must be listed in the lexical entry for *open*. In *Seymour feels inadequate* we find no obvious action at all. In this case *Seymour* is the *experiencer*. The next example (*Sue seemed hesitant*) is even more complicated. Here, Sue is not doing any "seeming," and bears no thematic role to *seem* whatsoever. *Sue* is an *argument* of the adjective *hesitant*, explaining why *It seemed Sue was hesitant* is a close paraphrase of the original sentence. The final pair of examples shows that thematic roles can "flip" when we compare active sentences to their passive counterparts.

Thematic role assignment in passives.

Identify the thematic roles assigned to the underlined expressions in the following:

a. The cow jumped over <u>the moon</u>.

b. <u>John</u> rolled down the hill.

c. <u>There</u> seemed to be no excuse.

d. <u>What</u> John ate was beans.

We have concentrated on the thematic properties assigned by verbs, but we may also inquire about the thematic properties of other parts of speech. We have just seen that adjectives like *hesitant* can assign thematic roles. It turns out that other syntactic categories may also participate in thematic relations. In sentences like *I consider John a fool* we find the phrase *a fool* acting like a predicate and applying to the theme *John*. In examples like *The decision of the committee is final,* the preposition *of* assigns the thematic role *possessor* to the phrase *the committee*. In general, then, the lexical entries for each thematic role-assigner must indicate which thematic roles to assign and which linguistic elements the roles should be assigned to.

When we try to spell out the semantic change associated with a particular morphological rule, it often becomes necessary to consider how the thematic structure of a root is affected by applying the rule. Consider, for example, the prefix *re-* that attaches to transitive verbs with the rough meaning 'to do X again.' So, *re-read* means 'to read something again' and *re-wash* means 'to wash something again.' If we look more carefully at these two examples, we notice a subtle difference between them with respect to their thematic interpretations. *I re-read the article* entails that I have previously read the article, but *I re-washed the dishes* does not presuppose that I washed them the first time. *Re-read* requires that the same agent repeats the action, but *re-wash* requires only that the action be repeated (by the agent or by someone else). A full analysis of the interpretation of morphologically complex lexical items must account for these kinds of dependencies between derivational rules and thematic role assignment.

3.19 Feature Representation

The final aspect of lexical interpretation we consider is the role semantic features play in the representation of meaning. Feature-based representations are a way of recognizing and formalizing

sub-classifications within groups of items that would otherwise be grouped together. A plural noun is still a noun, which we explain by treating plurals as instances of root nouns to which the feature value *[PLURAL]* has been added by a *lexical redundancy rule*. In this way we can refer to the linguistic category of nouns or, alternatively, the category of singular nouns or plural nouns. In English, for example, nouns with the value *[PLURAL]* for the *NUMBER* feature are items that are run through the morphological rule that attaches the plural marker.

Other feature values may be written into lexical entries to represent types of semantic information that we want to associate with individual lexical items. We have already discussed the distinction between action verbs like *kick* and stative verbs like *know*. We can formally mark this contrast by introducing the feature *V-TYPE* (for "verb type") with the values *[STATIVE]* and *[ACTION],* using them to properly subcategorize verbs in the lexicon. Morphological rules like the one that attaches the progressive suffix *-ing* can then be blocked from applying to verbs like *know* when they bear the feature value *[STATIVE],* and allowed to apply to verbs bearing the feature value *[ACTION]* like *kick*.

We also introduce the feature *KIND* with the values *[MASS]* and *[COUNT]* to mark the contrast between mass and count terms, and the values *[ALIENABLE]* and *[INALIENABLE]* can be introduced to distinguish body-part terms like *leg* and *arm* from the names of common objects in languages that mark the distinction. As before, morphological rules are sensitive to these feature values. For example, since the English plural rule does not apply to mass nouns like *veal,* if we guarantee via a lexical redundancy rule that all nouns with the *KIND* feature value *[MASS]* lack the *NUMBER* feature value *[PLURAL]*, we can block the plural rule from applying to all mass terms.

Luiseño, a Uto-Aztecan language of Southern

California, distinguishes between animates and inanimates, using separate forms of some verbs to mark these properties (see Steele 1977). We can capture this contrast by assigning the *V-TYPE* feature values *[ANIMATE]* and *[INANIMATE]* to the relevant entries in the Luiseño lexicon. Apparently, different semantic features are important in different languages. This suggests that we need to determine which semantic features the morphological rules of each language are sensitive to, and then associate the proper feature complex with each of that language's lexical entries. In this way we can assure that all morphological derivations and the proper privileges of lexical occurrence are properly accounted for.

3.20 Lexical Items

We are finally ready to propose a tentative model of what a lexical entry looks like, and to use this hypothesis as a jumping-off point for asking further questions about the nature of the lexicon and the rules of morphology. Each root in the lexicon must be associated with a specification of its underlying phonemic representation, its part-of-speech classification, and information about syntactic subcategory information (for example, verbs are marked as transitive or intransitive). The semantic information for each item must include an account of thematic relations (as relevant) and the appropriate complex of features to mark the aspects of the interpretation of the item referred to by other rules and principles. We use the verb *kiss* as an illustration:

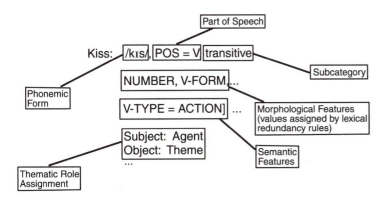

Partial lexical entry for *kiss*.

The information in this entry permits the application of the relevant phonological and morphological rules to *kiss*. For example, since the first segment of the phonemic form /kɪs/ is an unaspirated voiceless stop, the Aspiration Rule applies to eventually derive [kʰɪs].

Any lexical item based on the entry for *kiss* bears one of the alternative values for the feature *V-FORM* (for "verb form") that can be associated with transitive, active verbs to indicate their morphological category (e.g., *[PAST]*, *[PROGRESSIVE]*, and so forth). So *kissing*, for example, bears the *V-FORM* feature value *[PROGRESSIVE]* in addition to other feature values of *kiss*, which it inherits from the root. In turn, the presence of the *V-FORM* feature value *[PROGRESSIVE]* triggers the affixation of the suffix *-ing*. Notice that we do not need a separate lexical entry for *kissable, kisses, kissed, kisser,* or for any other forms that can be derived by rule. These forms are generated from the basic form *kiss,* and are not treated as independent lexical items. In this way, we can develop a model of the lexicon that captures significant linguistic generalizations.

How many other derived forms based on the verb kiss *can you think of? List them.*

IN DETAIL 3.20

Morphological features like *V-FORM* play four roles in our analysis. First, notice that the lexical entry for *kiss* has the *V-FORM* feature, but no values have been assigned. This is because *kiss* is a root form — a basic lexical entry that lists only the idiosyncratic information that must be specified to capture what is unique about this item. When we wish to derive a lexical item from the root *kiss,* we can apply one of a set of *lexical redundancy rules* that adds feature values to the feature complex associated with *kiss.* For example, since *kiss* is an action verb (that is, it is marked with the semantic feature value *[ACTION]*), the lexical redundancy rule *V-TYPE = [ACTION] → V-FORM = [PROGRESSIVE]* can apply to associate the *V-FORM* feature value *[PROGRESSIVE]* with the verb. (We read the → symbol as "if...then.") Alternatively, since verbs in general may appear in the past or present tense, the lexical redundancy rules *POS = V → V-FORM = [PAST]* or *POS = V → V-FORM = [PRESENT]* can apply to add the values *[PAST]* or *[PRESENT]* to the entry for *kiss.*

The second role that morphological features play involves the application of morphological rules. The assignment of a feature value like *[PAST]* (generally — see below) triggers the application of Past-Tense rule, attaching the past-tense suffix to the root form (turning *kiss* into *kissed*). Parallel comments about the feature value *[PROGRESSIVE]* triggering the *-ing* rule apply. In some cases, however, lexical items that come to be associated with a particular feature value (*[PAST]*, for example) fail to undergo the correlated morphophonemic rule. Here we have in mind irregular verbs like *go* and *understand* that do not have the past tense forms **goed* or **understood.* For these verbs, we have to list the appropriate past-tense forms (*went* and *understood*) as a part of the lexical entry for the root verbs *go* and *understand,* respectively. By providing this specific information in a lexical entry, we can override the more general Past-Tense rule.

The third role that morphological features play concerns semantic interpretation. Feature values like *[PAST]* and *[PROGRESSIVE]* modify the meaning of the expressions in which they appear. In the cases at hand, we might conclude that it is unnecessary to attribute this semantic consequence to abstract morphological features, since there is always some overt phonetic manifestation of either the past tense or the progressive (even in the irregular cases). So we might just as well assume that the interpretation of complex lexical items can be assigned directly, without having to consider feature representations. However, the case of the

3.21 Morpho-phonemics

We have developed an account of lexical representation that provides a wide range of syntactic, semantic, and phonemic information associated with each lexical entry. As we have seen, part of the motivation for this approach is to allow other linguistic rules to apply to the proper subsets of lexical forms as delimited by the lexical information that is provided. The application of a morphological rule has the potential to affect a basic lexical entry by changing its phonetic form, part of speech, and syntactic category. In the next few sections, we want to explore the first of these, phonetic form, in more detail. In doing so we can examine the operation of a new domain of rule application that plays an important part in English grammar.

IN DETAIL 3.20

singular verb complicates this story. In most of its forms, the present-tense verb is phonetically indistinguishable from the root form — there is no present tense suffix on *kiss (I/you/we/they kiss)*.

Assuming a lexical redundancy rule *POS = V → V-FORM = [PRESENT]*, we can anchor the interpretation of the present tense verb to the presence of the feature value *[PRESENT]*. Similar comments apply to the English plural, specifically with respect to the irregular forms like *fish* and *deer*. We want to associate the appropriate interpretation (i.e., either singular or plural) with any occurrence of these nouns, again, without the benefit of an overt phonetic clue as to the intended meaning. By positing the lexical redundancy rules *KIND = [COUNT] → NUMBER = [SINGULAR]* and *KIND = [COUNT] → NUMBER = [PLURAL]* and listing irregular plurals for words like

fish and *deer,* we can override the application of the usual plural rule in these special cases. Since fish *[SINGULAR]* is distinct from fish *[PLURAL]*, we assign the correct interpretation even in the absence of phonetic marking.

Fourth, and finally, morphological features are important in syntactic analysis. To return to *[SINGULAR]* and *[PLURAL]*, notice that nouns bearing one or the other of these feature values are introduced by different types of determiners. So, we say *one dog* but *two/three/four…dogs* — *one dogs* and *two dog* are ungrammatical. We return to this matter below.

Exactly how the morphological feature system of English looks is an open question. To consider a hypothetical case, suppose someone proposed the feature *ABLE* along with a putative lexical redundancy rule that established the value of this

feature as *[TRUE]* for transitive verbs, claiming that this feature value triggered the application of the *-able* rule that converts root verbs like *kiss* into adjectives like *kissable.* Although there is nothing wildly implausible about this analysis, it is not sufficiently well motivated. If we could find evidence that verbs without the *-able* suffix nevertheless have "able" interpretations, or that there is some morpho-syntactic dependency that requires us to posit *ABLE* as an abstract feature, then we might accept the proposed analysis. But in the absence of such independent motivation, we conclude that the *-able* rule applies to transitive verbs, making the analysis more indirect but the feature system simpler. ■

With the exception of the special case of phonetically unrealized morphological features, each morphological rule we have investigated has changed the phonetic form of the input to the rule. Rules that add prefixes attach phonetic segments to the beginning of a linguistic item, rules that add suffixes attach phonetic segments to the end, and infixing rules insert phonetic material into a linguistic item.

In each case, the phonetic effect triggered by applying the morphological rule involves the straightforward process of incorporating a new morpheme and attaching its phonetic form to the root (or derived root) to which it is affixed. Suppose we examine this process more carefully with the English past tense.

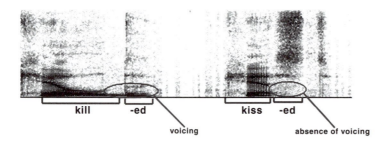

Spectrograms for *killed* and *kissed*.

The above spectrogram shows the past tense of *kill* followed by the past tense of *kiss*. If you say the two words out loud, you will hear that the two instances of the past tense do not sound alike. Furthermore, you can see the difference by inspecting the two circled regions above. The final segment of the past tense morpheme in *kill* is a voiced [d], and the parallel segment in *kiss* is a voiceless [t]; or, phonetically, [kɪl+d] and [kɪs+t]. To make matters more interesting, notice that two forms of the past tense morpheme cannot be reversed in these cases. If, for example, we put a [t] at the end of [kɪl], it becomes [kɪl+t], which in most dialects of English sounds like the name for a type of Scottish skirt, but not like the past tense of *kill*.

We could avoid the conclusion that there are two forms of the English past tense if we could show that either *kill* or *kiss* is irregular, and that its past-tense form should be handled outside the scope of the general form of the past-tense rule. To test this claim, let's examine a larger set of data. We need to establish what form the past tense takes in each of the following examples:

kick/kicked	[kɪk]	jog/jogged	[jag]
sack/sacked	[sæk]	sag/sagged	[sæg]
grip/gripped	[grɪp]	grab/grabbed	[græb]
hiss/hissed	[hɪs]	fizz/fizzed	[fɪz]
push/pushed	[puš]	bribe/bribed	[braib]
miff/miffed	[mɪf]	pave/paved	[pev]

The items in the first column take a final [t] in the past tense, and those in the second column take a final [d]. Again, you can verify that these patterns cannot be reversed by considering the status of a form like [fɪz+t] as a candidate for the past tense of *fizz* — not a normal English pronunciation.

We have discovered that the form of the English past tense varies depending on the particular verb to which the rule is applied. Furthermore, we have established that there is no motivation for treating the problem as a case of irregularity, since there are many instances of each type of past tense form. To buttress this conclusion, we might note fact that any new verb added to the language is automatically and uniformly judged by native speakers of English to take one of these two past-tense forms. For example, if we add *drix* to the lexicon, its past tense must be [drɪks+t]; and if we add *flug,* its past tense form must be [flʌg+d]. This confirms that we are dealing with a productive process that must be accounted for.

The challenge remains to figure out which past tense forms go with which verbs. Some property of verbs like *kick* (which takes [t]) must distinguish them from verbs like *jog* (which takes [d]). In principle, it could be a feature of meaning or a syntactic feature that distinguishes the two classes of cases. But since *kick* and *jog* are both action verbs with related meanings, these avenues do not seem fruitful. We do better to consider the phonetic form of the two classes of verbs and in particular, to consider the phonetic properties of the final segment of the root to which the past tense is attached. Let's look again at the previous data set to see what we find.

Our goal is discover a generalization that allows us to identify each of the two kinds of verbs as a natural class. Since the final segments of the roots in the first column, [k], [p], [s], [š], and [f], are voiceless sounds, and the final segments of the roots in the second column, [g], [b], [z], and [v], are voiced, we can advance the following generalization:

Past-Tense Rule (Phonetic Change)
Words ending in voiced sounds take [d] as the past tense. Words ending in voiceless sounds take [t] as the past tense.

Notice that this rule applies to the phonemic form of the root and attaches the correct form of the past-tense morpheme according to the character of its final segment. We call such rules *morpho-phonemic* rules, because they affect the sound shape of lexical items as a consequence of applying morphological rules. Morpho-phonemic rules resemble the phonological rules we examined in chapter 2 in that they operate on underlying representations to derive output forms by modifying the phonetic character of the input.

We can now push our analysis of past-tense formation a bit further by asking why there is a correlation between voiced final segments and the [d]-form of the past tense and voiceless final segments and the [t]-form of the past tense. Would it have been possible for the correlation to be reversed? If we consider the phonetic character of [d] and [t], we will see the generalization more clearly: [d] is a voiced sound and [t] is voiceless. This suggests the following modified version of the phonetic change involved in the Past-Tense Rule:

Past-Tense Rule (Phonetic Change) (revised)
The past tense ([d] or [t]) must agree in the value of voicing with the final segment of the root to which it is attached.

Rules that enforce feature agreement of this type are called *assimilation* rules. Construing the sound change associated with the Past-Tense Rule as an assimilation rule allows us to explain why words ending in voiced sounds take voiced past-tense endings, and those ending in voiceless sounds take voiceless endings.

Can you think of any counterexamples to the current analysis of the English past tense? Explain your answer.

The derivational prefix in- *attaches to adjectives to form new adjectives with the meaning of 'not X.' Consider the following examples:*

a. *indifferent*
b. *inanimate*
c. *incorrigible*
d. *intolerant*
e. *implausible*
f. *impossible*
g. *indecisive*
h. *insubstantial*
i. *inconsiderate.*

Can we predict if the nasal will be [n], [ŋ], or [m]?

3.22 More Past Forms

We have discovered a generalization that determines the form that the past tense ending takes, based on phonetic character of the final segment of the root it is attached to. Now, however, we encounter a complication in the form of new data that are inconsistent with our analysis:

putt/putted	fold/folded
melt/melted	meld/melded
salt/salted	load/loaded
hate/hated	weld/welded
paste/pasted	braid/braided

If you listen carefully to these data, you will hear that the past-tense ending is neither [t] nor [d] but [əd]. Worse, the [əd] ending seems to be independent of whether the root ends in a voiceless sound or voiced sound.

There are two problems: our Past-Tense Rule over-generates (produces ungrammatical forms); for example, *[lod+d] is derived as the putative past tense of *load,* and we seem forced to admit a third past-tense form, [əd], with a surprising distribution. Let's deal with the distribution first. The [əd] past-tense form seems to be limited to roots that end in [t] or [d]. In such cases, a schwa is inserted before the past-tense morpheme [d]. We can capture this complication by adjusting our statement of the phonetic change portion of the Past-Tense Rule as follows:

Past-Tense Rule (Phonetic Change) (re-revised)
The past tense ([d] or [t]) must agree in the value of voicing with the final segment of the root to which it is attached except for roots ending in [t] and [d], which take [əd].

Unfortunately, this statement of the rule is most unsatisfactory; it is little more than a description of a curious set of facts that fails to explain the linguistic patterns that we have discovered. More specifically, although this past-tense form [əd] is obviously phonetically related to the other past-tense forms, there is no account of this relationship; moreover, we have no explanation for why words ending in the voiced [d] or the voiceless [t] both take the same past-tense form, in contrast to the other cases of the past tense we have studied. We can improve our analysis by noticing that the three forms of the past tense are predictable in their distribution, and this predictability is expressible in the form of phonological rules in the theory developed in the previous chapter. What would such rules look like in the case of the English past tense? There appear to be three generalizations at work here: (1) if a verb ends in a voiced sound it takes a [d] ending; (2) if a verb ends in a voiceless sound it takes a [t] ending; unless (3) a verb ends in a [t] or [d] sound, in which case it takes an [əd] ending.

We can capture the unity of this phenomenon by positing a single underlying form for the past-tense morpheme, by hypothesis, /d/. The process of forming the past tense consists of affixing the past tense /d/ to a verb stem in an underlying phonological representation. Consider the verbs *kick, jog,* and *load.* These have the phonemic forms [kɪkt], [jagd], and [lodəd], respectively. In order to account for the [d] that occurs at the end of forms with final voiced segments like *jog,* we need do nothing at all, and /jag+d/ surfaces phonetically as [jagd], with no additional steps. In order to account for the [t] that occurs at the end of words like *kick,* we posit the following rule:

Devoicing
When a morpheme /d/ is preceded by a final unvoiced segment, devoice the /d/; that is, convert it to [t].

The Devoicing Rule does not apply to /jag+d/, because the final [g] of the root is voiced, but does apply to /kɪk+d/, because the final /k/ of the stem is voiceless; hence the /d/ past -tense affix is converted by devoicing to [t], yielding [kɪk+t].

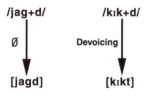

Derivations for *jogged* and *kicked*.

It remains to account for the past tense of words like *load*. The underlying representation of *loaded* is [lod+d], and [ə] must eventually appear between the /d/ of the root and the past-tense affix. Since this vowel is not present in the underlying representation under this account, we must postulate a rule to accomplish its insertion into the representation.

[ə]-Insertion
When a /d/ morpheme is affixed to a root with a final alveolar stop, insert [ə] between the root-final segment and the affix.

We have streamlined the description of the environment for [ə]-insertion by referring to [d] and [t] as alveolar stops. The rule applies to /lod+d/, yielding [lodəd]. The Devoicing Rule does not apply in this case, since the final segment of /lod/ is voiced.

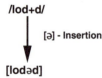

Derivation of *loaded*.

The final case we need to consider is that of verbs like *melt* — those that end in the voiceless alveolar stop [t]. The past-tense form of *melt* is [mɛltəd] which must be derived from the underlying form /mɛlt+d/. If we apply the [ə]-Insertion Rule to the underlying form,

Draw analysis trees for the underlying representations for the following:

a. smelled
b. xeroxed
c. rushed

Describe how Devoicing applies in each case.

Draw analysis trees for the underlying representations for the following:

a. folded
b. unmolded
c. wadded

Explain how [ə]-insertion applies in each case.

we get [mɛltəd]. The Devoicing Rule cannot now apply to [mɛltəd]: the schwa directly precedes the affix [d] at this stage in the derivation; and, like all English vowels, [ə] is a voiced sound.

/mɛlt+d/

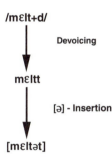

[mɛltəd]

A derivation for *melted.*

In the derivation of [mɛltəd] that we just discussed, we attempted to apply [ə]-Insertion prior to Devoicing, and applying the former rule blocked the application of the latter.

Suppose we try to apply the rules in the opposite order? The result of applying the Devoicing Rule before the [ə]-Insertion Rule is disastrous. The Devoicing Rule is responsible for changing [d] into [t], and when the [ə]-Insertion Rule applies it is too late to maintain the [d] past-tense marker that [mɛltəd] requires.

/mɛlt+d/

| Devoicing

mɛltt

| [ə] - Insertion

[mɛltət]

Alternative derivation for *melted.*

Since the derivational order that produces the correct result for *melt* requires [ə]-Insertion to apply before Devoicing, we must establish this order of application in our rule system. Thus, in addition to the morpho-phonological rules themselves, the ordering relation [ə]-Insertion > Devoicing must be incorporated into the grammar of English. Our analysis of the English past tense involves positing [d] as the underlying form for the past-tense morpheme, coupled with a Devoicing Rule and a [ə]-Insertion Rule to derive the correct phonetic form of the past tense.

Draw analysis trees for the underlying representations for the following:

a. pelted
b. molted
c. recounted

Explain whether Devoicing and/or [ə]-insertion apply in each case.

One interesting additional property of past-tense items is the syllabification of the phonetic form. In most cases of affixation, the incorporation of an affix adds at least one more syllable to the root. So, *kill* is a one-syllable word, whereas *killing* contains two syllables. However, when the past-tense marker is either [d] or [t], as in *killed* ([kɪl+d]), the phonetic form remains one syllable in length (rather than two, as we might expect). We would like to explain these facts, but our present analysis does not account for the differences in the two classes of cases. And, as we shall see, there are important further implications of the problem for our general conception of morpho-phonemic derivations.

An answer to the puzzle about the syllabification of *killed* can be found by undertaking a close examination of the assumptions we have been making about the representation of /d/. Unlike such affixes as *pre-* and *-ing* that are legal syllables, the past-tense morpheme is a member of a special class of affixes that cannot easily be assigned a syllabic structure in their own right. More specifically, note that the affix /d/ lacks a vowel nucleus, which contravenes the Nucleus Constraint, discussed in chapter 2.

Furthermore, if we attempt to associate a full syllabic representation with /d/, we encounter a puzzling potential ambiguity in the analysis. Let's consider the analysis tree for *killed* to illustrate the problem. The root *kill* will look like this:

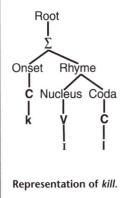

Representation of *kill*.

If we posit an underlying syllabic representation for /d/, we must decide whether to attach it to (1) the onset slot or (2) the coda slot of the affix.

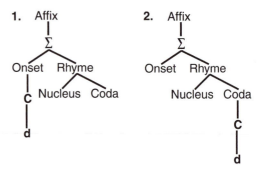

Alternative representations for the past-tense suffix.

A more straightforward analysis admits that the affix /d/ does not constitute a syllable in underlying representation, assigning it a simpler extrasyllabic representation.

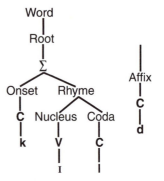

Extra-syllabic representation for *killed*.

Next, suppose we adopt the following principle, which we call the Syllabification Principle:

Syllabification Principle
Every segment must be associated with a syllable.

Since the past-tense marker /d/ is not associated with a syllable in the underlying representation of /kɪl+d/, this structure may be brought into line with the Syllabification Principle if the affix /d/ attaches to the root.

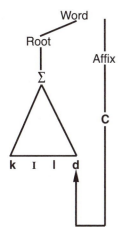

Resyllabified representation for *killed*.

Let us now reconsider the analysis of *melded* in the light of our current observations:

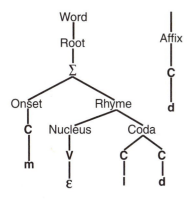

Underlying representation for *melded*.

The underlying form is presented above. Here, the application of [ə]-Insertion introduces a second vowel nucleus, [ə]. This allows the underlying /d/ to be associated with a second syllable, yielding the syllabification *meld-ed*, a

point of contrast with respect to the monosyllabic form *killed* discussed above.

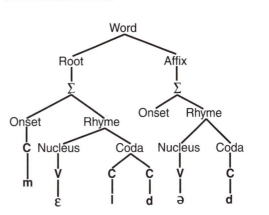

Representation for *melded*.

This analysis offers an interesting account of the facts, but also forces us to revise a fundamental assumption that has undergirded our analysis thus far: We are no longer deriving syllable structures from fully represented underlying syllable structures. Instead, we have assumed that a special class of affixes, including /d/, must get incorporated into a syllabic representation in a way that is *optimally* consistent with the principles of English. Such an approach is not strictly linear, and it adopts a rather different conception of the phonological derivation from the one we had been developing.

Although we do not incorporate this approach in our formal analysis, many contemporary linguists consider it to hold great promise (see Prince and Smolensky 1995, and the references cited there). There are, furthermore, many other open questions about the proper representation of affixes. Just the same, our discussion should give you the flavor of an explanatory approach to a broad range of linguistic problems. Perhaps the most interesting property of our analysis is the way in which independently motivated principles like the Nucleus Constraint, [ə]-Insertion, and so forth, conspire to

IN DETAIL 3.22

constrain the range of possible analysis available within our theory.

Linguists argue that children's ability to learn language is bootstrapped in the same way. By developing principles that serve to limit the hypothesis space, children become more powerful learners, able to ignore misleading, false, or nonoptimal analyses on the basis of deep principles of their language-acquisition device. ■

The alternative surface forms that a morpheme can take are called *allomorphs*. By deriving the three allomorphs of the past tense from a single underlying form we can simultaneously account for the distribution of the past-tense forms and for the unitary nature of the past-tense morpheme.

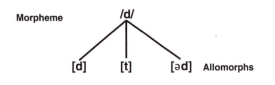

Allomorphs of the morpheme /d/.

3.23 The Plural Revisited

We would now like to extend the generality of this analysis by reconsidering our analysis of the English plural. All native English-speakers know that the plural of *dog* is *dogs,* and that the plural of *cat* is *cats*. When English-speakers produce these plurals, they instinctively sound the plural marker as [z] in the first case, and as [s] in the second. In our earlier discussion of the English plural, we argued that plurals were to be derived by applying a morphological rule (the Plural Rule) to nouns. In the regular cases, this rule adds a plural suffix to the input form. We went on to add the requirement

that the rule be restricted in its application to count nouns; that is, nouns listed in the lexicon that are marked with the feature value *[COUNT]*. At this point, some of the parallels with the case of the English plural should be clear. The distribution of the past-tense allomorphs [d] and [t] depends on properties of the root, and so does the distribution of [z] and [s].

ship/ships	hub/hubs
gnat/gnats	dud/duds
tick/ticks	bag/bags
laugh/laughs	shill/shills
depth/depths	hoe/hoes

Each of the items in the first column takes an [s]-plural, and each in the second column takes a [z]. In order to develop a complete analysis of the plural, we need to be able to predict which of these forms the plural takes for any given input.

We could, of course, simply list each English noun in the lexicon with its appropriate plural form but, as in the case of the past tense, to do so would be to miss a generalization, since the distribution of [s] and [z] is not random. Indeed, the factor that conditions the choice between [s] and [z] is precisely the one that decides the distribution of the past-tense allomorphs: roots like *cat* ending in voiceless sounds take [s]-plurals ([kæts]) and roots like *dog* ending in voiced sounds take [z]-plurals ([dɔgz]). Furthermore, since [s] is voiceless and [z] is voiced, we once again find a pattern of agreement in the value of voicing between the plural affix and the final segment of the root.

Suppose we try to capture the dependency between the form of the plural and the phonetic character of the final segment of the root (as well as the obvious analogy to the past-tense cases) by treating [s] and [z] as allomorphs of an underlying plural marker. The first decision we face is what to choose as the phonemic representation of the plural. It is tempting to posit /s/ as the underlying form of the plural, since *s* is the typical spelling for the English plural. If we adopt this strategy, the underlying form for *dog* is /dɔg+s/, and the underlying form for *cat* is /kæt+s/. The second case is unproblematic, since we already have the correct segmental sequence for the output form [kæts] without applying any morpho-phonemic rules. The first case, however, requires further analysis.

Somehow, the underlying [s] of /dɔg+s/ must surface as a [z] to derive [dɔgz]. We could invent a new morpho-phonemic rule that voices [s] (turning it into [z]) before root-final voiced segments:

Voicing
When a morpheme /s/ is preceded by a final voiceless segment, voice the /s/; that is, convert it to [z].

This rule applies to /dɔg+s/ to change the final [s] to a [z], yielding [dɔgz], the correct phonetic form. However, this is a very unsatisfying solution in that we have failed to capture the superficial similarity between the past tense and the plural that cries out for an explanation. By positing a Voicing Rule to go along with the Devoicing Rule required for the past-tense cases, we have treated these obviously related phenomena as if they were unrelated. We do better to revise our assumption about the phonetic character of the underlying form of the plural. After all, it was our decision to adopt /s/ as the underlying form of the plural that led to the necessity of recruiting a Voicing Rule in the first place. Suppose we adopt [z] as the underlying form of the plural, and generalize the Devoicing Rule so that it applies in the case of both the past tense and the plural.

Devoicing
When a past or plural morpheme is preceded by a final voiceless segment, devoice it.

The derivation of cases like [dɔgz] is straightforward. The underlying form is /dɔg+z/, and no rules apply, resulting in the surface form [dɔgz]. Examples like [kæts] will require the application of the Devoicing Rule.

By adopting [z] as the underlying form of the plural, we have regained parallelism with the treatment of the past tense. In the next section we take the resemblance even further.

Draw analysis trees for the underlying representations for the following:

a. smells
b. writes
c. graphs

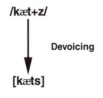

/kæt+z/

Devoicing

[kæts]

Derivation of *cats*.

3.24 A Third Plural

Our analysis of the English plural has successfully captured significant linguistic generalizations. Still, one point of asymmetry with
respect to the analysis of the past tense remains. In the latter case,
but not the former, we observed a third form, [əd], the derivation of
which required the application of a second morpho-phonemic rule,
[ə]-Insertion. It remains to be seen whether [ə]-Insertion applies in
the derivation of the English plural. The likely cases to investigate
are nouns that end in voiced or voiceless alveolar stops ([d] or [t]),
since those were the root-final segments that triggered [ə]-Insertion
in the past tense cases. But we have already examined words like *cat*
and *dud,* examples that take [s] and [z] for their respective plurals,
and do not require us to recognize a third plural form.

It does turn out that there is a third form of the plural, as the
following data attest:

glass/glasses	gaze/gazes
lash/lashes	rouge/rouges
latch/latches	fudge/fudges

Furthermore, the form of this third type of plural is [əz], suggesting
that the [ə]-Insertion Rule is implicated in the derivations of these
forms as well. The problem is that the phonetic factor that governs
the distribution of [əz] does not appear to be the same as that for
[əd].

We must first discover what linguistic generalization determines
the distribution of [əz]. The first step is to transcribe our data to
make it easier to see the pattern.

glass	[glæs]	gaze	[gez]
lash	[læš]	rouge	[ruž]
latch	[læč]	fudge	[fʌǰ]

The root-final sounds that trigger the [əz] form of the plural are [s],
[z], [š], [ž], [č], and [ǰ]. The phonetic property that unifies this set of
segments is that they are all *strident* (hissy) sounds. Suppose we try
to incorporate this generalization into the [ə]-Insertion rule as
follows:

[ə]-Insertion (revised)
When a past-tense morpheme is affixed to a root with a final
alveolar stop or a plural is affixed to a root with a final strident
segment, insert [ə] between the root-final segment and the affix.

Although this statement of [ə]-Insertion seems to be adequate to the facts, it still amounts to little more than a conjunction of two rather different statements about the environment in which the rule applies. A better explanation would provide some insight into why alveolar stops trigger the rule for the past-tense morpheme, and strident segments for the plural. One approach this problem is to ask what the phonetic form for [əz] plurals and [əd] past-tense forms would look like if the [ə]-Insertion Rule did not apply. That is, suppose that we remove [ə]-Insertion from our list of rules. Assuming that the underlying form for the past tense is [d], and the underlying past tense for the plural is [z], the putative phonetic forms for words like *putted, folded, glasses,* and *gazes* would be: [pʌtt], [foldd], [glæss], and [gezz]. Notice that each example involves a sequence of two identical final sounds. Such sequences, called *geminates* (from the Latin for 'twins'), are not possible in well-formed English words: there are no possible English words like [brʌšš] with a double [š] *coda* (the end of the syllable) that could contrast with the actual English word *brush* ([brʌš]).

In fact, English sometimes goes to great lengths to avoid geminate sequences even across morpheme boundaries. Consider, for example, compounds like *horse sense* that involve the underlying sequence /hɔrs+sɛns/, which contains an *s-s* sequence. In normal speech, *horse sense* is pronounced [hɔrsɛns] rather than [hɔrssɛns], avoiding the incipient geminate. When we notice that geminate sequences violate the principles of English phonotactics, the environment for the [ə]-Insertion rule makes sense: the affixation rules involved in past-tense formation and plural formation run the risk of creating illicit *t-t, d-d, s-s,* and *z-z* sequences; and [ə]-Insertion serves to break up geminates to preserve well-formed English syllable structures, applying in cases in which a phonotactic violation is imminent.

We have now unified our accounts of the plural and the past tense. The analyses involve positing [d] and [z] as the underlying forms of the past tense and the plural, respectively. We have also devised two morpho-phonemic rules — Devoicing and [ə]-Insertion — as well as an ordering relation ([ə]-Insertion > Devoicing) that governs the sequence in which the rules are eligible to apply.

3.25 Morpho-syntax

Our investigation of lexical rules and processes has mostly concentrated on the analysis of words in isolation. We have discussed aspects of meaning, structure, and pronunciation that are relevant

Draw analysis trees for the underlying representations for the following:

a. *bridges*
b. *paths*
c. *britches*

to individual words without regard to the ways in which the properties of other words in a phrase or sentence might bear on lexical representations. We now turn to a series of topics in *morpho-syntax*, the subfield of morphology concerned with points of interaction between the lexicon and the syntactic component of the grammar. Here we are especially interested in studying the ways in which the lexical properties of individual lexical items and aspects of the syntactic context influence each other.

We begin our inquiry into morpho-syntax by examining some of the roles lexical features play in the organization of phrases and sentences. We also look at the *agreement* system in English — the mechanism responsible for insuring that certain lexical items share lexical features with other lexical items. Next, we introduce and discuss the English *case* system, a module of the grammar that is concerned with the distribution of features such as the possessive marker *'s,* among other things. We then examine certain parallels between morphological and syntactic processes, particularly with respect to thematic role assignment. We close the discussion by reconsidering the contraction process, which displays an interesting sensitivity to aspects of syntactic analysis that we will discuss further in the next chapter.

3.26 Lexical Features

Up to this point, we have used lexical feature values like *[PLURAL]* and *[STATIVE]* to identify a part of the membership of a lexical category, by allowing a subset of that membership to share a particular feature or features. Lexical features form a part of the lexical entry associated with an individual lexical item, formalizing aspects of interpretation and triggering the application of relevant morphological and morpho-phonemic rules. In addition to their role in morphological and morpho-phonemic processes, lexical features are also important in syntactic analyses. In the next few sections, we examine several ways in which lexical features figure in the organization and interpretation of sentences, beginning with the *tense* system.

How many tenses are there in English? This is a trick question: It depends what you mean by a tense. Languages have many ways to encode information about time. For example, helping verbs *(will)* and adverbs *(tomorrow)* are two kinds of temporally oriented items in English. But linguists reserve the word *tense* to signify a verb form that establishes a temporal reference point. Thus, there are only two tenses in English: past and present, and even the existence of the latter is not beyond dispute. Minimally, we must recognize a contrast between forms like *walk* and *walked*, *sing* and *sang*, and *understand* and *understood*, which seems to require a distinction between past and present tense. Since the past is typically marked by an affix or other sound change, its status is secure. But, in most cases, the present tense form looks suspiciously like the root form.

We are convinced that we must recognize a present-tense form (that is distinct from the root form) because of the contrast in the third-person singular: We say *John walks* not **John walk*. In addition to this evidence, we also find a more full-blown set of distinctions in the conjugation of the irregular verb *be*. Here the contrast between the present tense forms *am, are,* and *is* is paralleled by the past tense forms *was* and *were*.

You might be wondering about the future tense in English. We can express futurity in a number of ways: *Tomorrow, he leaves* is surely about the future, as is *She is gonna leave*. But in both cases the verbs (*leaves* and *is*) are in the present tense. Similarly, *The committee will decide our fate* involves a reference to the future, but the device that establishes it is the helping verb *will* rather than a future-tense form. The contrast with French may help to clarify matters here. French, like English allows futurity to be expressed with a helping verb construction; *Je vais chanter* (literally, *I go to sing*) means what *I will sing* means. But French also can express this proposition with the bona fide future tense form *Je chanterais* in which *chanterais* is the future tense form of the verb *chanter* (*to sing*). English lacks a counterpart to *chanterais,* and must rely solely on other devices to convey this meaning.

In our analysis of the past tense, we posited a past-tense morpheme /d/ that surfaced as one of three allomorphs, [d], [t], or [əd] by applying Devoicing and [ə]-Insertion rules. Exhibiting a pattern that by now is becoming familiar, we find the following third-person-singular present-tense data:

walks	[wɔk+s]	sings	[sɪŋ+z]	hisses	[hɪs+əz]
hits	[hɪt+s]	fibs	[fɪb+z]	fizzes	[fɪz+əz]
jumps	[jʌmp+s]	hug	[hʌg+z]	axes	[æks+əz]

The distribution of phonetic forms in the third-person singular is the same as that in the past tense (and the plural), displaying the usual pattern of voicing assimilation. If the feature value *[PRESENT]* is listed as an alternative to *[PAST]* in each verb's lexical entry along with a person feature value (e.g., *[3 PERSON]* for third person) and a number feature value *([SINGULAR] or [PLURAL]),* we can trigger the relevant morpho-phonemic rules. If we posit [z] as the underlying form for the present-tense third-person singular morpheme, and apply Devoicing and [ə]-Insertion, as appropriate, we will account for the present data.

As noted above, all present-tense forms of the verb other than the third-person singular do not participate in the sound change associated with the third-person singular forms. So, we find *I/you/ we/they kick* each without any overt marker of tense, number, or person. But despite their absence of morphological marking, these verbs are nevertheless associated with the feature value *[PRESENT]* as well as a number feature value (*[SINGULAR]* or *[PLURAL]*) and person feature value (*[1 PERSON], [2 PERSON]*, or *[3 PERSON]*). In this regard, such verbs are like plural nouns that lack an overt plural marker (but are still marked *[PLURAL]*). In other words, in making the assignment of features values more general, we are claiming that even verbs lacking overt affixal morphology must comprise a complete tense, number, and person feature bundle. This explains why sentences like *The gamblers want to leave* are interpreted as present-tense utterances despite the lack of a phonetically marked present tense. The lexical feature value *[PRESENT]* associated with *want* is enough to establish the appropriate interpretation.

3.27 Lexical Dependencies

What do we mean by a dependency? In very abstract terms, a dependency is linguistic connection that somehow links two independent items. An example of a dependency that we have previously studied is the assimilation relation between certain inflectional morphemes (like past tense or plural) and a root-final segment with respect to the phonetic feature of voicing.

Features can also be involved in dependencies that involve other lexical items. Reconsider, for example, the English progressive form of the verb, *hoping* being a case in point. Suppose we want to characterize where progressives can appear in well-formed English sentences. We begin with the following data:

1. Mary could be leaving.
2. *Mary could leaving.
3. John thought that he was winning.
4. *John thought that he winning.
5. The committee is considering the problem.
6. *The committee considering the problem.
7. Sally could have been faking it.
8. *Sally could have faking it.
9. I am flying.
10. *I must flying.

In the examples that are well formed, the progressive verbs follow *be, was, is, been*, and *am*, each of which is functioning as a so-called helping verb. Sentences in which the progressive follows the subject or a helping verb like *could* or *have* are ungrammatical. In short, progressive verbs must follow forms of the helping verb *be*. Furthermore, as the data below show, it looks as if there is also a dependency in the opposite direction: Forms of the helping verb *be* cannot appear freely next to past, present, or other forms of the main verb; but they can appear next to its progressive forms:

1. The wound could be oozing.
2. *The wound could be oozed.
3. John thought that he was deteriorating.
4. *John thought that he was deteriorate.
5. You should be reevaluating the solution.
6. *You should be reevaluated the solution.
7. I must have been singing.
8. *I must have been sang.
9. Sue is trying pizza for the first time.

We can capture the dependency between the helping verb *be* and the progressive by adding the following restriction to the lexical entry for *be*: forms of the helping verb *be* must "help" a verb that is in the progressive. This condition permits a form of *be* to take as its *complement* (i.e., its "helpee")

a verb marked with the *V-FORM* ("verb-form")
value *[PROGRESSIVE]*. Since verbs with this feature
value must undergo the morphological rule that
attaches the suffix *-ing,* we establish that the
complement to the helping verb *be* is a progressive
verb:

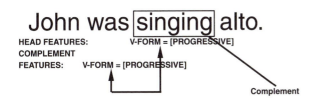

The progressive.

The head features of a lexical item are the features
that "belong" to it. So, *was* is marked with the
head *V-FORM* value *[PAST]* because it is the past-
tense form of *be,* and *singing* is marked *[PROGRES-
SIVE]* because it is in the progressive. The complement features of a lexical item specify which head
features its complement must have. *[PROGRESSIVE]*
is listed as a complement *V-FORM* value for the
helping verb *was,* not because *was* is a progressive
(which it is not), but because the complement of
was must be a progressive; that is, its complement
must bear the head *V-FORM* feature value *[PRO-
GRESSIVE]*. By introducing complement features
into lexical entries we can formalize the dependencies inhering between items and their complements. We now turn to a consideration of the
number features, which involve a more complicated featural dependency.

3.28 Number Agreement

Our earlier discussion of the feature values *[SIN-
GULAR]* and *[PLURAL]* concentrated on two problems: the phonetic form that the plural takes, and
the proper morphological analysis of words that
lack an overt plural form. Up to this point, we

have assumed that *NUMBER* values can be established without considering the context in which
an item appears. Consider, in this regard, the
following data:

1. Dogs have no chance.
2. *Dogs has no chance.
3. A linguist solves the problem.
4. *A linguist solve the problem.
5. We know when to quit.
6. *We knows when to quit.
7. It is raining.
8. *It are raining.

In each case, the form of the noun in subject
position depends on the form of the verb. More
specifically, if the subject noun is singular, the verb
must be singular, and if the subject noun is plural,
the verb must be plural.

Dogs   have   no   chance.

NUMBER =   NUMBER =
[PLURAL]   [PLURAL]

Number agreement.

To capture this dependency, we must associate
NUMBER features with both nouns and verbs, and
require that in any given sentence, the subject's
NUMBER feature value must match the verb's
NUMBER feature value.

We can extend the technique we used to establish a featural dependency between a progressive and its helping verb to account for the number agreement data. Let's posit a set of *specifier (Spec)* features (parallel to the complement [Comp] features we posited earlier) that impose featural restrictions on the subject of the sentence. In this case, the subject's head features must include the *NUMBER* value *[PLURAL]*.

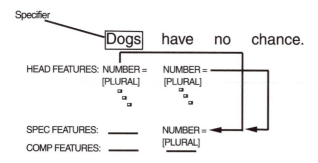

Number agreement.

Note that the head *NUMBER* feature value of the subject must be the same as the specifier *NUMBER* feature value of the verb. This principle is what ultimately guarantees that the number head-feature value of the subject agrees with the number head feature value of the verb. It functions as a kind of lexical well-formedness condition that must be imposed on the feature bundle associated with every verb.

3.29 Pronouns and Case

Our analysis of English nouns has identified contrasts between singular and plural, and between mass and count. This pair of alternations is sufficient to characterize most English nouns, but there is one special subcategory of noun that requires further analysis: the class of *pronouns*. We begin by noting that the usual alternation between singular and plural obtains in the pronoun system; but it is not marked by any of the three plural allomorphs [s], [z], or [əz]. So, alongside *I* we find *we; you* lacks an overt sign of the plural; and *he, she,* and *it* all alternate with the plural form *they*. Pronouns also tend to irregularity in their possessive form. Whereas most nouns add a suffix (written *'s*), here we find the alternations *I/my, you/your, he/his, she/her, we/our,* and *they/their*. Only in the case of *it* do we find the expected possessive *its*, which is pronounced [ɪts] (and note the curious fact that the apostrophe is suppressed in the spelling). We can distinguish between the root form and the possessive form of a noun by assuming that only the latter incorporates the feature value *[POSSESSIVE]*. In the normal case of possessives like *Mary's* we posit /z/ as the underlying form for the possessive, deriving [mæriz] from /mæri+z/ in the usual way. In the case of the pronouns, we can account for their irregular possessive forms by assuming that these phonetic forms are specially listed in the lexicon.

The marking of a pronoun's possessive form is an example of a *case* distinction — a variation in the form of a lexical item that depends on its syntactic function. If we look closely at the distribution of English pronouns we notice other types of case marking as well. In general, pronouns in subject position take *nominative* case, and pronouns in other positions take *accusative* case. *I, he, she, we,* and *they* are nominative, and *me, him, her, us,* and *them* are the corresponding accusative forms. Even though *you* and *it* do not have distinctive nominative and accusative forms, we assign them the abstract *CASE* feature values *[NOMINATIVE]* or *[ACCUSATIVE]* depending on their distribution according to the above case generalizations. Circumstances such as these, in which there is no phonetic manifestation of the associated case feature involve what is sometimes called *abstract case*.

Francis (1958) points out that the plural morpheme bears a different meaning in its role in marking number in the pronoun system than it does as a marker on nouns. Describe the two different kinds of semantic changes that the plural contributes.

Draw analysis trees for the underlying representations for these possessives (use /z/ as the underlying form for the affix):

a. John's
b. Pat's
c. Trish's

Explain whether Devoicing and/or [ə]-Insertion apply in each case.

HISTORY 3.29

English has been losing its case markers for centuries. Whereas in Modern English nominative and accusative case are marked only in the pronoun system, in Old English we find a very rich system of case marking that includes different inflections for common nouns. Above, for example, is the paradigm for *stan,* the Old English word 'stone.'

Typically, the nominative case marked the subject of the sentence and the accusative marked the object. One of the uses of the dative was to mark the indirect object, and the *genitive* marker identified posses-

Case	Singular	Plural
Nominative	stan	stanas
Genitive	stanes	stana
Dative	stane	stanum
Accusative	stan	stanas

sive nouns. Notice that each of these case markings were different in the singular and the plural.

As the sound system of Old English changed, two of the case endings (the dative singular and the genitive plural) were reduced in pronunciation to [ə]. What is more, these schwas began to be omitted from pronunciation, as part of a

more general sound change. The result was that the different case markers became progressively less phonetically distinct from one another, and over time, these markers fell into disuse (see Gee 1993:369). ■

Although virtually all nouns can be marked with the feature value *[POSSESSIVE]*, nonpronominal nouns do not appear to inflect for nominative and accusative case. We will return to the question of whether such nouns should bear abstract *CASE* feature values in the next chapter.

3.30 Morphological Gender

The pronoun system of English also is capable of reflecting distinctions of *gender*, at least in the third-person singular. Here we find a three-way contrast among *he, she,* and *it*, respectively exemplifying the genders masculine, feminine, and neuter. These contrasts are not generally marked in the rest of the English pronoun system, qualifying English as a relatively impoverished gender-marking language. Notice that the sense in which *he* is masculine is what we might call the biological sense of gender. This is as opposed to the conventional basis for gender-marking in nonpronominal nouns like *ship* (which is conventionally feminine) and *God* (which is conventionally masculine). In these cases, it is not the biological gender of the named objects, but rather an arbitrary convention that determines the "gender" associated with them. Other languages also employ these two systems of gender marking, and often more systematically. For example, in French we find a gender contrast in the *determiner* system. The English word *the* has three French counterparts: *le, la,* and *les. Le* is the masculine definite determiner, and *la* is the feminine definite determiner. The masculine/feminine contrast in the determiner system is lost in the plural, with *les* appearing before both masculine and feminine plural nouns.

The gender of the singular *determiners le* and *la* must agree with that of the nouns they introduce. Thus, we find *le chat* and *la chatte* (both mean 'the cat'), the former standing for a male cat and the latter for a female. *Chat* and *chatte* derive their gender from biological considerations, but French also establishes arbitrary gender categorizations for many common nouns. For example, *le livre* ('the book') is masculine by virtue of the masculine form of the determiner, but there is obviously nothing biologically gendered about books that grounds this assignment. There are even cases like *le docteur* ('the doctor') in which a female individual can be picked out by a masculine construction. What's more, to refer back to a female doctor we use the third-person singular feminine pronoun *elle* ('she') (since French pronouns, like their English counterparts manifest biological gender [Martinet 1960:115]).

Gender is important in the English pronominal system as well, although it is marked only in the third-person singular. Here, we find contrasts between *she/he, hers/his,* and *her/him,* and between *himself/herself.* There is also a pattern of gender agreement that obtains between pronouns and names:

1. *Mary thought Sally disqualified himself.
2. Mary thought Bill disqualified himself.
3. John thought he won.
4. John thought she won.
5. His father loved Mary.
6. Her father loved Mary.
7. Everyone thought he had voted correctly.
8. Everyone thought they had voted correctly.

The first two examples show that *reflexive* pronouns (*-self* forms) must agree in gender with a linguistic *antecedent.* Since that condition cannot be met in the first example, it seems anomalous. The next pair of cases demonstrates that personal pronouns like *he* and *she* can also take a linguistic antecedent, provided there is agreement in the feature of gender. However, unlike in the case of the reflexives, if a gender-matched linguistic antecedent is not available (and even if one is), it is possible to interpret the pronoun with respect to the context, as for example, in the case of *John thought she won.* The last two cases, *Everyone thought he/they had voted correctly* illustrates an interesting aspect of the English pronoun system as well as a change in progress. This case involves the grammatically singular antecedent *everyone,* which quantifies the domain of discourse (and hence seems semantically plural in some sense), and the third-person masculine pronoun *he.*

Obviously, *everyone* might comprise males and females in any number of discourse situations, raising the question of why the masculine pronoun appears in this construction. Indeed, many commentators see this usage as contributing to the gender inequities in our society (see Lakoff 1975). In some dialects of English, the gender-neutral third-person plural pronoun *they* substitutes for *he* resulting in *Everyone thinks they voted correctly.* This construction is unusual in that the expected agreement in number that inheres between a pronoun and its antecedent is not manifest. This is a recent linguistic change that is in action, and one that is pitting a consciously constructed principle of politically correct gender-marking against the grammatical process of number agreement. It will be interesting to see how it resolves. We say more to about

In addition to masculine and feminine gender-agreement, there is a third agreement form in English illustrated by the following data:

a. *The baby couldn't care for itself.*

b. *The committee dissolved itself.*

c. *The table, itself was destroyed.*

Explain the circumstances in which itself *is used by formulating a rule that captures its distribution.*

Suppose someone were to argue that they *is becoming a singular (gender neutral) pronoun through a process of linguistic change. How does the following evidence bear on this claim?*

a. *Everyone thinks they know/ *knows best.*

b. *John thinks he/*they will win. (he, they = John)*

PRO 3.30

The language you speak influences how you think, and sexist language leads to sexist thinking. It is well known that the language does not treat the genders equally, and this linguistic inequity translates into unfortunate gender inequities in the workplace, the home, and even in everyday conversation. For example, English uses the masculine form of a word to refer to groups of mixed gender. We have already considered the case of *he,* but note also the way the feminizing suffix *-ess* works: We have actors and actresses, but a group of males and females who act are called, simply, *actors.* Even the word *man* is used to refer to the species as a whole (*Man is a rational animal*) (Pfeiffer 1994).

The masculine form is the default in language as in life. English also treats gendered descriptive terminology asymmetrically. While people may be derogatively labeled *bastards* or *bitches,* according to their gender, women may also be called *witches* or *whores* (or *hos*), without men being referred to as *warlocks* or *Johns* with the same extended meanings. There are many other terms that appear to be gender-neutral, but are nevertheless applied discriminatorily. For example, we describe certain kinds of women as being *easy,* but we call men *studs.* The feminine descriptor has negative connotations, while the masculine term has positive associations, despite the fact that both terms describe similar personal characteristics.

There is also evidence that women's language is different than men's language, and that this discrepancy also works to keep women in their place. Perhaps the most outstanding example is that women frequently use question intonation when making assertions. Lakoff (1974) claims that women's use of this intonation reducing their assertiveness, is a reflection of a lack of self-confidence and a marker of inferiority for the female class. She argues that women more frequently than men tend to use empty adjectives (like *divine* and *cute*), to use intensifiers like *so,* to use tag questions at the end of assertions (*I was right, wasn't I?*) and to use linguistic hedges like *I think* or *kinda* to soften their claims (Lakoff 1975). More generally, she suggests that women tend to speak politely — to avoid swearing and telling jokes; in short, women have a different linguistic style than men.

How do these linguistic facts manage to perpetuate gender stereotypes, in effect contributing to the low social status that they reflect? Lakoff suggests that women's language is frequently role-modeled by female television characters. She also argues that women's linguistic style is more constraining than men's, and that, paradoxically, the societal advantages of successfully adopting women's style are slight compared to the benefits of adopting men's. Moreover, women are taught a very different conversational style than men which Lakoff (1974) suggests incorporates the following principles: (1) keep aloof; (2) give options; and (3) show sympathy (with the consequence that men interrupt more and women ask more questions, see Pfeiffer 1994). It should be clear that anyone who hopes for gender equality has to consider language part of the problem. ■

pronouns, antecedents, and agreement in the next section; but for now we shall assume that the *GENDER* feature values *[MASCULINE]*, *[FEMININE]*, and *[NEUTER]* are included in feature complexes associated with lexical items, and that there is a mechanism responsible for establishing gender agreement in the proper range of cases.

Although it is tempting to interpret the parallelisms between women's language and women's place in society to mean that "women's language" both creates and perpetuates women's low social status, the conclusion is unwarranted. As a first observation we note that, throughout the history of linguistics, scholars have debated the extent to which language shapes thought and action, compared with the extent to which it merely reflects underlying realities. Pretheoretically, many of us reflexively embrace the notion that language plays a deterministic role with respect to culture and cognition, but there is little supporting empirical evidence. There is also a lack of evidence for the claim that sexist language causes low social status, without which the implication that changing women's language will change women's status is unjustified.

English is a sexist language. This conclusion follows from the observation that women's speech is different from men's speech. And there is little doubt that, to the extent that linguistic roles conspire to dictate that women should be nonassertive and overly polite, women's linguistic style is detrimental. But it is an open question whether these linguistic differences cause and reflect lower social status as opposed to some other factor; for example, women's differential role in society. Crosby and Nyquist (1977) argue that the evidence supports the latter interpretation. In a series of experimental studies they determined that women do exhibit a special speech style in that they use the so-called female register more frequently than men do. However, they also noted that there was no evidence that

...women's speech reflects (or is caused by) the low status of women in our society. If we assume that the obtained sex differences in speech were due primarily to sex-status differences, then we should also expect that other types of status differences...[parenthetical omitted]...would affect speech. Such was not the case. (p. 320)

Crosby and Nyquist conclude that

...we will not create a more egalitarian society by eliminating the female register. Rather, as our society becomes increasingly androgynous, sex differential usage of the female register ought to diminish, and hopefully, one day, disappear. (p. 321) ∎

CON 3.30

3.31 Person, Number, and Pronouns

In the previous section, we alluded to the fact that third-person pronouns must typically agree with their antecedents in number as well as in gender. This explains the contrast between *Mary thinks she will win* and *Females think she will win*. In the first case, *she* receives either a discourse-bound or an antecedent-bound interpretation, but in the second, only a discourse-bound interpretation is possible. This is because *Mary* and *she* agree in number and gender; but in the second example the only possible linguistic antecedent for *she, females,* agrees in gender but not number.

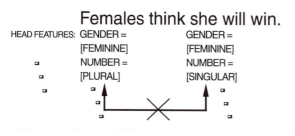

Females think she will win.

HEAD FEATURES: GENDER =   GENDER =
            [FEMININE]   [FEMININE]
            NUMBER =   NUMBER =
            [PLURAL]   [SINGULAR]

Pronominal gender agreement.

Since, unlike gender features, number features are more richly phonetically marked, we observe a broader range of potential number conflicts between a pronoun and its antecedent. The effect is easiest to detect in the reflexive system, because reflexive pronouns must have antecedents, and these antecedents must agree with the reflexive in number as well as gender. This accounts for contrasts like the following:

1. I like myself.
2. *I like ourselves.
3. *We like myself.
4. We like ourselves.
5. *They like himself.
6. They like themselves.

Finally, reflexives and their antecedents must also agree in person (in addition to number and gender). We can account for this by employing the feature *PERSON* with the values *[1 PERSON], [2 PER-SON],* and *[3 PERSON]* for first, second, and third person, respectively. The resulting patterns of agreement dramatically reduce the range of possible antecedents for a given pronoun.

The agreement in number, person, and gender that obtains between a pronoun and its antecedent reminds us of the agreement in number that applies to subjects and verbs, detectable in the present-tense third-person contrast between singular and plural verbs (e.g., *She drives/They drive*). It therefore seems reasonable to extend the use of features and feature matching to enforce the agreement dependency here as well. There is, however a residual problem. In the case

HISTORY 3.31

Earlier stages of English involved a good deal more inflection than we find in the English we speak today. For example, in Old English, around 500 AD, verbs were richly marked for person. Here are the singular present tense forms for the verb *fleogan* 'fly' (see Lehman 1962:184):

First person singular   fleo
Second person singular   fliehst
Third person singular   flиehð

By the time of Shakespeare at the beginning of the seventeenth century, this paradigm was changing. The third-person-singular marker, which used to be *-ð*, began to alternate with *-s*. Thus, we find *The sight of love feedeth those in love* in As You Like It, but *Winter tames man, woman and beast* in The Taming of the Shrew (see Radford 1997 for discussion). Eventually, this variation was resolved in favor of the *-s* ending in the third-person-singular, and in the same time period, the second-person ending *-st* dropped out of the language, except for a limited use in religious language. ■

of subject-verb agreement, we established the required dependency by introducing the mechanism of specifier, head, and complement features, along with the principle that a verb and its specifier (that is, its subject) must agree in number. It is clear, however, that the dependency between a pronoun and its antecedent cannot be captured in these terms:

1. *Mary thinks the committee demoted herself.
2. The committee thinks Mary demoted herself.
3. Bill thinks Fred likes him.
4. Sue thinks Bill likes him.
5. Harry believes himself to be unlucky.
6. *Harry believes himself is unlucky.

In the first example *Mary* appears to be ineligible as an antecedent for *herself* despite agreeing in the relevant feature values (as the second example illustrates). In (3), *him* can be Bill, but not Fred, again despite that both potential antecedents have the correct feature values (i.e. *[SINGULAR]*, *[3 PERSON]*, and *[FEMININE]*). (4) requires a contextual interpretation for *him* (but why can't *Bill* be its antecedent?). Finally, (5) and (6) illustrate a subtle contrast that concerns the appropriateness of *Harry* as the antecedent for the reflexive *himself*.

Obviously, bearing the correct features is a necessary but not a sufficient condition that a potential antecedent must meet in order to link to a pronoun or reflexive pronoun. There seem to be additional restrictions on this dependency that eliminate certain potential antecedents despite their featural appropriateness. We return to this interesting question in the next chapter.

4. Sentences

4.1 From Word to Sentence

Linguistics is the branch of cognitive science concerned with human language. Its goal is to understand how linguistic knowledge is represented in the mind, how it is acquired, how it is perceived and used, and how it relates to other components of cognition.

A language is a system that uses a physical signal (a sound, a gesture, a mark on paper) to express meaning. Our inquiry into the nature of this system has lead us to investigate the structure of sounds and words in an attempt to understand what linguistic knowledge comprises. We have seen that languages may be described by systems of rules and principles that constitute scientific hypotheses about the nature of linguistic knowledge possessed by native speakers. These rules account for the patterns of language — the range of possible moves in the language game that are consistent with speakers' conventions.

Although we recognize that languages are sociohistorical objects, dynamic in nature, subject to change over time, and inextricably intertwined in the fabric of life, our approach to understanding sounds and words has been to develop formal theories of linguistic knowledge itself, independent of other aspects of cognition, socialization, or behavior. A *grammar* — a theory of linguistic knowledge — must characterize what we know about the physical signals on one end of the linguistic equation, and what we know about meaning on the other. We have argued that a grammar constitutes a description of the underlying knowledge reflected when people use language. We are not interested here in legislating linguistic norms or rendering aesthetic judgments about language usage.

Even before you began to study linguistics, you probably knew that any analysis of language must concern itself with the nature of sounds and words. The most casual observer of the linguistic scene notices that different languages have different inventories of sounds and words; and nearly everyone celebrates two great milestones of a child's linguistic development: the first sound and the first word. The course of our investigation and the course of language acquisition, to some degree, parallel each other (pedagogy recapitulates ontogeny?). Both start with lower-level units (sounds) and move on to higher-level units (words); and the latter seem, at least on the surface, to contain combinations of the former. In this chapter we

Does abstracting away from social, historical, and political factors seem to be a reasonable idealization? Discuss the implications of this decision (you may want to consider idealizations in other fields to frame your answer).

PRO 4.1

A theory of language is simultaneously an account of the nature of language and of language acquisition (Chomsky 1965). Consequently, a linguistic theory is a psychological theory in that it not only provides linguistic descriptions, but also contributes to our understanding of the mind. The connection between grammatical description and language acquisition depends on our assumption that the language learner acquires linguistic competence from information-processing principles that guide the course of language development. These principles must be general enough to support the acquisition of any natural language, but specific enough to appropriately constrain the description of a given child's particular target language.

For example, suppose we adopt the generalization that all complete sentences must minimally contain a subject noun and a verb as a principle to bootstrap the acquisition process. According to this principle, sentences like *Ringo sang* and *Mick contorted his face* ought to be possible in English, but ones like **sang* and **contorted his face* are prohibited. Moreover, children learning English would be guided by this principle, inclining them to build a grammar consistent with it, and ignoring even plausible linguistic generalizations that run afoul of it. We can investigate a wide range of English constructions to determine whether the generalization is accurate. We encounter constructions like *Says who?, Eat your Wheaties, Looks like rain, From here to Tucson is a long way,* and *Me, too* that seem to challenge this claim, each of which requires an explanation if we are to preserve the principle.

Furthermore, since this principle is supposed apply to all languages, we need to carefully examine *pro-drop* languages like Hebrew and Spanish that seem to leave out the subject in certain types of sentences. Finally, if we can maintain this principle in the face of all this linguistic evidence, we must also look for evidence from the domain of language acquisition. For example, in a study of the acquisition of the pro-drop language Italian, Hyams (1987) has argued that children pass through a stage in which they assume that Italian sentences require subject nouns, even though the primary linguistic data do not warrant this conclusion. Hyams explains this interesting learning profile by arguing that children approach the task of language acquisition with the default assumption that sentences must have subjects, even though this principle happens not to apply to Italian.

Although the fate of our generalization is not yet fully decided (and it won't be until we have analyzed all the data we have collected in this discussion, some of which we take up later in this chapter), you can see that a linguistic principle may be justified on three levels: It can be useful in describing a particular language, it can be part of a set of generalizations that fit all languages, and it can provide the basis of an explanation for language acquisition. Any linguistic theory that proves adequate at each of these levels of analysis deserves to be recognized as a psychological theory of the human mind. ■

There are a small number of counterexamples to the generalization discussed in the text, some of which are illustrated below:

1. *Eat your Wheaties!*

2. *Seems like a long way to Tucson.*

3. *Wanna dance?*

How can we maintain our generalization in the light of these data? Discuss.

Consider the following fantastical circumstance: You encounter a creature from another planet doing subtraction problems in your kitchen. Here is some of the work you see scratched on the wall:

$$
\begin{array}{r} 267 \\ -\ 19 \\ \hline 248 \end{array}
\qquad
\begin{array}{r} 119 \\ -\ 77 \\ \hline 42 \end{array}
\qquad
\begin{array}{r} 42 \\ -\ 3 \\ \hline 39 \end{array}
$$

Being scientifically inclined, you attempt to form a hypothesis about how the creature subtracts. You are buoyed by the fact that the creature's answers are the same as yours, you conclude that mathematics is a universal language, and you conjecture that the creature's mind is like your own, at least as far as subtraction is concerned.

Months pass; and after you learn Creaturese, weighty discussions of how the creature subtracts ensue. You discover that although the creature derives the same answers that you do, that is where the commonality ends. For example, in cases in which the bottom digit is smaller than the top digit, you borrow ten from the top digit to the left (reducing its value by 1), and subtract away. The creature takes the bottom digit, subtracts it from 10, adds the result to the top digit, prints this result on the answer line, and adds 1 to the value of the next digit to the left on the bottom line. Although the results are the same, the process is obviously different. As a consequence, the creature makes different kinds of mistakes than you do and tends to work at a slower rate.

Linguists who make claims about language acquisition without gathering experimental data (about errors, performance rate, and so forth) or building psychological models are like you trying to investigate how the creature subtracts. Although one may be in a position to determine whether or not certain formal laws (like the principles of mathematics) are consistent with the performance of a subject under investigation, it is not possible to find out how the subject's mind works simply by observing and modeling the subject's linguistic (or mathematical) competence.

Linguistics, properly construed, is about the description of language. Any extension of the results of linguistic inquiry into the domains of learning, language use, and so forth, requires psychological evidence not normally considered in constructing linguistic theories (see Gazdar et al. 1985). ∎

CON 4.1

---

continue to work our way up the levels of linguistic analysis by turning our attention to the structure of phrases and sentences.

We call the part of the grammar that concerns itself with sentence and phrase structure *syntax*. A syntactic theory must provide a systematic account of the connection between sound and meaning. As before, we measure our progress according to how well we can explain what English-speakers know about the syntactic patterns of English, aiming to generalize our analysis to also account for the facts of all other natural languages. Ultimately, we hope to find a basis for a systematic explanation of general linguistic knowledge, with the concomitant ability to explain how children acquire the linguistic knowledge we now set out to describe.

We begin on a rhetorical note: What more is there to know about the pattern of a language besides its sound system and lexicon, along with the rules and principles of its phonology and morphology? Imagine trying to learn a foreign language, say Sinhala, a language of Sri Lanka. Suppose you mastered its sound inventory, learned all its vocabulary, and even acquired a native speaker's grasp of its phonological and morphological rules. Despite your efforts, it is unlikely that you would be able to muster very many well-formed utterances in Sinhala, because you would not be able to reliably assemble groups of Sinhala words in a way that other Sinhala speakers could recognize as part of their language. Only certain patterns of words constitute well-formed sentences in Sinhala (or any other natural language), and many other patterns are systematically excluded.

For example, English-speakers register the following judgments:

1. The dog annoyed Mary.
2. Mary annoyed the dog.
3. *Dog the Mary annoyed.
4. *The Mary annoyed dog.

Only (1) and (2) are well-formed English sentences; we characterize them as grammatical sentences. (3) and (4) are ungrammatical strings of words. These discriminations are like second nature to us once we have acquired the relevant body of linguistic knowledge. But we must not lose sight of the complexity and variety of the patterns we have learned.

Suppose, for example, we tell you that in Sinhala, *noona* means 'the woman,' *kanəwa* means 'eats,' and *bat* means 'rice.' How would you construct the Sinhala equivalent to the English sentence *The woman eats rice?* In Sinhala declarative sentences, the order of elements is S(ubject) O(bject) V(erb); English is SVO. Thus, the Sinhala equivalent to *The woman eats rice* is *Noona bat kanəwa,* with the verb *kanəwa* at the end of the sentence. It is incumbent on every language-learning child to determine the syntactic pattern for a target language, and determining word order is an important part of this task.

To make matters more interesting, all native speakers also recognize a vast array of more complicated linguistic structures, over and above the simple declaratives: questions such as *Did the dog annoy*

Make a list of the kinds of things you need to learn to become a fluent speaker of a second language. Does this list correspond to the list of things children must learn to become native speakers of their language? Discuss.

Strings like Me Tarzan, you Jane *are readily interpretable, but do not follow the syntactic pattern of English. What would you say to a skeptic who suggests that if you can interpret a string, then it is part of the language, dispensing with the distinction between grammatical and ungrammatical strings? What evidence could you find to justify the category of grammaticality against the skeptic's challenge?*

There are more languages with SOV order than any other word order. How many SOV languages can you name (list at least three)? Can you name a language that has any other basic word order (other than SVO and SOV)?

Mary?; negations such as *The dog did not annoy Mary;* sentences with parts emphasized such as *It was the dog that annoyed Mary;* sentences with parts truncated such as *The dog did* (in answer to the question *What annoyed Mary?*); and so forth. As before, different languages associate different patterns of words with these different kinds of sentences. For example, one way to form negations in Hebrew is to put *lo,* the word for 'no,' at the front of the sentence. In French negations, the dual elements *ne* and *pas* flank the verb. As a final example, compare the English question in (1) with its German equivalent in (2).

1. Did John see the man?
2. Sah Johann den Mann?
    saw John the man

Sentences (1) and (2) no doubt mean the same thing, and even contain words that bear a historical relationship to one another. The difference between them falls in the domain of syntax. We now examine some of the major syntactic structures of English, seeking to develop an analysis of these data that deepens our understanding of the nature of linguistic competence. We begin by getting a feel for some linguistic paradigms that point to the kinds of phenomena that our theory must explain. Next, we introduce *phrase-structure grammars* — a formal system of analysis that allows us to capture many interesting linguistic dependencies. We investigate how phrase-structure grammars can be integrated with the analysis of the lexicon introduced in the previous chapter, including a discussion of how some of the work traditionally done by phrase-structure grammars can be reassigned to the lexicon. Then we consider other syntactic phenomena that cannot be explained using standard phrase-structure approaches. In this section, we reconsider topics such as pronouns and thematic roles. We also study linguistic dependencies, such as questions and passives, to broaden our analysis. Throughout these discussions we have occasion to reflect on some of the conclusions established in previous chapters about the nature of linguistic knowledge, in an attempt to further elucidate and consolidate our theoretical positions. We also investigate some of the more important philosophical and psychological implications of our analysis.

It is often contended that people who speak different languages mean (slightly or radically) different things by what are apparently intertranslatable sentences. (A) Discuss the difficulties introduced by this problem in rendering accurate translations. (B) How could we go about determining if an alleged semantic difference is really there, in any given case?

4.2 The Case of *That*

As an illustration of the complexities of syntactic patterns, consider some examples involving the word *that*.

1. Irving believed <u>that pigs can fly</u>.
2. Irving believed <u>pigs can fly</u>.
3. The pain <u>that I feel</u> is most unpleasant.
4. The pain <u>I feel</u> is most unpleasant.
5. <u>That sugar is sweet</u> is obvious to everybody.
6. *<u>Sugar is sweet</u> is obvious to everybody.
7. The dog <u>that bit me</u> is missing now.
8. *The dog <u>bit me</u> is missing now.
9. *The dog <u>Mary hoped that bit me</u> is missing now.
10. The dog <u>Mary hoped bit me</u> is missing now.

That plays several distinct roles in English sentences. It can appear prenominally (before nouns) in noun phrases like *that turkey*. It can also function as a pronoun, as in examples like *Please don't touch*

PRO 4.2

Although it might seem at first that the only way to amass the kind of linguistic data that allows us to investigate the nature of grammars is to gather actual utterances by native speakers, this is often not the most productive approach. For one thing, native speakers sometimes make performance errors, which means that a record of their verbal output does not reliably indicate their linguistic competence. Furthermore, in cases like our investigation of *that*, we might wait a very long time before a speaker produces an example that may be crucial for our analysis. Finally, it often turns out that the most important bits of evidence in favor of a well-motivated analysis are ungrammatical strings that are not part of the language under investigation. Obviously we cannot systematically wait to see whether or a string that we predict to be ungrammatical is ever produced by native speakers; there is no obvious way to determine how long would be long enough to wait before concluding we were on safe ground.

Our recourse is to ask native speakers for their intuitions of grammaticality; that is, we simply produce a string that may or may not be grammatical in a given language, and ask a native speaker for a judgment. Although this process is informal compared with many other kinds of data-gathering experiments, it can nonetheless produce reliable results that often are more dependable than real-time transcripts. We can improve the reliability of these data by consulting several native speakers, providing an appropriate context, and trying out several tokens of a particular construction, to determine if extraneous factors are at work. In the long run, there may be some linguistic phenomena sufficiently difficult for native speakers to judge that other data-gathering techniques (including more formal psychological experiments) may need to be used. But for the purposes of our inquiry — even as we descend into levels of considerable complexity — the intuitions of a native speaker usually suffice as a source of useful linguistic data. ■

that. In the above list of sentences, we concentrate on the use of *that* as a *complementizer,* a word that introduces *subordinate clauses* (underlined in the previous data set). In some of these constructions, *that* seems to be optional, in others it is obligatory, and in still others it is prohibited. The principles governing the distribution of *that* seem to have nothing to do with the meanings of the sentences. In fact, it is not immediately clear how to characterize the privileges of occurrence for *that,* even though native speakers of English "know" its distribution. Although all native speakers have a tacit knowledge of the syntactic patterns for *that,* these are aspects of English grammar that are never taught in school, and it is exceedingly unlikely that parents ever instruct their children regarding them. How do we characterize the linguistic knowledge of *that* possessed by native English-speakers? How do we come to have such knowledge? In what form is such knowledge represented in the mind? Questions of this order, posed at a fine-grained level of detail, are paradigmatic examples of problems in contemporary linguistic theory.

CON 4.2

Although native speakers' intuitions may be of some use in constructing linguistic analyses, it is easy to overestimate their value. The problem is that native speakers are simply not dependable (indeed, can you think of any other science in which subjects provide researchers with data based on intuitions?). There are cases in which intuitions are too generous, and others in which they are too restrictive. For example, many speakers — even ones who freely produce such strings — will judge strings like *It was just between you and I* as ungrammatical. When they reflect on the string, they apply a prescriptive rule, even though they tend to follow it in the breach in actual production. In other cases, speakers accept strings like *This is the kind of song that if you listen to it it sounds good* because they can make sense out of it, even though it is not consistent with the syntactic pattern of the language.

It is also very difficult to judge sentences outside of a linguistic context and without an appropriate intonation. For example, if you go up to a randomly chosen English speaker and ask, "Is *This book, John read* a sentence of English?" most speakers will say "No." However, if you embed it in an appropriate context (Speaker *A:* Did John read this book and that one? Speaker *B:* This book, John read [that one, he didn't]."), it is acceptable. Finally, there are many kinds of systematic variations and dependencies that will never be noticed if we restrict our data to judgments of grammaticality. Many subtle factors such as the formality of the speech circumstance; the purpose of an utterance; the relative status of the interlocutors; and interplay of other sociolinguistic variables such as race, class, gender and socio-economic status are ignored or underestimated if the only question we ask is "Is *X* grammatical in your language?" ■

We can explain the cases in which *that* is optional by assuming that one type of English complementizer is the "null" complementizer, denoted Ø, a linguistic item with syntactic status but no phonetic realization. The other possibility is to assume that complementizers are simply optional elements in English sentences. It is difficult to choose between these two possibilities in this case, but there are several other English sentence structures that invite the first, more abstract analysis.

For example, English commands like *Don't do that* seem to be missing overt subjects, but are still interpreted as if they contained a second-person subject *(you)*. Such command constructions can even contain reflexive pronouns that must agree with the missing subject (*Don't do that to yourself* is an example). And in sentences like *I want to eat,* the subject of the verb *eat,* sometimes called an "understood" subject, also seems to be missing. In this case (referred to as a control structure), the subject of *eat* is construed as identical to the subject of the verb *want,* namely as *I.* Although different syntactic approaches handle these kinds of cases somewhat differently, the possibility of syntactically or semantically present but phonetically absent linguistic elements considerably complicates the basic working assumption that sentences are merely strings of words.

Cases in which *that* is a required element pose the opposite kind of descriptive challenge for an analysis of the complementizer system. For, no matter how we capture the usual optionality of *that,* it is not clear why it cannot be missing in cases like *That sugar is sweet is obvious to everybody* and *The dog that bit me is missing now.* One intriguing possibility is that its mandatory presence is due to sentence-processing considerations. Notice that if we leave the *that* out of the sentences in question, the resulting strings each begin with sequences of words that look like they could be complete sentences on their own:

1. *Sugar is sweet is obvious to everybody.
2. *The dog bit me is missing now.

Without the complementizer *that,* it is difficult to *parse* (assign a structure to) these strings in real time because the initial few words tempt the hearer into mistaking them for a sentence in their own right, leaving the rest of the string uninterpretable.

How many other English complementizers can you think of? Provide two example sentences for each one you discover.

This sort of explanation for the obligatory presence of a normally optional linguistic element is controversial, partly because it assumes that the grammar of the language is responsive to the sentence-processing needs of a speaker. While this may not seem terribly far-fetched, there are three considerations that may make us question this assumption, at least here. The first concern has to do with a famous and very well-studied example:

The horse raced past the barn fell.

Most speakers cannot persuade themselves that this is a grammatical English sentence, even if they stare at it for quite awhile. But consider the close counterpart *The horse that was raced past the barn fell* which is fully grammatical. When the complementizer *that* appears, the string is easily interpretable to mean that the horse was raced (by someone) in the vicinity of the barn. Without the *that,* the string *The horse raced past...* is so easily parsed as a complete sentence that it induces what is called a "garden path" effect, and you are persuaded (or fooled) into rejecting the sentence as ill-formed. Now here is the complication with respect to our explanation for the obligatoriness of *that:* In the previous cases, the absence of *that* produced outright ungrammaticality; whereas in the garden-path case above, the sentence may have initially seemed unacceptable but turns out, on reflection, to be grammatical.

Explain what it was about the garden-path sentence discussed in the text that temporarily convinced you that it was ill-formed.

If we concentrate on the garden-path cases, we are left with the surprising conclusion that parts of English may be grammatical yet difficult to use. Here is a second kind of example that supports this conclusion:

Oysters oysters oysters eat eat eat.

The simple sentence *Oysters eat* is obviously well formed. If you add another level of embedding, building a second clause inside the first clause, you get *Oysters oysters eat eat*. Although this may seem like an unstructured string of words, if you study it carefully, you will discover that it is well formed, and means that oysters that are eaten by oysters, themselves eat (whatever). This particular way of forming complex clauses is called "center embedding," an operation producing strings that are notoriously difficult

to parse. Suppose we kick it up a notch and try a third degree of embedding, yielding *Oysters oysters oysters eat eat eat*. Even upon reflection, this string is a hard row to hoe (a tough shell to crack?). Adding in the complementizer *that* to mark off the clauses doesn't even seem to help much (consider: *Oysters that oysters that oysters eat eat eat*). Still, we must conclude that these strings are grammatical (that is, they fit the pattern of English), despite the fact that they appear unacceptable. One reason to do so is that changing the vocabulary helps to reduce the unparsability of the sentence. So, *Diseases people doctors treated have spread* is perhaps manageable. Once we see the trick to these types of sentences, it seems best to conclude that the problem lies in the sentence processor, not in the grammar. Thus, we have a second case in which the grammar and the processing system seem to be at odds with one another.

A final complication for our claims about the mandatoriness of *that* concerns dialect variation in the English complementizer system: British English has some dialects that

IN DETAIL 4.2

allow constructions like *The person beats me is the winner,* in which the absence of *that* does not render the sentence ungrammatical. In the same vein, Traugott (1972) reports that constructions of this sort appeared in earlier stages of English. Since our presumption is that speech-processing effects ought to be uniform for all speakers, this is a puzzling result.

Although we have not settled on a final analysis of *that* (indeed, it remains an open research topic in the field, e.g., see Pesetsky 1998 for one recent analysis) we have accomplished two things: The challenge of doing real linguistics "in the raw" (i.e., with raw data) has been revealed, and we have begun to explore the relationship between the grammar and the sentence-processing system (another central question guiding current research in the field; see Frazier and de Villiers 1990). ∎

4.3 Syntactic Representation

These recent discussions about word order and the distribution of *that* are meant to demonstrate that English-speakers possess intricate knowledge pertaining to the organization of phrases and sentences. It remains to discover the extent of this knowledge and how to best represent it in our linguistic theory. As with lexical knowledge, there is ample reason to believe that syntactic knowledge cannot be represented in the form of a list; in this case, a list of sentences. We have already examined arguments demonstrating that there is no longest English sentence, and that English contains an infinite number of sentences. These arguments are calculated to show that a list of sentences is a poor data structure for syntactic knowledge, because it cannot account for the unbounded character of all natural languages — a finite list is not an adequate representation for an infinite capacity. Conceiving of syntactic knowledge as a list of sentences treats every sentence of every language as a kind of linguistic accident.

Consider the following claim: Many of the sentences that you produce have never before been produced in the history of the world, and will never be produced again. Can you think of an example of such a sentence? Discuss the implications for the possibility of representing syntactic knowledge as a list of sentences. What kind of model of how we produce sentences seems to explain this capacity?

But even if we concentrate on the finite subset of English that any single native speaker produces in a lifetime, we must still reject the idea that syntactic information takes the form of a list. We have argued that all native speakers are creative in their use of language; the sentences we construct are frequently novel utterances, never before produced, yet instantly recognized by other speakers of the language as well formed and interpretable. The extensibility of a language is a consequence of the way in which syntactic information is represented. Speakers must have access to generalization-capturing rules and principles that can recombine familiar items in novel arrangements. For example, the rule for conjunction, which as a first approximation we might write as:

$$S \rightarrow S \text{ and } S$$

says that a sentence can consist of any sentence followed by *and* and then another sentence. This single rule establishes a generalization about conjunctions that immediately accounts for the fact that conjunctions can contain any number of conjuncts; for example, the sentence below can be repeatedly extended by adding more conjuncts to

---

IN DETAIL 4.3

In a more thoroughgoing analysis of conjunction, we would like to generalize this analysis to account for the fact that categories other than S can be conjoined. In fact, virtually every syntactic category of English participates in this generalization. Here are a few examples:

1. John is old and tired.
2. Paul and John had the talent.
3. Ringo tried and failed to keep the beat.
4. George played quickly and nicely.

We see that adjectives, nouns, verbs, and adverbs are each capable of appearing in conjoined structures. There is also a deeper generalization in play here: Only like syntactic categories can conjoin. So, even though *George played rock* is well formed,

and *George played nicely* is as well, *George played nicely and rock* is not. The adverb *nicely* cannot be conjoined with the noun *rock*.

Can you think of any syntactic categories that cannot be linked by and *to form a conjunction? Is there a generalization that explains any examples you may have discovered?*

We can explain these observations about conjunction by replacing the rule under discussion, S → S and S, with a generalized schema of the form X → X and X, where X is construed as a variable ranging over the different syntactic categories. In effect, this schema is an abbreviation for a series of rules that includes N → N and N, V → V and V, and so forth. We would also like to generalize our analysis of the conjunction *and* to include other English conjunctions. For example, *or* has essentially the same distribution as *and,* suggesting that we might introduce the category Conj (understood to include *and* and *or*), modifying the schema under discussion to X → X Conj X.

The function word but *is also frequently analyzed as a conjunction on the basis of its distribution in examples like* Ella sang but Louis hummed. *Suppose we incorporate* but *into the schema for conjunction. What difficulties do you perceive (if any) with this proposal?*

One final complication that needs to be addressed is the occasional optionality of conjunctions in conjoined structures. Consider the following examples:

5. John and George and Paul and Ringo were best buds.
6. John, George, Paul, and Ringo were best buds.
7. *John, George, Paul, Ringo were best buds.
8. *John and George, Paul, Ringo were best buds.
9. John and George, Paul and Ringo, and Mick and Keith were best buds.

In our analysis up to this point, we have treated the conjunction (*and* or *or*) as an obligatory part of conjoined sentences, explicitly mentioned in the rule that accounts for these structures. The contrast between examples (5) and (6), however, suggests that the conjunction may be an optional element, in that two of the three conjunctions of (5) have been omitted in (6). But the seventh example, leaves all three of the conjunctions in (5) out, producing an ungrammatical result. Example (8) shares with (6) the property of having only one conjunction; but curiously, unlike (6), it is ungrammatical. (9) introduces further complications: The elements in a conjunction (*John and George, Paul and Ringo,* and *Mick and Keith*) are themselves conjunctions. The distribution of the conjunction *and* is extremely interesting in these kinds of cases. Notice that we can put *and* in between the major conjuncts (*John and George and George and Paul and Mick and Keith were best buds),* which subtly changes the range of interpretations for the string.

Our goal in understanding the distribution of conjunctions like *and* and *or* is to somehow reduce all this complexity to a relatively straightforward pattern. We conjecture that for language to be learnable by children in the actual circumstances of language acquisition, there must generally be relatively simple generalizations that lurk below the surface of apparently complicated streams of data. And, correspondingly, children must be equipped with the ability to process linguistic information in such a way that they can efficiently see the operative patterns in the primary linguistic data. It is well known that adults who put their conscious minds to the task just described are far less successful at unearthing linguistic patterns than young language learners in the process of acquisition. Even the achievements of scholars trained in and practiced at linguistic analysis pale in comparison to those of the average three-year-old. ■

IN DETAIL 4.3

it. The result may be clumsy or redundant, but arguably still a sentence of English:

> Our backs were against the wall, and you were next, and we knew it would be OK, and the results would be in soon, and Mary knew that we gave it our all...

The trick is that any conjunction is itself a sentence, and can appear as a conjunct in a larger conjunction. So, since *John is a Beatle* and *George is a Beatle* are both sentences, so is *John is a Beatle and George is a Beatle*. But since *Paul is a Beatle.* is also a sentence, it can combine with *John is a Beatle and George is a Beatle* to form *John is a Beatle and George is a Beatle and Paul is a Beatle*. The resulting sentence is getting long and unwieldy, but there is no grammatical consideration to stop it from combining with other conjunct sentences to form a still-longer conjunction, and so, on ad infinitum.

Although we could certainly list the conjunctions that a given speaker might produce, the only way to model the syntactic knowledge underlying the production of conjunctions is to posit a rule that describes what a well-formed conjunction is, rather than merely listing some of the outputs that are consistent with that rule. As we shall see, there are certain dependencies that are frequently encountered across the languages of the world (such as conjoined sentences), and others that are non-existent (see Sag and Wasow 1996 for discussion). There are, for example, no languages that require a negation to be placed in the middle of a sentence for it to be a well-formed negative sentence. If we attempt to list the well-formed sentences of English we fail to account for which kinds of sentences may or may not appear on that list. We also fail to capture important *cross-linguistic* generalizations. In the next section, we consider a more sophisticated conception of syntactic information that brings us closer to a fruitful account of linguistic competence.

Do you know any languages in which the process of combining conjuncts indefinitely is not available? Discuss.

4.4 Parts of Speech

In our analysis of English phonology in chapter 2, we concluded that the simplest analysis of the word, as a sequence of sound segments, was inadequate. We were moved to posit a level of phonemic representation that specified unpredictable aspects of pronunciation, coupled with a set of phonological rules that applied to these representations to derive phonetic forms. A phonological rule affects a group of phonemes known as a *natural class* — a collection of sounds that share phonological features in common (for example, the voiced sounds or the alveolar sounds). By stating rules and principles that refer to classes of linguistic items, we gain generality, avoiding the inadequate list structures we have been at pains to avoid. Suppose we apply the same insight to our analysis of syntactic structure. Our goal is to identify the groups of syntactic items that function as a class, and to understand how they are organized.

Traditional analyses of syntactic structures posit grammatical categories known as parts of speech to anchor the analysis. These categories come with familiar names like *noun* and *verb*, and they tend to be defined in semantic terms (a noun is the name of a person, place, or thing). Although these semantic definitions head us in the right direction, they are too imprecise to be of use in a formal theory. Consider the example of the noun *rain*. Rain is not just a thing (water), but rather a thing in action. One of its meanings is *a rapid falling or propulsion of many small particles*. In what sense is a falling (this kind or any other) a thing? A slender sense, indeed; English seems to have the means to objectify actions at will. Luckily, there are other techniques for establishing grammatical categories that supplement our semantic definitions. Nouns like *rain* can appear after determiners like *the,* function words that serve to introduce nouns. How did we know that *the* was a determiner? Well, determiners introduce nouns, and since *rain* is a noun…

No doubt you have noticed the circularity. But unlike circularity in argumentation, this circularity is not dangerous: We depend on simultaneous functional definitions of parts of speech in order to categorize lexical items. This categorization is functional because we conceive of grammatical categories like *noun* and *verb* as equivalence classes of linguistic items whose members can be substituted freely for one another, in that they serve the same syntactic function. So, if *the* is a determiner because it can introduce (or *specify*) *rain, some* must be a determiner, too (since *some rain* is well formed); and *dog* must be a noun since *the* and *some* can introduce it.

We can take a similar approach to establishing the class of verbs. In this case, we identify some morphological criteria: verbs inflect for tense and for number (in the third person), and can appear in the progressive when introduced by a form of the helping verb *be.* So, if a lexical item (say, *kick*) has progressive, third-person-singular, and past-tense allomorphs (*kicking, kicks* and *kicked)*, it is a verb.

In addition to the morphological criteria for identifying verbs, there are a number of distributional criteria. Verbs are the only

Using the criterion discussed in the text, which of the following would count as nouns (defend your answer)?

a. *Mary*
b. *drinking*
c. *like (as in* The, like, biggest dog I ever saw bit me.)

category that can appear systematically after helping verbs like *can* and *would*. So, if a lexical item can appear in the sentence frame

If it/they would __ I'd be surprised.

it is a verb. In the same spirit, the function word *to* (not to be confused with the preposition *to*) introduces verbs in their root forms — the so-called *infinitive* form. So, in *I think I want to leave* we know that *leave* is a verb because its specifier is *to*.

We can identify nouns with the same strategy. The chief morphological criterion for nouns is the ability to inflect for number. An alternation between a singular allomorph and a plural allomorph (*dog/dogs*) is a sure sign that something is a noun. We can establish other morphological criteria as well; for example the presence of the noun-forming suffix *-er*. The distributional test that characterizes nouns is their ability to be specified by a determiner. Nouns are generally able to appear in the frame *The __ exist(s)*.

Once we have identified determiners, nouns, and verbs, we can isolate many other grammatical categories by their patterns of combination with the above parts of speech. Adverbs (*happily*) and adjectives (*happy*) are the only grammatical categories that appear after *very* (*very happy/happily/*dog/*run*). The difference between these two categories is in the kind of categories they modify. Adjectives like *happy* can modify nouns (*happy children*) and can appear in the frame *They seemed __* . Many adjectives also have comparative and superlative forms, for example *happier* and *happiest*. There are other morphological clues as well, including the presence of the suffix *-able* on adjectives such as *readable*, that have been derived from verbs.

Adverbs tend to have opposite properties from adjectives. They cannot appear in the frame *They seemed __* (**They seemed happily*), they do not have comparative and superlative forms (**happilier, *happiliest),* and they never appear with the *-able* suffix. While adjectives modify nouns, adverbs modify other parts of speech, for example verbs (*I ate happily*) and adjectives (*It was extremely quick*). Finally, many adverbs have the distinguishing suffix *-ly,* an ending that marks the derivation of an adverb from an underlying adjective.

One final category that merits discussion is the *preposition*. Prepositions (for example *near* and *to*) take noun complements, as in *near John* and *to Bill*. Many prepositions can be modified by *right* (*right near Bill*). These prepositions usually designate a location or direc-

Which of the following words lack regular plural forms? How can we justify their status as nouns? Discuss.

a. *octopus*
b. *data*
c. *deer*
d. *fish*

Discuss any counterintuitive results you discover.

tion. Other prepositions, like *of* and *to* can play a strictly grammatical role in English — *of* can indicate possession (*the decision of the committee was final*) and *to* can introduce an *indirect object* (*I gave the gold to Mary*). Unlike verbs, some of which also take noun complements, English prepositions do not inflect for tense or number. Finally, prepositions along with their noun complements can be complements to other nouns, as in *a picture of Bill*. Although these diagnostics are far from complete (and they may need modification as we go along), they should help us begin our grammatical analysis. We turn next to a discussion of how grammatical categories are organized in phrases and sentences.

4.5 Categories and Rules

We have previously introduced the rule $S \rightarrow S$ *and S* ('a sentence can consist of a sentence followed by *and,* followed by another sentence') to account for the pattern of sentence conjunction in English. To fully explicate this analysis, we need to spell out what sort of English expressions count as constitutive sentences. This, in a nutshell, is the central descriptive goal of syntactic theory. The list hypothesis, discussed (and rejected) would have us add rules of the form:

S → Mary won the race easily.
S → Old Atlas shrugged.
S → The boy on the left is the bomb.
S → I know you know she knows Bill died.

We can improve on this approach considerably by characterizing well-formed English sentences in terms of permissible sequences of grammatical categories. In this view, the rules for the prior group of sentences would look like this (using the abbreviations N for *noun,* V for *verb,* Det for *determiner,* Adv for *adverb,* Adj for *adjective,* and P for *preposition*):

S → N V Det N Adv
S → Adj N V
S → Det N P Det N V Det N
S → N V N V N V N V

Each of these rules defines a template for a set of English sentences. The first rule, for example, characterizes the set of sentences containing the sequence N-V-Det-N-Adv. So, not only have we accounted for *Mary won the race easily,* but also for *Bill shucked the*

List three sentences that do not fit any of the patterns discussed in the main text. Next, try to describe the patterns for the sentences you have chosen by writing new rules for S in the style under discussion.

The research program that most immediately precedes the contemporary linguistic tradition was developed by Noam Chomsky's mentor, Zellig Harris. Harris was one of the innovators of a style of syntactic analysis known as transformational grammar, later developed by Chomsky and his followers, which formed the basis of much current work in linguistic theory. We discuss *transformations* later in chapter 4, but here we want to present one of Harris's nontransformational analyses of sentence structure. Harris (1963) analyzed the English declarative sentence as follows (we use *N'* for *N* with a line over it, for typographical reasons):

APP   N'   APP   V   OBJ   APP

He comments:

APP means zero or more sentence appendices (words, phrases, or clauses) listed below; APP can also occur before obj, if obj does not begin with a short [N']. (e.g. He relies on his charms at such times. He avoids at such times the more dangerous curves of the road. He avoids the more dangerous curves of the road at such times. He avoids the road at such times. There does not occur: He avoids at such times it.)

[N'] means noun-phrase of any type listed below.

V means a single verb word, from the verb subclasses...

OBJ means whatever object is appropriate to the preceding V... (Harris 1963)

Harris also provides examples of vocabulary for each of these categories of analysis, and illustrations of constructions that exploit many alternative subclasses and combinations of items. He concludes his analysis by presenting a list of sentences that do not fit the pattern above, some of which are discussed below. For example, Harris mentions cases like *Him I told that they came,* in which the word *him* seems to be displaced to a position at the front of the clause (see below). These types of examples proved to be extremely important in the development of contemporary syntactic analysis. ■

corn quickly and *Democracy ruined the economy completely.*

Putting aside the occasional semantic anomaly (a topic we will return to below), the rule, S → N V Det N Adv, generates over three thousand different English sentences based on only five separate vocabulary items per grammatical category! In combination with the rule for conjunction, S → S and S, we have produced a grammar that generates an infinite number of sentences. There are important advantages to this approach to syntactic analysis and, as we shall see, some difficulties as well. By constructing rules that reference syntactic categories, we can account for a core generalization of syntactic theory: Members of a single syntactic category can substitute for one another without affecting grammaticality (the *substitution test).* We have also overcome the finiteness of list-based models of syntactic knowledge, a very important accomplishment if our analysis is to account for all of English. With certain abbreviatory conventions we can also streamline our rules, to capture other linguistic generalizations.

The original form of the first five rules we have proposed is:

S → N V Det N Adv
S → Adj N V
S → Det N P Det N V Det N
S → N V N V N V N V
S → S and S

Suppose we add to our corpus *The boys won the race easily,* a close cousin to *Mary won the race easily,* which motivated the first rule. The new sentence seems to require adding the new rule S → Det N V Det N Adv to the grammar. We now add our first abbreviatory device: Let parentheses indicate that the item within is optional. This move allows us to collapse the two rules

S → N V Det N Adv

and

S → Det N V Det N Adv

into the single rule

S → (Det) N V Det N Adv

which generates both *The boys won the race easily* and *Mary won the race easily.* Once we notice that the adverb at the end, *easily,* is also optional, this rule can be further revised:

S → (Det) N V Det N (Adv)

(to account for *Mary/The boys won the race*) and revised once again when we notice that the second determiner position is also optional:

S → (Det) N V (Det) N (Adv)

Which of the following count as grammatical according to the rule S → (Det) N V (Det) N (Adv)? Discuss any problems you discover.

a. Mary saw Fred.

b. The fish saw a worm.

c. Fred saw a worm.

*d. *Fred saw worm.*

*e. *The Fred saw a worm.*

IN DETAIL 4.5

Semantic anomaly results when certain linguistic items are juxtaposed that place unhonored semantic restrictions on one another. Any syntactically based rule system that fails to enforce the appropriate dependencies ends up generating semantically deviant strings like *The lonely prime number explained the smallest water on itself,* among many other oddities; probably the most famous example of semantic anomaly is Chomsky's *Colorless green ideas sleep furiously.* The $64,000 question is, should we take steps to rule strings like this out on syntactic grounds, or should we assume that extrasyntactic principles of semantic interpretation account for their unacceptable status? An even more radical suggestion is to do nothing, concluding that the sentences under discussion are merely false sentences, colorful (!) as they may be. Perhaps they will have a use in poetry (Chomsky's sentence in fact appears in a poem), or perhaps they have no obvious use at all; but so long as they fit the syntactic pattern of the language, we can let them stand. If we go down this road, we draw the line between (2) and (3), but not between (1) and (2):

1. Colorful green toads sleep quietly.

2. Colorless green ideas sleep furiously.

3. *Colorful green toads sleeps quietly. ■

How would you go about answering the question about the proper treatment of semantic anomaly discussed in the text? What evidence could you gather that might bear decisively on the issue?

Consider, now, the second rule:

S → Adj N V

which generates the sentence *Old Atlas shrugged*. That *Atlas shrugged* is also grammatical convinces us that *old* is optional, and we revise the rule accordingly:

S → (Adj) N V

We might also note that in addition to the possibility of there being no adjective or one adjective in this sort of sentence, there may also be three or more adjectives:

1. Atlas shrugged.
2. Old Atlas shrugged.
3. Old, tired Atlas shrugged.
4. Old, tired, fat Atlas shrugged.
5. Old, tired, fat, unhappy, unappreciated Atlas shrugged.

Obviously we cannot add a new rule for every separate case (since there are an infinite number of cases). Suppose we introduce a second abbreviatory convention, "*" (called the Kleene star — not to be confused with the typographically identical marker of ungrammaticality) to indicate that an item can appear any number of times (including zero). We revise the last rule accordingly (notice that the parentheses are no longer necessary in this case):

S → Adj* N V

4.6 Constituents

We have progressed from an approach to syntactic analysis that treats sentences as sequences of words to one that treats them as sequences of syntactic categories. This allows us to deal in types of sentences rather than in individual tokens, on a case-by-case basis. But we are still considering the grammar as a list, albeit at a higher level of abstraction.

This approach has problems that force us to refine it further. For one thing, it is not obvious that, even with our abbreviatory conventions, we can enumerate enough syntactic rules to account for every grammatically possible combination of syntactic categories in English. But the most telling concerns have to do with our assumption about the units of analysis that a sentence comprises.

We can illustrate the kind of analysis we are ascribing to English sentences by appealing to a tree diagram (similar to those we used in phonological and morphological analysis). The syntactic tree for *Most books on the tables outweighed John,* sanctioned by the rule S → Det N P Det N V N, looks like this:

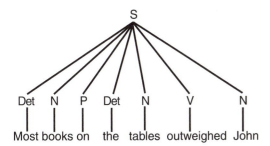

Representation for *Most books on the tables outweighed John.*

The tree is a pictorial representation of the structure assigned to a sentence by our grammar. The vocabulary words are called the *terminal nodes,* and all other nodes are *non-terminals.* Each node is connected to at least one other node by a branch. Nodes connected in this way are referred to as *mothers* and *daughters.* Mothers are one node higher up in the tree than their daughters, and are said to *dominate* them. In the previous example, S is the mother of Det, N, P, Det, N, and V; and they in turn are the mothers of the terminals they dominate. Finally, nodes that are to the left of other nodes are said to *precede* them (so *outweighed* precedes *John,* in this case).

We can refer collectively to all of the daughters of S as a *constituent* (more specifically, an S-constituent). Constituents are the units of analysis out of which a sentence is constructed. Importantly, other than the S-constituent, the only other constituents in this analysis are the nodes labeled with a part of speech (Det, N, P, or V), each of which dominates a single terminal element. Here simple sentences are considered sequences of one-member constituents, each of which functions as an independent item. Unfortunately, there are many reasons to think that this account of the internal structure of the sentence is incorrect.

We can start investigating this question by considering the traditional grammatical distinction between subject and predicate.

Our approach to syntactic analysis treats a sentence as a series of items arranged in a particular order. One precursor to this approach popular in the middle of this century was called immediate-constituent (IC) analysis (Bloomfield 1933). One of the best-known syntacticians of 1950s, Eugene Nida, described the sentence from an IC point of view as "…a framework having certain compartments into which various classes of words may fit." (1966:52) IC analysis involved breaking a sentence down into its parts, the result of which could be represented by diagrams that resemble upside-down versions of analysis trees:

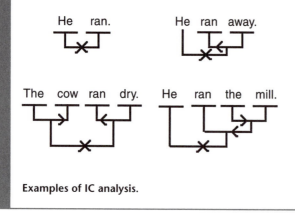

Examples of IC analysis.

Each constituent is underlined, and items that modify each other are linked together with connecting lines bearing either a < or a > to indicate the direction of the modification (although Nida indicates that the type of modification involved is different in the case of a verb followed by an noun than with an adjective modifying a noun).

Items that are next to each other but are not involved in a modification relation are also connected by a line, this time annotated with an X. Nida applies this analytic framework to provide an inventory of many major sentence types in English, and as we shall see, the sorts of structural claims he makes bear more than the occasional similarity to the analyses developed below. ∎

According to traditional wisdom, sentences comprise two parts, a subject and a predicate, although it is difficult to define these categories precisely. In the sentences we have examined so far, the subject corresponds to the first noun, along with its specifier and complements (if any). In a very simple sentence like *Atlas shrugged* the subject is a single word (*Atlas*), but in a more complicated example like *Most books on the tables outweighed John* the subject is the phrase *Most books on the tables*. The predicate consists of the verb and its complements (or other modifiers). The single word *shrugged* is the predicate in *Atlas shrugged*, and the phrase *outweighed John* is the predicate in *Most books on the tables outweighed John*.

It is our analysis of this second example that poses problems: Neither the subject *Most books on the table* nor the predicate *outweighed John* is analyzed as a constituent; each is a sequence of independent items. A better analysis would look like this:

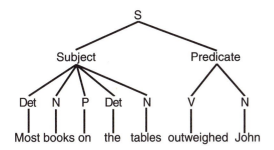

Revised representation for *Most books on the tables outweighed John*.

By grouping the items Det, N, P, Det, and N (and their daughters) into a single subject constituent that combines with a predicate constituent consisting of the verb *outweighed* and the noun *John,* we can represent the traditional subject/predicate analysis. We can — but should we? How can we choose between these different representations for *Most books on the tables outweighed John?*

Our first line of attack might be to consult native speakers' intuitions (introspective judgments) about the structural categorization of sentences. Asking a native English-speaker to divide the sentence *Most books on the tables outweighed John* into two main parts reliably yields an analysis into subject and predicate. In many cases, however, the analysis gets complicated, our intuitions about syntactic structure become less clear, and there even may be disagreements among native speakers. Moreover, we ought not investigate the structural properties of languages by relying on speakers' intuitions. Although people often believe they have reliable insights into these matters, it does not make for good science to rely on the layperson's hunches about scientific analysis, any more than it would in the study of the brain or digestion.

Luckily, there are experimental results to support the claim that syntactic representations of sentences involve higher-order structures. Fodor et al. (1975) provide a nice overview of some of these results. Levelt (1970) showed that when subjects are asked to judge the relative relatedness of adjacent words in a sentence, responses showing a high degree of relatedness cluster around syntactic boundaries like those proposed here. In other experiments, Fodor and Bever (1965) inserted brief clicks into sentences, and asked subjects to identify a click's location. Subjects' performance was best when the click coincided with a major constituent boundary.

However, in cases when experimental evidence is unavailable, or when it is unclear how to establish this kind of confirmation, we require other ways to determine the structure we associate with sentences. As we see in the next section, several syntactic tests can be applied to provide linguistic evidence for assigning structure.

4.7 Tests for Constituency

Our current analysis of *Most books on the tables outweighed John* posits a subject phrase and a predicate phrase, each of which dominates a sequences of nodes that each exhaustively dominate terminals. We now want to determine whether any of the constituents of the subject and predicate phrases are themselves organized into intermediate constituents. One way to pursue this question is to

HISTORY 4.6-B

The analogizing of language to other biological processes (like digestion) is a calculated move on the part of contemporary linguists to emphasize the point that cognitive capacities are no less biological for being mental organs (rather than physical organs). The analogy is sometimes invoked to stress methodological parallels between linguistics and other sciences, and occasionally to counteract the bias that mental properties are somehow mystical or beyond our ability to understand. It is also important to consider how much our understanding of other organ systems' development informs our grasp of language development. In this regard, it is easy to find historical precedents for drawing these types of comparisons. For example,

Otto Jespersen, writing in 1922, wondered whether "...little brains think about these different forms [of language] and their uses? Or is the learning of language performed as unconsciously as the circulation of blood or the process of digestion?" (Jespersen 1968:130)

He goes on to conclude that there is some conscious effort expended in the mastery of language (which he describes as "slow and painful"), and that the learning process involved "some thinking over." He decides that language development occupies a middle ground between completely unconscious processes (like digestion) and conscious learning activities (like memorizing grammar lessons). Jespersen is persuaded of language learning's semireflective

character by incidents in which children comment on their own linguistic systems. For example, Jespersen reports a case in which a child produced an incorrect past tense, saying *I sticked it in*, immediately changing it to *I stuck it in*. He concludes that this self-monitoring behavior requires some conscious access to one's internal rule system. ■

How many other mental processes can you think of for which you can identify a biological basis? Explain your reasoning.

reemploy the substitution test. According to this test, items that can be freely intersubstituted are members of the same syntactic category. Notice in this regard that, in the previous example, the subject *Most books on the tables* and the object *John* can be substituted for one another, yielding *John outweighed most books on the tables*. On our current analysis, the tree for this new sentence would look like this:

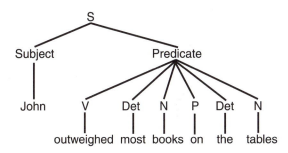

Representation for *John outweighed most books on the tables.*

Unfortunately, our analysis does not predict this possibility since one of the substituents is S and the other is the nonconstituent sequence Det-N-P-Det-N. We can remedy this problem by revising our analysis as follows:

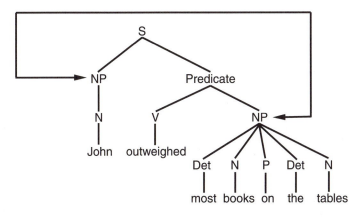

Revised representation for *John outweighed most books on the tables.*

In order to preserve the generalization that only like constituents can be substituted for one another, we have revised our assumption that the subject of the sentence is dominated by a node labeled *subject*. This revision is motivated by the observation that subjects and objects seem to be intersubstitutable. By labeling subjects and objects with the common node label NP (*noun phrase*) we can capture this important generalization. Although the old analysis of sentences into subjects and predicates may have had tradition on its side, the new analysis has something more persuasive going for it: evidence (in the form of the substitution test). By this account, NPs are phrases that minimally dominate Ns, but may also include specifiers of and complements to N. Once we see this generalization, we might well become suspicious of our position on the internal structure of the NP *Most books on the tables*. Notice, for example, that the object NP *John* can substitute for the Det-N sequence at the end of the subject NP, yielding *Most books on John outweighed the tables*. This suggests that *the tables* must also be a NP, forcing us to revise our analysis as follows:

Use the substitution test to break the following examples down into constituents. You can use brackets to show constituency (see below). Discuss.

Example: [John] [sang a cappella]

1. *John and Paul sang duets.*

2. *John wrote songs daily.*

3. *Last Tango in Paris was a dirty movie.*

4. *Marlon could have been a contender.*

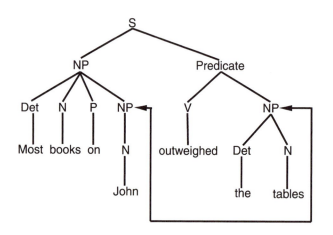

Revised representation for *Most books on John outweighed the tables*.

There is a variation on the substitution test that we might call the *incredulity test* that will help us to further refine our analysis. Notice that each of the phrases we have posited can serve as an incredulous rejoinder to an apparently dubious assertion:

Speaker A: The books on the tables outweighed John!

Speaker B: a. John?
              b. Outweighed John?
              c. The books on the tables?
              d. The tables?
              e. The books?

However, nonconstituents cannot serve as replies in this circumstance:

Speaker A: The books on the tables outweighed John!

Speaker B: a. *The books on?
              b. *On the?
              c. *Books on the?
              d. *The tables outweighed?
              e. *On the tables outweighed John?

We can use this new test to check to see if we have missed any constituents in our current analysis. It turns out that one has escaped our notice: The P-NP sequence *on the tables* constitutes a *prepositional phrase* (PP), a phrasal constituent consisting of a preposition followed by an NP complement. The incredulity test provides evidence for this claim: *On the tables?* is a well-formed reply to the example under discussion.

A closely related test, the *interrogation test,* can also be used to confirm our analysis. In this paradigm, we discover that constituent phrases can typically form the answers to questions:

1 a.   Who did most books on the tables outweigh?
  b.   John.

2 a.   Where were most books that outweighed John?
  b.   On the tables.

3 a.   What was it that outweighed John?
  b.   Most books on the tables.

4 a.   What were most books that outweighed John on?
  b.   The tables.

5 a.   What did most books on the tables do?
  b.   Outweigh John.

In contrast, there are no questions to which nonconstituents like *on the* or *tables outweighed* can be provided as answers. Taking all

Use the incredulity test to break the following sentences down into constituents. You can use brackets to show constituency (see below). Discuss.

Example: [John] [sang a cappella]

1. *John sold his favorite guitar to George.*

2. *I ran over the river and through the woods.*

3. *To be or not to be, that is the question!*

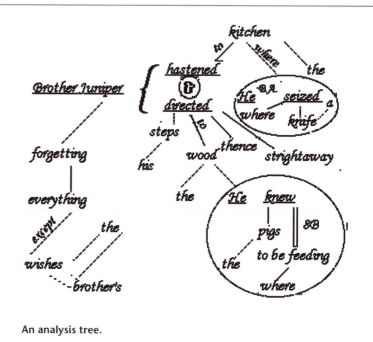

HISTORY 4.7

The idea of representing the syntactic structure of a sentence in the form of an analysis tree is actually quite old. The diagram below comes from a grammar book written by Isabel Fry in 1925 in London (cited in Jespersen 1969). It is an analysis of the sentence *Brother Juniper, forgetting everything except the brother's wishes, hastened to the kitchen, where he seized a knife, and thence directed his steps straightaway to the wood where he knew the pigs to be feeding.*

This rather opaque diagram is discussed by Jespersen, who comments, "Her diagram on pg. 83 is even more forbidding, though done with extreme care." ■

An analysis tree.

these arguments into consideration, our current analysis of *Most books on John outweighed the tables* looks like this:

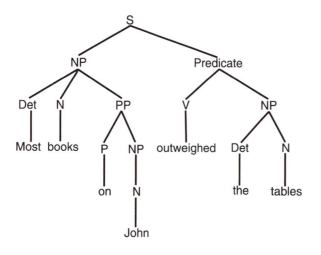

Revised representation for *Most books on John outweighed the tables*.

Finally, a theoretical consideration; NP and PP are each phrases with a *head* (N in the case of NP and P in the case of PP) with specifiers and complements, as appropriate. Our commitment to a predicate phrase, however, is a holdover from an early stage of our inquiry. We can unify our analysis by renaming this node VP for *verb phrase,* in this case dominating a verbal head and an NP complement.

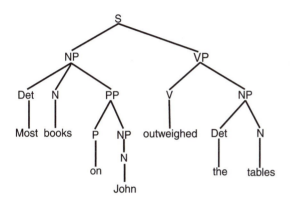

Revised representation for *Most books on John outweighed the tables.*

4.8 From Rule to Tree

The substitution test, the incredulity test, and the interrogation test combine to provide a method for establishing a sentence's syntactic structure based on empirical considerations. Viewed in this way, a syntactic structure constitutes a hypothesis about a speaker's linguistic representations that can be confirmed by describing and predicting a sentence's systematic syntactic properties. More generally, we can abstract a set of phrase-structure rules that define the set of representations we hypothesize to be available to a native speaker. The following phrase-structure rules are sufficient to generate the analyses we have adopted in the previous section:

S → NP VP
NP → (Det) N (PP)
VP → V (NP)
PP → P NP

In addition to a set of phrase-structure rules, we also assume that a lexicon is available that contains entries marked for phonemic

Phrase-structure grammars such as the one under consideration were originally developed for formal languages; invented languages like logics or computer languages that have much simpler syntactic systems than do natural languages. Suppose, for example, that we imagine a formal language consisting exclusively of sentences that contain a single occurrence of the symbol *A* followed by any number of instances of the symbol *B*.

A grammar for this language contains the initial symbol A, and a rule that dictates that the symbol *A* can dominate the symbols *A B:*

$$A \rightarrow A\ B$$

Applying this rule yields the string *A B,* as the rule specifies. Notice, however, that this rule is *recursive* — it applies to its own output. If we apply it twice, we get the following result:

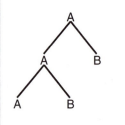

A simple analysis tree for a formal language.

There is, in fact, no limit to the number of times the rule may be applied in a derivation.

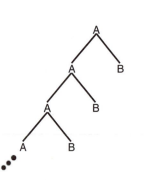

A recursive structure.

And since there is no upper bound to the number of times this rule can be recursively applied, there is an infinite number of sentences in this formal language. Accounts of syntactic patterns in languages like English hold that the syntax of natural languages can be characterized by a grammar that employs recursion in this sense to provide for the essential creativity of linguistic systems.

Notice that all of the sentences generated by our simple grammar are of the form $A\ B^n$ — one *A* followed by any number of *B*s. Any other string is ungrammatical — it is not part of the language and the grammar cannot generate (assign a structure) to it. ■

Make a list of at least three different kinds of English sentences that exploit recursive structures. If you speak a second language well enough to judge (or if you have access to a speaker of another language), determine whether the constructions you identified are possible in that second language. Discuss.

representation, part of speech, and so forth. The phrase-structure rules define syntactic representation up to but not including the level of the terminal vocabulary. For example, our current rules sanction the following representation:

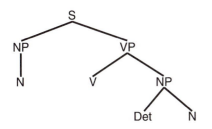

A syntactic representation without lexical items.

Next, a process known as *lexical insertion* applies; that is, each nonphrasal node is associated with a corresponding terminal lexical item. The part of speech of the terminal must match the syntactic category of its mother; e.g., nouns are inserted under N and verbs under V. The result is a fully specified analysis tree that assigns a particular representation to a given sentence based on the dominance and precedence relations that are expressed.

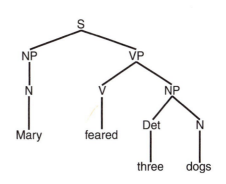

A syntactic representation after lexical insertion.

4.9 Binary Branching

Let us return one last time to our analysis of *Most books on the tables outweighed John,* concentrating on the structure proposed for the subject NP.

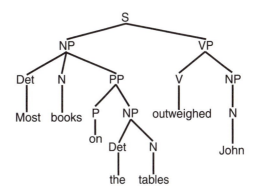

Representation for *Most books on the tables outweighed John.*

The maximal expansion of the NP rule allows three daughters in the sequence Det-N-PP. Since this is the only instance in which three daughters are permitted, we might suspect that there is more hierarchical structure within the NP than we have posited thus far. Let us consider two possibilities for the structure to be assigned. Both of these representations strictly employ binary branching, but they differ in internal constituency.

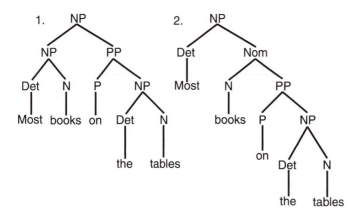

Alternative representations for *Most books on the tables*.

The first alternative, which requires the new phrase-structure rule NP → NP (PP), posits a noun phrase within a larger noun phrase with a PP complement. Although superficially plausible, there are several problems with this analysis. Notice first that the substitution test leads us to expect that other NPs should be freely intersubstitutable for the small NP *Most books*. Suppose we try to substitute the pronoun *they,* (which is substitutable in simpler examples like *Most books/They outweighed John*). The resulting string, **They on the tables outweighed John* with the following putative analysis tree, is ungrammatical:

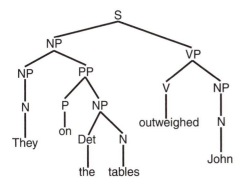

Putative structure for *They on the tables outweighed John.*

There is also a subtle aspect of interpretation not easily explained by this approach. *Most books on the tables outweighed John* means that (roughly) more than half of the books on the tables weigh more than John. It does not mean that more than half of the books in the universe (or the universe of discourse) have this property. That is, *Most* specifies *books on the tables* not just *books*. Although this constituency is not captured by the first analysis, the second alternative does account for it (we return to this matter in chapter 5).

Another kind of evidence gives us further confidence in this proposal. Cardinal numbers such as *one* or *two*, as in *I want that one* can be used in certain discourse situations as pronominal substitutes for nominal constituents. If someone heard you assert *Most books on the tables outweighed John,* and was not clear which books you meant, he or she might respond: "Those three?" an NP with the structure illustrated below.

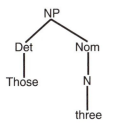

Representation for *Those three.*

We have introduced new syntactic category, *nominal* (abbreviated *Nom*), which dominates the noun and its complement. This squares nicely with the kind of interpretation we assign to Det-N-PP sequences. It is the interpretation of *three* that we are particularly interested in. Notice that *three* can be used here to stand for *books on the tables*. Again, our present analysis of the noun phrase lets us describe the type of interpretation exhibited by this class of pronouns (or, better, proforms) by positing the category Nom as a basic constituent

IN DETAIL 4.9

There is a more subtle argument in favor of the Nom analysis that turns on the semantic interpretation of proforms like *three* and *one* that take Nom antecedents. Consider, in this regard, the structure for *a teacher of Spanish from Mexico,* which can be assigned as follows:

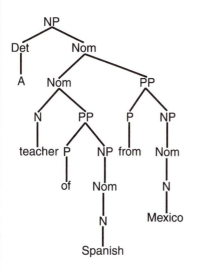

Representation of *a teacher of Spanish from Mexico.*

Notice that in this example we have two PPs in the largest NP, each of which has been assigned a phrase-structure position as a sister under Nom. Suppose, now that a certain speaker *A* says, "I know a teacher of Span-ish from Mexico," and a speaker *B* responds, "Oh yeah? I know one too." One what? It seems that *one* could mean *one teacher of Spanish from Mexico,* but it could also mean just *one teacher of Spanish,* a reading that can be brought out by adding:

B': Oh yeah? I know one from Spain too.

If you go back and inspect the analysis tree above, you will see that this ambiguity in interpretation for *one* is predicted by the current analysis. Since both *teacher of Spanish* and *teacher of Spanish from Mexico* are dominated by a Nom, and since *one* is free to take any Nom antecedent, both readings ought to be possible.

There is also a difference in status between the PP complement *of Spanish,* which is a sister to N, and the PP *from Mexico* that appears as a sister to Nom, higher up the tree. The former receives a complement interpretation that is integrated into the thematic structure of the NP as a theme, whereas the latter is a modifier phrase. Notice, for example that if we try to swap the two PPs yielding **a teacher from Mexico of Spanish* the result is clumsy. It turns out that certain prepositions like *of* act like function words that allow a complement interpretation for the PP, whereas contentful prepositions like *from* can only introduce modifier PPs. The awkwardness of switching the order of the two PPs results from installing a PP that invites a modifier-type interpretation into a thematically assigned complement PP slot. ■

available in syntactic representation. A second benefit of this analysis is that we can generalize our commitment to (at most) binary branching in our syntactic system, in principle ruling out all other types of representations. We should emphasize that this move is theoretical, subject to revision in the face of contravening evidence. But we are motivated to adopt it in order to restrict the range of possible grammars admitted by our theory, aiming to provide an account of grammatical knowledge that helps to understand how children can, in a limited time period, attain systems of great apparent complexity (i.e., grammars) on the basis of limited exposure to primary linguistic data. By radically restricting the form that grammars can take, and by positing that children are themselves restricted to considering only the "available" grammars, we hope to begin to illuminate the process of language acquisition — the ultimate goal of linguistic theory.

4.10 Syntactic Ambiguity

We have now arrived at a phrase-structure grammar with the following rules:

S → NP VP
NP → (Det) Nom
Nom → N (PP)
VP → V (NP)
PP → P NP

Next, let us turn to the VP rule. As it stands, we have provided for transitive VPs like *saw a ghost* and intransitive VPs like *elapsed*. However, there are other VP structures that we would like our rules to account for. Notice, for example, that intransitive verbs can generally co-occur with a PP (*Mary ran out the door*). We can account for this type of VP by replacing our single VP rule with two new ones:

VP → V (PP)
VP → V NP

We can now generate sentences like *Mary ran with abandon*, as well as *Mary ran*, and *Mary hit the ball*.

Let us now consider the analysis of the sentence *The people talked over the noise*. Our revised rules for VPs allows us to assign the following analysis tree to this example:

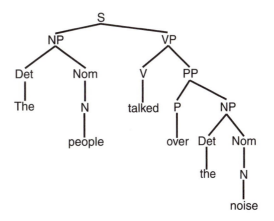

Representation for *The people talked over the noise*.

In the main discussion, we mentioned incorporating modifierlike PPs into the formal analysis. This brief discussion will help to keep in mind the extra degree of complication in the internal structure of the Nom constituent that must be accounted for in a complete account of the English NP. Our current rule system is also conspicuously missing adjectival modifiers in the NP. It might seem that the approach to adjectives discussed earlier (in which we employed the Kleene star to capture the fact that an infinite number of adjectives can precede a noun) ought to be incorporated into our current analysis. However, a Kleene star-based analysis is incompatible with binary branching, as illustrated by the following analysis tree:

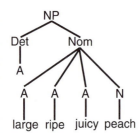

Representation of *a large juicy ripe peach.*

There is available, however, an alternative account of adjectives that incorporates essentially the same recursive analysis of Nom that was introduced to explain the distribution of PPs. In this approach, adjectives are introduced as shown at top right.

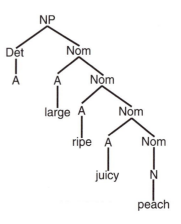

Alternative representation of *a large juicy ripe peach.*

Notice that each adjective has a Nom sister that corresponds to its scope of modification. So, *large* modifies *ripe juicy peach, ripe* modifies *juicy peach,* and *juicy* modifies *peach.*

Once again, strategic deployment of the Nom proform *one* confirms this analysis. Consider, in this regard, the following conversational rejoinders:

Speaker A: I'd prefer a large ripe juicy peach.
Speaker B: a. I'd prefer one too.
              b. I'd prefer a small one.
              c. I'd prefer a small meaty one.
              d. I'd prefer a small meaty hard one.

Each of speaker *B*'s responses involves a progressively smaller Nom antecedent for *one.* The availability of each of these readings provides additional support for our claim that adjectives are dominated by Nom in a potentially recursive structure. Even though our desire to seek an alternative account for adjectives was motivated by an essentially theoretical consideration, in the process we have gained an descriptive advantage in our analysis of the English NP. ■

So far, so good. However, if we consider the interpretation of this example carefully, we will detect a subtle *ambiguity*: A single string of words can be assigned more than one semantic interpretation. On one reading, the sentence means that the people spoke so as to overcome an interfering sound; and on a second reading, it means that the people discussed the noise. The first representation is appropriate for the first reading, but the second interpretation is better represented as follows:

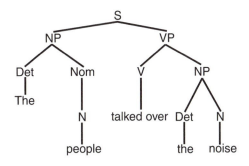

Alternative representation for *The people talked over the noise.*

This analysis treats *talked over* as a two-part verb, consisting of the verb *talk* and the particle *over* that have been combined to form a complex transitive verb taking an NP complement. If this structure is correct, and the string *talked over* forms a constituent, we should be able to substitute another verb for it — for instance, *discussed* — and still have a sentence that preserves the same grammatical relations. In the first representation, *talked over* does not form a constituent, but *over the noise* does. This explains why in this representation (but not in the second one) *over the noise* can be substituted for by another PP say, *despite the racket,* preserving grammatical relations.

The incredulity test helps to confirm this analysis. Suppose a skeptic responded to your assertion, *The people talked over the noise,* by saying *Over the noise?* This reply is only consistent with the 'interfering sound' interpretation, since it must be analyzed as a PP constituent. We conclude that meaning must be assigned to sentences on the basis of syntactic structure, and not directly to words and phrases themselves. Thus, by determining constituency relations, we are not only fixing the syntactic analysis of language, but also establishing aspects of semantic interpretation.

Determine which of the following sentences are ambiguous, and describe each of their interpretations:

1. *Flying planes can be dangerous.*

2. *The chickens are too hot to eat.*

3. *We are visiting kin.*

4. *John saw Paul with a telescope.*

5. *John thought Paul left yesterday.*

4.11 Subordination

In the previous section we added a new VP rule to generate V-PP sequences. In this section, we consider another type of English VP in which sentences are introduced as complements to a verb; for example, *John admitted that Mary won*. Notice that the sentence *Mary won* is a constituent of the larger sentence, and that it is introduced by the complementizer (abbreviated *Comp*, not to be confused with *complement*) *that*.

Subordinate clauses are sentences that appear as subconstituents of larger sentences. These clauses generally have the same syntactic properties as simple sentences, a fact captured by introducing the following rule:

S' → Comp S

S' (read "S-bar") dominates the sequence Comp-S, with Comp serving as the specifier for the subordinate sentence. In this approach, the subordinate clause *that Mary won* will have the following analysis.

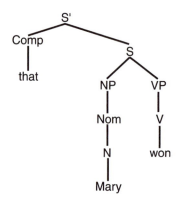

Representation for *that Mary won.*

It remains to attach the subordinate clause to its containing clause (the main clause). We can appeal to our constituency tests to anchor our analysis. The substitution test is consistent with our assumption that the subordinate clause is a subconstituent of the VP because the string *admitted that Mary won* in the sentence *John admitted that Mary won* can be substituted for by a well-formed VP, for example *forgot the result,* yielding *John forgot the result.* The incredulity test applies as well, and since *Admitted that Mary won?* is an acceptable response, we have additional evidence for the VP-constituency of the subordinate clause. Finally, *Admit that Mary won* is a possible answer to the question *What did John do?* further confirming our analysis. To formalize this approach, we add the following VP rule to our grammar:

VP → V S'

This change leaves us with the following rules:

S → NP VP
S' → Comp S
NP → (Det) Nom
Nom → N (PP)
VP → V (PP)
VP → V NP
VP → V S'
PP → P NP

This grammar assigns the following analysis tree to *John admitted that Mary won:*

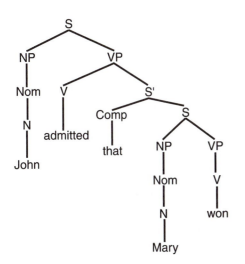

Representation for *John admitted that Mary won.*

Not only is this account of the facts plausible, it also introduces an important feature of our grammar that merits some discussion — it is possible to have more than one subordinate clause per sentence; indeed, there is no limit to how many can be in a sentence *(John believes that Bill believes that Sue believes…that fish fly)*. It turns out that our analysis explains these facts as it stands. Since there is a rule for VP that introduces an S' complement that in turn dominates a VP that can dominate an S' (and so forth), our rule system has a recursive character. We can present the situation schematically, as follows:

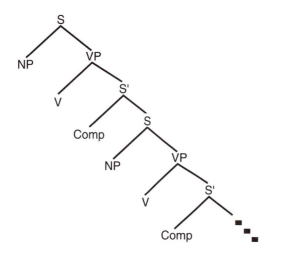

A recursive structure.

Because of its recursive character, our rule system is able to generate an infinite number of sentences (of a certain type) on the basis of a small, finite rule system. This is an important characteristic for any grammar intended as a model for linguistic competence.

IN DETAIL 4.11

The type of subordinate clause introduced in the main discussion is more properly called a tensed subordinate clause. English also has a number of other complex constructions that involve several different untensed forms of an embedded verb:

1. John prefers that Paul leaves.
2. John prefers for Paul to leave.
3. John prefers Paul to leave.
4. John prefers to leave.
5. John saw Paul leave.
6. John admired Paul's leaving.
7. John considered Ringo a fool.

In example (1), *prefers* takes a tensed subordinate clause for its complement. In (2), however, we find an infinitival construction that differs in several ways from (1). First, the tensed complementizer *that* has been substituted for by the infinitival complementizer *for.* The second change is that the infinitival marker *to* appears in the position normally occupied by a helping verb. Finally, the verb itself is in the root form, appearing without the third-person-singular agreement marker *-s* that we would normally expect.

Example (3) is identical to (2) except that the complementizer *for* is missing. In this regard, *for* behaves like *that,* which can be missing from subordinate clauses in certain circumstances. The fourth example is also based on *prefers,* but this time the complement appears to consist solely of the infinitival phrase *to leave.* Notice that there is no embedded subject appearing in the vicinity of the embedded verb: The subject of *leave* is understood to be identical to the main clause subject *John* (thus the understood subject is "controlled" by the main clause subject.)

The final three examples involve still other complex embedded complement constructions. Example (5) looks like (3), but there are two significant differences. First, the complementizer *for* is prohibited in this case (*John saw for Paul leave). The second point of contrast is that the embedded verb is not (and cannot be) introduced by the infinitival marker *to* (**John saw Paul to leave*). The penultimate example involves a possessive form of the NP *Paul* followed by a form of the verb marked with the suffix *-ing* (not to be confused with the progressive *-ing*). The last example is perhaps even more remarkable in that there seems to be an understood verb *to be* (which can appear — *John considers Paul to be a fool*) linking the NP *a fool* (here functioning as a predicate!) with its argument *Paul*.

Collectively, these constructions have been the subject of tremendous debate and conflicting analyses. Roughly speaking, there have been two approaches that we can call the "clausal analysis" and the "nonclausal analysis." The clausal analysis treats all of these embedded constructions as subordinate clauses, assigning them essentially the same structure as that assigned to tensed subordinate clauses. Here is the analysis tree for example (2):

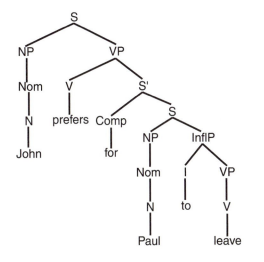

Representation for *John prefers for Paul to leave*.

The node label InflP stands for inflection phrase, the phrase taken to dominate infinitival phrases, with I standing for inflection. It is also possible to generalize this analysis of the InflP, locating helping verbs (like *can* or *should*, for example) in I-position in tensed clauses.

Where the subject of the infinitival is understood, proponents of this style of analysis posit the existence of a silent pronoun notated Pro, which occupies the embedded subject position:

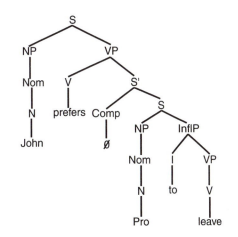

Representation for *John prefers to leave*.

One virtue of this approach is that it allows us to maintain a simple lexical analysis for verbs like *prefer*. We need only mark *prefer* as accepting an S' complement, and it automatically inherits the option of taking either a tensed or infinitive subordinate clause as its complement.

There are, however, many questions that must be addressed in order to make this account complete. Much debate has centered on the status of Pro (see Radford 1997 for a recent discussion) and on the mechanisms available to correlate the different types of verbs with the various complement structures they accept. For example, *try* requires a Pro subject in its complement *(I tried (*Paul) to audition), believe* prohibits a Pro subject *(*I believe to be dead), want* is happy in either circumstance *(I want (Paul) to sing)*; in short, there are many complications that must be addressed on the assumption that all of the complements under investigation are Ss.

Proponents of the nonclausal analysis tend to treat each of the complement structures involved in these examples as a series of constituents, avoiding any commitment to silent subjects and silent complementizers. In this view, *prefer* can take an NP followed by an infinitival phrase as its complement, or just a bare infinitival phrase. Here is an analysis tree for the VP *prefers Paul to leave:*

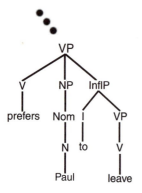

Alternative representation for *prefers Paul to leave.*

If we follow this approach, we must enter each verb in the lexicon in such a way that its complement possibilities are spelled out properly. You will also note that the constituency assigned to the VP is inconsistent with the principle of binary branching. Finally, since the understood subject of *leave* is not marked in this syntactic analysis (right), we must provide a semantic interpretation for the infinitival phrase that introduces a subject

argument identical to the main-clause subject (see Sag and Wasow 1996 for details).

Although we will not resolve the debate about the proper analysis of subordinate clauses here, we have presented two opposing points of view to give you a feel for the layers of descriptive and theoretical considerations that complicate linguistic analysis.

It is fair to say that the grammar of subordinate clauses remains a lively open research question in the field. ■

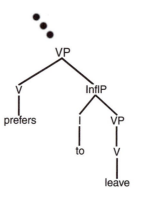

Alternative representation for *prefers to leave.*

Here is another class of examples that features a different complement structure for verbs like consider *and* strike:

1. Bill considered Ella a giant.

2. Billie struck Sarah as an inspiration.

How would you describe the complement structure illustrated in these examples? How could we incorporate these data into our analysis? Discuss.

4.12 Subcategorization

In order create a representation for a sentence, we first generate a syntactic structure that is consistent with our phrase-structure grammar, and then apply lexical insertion. Thus far we have assumed that the only condition potential lexical entries must meet is the appropriateness of their part of speech, which must match the category label of the node that directly dominates them. In this section we will explore further conditions on lexical insertion.

In the previous chapter, we discussed two subcategories of verbs, transitives and intransitives. Transitive verbs such as *nominated* require NP objects, and intransitive verbs such as *died* may not co-occur with NP objects. We have anticipated this contrast in two ways: We have marked verbs in the lexicon as transitive or intransitive, and we have proposed separate phrase-structure rules to expand VP to accommodate either case. Still, one problem remains: matching up the right verbs with the right syntactic structures. To see this problem more clearly, consider the analysis tree at right.

Strings like *John worried that song (as well as *Ringo arrived a bass and *Mick slept a tune) are ungrammatical outputs generated by our grammar in its current state. Since *worried, arrived* and *slept* are intransitive verbs they cannot co-occur with an NP object (compare *Ringo arrived with a bass* and *Mick slept during a song*). We can produce a parallel problem by freely substituting verbs in intransitive VPs, resulting in strings like *Nixon liked and *Regan nominated, cases in which a transitive verb has been inserted in a slot that should be reserved for intransitive verbs. It is not enough to have two kinds of VP structures and two kinds of verbs; we must ensure that transitive verbs end up in transitive positions and intransitive verbs in intransitive positions.

The solution is mechanically simple but theoretically far-reaching: we need to check the complement structure associated with each verb that is a candidate for lexical insertion and make sure that what Sag and Wasow (1996) call its *valence* is appropriate for insertion into a particular VP. (The term is borrowed from chemistry to suggest that intransitive verbs can constitute "complete" predicates, but transitive verbs — those requiring NP objects — cannot.) This will establish the correct correspondence between lexical item and syntactic representation and will solve our problem with *overgeneration*.

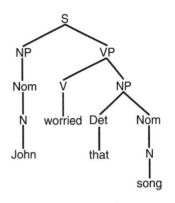

Representation for *John worried that song.*

List five intransitive and five transitive verbs. Can you think of any verbs that can appear on both lists?

We can extend this idea to other cases that require selecting the appropriate subcategory of lexical item in the process of lexical insertion. For example, in addition to transitive and intransitive verbs, we discovered in the previous section that verbs like *believe* and *hope* can take subordinate clauses as complements (*Mary believed/hoped that it wasn't true*). However, intransitive verbs (like *dined*) and transitive verbs (like *devour*) cannot select S' complements: **Sue dined/devoured that Bill won*. Verbs selecting S' complements have a distinct valence from transitives and intransitives. This suggests that we should replace the two-way distinction between transitive and intransitive with a more general specification of the type of complement selected by a given verb.

We can record the valence of a verb in its lexical entry by employing the feature *POS* (part of speech) and distributing it in the matrix of head features, as well as in the matrix of complement features. For example, the value of the head feature *POS* for the verb *hope* is *[V]* (since it is a verb), and the value the complement feature *POS* is *[S'],* indicating that *hope* selects for an S' complement.

List five verbs that select subordinate clauses for their complements. Provide one example sentence for each verb.

Hope: /hop/
          Head Features: POS = [V],...
          Specifier Features: _____
          Complement Features: POS = [S'],...

          ...

Partial lexical entry for *hope*.

The lexical entry for intransitive verbs like *dine* contains *null* for its complement *POS* feature value (meaning that it selects for no complement); and for transitive verbs like *devour,* the value of the complement *POS* feature is *[NP].*

4.13 Modifiers

Our previous analysis of subcategorization makes use of the distinction between head features and complement features introduced earlier. By specifying for each verb what its complement must be, we can control the process of lexical insertion more precisely. In the case of transitive verbs and verbs that select an S' complement, the analysis is quite straightforward; but our analysis of intransitives has some implications that merit discussion.

We have already noted that intransitive verbs can appear freely with prepositional phrases. So, with *Nixon resigned,* we also find *Nixon resigned in disgrace; Nixon resigned for his own good;* and so forth. However, if, as we have proposed, the value for the complement *POS* feature for *resigned* is *null,* this rules out the possibility of inserting *resigned* into a VP with the following structure:

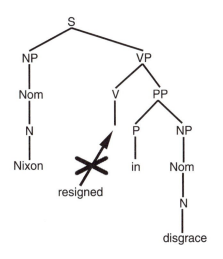

Lexical insertion blocked for *Nixon resigned in disgrace.*

We could, of course, change the value of the complement feature *POS* for the verb *resigned* to *[PP],* but that would block lexical insertion in cases in which the verb is the only daughter of the VP. There is, however, another possibility worth exploring: perhaps the PP is not the complement of verb in the examples under discussion. One important argument for this conclusion concerns the iterativity of PPs, as illustrated by examples like *Nixon resigned for his own good, by prior arrangement, in extreme circumstances...*

Apparently, there is no limit to the number of PPs that can co-occur with *resign.* Contrast this behavior with that of the NP complement to a transitive verb; in the latter case only one NP complement is permitted (**John touched the guitar the piano the bass*). To account for these facts, we revise our assumption that the PPs co-occurring with intransitive verbs are complements, reanalyzing them as modifiers. Modifiers are optional elements and can

IN DETAIL 4.13-A

There is another class of verbs for which the analysis for *resigned,* rejected in the main discussion, seems appropriate. In this regard, consider the following data:

1. John relied on Paul.
2. *John relied.
3. *John relied Paul.

Rely represents a small class of verbs that take PP complements (rather than PP modifiers). As evidence in favor of this conclusion we note that neither (2), which lacks a PP complement, nor (3), which incorporates an NP complement, is grammatical. There is also another curious thing about *rely* — it requires the preposition that is the head of the PP to be *on* (**John relied near Paul*). We need to list this idiosyncratic information in the lexical entry for *rely,* since it is not predictable from other considerations.

Build a rule system that generates PP complements. Draw a tree for John relied on Paul *using the rule system you have created.*

We should also take notice of verbs like *put,* which require both an NP and a PP in their complement structure:

1. John put his guitar on the stage.
2. *John put on the stage.
3. *John put his guitar.

In this case, *put* requires a PP that specifies a location (a *locative* PP). Although it is relatively straightforward to capture this generalization in the lexical entry for *put,* the constituency of the complement raises an interesting problem: The most obvious analysis is inconsistent with our commitment to binary branching.

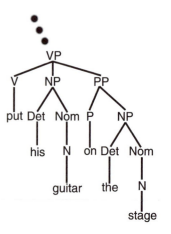

Representation for *put his guitar on the stage.*

We leave this question open, encouraging you to develop plausible alternative analyses that are consistent with a binary approach to phrase structure (see Larson 1988 for a proposal). ■

appear iteratively in a phrase. We introduce PP modifiers into the VP, as follows:

VP → V'
V' → V' PP
V' → V
V' → V NP
V' → V S'

These rules posit a new node, V', that expands in one of four ways. The first option is to rewrite V' as V' PP. This rule is recursive, allowing an arbitrary number of PPs to be introduced. In this example, there are two PP modifiers.

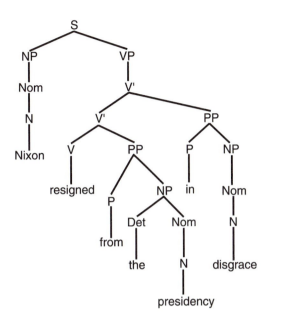

A sentence with two PP modifiers.

The other three V' rules introduce transitive, intransitive, and subordinate-clause-taking verbs, respectively. We can now formally define a complement to the verb as a *sister* of V under V'. In contrast, modifiers are constituents introduced as sisters to V'.

We can also generalize this analysis of the complement/modifier distinction to refine our analysis of the NP. Suppose we rename the category Nom as N', to achieve parallelism in nomenclature with V'. Notice that in both cases these categories are intermediate between the phrasal category (NP or VP) and the head (N or V). Suppose, further, that we revise the rules that expand NP and N' as follows:

NP → Det N'
N' → N' PP
N' → N

This allows us to capture the fact that these PPs are actually modifiers as well, explaining why they are optionally occurring and capable of iteration:

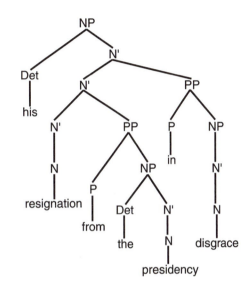

An NP with two PP modifiers.

More impressively, we have identified a cross-categorical generalization about the structure of modifiers: Modifiers are introduced by recursive rules as sisters to X' categories where X can be either N or V.

Discuss any problems posed by the following examples for the current analysis of modification:

1. *On his own, John learned the guitar.*

2. *George saw Paul without his glasses.*

3. *In 1972 John thought the Beatles would disband.*

One of the most interesting versions of X'-theory aims at reducing the phrase-structure rules for a language to a schema acting as a template that constrains phrase structure. We have already observed that both NPs and VPs can be hierarchically analyzed to contain a projection from XP (or X") to X' to X. So, an NP can dominate an N', which in turn dominates an N; and a VP can dominate a V', which dominates a V:

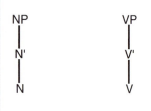

Some X' structures.

In our present grammar, we treat this parallelism as accident; it would be just as easy to handle the two kinds of phrases completely differently from one another. By introducing the following template, we can restrict phrase structure to the observed cases:

XP → (Spec) X' (Mod)
X' → X' (Mod)
X' → X (Comp)

Spec (specifiers), Mod (modifiers) and Comp (complements) are optional elements that need to be further specified depending on the value for X (namely, N, or V). For example, the lexical entries for the head noun or verb include feature specifications that determine the nature of the specifiers and complements they select (if any). Some further specifications must restrict the type of modifiers that are appropriate.

We would also like to generalize this schema to account for the phrase structure of other types of phrases. For example, we might

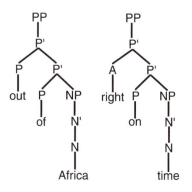

Representations for *out of Africa* and *right on time*.

reconsider the internal structure of PPs, looking for evidence to support positing an intermediate P' constituent, in analogy to V' and N', preserving the parallelism across these three categories. The possibility of examples like *out of Africa* and *right on time* is consistent with this extension of the X'-based analysis. ∎

Cross-categorical analyses of this sort have been investigated in contemporary linguistic research under the rubric of *X-bar syntax*, with the goal of discovering and explaining these types of phrase-structure generalizations (see Jackendoff 1977 for discussion). Central to this approach is the claim that major phrasal categories have a unified phrase structure involving a progressive expansion from a phrase of type XP (sometimes written X") to an X' constituent to head of type X, for each syntactic category X. The aim of this research program is to restrict the range of possible phrase-structure analyses available within the theory of language, consistent with our overall goal of describing language so as to explain how children are able to efficiently acquire linguistic competence. Generalizations such as the one about modifiers reveal an underlying organizational structure in language that a child can discover on the basis of less direct evidence than it would take to learn the structure of each phrase individually, thereby simplifying the learning task. We return to this point below.

Finally, we can reconsider our analysis of adjectives. Recall that adjectives, like PPs, can be iterated arbitrarily many times in prenominal position. We might also notice that adjectives are also optional in the NP, as the contrast between *this old man* and *this man* illustrates. In short, adjectives have the two hallmark properties of modifiers. Suppose we extend our analysis of the N' constituent to capture these generalizations. The following rules for NP and N' do the trick:

NP → (Det) N'
N'→ N' Adj
N' → N' PP
N' → N

These rules allow us to associate the structure below with the NP the last angry man.

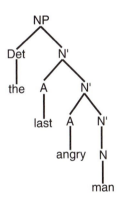

Representation for *the last angry man.*

The constituency associated with the NP treats each adjective as a modifier of its sister N'. That means that *angry* modifies the N' *man* and *last* modifies the N' *angry man* (not just *man*) — an analysis that accords with intuition nicely. Furthermore, if I say, "He is the last angry man," and you reply in disbelief, "I don't think he is the last one," we can explain the most natural interpretation of *one* straightforwardly: *one* stands for the antecedent N' *angry man*, consistent with its usual behavior as an N' proform (see Lightfoot 1991 for related discussion).

IN DETAIL 4.13-C

In our previous discussion of modifiers, we suggested that it would be desirable to extend the X'-analysis of canonical phrase structure to as many phrase types as possible. Against this background, it seems unusual that adjectives would be introduced into phrases dominated by the lexical category Adj, with no superordinate X'- or XP-level projections. As it turns out, there is evidence that adjectives can take complements and modifiers, justifying a more complete analysis assigning the same overall structure to adjectives that is assigned to other phrasal categories. Consider, in this regard the adjectival phrase *proud of Mary* as in *John was proud of Mary*, in which the adjective *proud* takes a PP complement (notice that *proud* takes on a different sense in its intransitive use — *John was proud*). There are also complex adjectival phrases like *happy because he was green* (as in *John was happy because he was green*) that consist of an adjective (*happy*) that is modified by the optional phrase (*because he was green*). On the basis of this evidence we might posit the Uniform Phrase Structure Hypothesis, requiring that all major phrasal categories have the same internal structure, tentatively captured by the X'-schema. ■

Build a rule system that generates the AdjPs with PP complements. Draw a tree for John is proud of Ringo *using the rule system you have created.*

4.14 More Modifiers

Before leaving the topic of modifiers, we should briefly discuss adverbs, a notoriously complicated aspect of English grammar. Part of this complexity stems from the fact that adverbs fall into several different classes with subtly different distributions. Often classified by their interpretation type, we find time adverbials (like *frequently),* manner adverbs (like *quickly*), place adverbs (like *outside*) and a variety of other adverbs like *even* and *only* that are more difficult to categorize. There are adverbs that seem to modify sentences rather than verbs or verb phrases (adsentences?); *obviously,* as in *Obviously two plus two equals four* is a relevant example.

A second interesting property of adverbs is their ability to appear in multiple phrase-structure positions within a sentence:

1. Suddenly, I lost my grip.
2. I suddenly I lost my grip.
3. *I lost suddenly my grip.
4. *I lost my suddenly grip.
5. I lost my grip suddenly.

Notice, however, that even though there are several acceptable positions, the adverb cannot be located between the verb and its object, or between the determiner and the noun. Adverbs resemble other modifiers in that they are, in general, optional. However,

Consider the distribution of the intrusive like *in the following examples:*

1. I was, like, obese.

2. The, like, only reason you're here is to bring food.

3. I was, like, totally bummed out.

Characterize the distribution of like *(feel free to make up your own examples). Can it go anywhere?*

many adverbs do not allow iteration the way other modifiers do. So, whereas PPs can stack up at the end of the VP in examples like *Mary quit the team in a sudden move without warning on purpose,* the semantically similar **Mary quit the team suddenly unexpectedly purposely* seems odd. Although we cannot do justice to all these facts about adverbs in our analysis, we will incorporate the subclass of manner adverbs in at least one of their positions at the end of the verb phrase. We have introduced other modifiers as daughters of V' but our approach to adverbs must be different to account for their noniterability. The following rule accomplishes this:

VP → V' Adv

The Uniform Phrase Structure Hypothesis seeks to establish a common phrase structure for each major phrasal category based on the principles of X'-theory. In addition to being descriptively motivated, this hypothesis restricts the range of available grammatical options allowed by our theory, consistent with the aim of developing a feasible account of language acquisition. As with our initial analysis of adjectives, our current account of adverbs stands out as inconsistent with the phrasal profile displayed by the other major categories. Here, too, we would expect to find more complicated phrases that invite analysis in terms of heads, specifiers, complements, and modifiers. And once again, we are not disappointed. Adverbs like *quickly* can be modified by other adverbs *(breathtakingly quickly)* or prepositional phrases *(quickly for a duck).* It is also plausible to analyze adverbial phrases like *more quickly than Mary* into the specifier *more,* the head adverb *quickly,* and the complement phrase *than Mary* (although other analyses may be also be possible). We can even combine specifiers and modifiers into a single phrase, like *more breathtakingly quickly than Mary.*

The uniformity of phrase structure across phrasal categories seems to be a design feature of language that is available to be exploited by the child in the process of language acquisition. To the extent that the proper analysis of each phrasal category is analogous to that of every other category, the child is in a position to parlay a relatively small amount of linguistic evidence about the structure of a particular phrase into a far-reaching hypothesis about the structure of all phrases. Of course, being in a position to take advantage of powerful linguistic generalizations is only half the battle: The child must (and does) possess the mental faculty capable of processing information so that the relevant identifications become salient and the useful regularities are extrapolated. And when we develop this sort of hypothesis concerning the nature of linguistic representations and the course of language acquisition, we are on the way to justifying the conviction that language is a "mirror of mind." ∎

IN DETAIL 4.14

Build a rule system that generates AdvPs with PP complements and Adv specifiers. Draw a tree for John ran quickly for a duck *and* John ran awfully fast *using the rule system you have created.*

In conjunction with our other rules (summarized at the beginning of the next section), this new rule allows us to assign the structure below to *I lost my grip suddenly.*

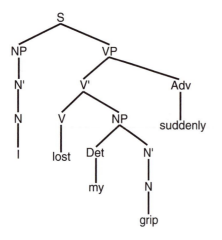

Representation for *I lost my grip suddenly*.

4.15 Specifiers

The current form of our grammar, incorporating the revisions discussed in the previous section, is as follows (eliminating parentheses or other abbreviatory notations):

S → NP VP
S' → Comp S
NP → Det N'
NP → N'
N' → N' PP
N' → Adj N'
N' → N
VP → V' Adv
VP → V'
V' → V' PP
V' → V NP
V' → V S'
V' → V
PP → P NP

Although these fourteen rules are far from exhaustive and are, in places, controversial, they provide a reasonable example of a phrase-structure grammar that generates an impressive portion of English, and reflects some of the insights and analyses found in contemporary linguistic theories. We now move on to develop our account of the interaction between lexical features and phrase-structure rules to further constrain the analysis, concentrating in this section on the head-specifier relationship in the NP.

In our informal characterization of specifiers, we stipulated that the subject NP is a specifier with respect to the VP. We would now like to generalize this analysis and extend the specifier-head relation to the determiner with respect to the head noun in the NP. There are a number of motivations for this move. First, there are close structural parallels between the sentence and the noun phrase that ought to be captured. Notice, for example, that a sentence like *Ringo played the drums* correlates with the NP counterpart *Ringo's playing of the drums,* in which the subject of the sentence appears in the possessive as the determiner of the NP. It is natural to connect these two constructions by assuming that the two forms of *play* are derived from the same root, but there is a deeper generalization we would like to account for: the thematic role *agent* is assigned to the subject in the sentence, and to the determiner in the NP. If we assume that the root *play* assigns the thematic role *agent* to its specifier, and that both the NP subject and the determiner are specifiers in their respective domains, we can unify this analysis, revising our prior account. Finally, there are featural dependencies between the determiner and the head noun that have some of the same properties as the dependencies between the subject NP and the VP. This suggests that we might exploit the same mechanism of feature agreement between the head and its specifier to generalize our account here as well.

More specifically, our earlier observation that the subject and main verb in a clause must agree in the features of number and person (*John walks/*walk into the room*) is paralleled by the new observation that the determiner must agree in number with the head noun (*A dog/*dogs*). Unfortunately, our current grammar does not respect this condition, overgenerating strings like **A dogs died* and **Dog died* as a result. We can enforce number agreement between determiner and the head noun by providing a specifier feature in the lexical entry for each noun indicating what its specifier's number feature value must be. A partial feature assignment for the plural noun *dogs* illustrates our approach:

Dogs	Head Features:	POS = [N], NUMB= [PLURAL],...
	Complement Features:	POS = Null
	Specifier Features:	POS = [Det],NUMB = [PLURAL],...

This assignment guarantees that the plural noun *dogs* occurs with a plural determiner.

Unfortunately, the pattern of agreement between the determiner and the head noun involves more complications. Notice, for example, that singular count nouns like *dog* must co-occur with a determiner, whereas plural nouns like *dogs* take an optional determiner. So, **Dog died* is ungrammatical, whereas both *Dogs died* and *Some dogs died* are well formed. But grammatically singular mass nouns like *stuff* have a different distribution (consider: *Stuff happens, Some stuff happened,* and **Many stuff happened*). Let us revise our

Draw analysis trees for the following sentences:

1. *John fingered the guitar.*

2. *The drummer waited for a long time.*

3. *George brought a vintage guitar.*

4. *Paul wants the guitar on the stage.*

(There are two different trees for the last example.)

Draw analysis trees for One guitar fell *and* Most guitar fell *Discuss and explain the grammatical status of both examples.*

Draw analysis trees for Dogs fell, Guitar fell, The dogs fell, *and* One dogs fell. *Discuss and explain the grammatical status of each example.*

PRO 4.15

Our approach to analyzing English phrase structure has heavily emphasized developing a detailed set of phrase-structure rules that define syntactic structures. These rules have the advantage of being fully explicit, and can be relatively easily tested against larger and larger sets of linguistic data. In this regard, our approach to linguistic theory exhibits the hallmark of most classical approaches to cognitive science: We aim to construct a theory of the mind that contains formalized representations at several levels of analysis, levels that can be manipulated by established principles of information processing and that become invested with meaning in virtue of being "about" features of the world around us.

Construed as such a theory of mental representation, linguistic theory posits a set of rules and principles that characterize the knowledge a language learner brings to the task of language acquisition, as well as the body of linguistic competence attained by a native speaker. In this view, knowledge, be it information about the world, memory, or the representation of a linguistic generalization, takes the form of abstract rule systems and higher-order structures that are applied and instantiated in a derivational, computationally based theory of mind. ■

CON 4.15

Linguistic rule systems may be convenient descriptive devices; but when we intend to develop a theory of mental representation, we must replace higher-order constructs like phrase-structure rules and other linguistic principles with more fundamental units of processing and representation that correspond as nearly as possible to what we know about actual brain structures. In connectionist models, linguistic knowledge, as well as everything else in the mind, is ultimately composed of relatively homogeneous processing units resembling neurons that are not dedicated to any particular special tasks (like the representation of linguistic knowledge). In this view, an internal knowledge state is a network of weighted nodes (in a new sense of the term) directly representing probabilities that determine patterns of associations induced through a training process. During this process, the network learns to tune its internal representations to produce optimal input-output behavior relative to the examples in its training set.

Connectionist models have been developed in many linguistic domains, but one of the most influential is the study due to Rumelhart and McClelland (1986) that investigates the English past tense system and the nature of irregularity (which we discussed briefly in chapter 3). This system is trained on data including inflected and uninflected forms of verbs, and ends up doing a remarkable job of producing appropriate past-tense forms without ever representing a rule for the past tense. If connectionist models of this sort could accomplish their goals for the full range of linguistic generalizations identified by linguists, we would have developed an account of linguistic knowledge in which the very notion of an explicit rule system is unnecessary. In particular, there would be no grounds for positing a mechanism like a phrase-structure grammar, independent of other systems of knowledge; in effect, there would be no grammar at all (see Pinker and Prince 1988; Marcus et al. 1992; Elman et al. 1996). ■

analysis of plural nouns first. The generalization that we want to establish is that a Det is optional, but that if one does appear, it must be plural. Our first move is to restrict the specifier features of the noun to the effect that a specifier is optional, and that the number of the specifier is plural if it appears and null otherwise. Here is the revised partial feature specification for *dogs* that accomplishes this:

Dogs   Head Features: POS = [N], NUMB= [PLURAL],…
       Complement Features: POS = Null
       Specifier Features: POS = [Det]/Null,
                               NUMB = [PLURAL]/Null,…

The assignment for the singular noun *dog* differs in that its head number feature has the value *[SINGULAR]*, as does its specifier number feature.

The analysis for mass nouns like *stuff* involves a more complicated featural analysis. Mass nouns behave like plurals in that they may occur with or without a determiner; but in the event that a determiner is present, it must be a member of the special class of determiners, including *some, most, all,* and *the* (but not *a, one,* or *each*) that can specify mass quantities. We can establish this dependency by refining our earlier analysis of nouns to incorporate the feature *KIND* with the values *[MASS]* and *[COUNT]*, assigning the appropriate values to all determiners (for example, *[COUNT]* to *each* and *[MASS]* to *much*), and making feature assignments to mass nouns look like this (see Sag and Wasow 1996 for further discussion):

Stuff   Head Features: POS = [N], NUMB= [SINGULAR],
                                KIND = [MASS],…
        Complement Features: POS = Null
        Specifier Features: POS = [Det]/Null,
                                KIND = [MASS]/Null

Draw analysis trees for Time flies, Drummer flies, The Time flies, *and* Many time flies. *Discuss and explain the grammatical status of each example.*

English was not always so impoverished in its agreement system. And whereas Modern English largely only exhibits agreement between subjects and predicates, Old English (OE) not only had a much richer system of agreement, but it applied to determiners and nouns as well. For example, Traugott (1972) discusses the example *þis mann* ('this man'), which in OE involved agreement in number, gender, and case (in this case, singular, masculine, and nominative, respectively). Of these three distinctions, only number continues to play a small role in the dependency between determiners and nouns (consider *this man* and *these men,* for example), and even this distinction is not systematically marked in examples like *the man/men.*

What accounts for this type of change in the pattern of a language? Ultimately, we must admit that it is difficult to be sure of the causes for linguistic change in any given case, partly because these causes are wrapped up in social, historical, and political dynamics that defy our understanding (at least at the level of predictive science — see Lightfoot 1979). Despite this caveat, linguists have attempted to characterize the kinds of circumstances that can lead to change. Traugott suggests that the changes to the English agreement system that began insinuating themselves in the transition from Old to Middle English arise from a tendency toward the elimination of redundancy. She points out that the agreement markings in the cases under discussion appeared on both of the linguistic items involved in the agreement relation (the determiner and the noun). Since marking the noun alone suffices to indicate its linguistic status, there is no obvious function achieved by marking both items, and so change is invited. Of course, the change could go in either direction; and in this case, it did. In most English dialects, many of the distinctive forms of the determiners were eliminated to reduce the redundancy. But in AAE, Traugott argues, inflections were lost at the ends of the nouns, producing forms like *Ten boy came* in which the signifier of plurality is the plural determiner, and the noun shows no marking for plural.

Traugott (p. 16) also argues that the task of eliminating unnecessary linguistic redundancy falls to the children. For it is in the learning process that the primary linguistic data must be freshly analyzed by each successive generation of language learners, opening the door to a systematic restructuring of a language's grammar during the process of language acquisition. ■

Number agreement does not ordinarily involve dependencies between arguments and complements. So, although the subject *John* is singular in *John sees the fans,* the number of the complement is independent of this value; and in this case, the object NP *the fans* is plural. There are, however, a small number of cases involving verbs like *is, struck,* and *regard* that require agreement between an argument and a complement:

1. Ringo is a talented singer.
2. *Ringo is talented singers.
3. The other Beatles regarded John as a recluse.
4. *The other Beatles regarded John as recluses.
5. *The other Beatles struck John as a usurper.
6. The other Beatles struck John as usurpers.

In the first pair of examples, the singular subject *Ringo* must agree in number with the verbal complement *a talented singer.* Examples (3) and (4) involve the verb *regarded,* which takes as its complement an NP followed by an *as*-phrase. What is interesting about this example is that the object of *regarded* (in this case, the singular NP *John*) must agree in number with the object of *as.* The final pair of examples is superficially similar to the previous pair, except here, number agreement must obtain between the subject NP *John,* and the object of the *as*-complement. What unifies these three examples is the predicative role played by the NP complement participating in the number-agreement relation. That is, whereas the normal interpretation of an NP like *a singer* in a sentence like *A singer arrived* involves a singer to whom is attributed the property of arriving, in (1) the occurrence of this NP seems to express a property that the subject, *John,* is asserted to possess. Such occurrences are termed "predicative" because the NP in question plays the semantic role normally discharged by other property-expressing parts of speech (predicates) such as adjectives. (In support of this point, note the similarity in meaning between *John is foolish and John is a fool.*) The NP-objects of *as* in (3) through (6) also function as predicative NPs. The difference in agreement behavior between the last two pairs of examples correlates with the argument structure of the predicate NPs — in (3) and (4) the object NP *John* serves as the logical subject of the NP predicate, and in (5) and (6), the grammatical subject NP *the other Beatles* plays this role.

Although it may be possible to extend our feature-based approach

to number agreement to handle these cases by properly specifying the feature-assignment matrices for special verbs like *be, struck,* and *regarded,* to do so would introduce considerable complication. Especially in the case of examples (3) through (6), one of the items involved in the number agreement relation, the *as*-object, isn't even an argument of the verb (but rather, a subconstituent of the verbal complement), requiring some very fancy feature checking to describe the dependencies involved (see Sag and Wasow 1996). A second alternative would be to develop an independent account of predicate-argument structure, tying the number of the predicate NP to the number of its logical subject. In this view, logical subjects may participate in number-agreement dependencies, even when they do not appear as specifiers in the syntactic analysis. Developing principles that link the form of syntactic items to their functional role rather than to their syntactic role is what motivates the theory of grammar known as "Lexico-Functional Grammar" (see Sells 1985 for discussion).

Another possible line of attack (and one which we return to below in addressing a related problem), involves complicating the syntactic analysis of examples like (3) through (6) to include an understood subject in a complement phrase that includes the predicative NP. In this

approach, for example, the structure of the (3) might (informally) be

The other Beatles regarded John as Pro a recluse.

where Pro designates a silent pronoun that is semantically interpreted as the subject of *recluse,* but is phonetically null. In this analysis, number agreement can be analyzed as "local" between the predicate *a recluse* and its subject, Pro, with the feature value *[SINGULAR]* also needing to match that of the antecedent of Pro. In (3), the case at hand, the antecedent is the object *John,* accounting indirectly for number agreement between *John* and *a recluse.* In the contrasting case, (6),

The other Beatles struck John as Pro usurpers.

we find number agreement between *the other Beatles* and *usurpers* because the subject NP *the other Beatles* is the antecedent for Pro. ∎

4.16 Case

We noted earlier that pronouns can appear in a number of different case forms, as illustrated by the contrast between *she* and *her,* for example. In our lexical entries for pronouns, we assigned them *CASE* feature values such as *[NOMINATIVE]* and *[ACCUSATIVE]* to distinguish the different subcategories of items. There still is a residual problem, however. It is not enough to provide a means for generating alternative case forms for each pronoun; we must also ensure that the different case-marked forms are properly distributed. Nominative forms of pronouns are generally restricted to subject position in English (*I/*me won*), whereas accusative forms have a broader distribution. For example, objects of transitive verbs are in the accusative (*I saw him/*he*), as are the objects of prepositions (*I stood near her/*she*). We can establish these correlations by treating *CASE* as a head feature for pronouns. We must also exploit the feature system to capture the dependency between the case form of a pronoun and its surface structure position. Suppose we stipulate that the specifier features for a verb require that its specifier (that is, the subject of the sentence) must be an NP in the nominative case. Here is a sample lexical feature assignment for *dine* that illustrates this approach:

Dine	Head Features:	POS = [V],…
	Complement Features:	POS = Null
	Specifier Features:	POS = [NP],
		CASE = [NOMINATIVE],…

Dine is categorized as intransitive by virtue of the fact that its complement feature specification is *null*. Its specifier features require it to have a subject NP that bears the *CASE* feature value *[NOMINATIVE]*, sanctioning examples like *I won* and blocking **Me won*. Transitive verbs like *devour* will also have this set of specifier features since the case properties of their subjects are identical to those of the subjects of intransitive verbs. However, their complement features are, of course different:

Devour	Head Features:	POS = [V],…
	Complement Features:	POS = NP,
		CASE = [ACCUSATIVE],…
	Specifier Features:	POS = [NP],
		CASE = [NOMINATIVE],…

Draw analysis trees for They waited nervously *and* Them waited nervously. *Discuss and explain the grammatical status of both examples.*

Draw analysis trees for Ella brought her, Ella brought he, He brought me, *and* Him brought I. *Discuss and explain the grammatical status of each example.*

What kind of case do prepositions assign to their objects? Draw analysis trees for Billie waited for him *and* Billie waited for they *and discuss and explain the grammatical status of both examples.*

Here the feature assignment for the complement to *devour* requires an accusative NP, generating *I devoured them* but not **I devoured they.*

To this point, we have been implicitly restricting the range of our analysis to pronouns, since these are the only items in English that inflect for nominative and accusative case. For example, the form of the word *dogs* is invariant whether it is the subject *(Dogs run)*, the object *(I like dogs)*, or the object of a preposition *(Cats come before dogs)*. Now it is possible that nonpronominal nouns bear the abstract feature *CASE,* and even the feature values *[NOMINATIVE]* and *[ACCUSATIVE]*, although there is no phonetic manifestation of this marking. Another possibility is that the *CASE* feature distribution is restricted to pronouns, as we have more or less been assuming. As in other cases of featural analysis, we need evidence to settle the matter.

There are two considerations that bear on this question, one theoretical and one empirical. The first is that, as our lexical approach to case is currently framed, we actually have to complicate our analysis if we limit the distribution of the *CASE* feature to pronouns. That is, as they are written, the complement and specifier feature specifications for transitive and intransitive verbs and prepositions constrain the case-feature values for NP subjects and NP objects (if any) quite generally, independent of whether the NP is a pronoun or a common noun. If NPs like *dogs* do not bear *CASE* feature values, then they cannot appear as subjects, objects, or prepositional objects, since the presence of the appropriate *CASE* feature values is strictly required. Furthermore, we would have to extend our theory of feature assignments considerably to require that having the appropriate case values matters only if an NP is headed by a pronoun. It is simpler to assume that all nouns bear abstract case features (see Sag and Wasow 1996 for further discussion).

Second, we have been assuming that case dependencies are established by a verb or preposition, and that an NP bearing the appropriate *CASE* feature value must satisfy the case demands that are placed upon it (let's call this "having your case checked"). Suppose we generalize this requirement, making it more symmetrical, by also requiring every NP to appear in a position in which a verb or preposition can check the case of the NP. This is called the *Case Checking Principle.*

As our analysis stands, verbs establish featural requirements for their specifiers and complements by incorporating into their lexical entries specifier and complement features that must match the head features of the appropriate arguments. However, in circumstances in which arguments are rooted in phrasal projections like NP, we encounter a technical problem. Let's consider a simple sentence like *The critic dined* to illustrate the situation:

The features that we must check (like the case feature value *[NOMINA-TIVE]*) are listed in the lexical entry for the head noun *critic* of the subject NP, but it is the NP *the critic,* as a whole, that counts as the specifier of the verb *dine.* Although NPs do not manifest nominative case directly, we want to treat NPs dominating nominative nouns as themselves being nominative, in order for our feature-matching conventions to work properly.

We can accomplish this by associating feature matrices with X' and XP projections, and requiring that the values for certain features (including case features) for these projections must match the values for the head — a constraint called the Head Feature Constraint (see Sag and Wasow 1996). Notice that not all features are subject to this constraint. For example, the value for the *POS* head feature must not be inherited by X' and XP projections, since, by convention, the node label is really just a redundant way of stating the *POS* feature value. If we let *POS* feature values get inherited, we would have NPs with the *POS* feature value *[N],* which is a contradiction in terms.

On the other hand, the number and person features also fall under the Head Feature Constraint to allow us to treat branching NPs that dominate nouns with particular constellations of features as being marked just like their heads. (The theta features to be discussed below must also be treated in this way.) ∎

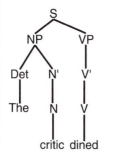

Representation for *The critic dined.*

The *CASE* feature.

Case Checking Principle
Every NP must have its case checked by a verb or a preposition.

We can exploit this principle to explain distributional patterns in English phrase structure that previously have been merely stipulated. For example, we noted above that there were interesting parallels between the structure of the NP and the structure of the sentence. In particular, both types of constituents have specifiers; Det in the case of NP, and NP in the case of S. In defense of this observation, we might note examples like *Pete destroyed the guitar* and *Pete's destruction of the guitar,* an S and NP, respectively. These data illustrate that the thematic relation between the form of *destroy* and its specifier is the same in each case. We might also note that the thematic role *theme* that is assigned to the object of the verb (*the guitar*) is assigned to the PP *of the guitar* in the NP, more evidence for the parallelism between the two constructions. But why, we may wonder, does the NP object of *destroy* turn up as a PP in the syntactic context of the NP; why not just have **Pete's destruction the guitar?* Moreover, why does the specifier for the NP turn out to be a determiner, whereas the specifier of the S is an NP? We might just as well expect **Pete destruction the guitar* as a legal NP.

One answer is that the phrase-structure rules prohibit these alternative constructions — NPs are subjects of sentences, not NPs; and nouns do not take NP objects. But if we inquire as to why these restrictions are the way they are, our theory of phrase-structure rules provides no answer. In fact, it is just as easy to write phrase-structure rules describing the ungrammatical possibilities as it is those describing the grammatical ones. The Case Checking Principle illuminates this mystery in a more satisfying way: a phrase with an N head could not have an NP specifier because the N is not capable of checking the case of its specifier (since only V and P can check case). Similarly, if an N head of an NP introduced an NP (for example, **Pete's destruction the guitar*), nothing would check the case of the NP *the guitar.* By incorporating this NP within a PP (*Pete's destruction of the guitar*), the Case Checking Principle is satisfied with respect to the NP *the guitar* by the preposition *of.* By applying this principle, we can begin to view the distributions expressed by the phrase-structure rules in a more principled light. As a consequence, we continue to extend our analysis of case to include the assignment of abstract case features to nonpronominal nouns in order to maintain our account of these kinds of generalizations (see Radford 1997 for further discussion).

The Case Checking Principle allows us to correlate the presence or absence of an object NP with the valence of a verb. We must also continue to constrain other combinations of verbs and complements. For example, intransitive verbs like *dine* can appear either alone (*I dined*) or with a PP modifier (*I dined on cod*), but they cannot take subordinate clause complements (**I dined that Paul sang*). In this regard, such verbs contrast with verbs like *hope*, which take subordinate clause complements, but cannot appear as simple intransitives (consider, **John hoped* and *John hoped that Paul was guilty*). For these circumstances, we must check the complement POS

Draw analysis trees for Ringo fingered the guitar, Ringo brought with Paul nervously, *and* Ringo waited the guitar. *Discuss and explain the grammatical status of each example.*

Investigations of the Case Checking Principle have yielded a number of interesting further restrictions on its application, one of which we have already encountered when we considered the distribution of adverbs like *suddenly,* which was of interest because such adverbs can appear in several different phrase-structure positions. Recall, however, that one position in which *suddenly* may not appear is in-between a verb and its object:

1. Suddenly I lost my grip.
2. I suddenly lost my grip.
3. *I lost suddenly my grip.
4. I lost my grip suddenly.

This restriction can be described by requiring that a case-checking verb

be adjacent to its complement NP. In the case of (3), the adverb *suddenly* intervenes between the verb and its object, running afoul of this adjacency requirement. In more complicated examples like *John wants him to leave* we see the same principle at work. Note first that *want* checks the accusative case of the pronoun *him.* Now, consider the following data:

5. Definitely John wants him to leave.
6. John definitely wants him to leave.
7. *John wants definitely him to leave.
8. John wants him definitely to leave.

Example (7) is ungrammatical because *definitely* interrupts the adjacency between *want* and *him.* Finally, notice that in each of these last paradigms it does not matter whether the case that is checked is overtly marked on the complement NP (as it is in [7]), or whether it is abstract (as it is in [3]). In both situations, the adjacency requirement must be respected. This counts as additional evidence in favor of the abstract-case hypothesis under discussion. ■

feature value for the verb, making sure that appropriate complements are selected. Here is the updated feature specification for hope:

Hope	Head Features:	POS = [V],…
	Complement Features:	POS = [S']
	Specifier Features:	POS = [NP],
		CASE = [NOMINATIVE],…

4.17 Theta Checking

Let us now explore one other checking principle, this one pertaining to thematic roles. As with the Case Checking Principle, our concern is to establish a kind of well-formedness condition on phrase structure by distilling a principle that ensures that thematic roles are properly assigned. Thus far we have considered thematic roles to be assigned on the basis of lexical information associated with the entry for each verb. In this view, the verb licenses thematic roles; and NPs simply bear them, provided the NPs are in the proper phrase-structure positions (for example, specifier position).

Draw an analysis tree for I said that he fell for her. *Draw a second tree in which you substitute* them *for* I, me *for* he, *and* she *for* her. *Discuss and explain the grammatical status of each example.*

There are two assumptions implicit in this approach to thematic role assignment that we want to make explicit and to challenge. The first is that any NP can bear a thematic role. This conclusion seems warranted, because there is no morphological inflection associated with different thematic roles. For example, the noun *dogs* takes the same unmarked form no matter be it the agent (in *Dogs make good pets*) or the theme (in *He walks dogs for a living*). However, there is a tiny number of lexical nouns that cannot receive a thematic role from a licensing verb; and our analysis must somehow capture this property. One example of a nonthematic-role bearing NP is the existential *there*. Not to be confused with the *homophonous locative there* (the *there* of *I stood there*), the existential *there* appears in sentences like *There is a fly in your soup.* Notice that this sentence means pretty much the same thing as *A fly is in your soup,* and that is the nub of the problem.

Once we characterize the thematic relations between the verb *is,* the NP *a fly* (its *theme*), and the NP *your soup* (which in the context of its containing PP is assigned the role *location*), there simply is no additional role to assign to *there.* Moreover, if we consider the interpretation of *There is a fly in your soup,* we notice that *there* does not refer to anything and does not play a role in the thematic structure.

A second example of a nonthematic NP is the pronoun *it,* again in some, but not all, of its uses. If we concentrate on constructions like *It is easy to win the game* and *It happens that you are right,* we see cases in which the *it* fails to refer to a theme or an agent that is implicated in the action structure of the sentence. We can call this type of *it* the "dummy" *it.* Both in the case of the existential *there* and the case of the dummy *it,* we must constrain lexical insertion so that these items are only inserted in phrase-structure positions in which they are not associated with a thematic role. If we violate this restriction, one of two things happens: we either produce an ungrammatical string (**There hit the ball*) or we read the occurrence of *there* or *it* as the homophonous locative or referential item (*It fell down*).

There is also a second assumption we need to reconsider. By incorporating information about thematic role assignment into the lexical entries for verbs, we have provided a mechanism to ensure that a verb with a thematic role to assign has an NP to assign it to. But what about the reverse situation? Suppose that an NP ends up in a phrase-structure position reserved for either the dummy *it* or

Draw an analysis tree for It seems that the slow, adventurous drummer waited for Paul. *Draw a second tree in which you substitute* hoped *for* seems. *Does the interpretation of* it *shift? Explain your answer.*

the existential *there*. The following data bear on this question:

1. It seems that you win.
2. *John seems that you win.
3. It is nice to see you.
4. *Bill is nice to see you.
5. It was believed that the earth was flat.
6. *Mary was believed that the earth was flat.
7. There exists no good solution.
8. *Collaboration exists no good solution.
9. Suddenly, there appeared a ghost in the garden.
10. *Suddenly, Hugh appeared a ghost in the garden.

In the ungrammatical examples, each of the verbs fails to assign a thematic role to the NP in the first subject position. For example, in *Mary believed the earth was flat, Mary* is not thematically linked to the passive verb *was believed,* making *it* the only item appropriate to this position (compare *Mary believed that the earth was flat* in which the active verb *believed* assigns the *agent* thematic role to *Mary).*

One way to ensure that all NPs except the dummy *it* and the existential *there* must receive a thematic role is to establish for all nouns the head feature *THETA,* with the values *[+]* and *[-]. [+],* which signifies that a noun must receive a thematic role, is the value for all nouns except for the two non-thematic elements *it* and *there,* which are assigned *[-].* Each verb incorporates the feature *THETA* into its specifier and complement features, as appropriate, with the value set according to whether the verb assigns a thematic role to each argument. There are other ways of implementing this generalization (perhaps collapsing the mechanism that checks the thematic status of an argument with the mechanism that assigns a particular thematic role); but more generally, we want to adopt the following principle:

Theta Criterion
Every thematic NP must receive a thematic role and every non-thematic NP must not receive a thematic role.

One interesting consequence of this approach is that it predicts that prepositions must also assign thematic roles and check the *THETA* feature, on pain of blocking NPs from appearing in PPs (since all thematic NPs must receive a thematic role). But this is a natural conclusion in that the choice of preposition often affects the thematic structure of a sentence. For example, in *John sang near Ringo, Ringo* is assigned a *locative* role whereas in *John sang to Ringo,*

Draw analysis trees for It snowed suddenly *and* I said that it seems that Ella waited. *Substitute another noun for* it *in both sentences. Discuss and explain the grammatical status of each example.*

IN DETAIL 4.17

The adoption of a phrase-structure grammar to capture the organization of English phrase structure has been a standard assumption in virtually every version of linguistic theory that has been developed from the early 1960s to the early 1990s. For while many linguists believed that standard phrase-structure grammars were not sufficient to describe the syntactic pattern of a natural language, most thought that they were at least necessary to accomplish this task. In the early 1990s, this assumption was challenged by an innovative approach to syntactic theory: Noting the kinds of information posited by newer versions of syntactic theory, proponents of *minimalism* began to argue that, in combination with other rules and principles, this enriched theory of the lexicon rendered the phrase-structure component otiose (see Chomsky 1995; and the essays in Barbosa et al. 1998). We can get some idea of the force of this argument by reminding ourselves of some of the dependencies we are currently capturing on the basis of lexical feature assignments. Since we can control values for features like *POS, NUMBER, PERSON, CASE, THETA,* and so forth for heads, specifiers and complements, we have the ability to match appropriate phrasal constituents with one another, strictly on the basis of lexical information.

And that is where the redundancy with respect to the phrase-structure rules is introduced. Suppose, for example, that we eliminate the phrase-structure component of the grammar and, throwing caution to the wind, allow any combination of constituents to form a V'. Suppose further that the verb we choose to incorporate into a putative V' is the transitive verb *devour.* Now, in a moment of syntactic bravura, we might try to build a VP out of *devour* and the PP *on the chicken:*

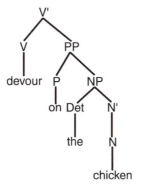

Representation of **devour on the chicken.*

However, since the complement features of *devour* require that it take an complement with the *POS* feature value *[NP],* a *THETA* feature value *[+],* and a *CASE* feature value *[NOMINATIVE],* this structure can be ruled out because it violates the feature-checking principles we have established. Perhaps now you can see why the phrase-structure rule V' → V NP is not strictly necessary: The generaliza-

tion that a verb can be followed by an NP is already written in the lexical entry for every transitive verb.

Of course, showing that one phrase-structure rule is redundant does not demonstrate that all phrase-structure rules are. And until we are certain that all of the regularities captured by these rules can be recaptured by lexical analysis, we are not justified in eliminating the phrase-structure component completely. Still, as the proponents of minimalism argue, it is clear that many phrase-structure generalizations already are restated in lexical terms; for example, the fact that the specifiers of nouns are determiners, that the objects of prepositions are NPs, and the subjects of sentences are NPs follows from feature specifications we have incorporated into lexical entries.

From this point of view, it seems reasonable to drop the phrase-structure component from the theory, replacing it with a far simpler operation called *merge,* which combines any two constituents together to form a new constituent.

Needless to say, we must also further develop our theory of the lexicon, buttressed by other linguistic principles, to filter out the (many) illicit combinations that the merge operation tolerates. Although minimalism is a very new approach to syntactic analysis, it has already been quite influential and equally controversial (see Radford 1997). ■

the *patient* role (indicating the receiver of an action) is assigned. We therefore modify our analysis of prepositions to allow them to check *THETA* status and assign thematic roles. An example feature assignment for *near* illustrates our approach:

Near	Head Features:	POS = [P],…
	Complement Features:	POS = [NP], THETA = [+],…
	Specifier Features:	POS = Null
	Thematic Assignment:	COMPLEMENT = [LOCATIVE]

4.18 Displacement

In our analysis of English syntax to this point, we have deployed a two-pronged analysis: (1) we defined a phrase-structure grammar, and (2) we developed an approach to lexical entries with a multi-level feature matrix that constrains lexical insertion in particular ways so as to capture dependencies among heads, specifiers, complements, and modifiers. We now discuss another syntactic dependency that goes beyond head-specifier-complement relations, what we might call a "nonlocal" dependency. As we shall see, there are several subclasses of nonlocal dependencies, each of which poses a slightly different challenge to our analysis. Our emphasis is on generally characterizing the phenomena in question, rather than on establishing any particular analysis.

Let us begin by returning to our account of *The people talked over the noise*. We argued that this example should receive two distinct syntactic analyses: one in which the complex verb *talked over* is a constituent, and one in which the PP *over the noise* is a constituent. Against this background, consider the following data:

1. The people shouted over the noise
2. Over the noise, the people shouted.

We have incorporated the verb *shouted* to force a PP constituency to be assigned in these examples. The second sentence can be seen as a stylistic alternative to the first in that both examples have the same *truth conditions* (the conditions under which a sentence is true), and both exhibit the same internal thematic relations. More importantly for our present discussion, in each case the PP *over the noise* modifies the verb *shouted*. Therein lies the difficulty. In our previous discussion of modification, we assumed that modifiers are sisters to the X' phrases they modify. This requirement is met in

Sentences like The people talked over the noise *are ambiguous (either they discussed the noise, or they shouted over it). Against this background, consider the following example:*

Over the noise, the people talked.

Explain why this example has only the shouted *interpretation and why the other reading disappears.*

example (1) (as it has been in all previously discussed examples), as the analysis tree below illustrates.

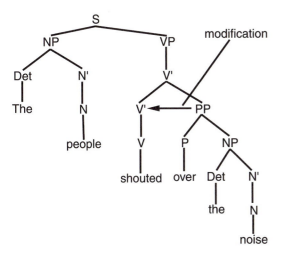

Representation for *The people shouted over the noise.*

However, in the structure assigned to the second example, the PP is obviously not a sister to the V' that it modifies. Here is one possible analysis of what this structure looks like (below).

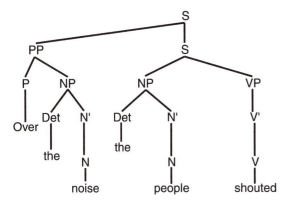

Representation for *Over the noise, the people shouted.*

In circumstances in which a normally local dependency (like the modification relation) must be enforced nonlocally we have a *displacement* effect. The descriptive challenge in such cases is to establish a linguistic dependency between items that are not in canonical phrase-structure positions with respect to one another.

The possibility of displacement complicates a linguistic system considerably. We must not only determine when a constituent exhibits the displacement effect, but we must also develop a mechanism that can establish the appropriate linguistic dependencies (in this case, the relation of modification) in a nonlocal domain. To put this point more simply, until now we have been tacitly assuming that English has the W.Y.S.I.W.Y.G. ("What you see is what you get") property in the following sense: the interpretation of each linguistic element is determined with respect to the phrase-structure position in which it occurs. While it is not obvious that this position cannot be maintained (see below), it is clear at least here that local constituent relations defined by phrase-structure grammar alone cannot systematically account for modification.

Consider the number agreement facts in the following examples:

1. That dog I know eats dry food.

2.*That dog I know eat dry food.

3.*Those dogs I know eats dry food.

4. Those dogs I know eat dry food.

Discuss the challenges these facts pose for the current analysis of number agreement.

4.19 Generalizing the Problem

Before discussing some possible approaches to the displacement problem, we need to appreciate how deep it runs in the grammar of English. After all, if displacement were only of concern in the case with PP modifiers, we might well be able to get by with an ad hoc explanation. On the other hand, if PP modification is only the tip of the iceberg, we are forced to develop a more systematic approach. As you might have guessed, displacement turns out to be a problem of titanic proportions. Let's begin our investigation by considering a class of constructions that involve the displacement of NP arguments. Here are some data to get us started:

1. Ollie clawed the sofa
2. The sofa was clawed by Ollie.
3. John started the car quickly.
4. The car started quickly.

The first and third sentences are unexceptional; it is the contrast of each of these examples with its successor that interests us here. In each of the latter cases, the subject of the sentence (*the sofa* and *the car*) is the *theme,* the thematic role normally assigned to the object of the verb. Moreover, in (2), a so-called passive sentence, the PP *by Ollie* is assigned the *agent* thematic role (which is normally assigned to the subject of the verb). Concentrating for the moment on the assignment of the role *theme,* we can identify the situation in (2) and (4) as an instance of displacement: *theme* is assigned to an NP located outside of verbal complement position (the phrase- structure position where *theme* is normally assigned).

A second facet to the displacement effect, as manifest in these examples, pertains to the checking of the verb's complement features. In each sentence, the verbs (*clawed* and *started*) are transitive — a fact that is motivated by the ungrammaticality of **Ollie clawed* and **John started* (in the relevant sense of *started*). In our current analysis, that means that these verbs have the *POS* feature value *[NP]* listed in their complement feature matrix.

Nevertheless, in (2) and (4) the object of the verb is missing, yet the sentence is grammatical. Furthermore, in the absence of an object, the verb cannot check accusative case, again in apparent violation of the complement feature specification associated with transitive verbs. In sum, it is as if the transitive verbs *clawed* and *started* in (1) and (3) have been detransitivized (in that they have lost an argument); and the one remaining argument, the subject, has been reassigned the thematic role normally reserved for the object.

In these examples, the displaced objects occupy subject position. Since the canonical position for these items is object position, and both subjects and objects are arguments to the verb, we refer to this type of displacement as argument displacement (A-displacement). A second class of phenomenon involving displaced constituents is called A'-displacement (read "A-bar displacement," where the bar is a set-theoretic notation meaning roughly 'the opposite of...' — not to be confused with N' or V'). In this type of case, the displaced element appears in a nonargument position; here are some examples:

1. That kind of person, I love.
2. Who do you love?
3. The person who I love is married.

The first sentence is an example of a *topicalization* — a construction in which an NP topic appears to the left of the subject, but still receives its thematic role from a nonlocal verb. Notice that the case checking of the topic NP is also a problem, since there is no obvious item that can check the case of an NP in this position. In this example, accusative case must be assigned, as the contrast between *Him, I love* and **He, I love* makes plain. The second example, a so-called *Wh-question,* also manifests these curious properties, with one additional complication: the mysterious appearance of the function word *do.* Notice that if we embed this type of example as a subordinate clause, the *do* disappears, as for example, in *I wonder who you love.*

Finally, in the third example, called a (restrictive) *relative clause,* we find an occurrence of the displaced item *who,* which seems to function here as pronoun (a relative pronoun) that plays two roles: It bears the *theme* thematic role that would normally be assigned to the object of *love,* and it somehow relays that role to *the person,* which determines the entity that the subject *I* is in the love relation to. A rather complicated state of affairs!

As with A-displacement, each of these examples of A'-displacement incorporates a transitive verb (*love*) that cannot check its complement features in the absence of a local object. A'-displacement also exemplifies another characteristic that makes the dependency between the verb and its displaced argument even more impressive: the displaced argument can be indefinitely far away from the verb that assigns its thematic role *(What did Bill think that Sue determined*

Here are some other main clause Wh-questions that do not involve the appearance of do. *Can you describe the conditions that seem to require* do? *(In other words, what makes these cases different from those that require* do?)*

1. What can you say?

2. Who would you think ate the beans?

3. Why should I help you?

The last two examples (repeated below) each involve a complex Wh-constituent of which the Wh-word is merely a part.

1. How tall did he seem?
2. Near whom did she stand?

The displaced constituent is therefore larger than the Wh-constituent. For example the displaced PP in (2) presumably has the following structure:

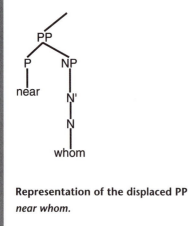

Representation of the displaced PP *near whom.*

Such cases are sometimes called *pied-piping* constructions, a term that recalls the mythic ability of the Pied Piper of Hamelin to induce large number of rodents to follow him helplessly to their deaths. In the case of linguistic analysis, the stakes are admittedly lower; but languages still differ interestingly in how they cope with pied-piping. Notice for example, that in there is a non-pied-piped alternative to (2), but not for (1):

1. How tall did he seem?
1'. *How did he seem tall?
2. Near whom did she stand?
2'. Who(m) did she stand near?

In fact, the non-pied-piped version in (2') is much more colloquial that the pied-piped alternative, an observation that contradicts the traditional prescriptive injunction against so-called dangling prepositions (which could in any event be rephrased as: "always pied pipe").

Although English is probably in the mainstream in requiring pied-piping in (1)–(1'), the optionality of pied-piping in (2)–(2') is relatively rare, especially in *Indo-European* languages spoken in Europe and the United States. To test this claim, you might check to see if you know another language that allows constructions like (2'). ∎

Many speakers of English say Near <u>whom</u> did she stand? *but* <u>Who</u> did she stand near? *Can you suggest a principle that explains these facts (you may want to consider grammar-based and non-grammar-based explanations).*

that Harry feared…that Mary knew?). And unlike A-displacement, some instances of A'-displacement can involve displaced constituents from one of several different syntactic categories. We use Wh-questions as an illustrative example:

1. <u>Who</u> did you know? (NP)
2. <u>How</u> did you know? (Adv)
3. <u>How tall</u> did he seem? (Adj)
4. <u>Near whom</u> did she stand? (PP)

In the following examples, identify the syntactic category to which each of the displaced items belongs. Justify your answers.

1. Who told the person to whom you spoke to leave?

2. How thin did he get?

3. How did you know where to go?

4. In the book, Bill knew why he lost.

4.20 Approaches to Displacement

Since all contemporary syntactic theories consider A-displacement and A'-displacement to be different classes of phenomena, we discuss them separately.

In the case of A-displacement, there are two major approaches, each of which has a following and is incorporated into modern research programs in linguistic theory. Our purpose here is not to settle on a particular analysis, but merely to describe the theoretical perspectives representing the current state of inquiry.

The first approach is known as the lexicalist approach. At the heart of this style of analysis is the intuition that a more sophisticated conception of lexical rules allows us to capture the dependencies between heads and displaced constituents. In this view, we must develop mechanisms that extend the domains in which lexical features are checked so that nonlocal dependencies can be established. There are two steps in this process. First, we posit a set of rules that derive new lexical items from existing roots. For example, in the case of a passive sentence like *The song was sung*, the root *sing* is entered in the lexicon with the complement *POS* feature value *[NP]* (since it is transitive), and with the complement *CASE* feature value *[ACCUSATIVE]*. It is also listed as verb that assigns the thematic role *theme* to its complement, and *agent* to its specifier. A lexical rule that we can call the Passive Rule derives a new lexical item based on the root *sing* (a passive verb) with a rather different feature matrix: The specifier and complement feature values for this new verb are set to "null," and only the single thematic role *theme* is assigned to its specifier. Finally, the *V-FORM* head feature value is set to *[PASSIVE]* to reflect that passive verbs have a special morphological marking (distinctive in the case of *sing/sung*, but sometimes indistinguishable from the past tense form of the verb — consider *John was killed* in which *killed* is the passive verb).

Sung	Head Features:	POS = [V], V-FORM = [PASSIVE],…
	Complement Features:	Null
	Specifier Features:	Null
	Thematic Assignment:	Specifier = [THEME]

We must also assume that the helping verb *was* is associated with a feature matrix that allows it to take passive verbs in its complement. This is accomplished by setting the value for the complement *V-FORM* feature for *was* to *[PASSIVE]*. This licenses the analysis shown at right (assuming that we adopt a new VP-rule that allows

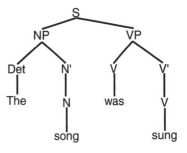

Representation for *The song was sung*.

VP to dominate V followed by V', which will be necessary in any event if we want to incorporate other helping verbs into the grammar).

This analysis raises many questions, and further complications need to be addressed to make it complete, but this overview should suffice to suggest how a lexicalist approach to passive (and other cases of A-displacement) would proceed.

We now briefly consider a second approach to A-displacement we will call the transformational approach, which adopts a quite different analytic framework. It provides a mechanism for deriving passive verbs like *sung*, but it associates somewhat different lexical properties with this class of verbs. As in the previous analysis, passive verbs are treated as detransitivized (meaning that their complement *POS* features and *CASE* features are erased); but they continue to assign the thematic role *theme* to their complement NP.

This decision is based on a commitment to a principle defended in Baker (1988), called "UTAH — the Uniform Theta Assignment Hypothesis" — according to which both the active and passive forms of the verb must assign *theme* to the same phrase-structure position (see Radford 1997 for further discussion). As a consequence, the analysis tree for the passive VP in the sentence *The song was sung* looks something like the one shown at right.

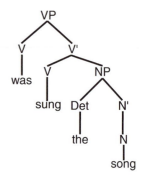

Representation for a passive VP.

The V' in this tree is identical in structure to one that dominates an active verb, with the NP object *the song* in normal object position. It is important to notice that in the transformational approach to passive, we build up the representation for the passive VP as a free-standing phrase. What remains is to incorporate the passive VP into a larger sentence structure. We accomplish this by *merging* the passive VP with an NP subject to form an S, at the same time *moving* the object NP *the song* into the newly incorporated subject position.

The operation that moves the object NP into subject position is called a *transformation,* more specifically, a *movement* transformation. Notice that the position evacuated by the object NP now contains a *trace* (abbreviated *t*) which is considered to be syntactically linked to the displaced NP constituent. The linkage between a displaced constituent and its trace forms a *chain* with a "head" (the displaced constituent) and a "foot" (the trace). After the passive VP gets incorporated into the larger S-structure, the passive verb can still assign *theme* to its complement, now construed to be the trace of movement. By convention, we allow any thematic roles assigned to the foot of a binding chain to be "inherited" by the head of the

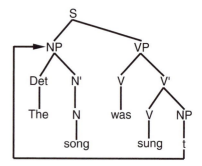

Merging to form a passive.

Harris (1956) proposed the following analysis of the passive:

It is possible to find in a language two or more constructions which contain the same constituents (in a different order, or with added material), e.g. N'$_i$ tV N'$_j$ and N'$_j$ is Ven by N$_i$ (People are killed by the bomb). In such cases, if the two constructions are satisfied by the same n-tuples of members of their constituents, we say that the two constructions are transforms of each other.

Harris uses N' where we would write NP, and he uses the separate category labels tV and V to mark the difference between transitive and intransitive verbs (Ven signifies a verb with passive morphology). But more importantly, his conception of a transformation is quite a bit different from ours: "…Transformations can be viewed as an equivalence relation among sentences or certain constituents of sentences." Construed in this way, transformations define sets of sentences whose correspondence to one another can be characterized as a transformational relation of a certain type (for example, the passive relation described above). In contrast, in contemporary transformational analysis, transformations have a derivational character, applying to phrase-structure representations to derive new phrase-structure representations.

In the four decades since Harris's initial proposal, the precise conception of the derivational characteristics of transformations has changed considerably. In the early generative analyses of the later 1950s, transformations applied to sets of basic representations for "kernel" sentences (a term introduced by Harris, incidentally), combining them in various ways to generate the set of derived sentences of a language (see Chomsky 1957 for an example of this type of analysis). In the 1960s, transformations were reconceived to apply to a single underlying representation (a *deep structure*), converting it eventually to a final representation (a *surface structure*) that

corresponded closely to the sentence as it was actually pronounced (see Chomsky 1965).

In this approach (developed at the same time that phonological derivations mapping from phonemic to phonetic representations were being developed, see chapter 2), the deep structure underlying the active form of a sentence could optionally undergo a passive transformation. This rule reordered the subject and object NPs, changed the verbal morphology, and built an agentive PP (converting the deep structure for *John sang harmony* into the surface structure for *Harmony was sung by John.* ■

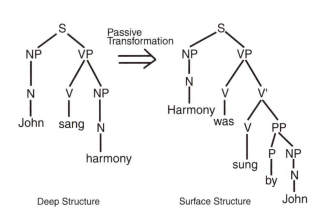

A derivation from deep structure to surface structure.

PRO 4.20

Within the linguistic framework under discussion, the recruitment of transformations to capture syntactic dependencies between a displaced item and its underlying position is motivated by the need to explain a cluster of properties that would otherwise be lost as a linguistic generalization. As a case in point, consider the behavior of three phenomena, Wh-movement, passive, and reflexive binding, in the context of coordinate structures (structures involving conjunction).

1. *Who did you see Bill and *t?*
2. *The book was stolen *t* and the magazine.
3. Mary nominated Seymour and herself.

Examples (1) and (2) illustrate the effects of a syntactic constraint called the Coordinate Structure Constraint, a principle that prohibits movement rules from applying unilaterally to constituents "inside" coordinate structures. In such cases, a movement option that is available in English involves moving the whole coordinate structure (as, for example, in *The book and the magazine were stolen*). Example (3) demonstrates that the Coordinate Structure Constraint does not apply in the case of reflexive binding. That is, it is possible for a reflexive pronoun (here, *herself*) to be a conjunct in a larger conjunction containing nonreflexive items, and be linked to an appropriate antecedent, under the same conditions as usual.

Although it might be possible to develop a single descriptive mechanism to analyze Wh-movement, passive, and reflexive binding (for example, lexical features), to do so would be to miss the generalization that movement rules apply to a natural class of phenomena distinguished by properties (including observance of the Coordinate Structure Constraint) that do not apply to other types of linguistic phenomena. ■

CON 4.20

Once we introduce the concepts of chains and traces into our theory of syntactic representation, it becomes possible to eliminate transformations simply by directly generating displaced constituents and their traces in their appropriate positions. Such an approach avoids the derivational character of the transformational approach, but can still distinguish displacement phenomena from other types of linguistic dependencies, in that the presence of trace-binding chains remains their distinctive characteristic.

Furthermore, this non-transformational approach is referable to its transformational alternative since "...eliminating [movement rules] genuinely simplifies the theory" (Brody 1995:12). So, while it is appropriate to debate the relative merits of a trace-theoretic approach versus one that exploits lexical features to analyze displacement phenomena, any syntactic theory that aims for a minimalist approach must reject the class of transformational rules (see Brody 1995; but also Chomsky 1998, for further discussion). ■

chain, accounting for the ultimate assignment of *theme* to the subject *the song*. We can also provide a principled account for why the NP object of *sung* must move out of object position and why the subject position is an available "landing site." The object must move because it cannot get its *CASE* feature checked in its initial position. This is a consequence of our decision to detransitivize passive verbs, "absorbing" their specifier *CASE* feature.

Linguists attribute the need for the object to move to a principle anthropomorphically known as "greed" — the object moves in order to satisfy its own case-checking requirements. But why does it move to subject position? Precisely because this is a position in which its case can be checked by the helping verb that introduces the passive verb (*was* in the case under discussion). Furthermore, if we strengthen the Theta Criterion so that thematic roles can only be assigned to either the head or the foot of a binding chain (but not both), then the object NP can only move to a position where it does not pick up a second thematic role. Once again, subject position qualifies, because the passive verb does not assign an independent thematic role to its subject (see Brody 1995:9 for discussion).

Like the lexicalist approach, the transformational analysis of passive presents an intriguing option that forces us to reexamine our grammar, introducing some incompatible assumptions and raising many new questions. For example, the idea that phrase structure is built from the bottom up by merging constituents to form larger constituents represents a quite different approach to the licensing of phrase markers. Perhaps most importantly, the advent of transformational operations that move constituents around in a phrase marker opens up new possibilities for phrase-structure analysis that has lead to some radical rethinking of sentence structure (see Radford 1997). Although it is beyond our scope to consider lexicalist and transformational alternatives in great detail, we briefly consider how each approach handles A'-displacement in the next section.

4.21 Lexicalism and A'-displacement

A'-displacement involves constructions containing constituents in nonargument positions that derive their thematic roles from nonlocal verbs (or prepositions). The lexicalist approach to capturing these dependencies again involves positing a lexical rule that introduces and distributes a new kind of feature, called *GAP* — intuitively, a feature that identifies missing constituents. The value for the *GAP* feature for "ungapped" categories of the sort we have been considering up to this point will be "null." "Gapped" categories are just like their ungapped counterparts except that they are missing a complement constituent, and the value for the feature *GAP* corresponds to the category that is missing. So, for example, a V' with the *GAP* feature value *[NP]* might dominate a subtree consisting of a transitive verb that appears without an NP complement (right).

The Gap Principle proposed by Sag and Wasow 1996 requires that in the normal case, the *GAP* feature values of the daughter(s) (in this case, the V) "add up" to the feature value of the mother (V'). This requirement is satisfied at the V' level in the example above because the mother V' only has one daughter, and their *GAP* feature values match. Following the same principle, the V' can be dominated by a

We have already discussed The people talked over the noise, *which is ambiguous between a* shouted *interpretation and a* discussed *interpretation. It is possible to apply the move transformation to* over, *moving it past the object* the noise *to the end of the sentence, yielding* The people talked the noise over. *Notice that one of the interpretations (which one?) disappears. Why?*

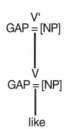

A V' with an NP gap.

VP with the *GAP* feature value *[NP]*; and the VP, in turn, can be the daughter of an S, again with the *GAP* feature value [NP] (suppressing the null *GAP* feature values on the subject NP).

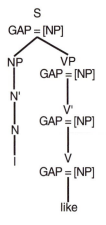

An S containing a VP containing a V' with an NP gap.

Finally, we need a rule that will combine the gapped S with a corresponding filler — a constituent that, intuitively, fills the gap created by the missing object. Suppose we want to generate the topicalization — *That kind of car I like*. The filler in this case is an NP in topic position:

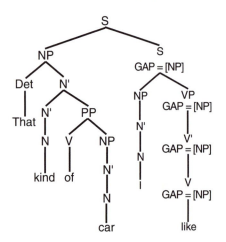

Representation of *That kind of car, I like.*

Sag and Wasow 1996 call the rule that combines fillers with gapped categories the "Head Filler Rule." Notice that in this case, the *GAP* feature value of the lower S is not matched by the (null) *GAP* feature value on the higher S — in effect, overriding the Gap Principle. When a filler is introduced into a sentence, the *GAP* feature value on the gapped constituent is canceled, and the resulting constituent is fully expanded and gap-free.

One important consequence of this analysis is a direct account of the unbounded character of filler-gap dependencies. Since a *GAP* feature can be discharged by the Head Filler Rule at any level of the phrase marker, we correctly predict that a displaced constituent can be an arbitrary distance away from the location of its corresponding gap. Here is an example in which a topic NP is one clause removed from its gap:

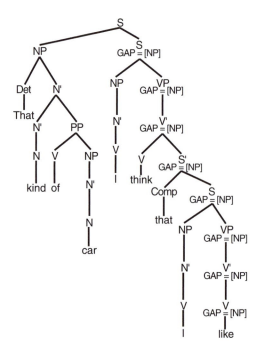

Representation of *That kind of car, I think that I like.*

Finally, we also can account for the possibility of topicalizations that are embedded in subordinate clauses, an automatic consequence of our analysis, as the next diagram illustrates:

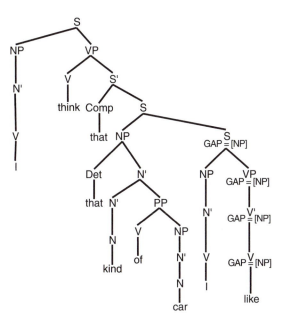

Representation of *I think that that kind of car, I like.*

The analysis of topicalization has an interesting extra complication involving the interpretation of the NP that is displaced. The following data illustrate the problem:

1. That kind of car, I like.
2. The Batmobile, I like.
3. Batman, I like.
4. *A cape, I like.

Although all topicalizations sound a bit odd out of context, for most speakers, the final example is beneath the threshold of acceptability (even with appropriate pause intonation, which we have tried to facilitate with comma punctuation). The difference between (4) and the other examples has to do with the definiteness of the topicalized NP: NPs introduced by determiners like *that, the,* and *this* are called definite NPs, and NPs introduced by determiners like *a* and *some* are called indefinites. In the majority of English dialects, NP topicalization works best in cases in which the topic NP is definite.

There is, however, a New York City-based dialect in which even indefinite NPs like the one in (4) are free to topicalize. Speakers of this dialect tend to be ethnically Jewish, and to have had some contact with the Yiddish language. It is worth noting in this regard that Yiddish is more liberal than English in allowing a wide range of topicalized phrases, suggesting that Yiddish has had an influence on English grammar for these speakers. ∎

IN DETAIL 4.21

Here, the topic of the subordinate clause cancels the *GAP* feature, yielding an S dominated by S'. Although we have barely scratched the surface in our exploration of the lexicalist approach to A'-displacement, we now turn briefly to the alternative transformational analysis. We then move on to consider another class of syntactic phenomena.

4.22 Transformations and A'-displacement

The transformational approach to A'-displacement has much in common with that approach to A-displacement, with some important differences. Once again we assume that displaced constituents are initially located in their canonical argument positions, and that movement of these constituents applies during the merging operation. Let's illustrate this style of analysis using the Wh-question *Who don't you love?* as an example. The initial state of the V' in this case will look something like this:

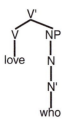

Representation of the VP *love who.*

Notice that we have located the interrogative *who* as the complement of *love,* consistent with the feature-checking requirements of this transitive verb. In particular, *love* assigns accusative case, as well as the thematic role *theme,* to *who* (which appears in some speakers' dialects as *whom*). Next, the V' is merged with *don't,* into a superordinate VP, and then with a subject NP into an S with the following structure:

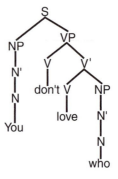

Representation of *You don't love who?*

If the derivation stops right here, we generate a type of Wh-question that is used with various intonations to serve a variety of discourse functions. For example, if one pronounces *You don't love who?* with a rising intonation on *who* (perhaps conveying incredulity), the result is called an echo question. Alternatively, if someone is asking a long series of questions — a lawyer interrogating a witness, for example — "…[And] you don't love who?" might well appear (with a rather different intonation pattern). Indeed, many languages other than English, such as Japanese and Chinese, employ constructions with unmoved Wh-words for asking neutral questions. In English, however, it is more common to use a displaced Wh-word for the common interrogative.

We should also say something about *don't*. Our approach assumes that forms of *do* appear in the same position as helping verbs, in our analysis, as a sister to V' under VP. (There are, however, several well-known complications in the analysis of *do*. For example, positive forms of *do* cannot generally appear in this position unless they bear heavy stress — compare **I do love you* with *I <u>do</u> love you*). The next step is to invert *don't* with respect to the subject NP *you*.

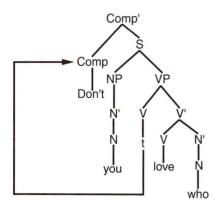

Inversion of *don't*.

Inversion is another instance of movement that relocates helping verbs to the left of the subject into Comp. Notice that this operation can apply independently in the absence of any Wh-words to form yes/no questions like *Don't you dance?* and *Was the song sung?* Also, we have changed the node label for the node that dominates Comp and S from S' to Comp', anticipating the next step in the analysis.

The final stage in the derivation of *Who don't you love?* involves moving *who* to the front of the clause, building a complementizer phrase (CompP) on top of Comp' to create the landing site:

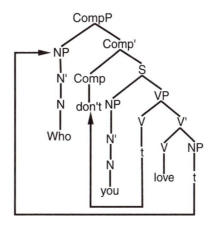

Representation for *Who don't you love?*

Although superficially, this derivation resembles the transformational analysis of passive, there are a number of important differences. With passive, case is assigned to the displaced subject after movement (indeed, the need for case is what motivates the object to move into subject position). In contrast, in question formation by Wh-movement, the displaced item receives case prior to being moved. This explains the following contrast: in passive, the moved item bears nominative case *(I/*me was duped)*; whereas in the questions, the presence of *whom*, at least for some speakers, is evidence that accusative case is assigned *(Whom did you talk to?)*. The thematic role borne by moved Wh-words is also assigned to their premovement position. As with passive, after movement, the trace that constitutes the foot of the chain will send the thematic role it receives up the chain to the head.

HISTORY 4.22

Helping verbs like *can* and *would* are called *modals* (or modal auxiliaries). There are currently nine modals in English (*could, will, may, might, must, shall,* and *should* are the others), but there is evidence that this category has been and continues to be involved in a linguistic change.

Traugott (1972) notes that contemporary modals behaved quite differently in Middle English; for example, constructions like *I shall may go* — so-called "double modal" constructions — were possible. Although this pattern survives in some dialects of English (e.g., in some types of AAE, some southern dialects, and some Caribbean dialects of English), double-modal sequences are not permitted in most English dialects.

There is also evidence that the modal system continues to evolve. Notice that *shall,* for example, has a distinctly formal ring to it, and is generally no longer used in colloquial speech — *Shall we dance* (compared to *Wanna dance?*) sounds very 1940s to our ears today. Other modals like *must* and *might* may be heading in the same direction, and have already begun to sound stuffy in their negative forms *mustn't* and *mightn't*. This sort of marginalization is often a telling sign of lexical loss in action. It is also common to substitute forms like *gotta,* and *usta* for modals, again, mostly in colloquial speech (which typically is in the vanguard of linguistic change). But these items are not exactly equivalent to modals in their syntactic behavior, despite supporting similar interpretations. For example, modals, like all helping verbs, can bear negation (*can't, wouldn't,* and so forth), invert in questions (*Can you sing?*), and form tags (*I can sing, can I*). Forms like *gotta* and *usta* do not play these syntactic roles.

The paradigm for modals (and other helping verbs) is quite unusual in English, and the substitution of *gotta* and its ilk may be an attempt to bring the overall grammar into line with patterns found more generally in the world's languages, an idea proposed by Lightfoot (1979), who argues that linguistic change happens partly by chance and partly by necessity. To illustrate, let us consider how English adopted the modal category in the first place. Originally, modals were derived from verbs, displaying atypical verbal behavior. It was by chance that over time, modals happened to accrue enough idiosyncratic properties (such as unusual inflectional alternations like *may/must,* and past-tense forms like *might* that do not have normal time reference) to stand out from other verbs. Once modals became opaque members of the verb category, linguistic change becomes necessary, since it is a condition of grammars that such opacity cannot be tolerated.

Lightfoot argues that English grammar was restructured in the transition to Early Middle English, introducing the new category *modal* in the phrase-structure grammar (along with other changes). He concludes that this type of change was sufficient to eliminate opacity yet subtle enough to "permit mutual comprehensibility with the earlier generation." (p. 406) The facts drawn from our discussion of the helping-verb system in contemporary English indicate that this process of change in still in progress. ■

Because Wh-moved constituents get their case checked in their original argument position and their thematic role assigned to this same argument position, they seem relatively free to move to different phrase-structure positions. However, as in instances of A-displacement, Wh-movement is constrained by the Theta Criterion. This means that the movement of Wh-word must, in effect, be to a position in the CompP, where no new thematic role will be inadvertently assigned.

The restrictions on movement leave open the possibility that Wh-words will move to Comp positions other than the one at the front of a main clause. Here is an example showing Wh-movement to an embedded Comp position for the sentence *I know what Bill wrote* (only the structure for the subordinate clause is shown):

I know...

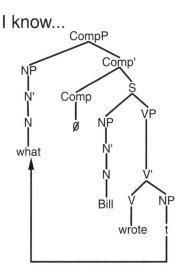

Partial representation for *I know what Bill wrote.*

The resulting construction is an indirect question. Notice that the Comp *that* is missing. Here is a more complicated example that involves two Wh-words, *what* and *where*.

I know...

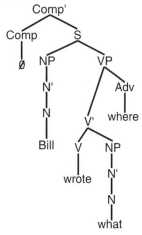

A partial structure with two wh-words.

To derive *I know what Bill wrote where* we move the object NP, or we could move the Adv to generate *I know where Bill wrote what*. But first moving the object and then the Adv, or vice versa, is not possible, because the first movement fills the CompP. This explains the ungrammaticality of **I know what where Bill wrote* and **I know where what Bill wrote*. The result is that English double questions like *I know what Bill wrote where* and *I know where Bill wrote what* require the second Wh-word to remain in argument position.

List all the sentences you can produce by locating what *in each of different CompP positions in the following sentence:*

You realized Bill knows Sue will decide to eat what?

4.23 Bounding Theory

As we commented earlier, the analysis of filler-gap dependencies (either in terms of movement or *GAP* features) introduces considerable complexity into the grammar, yielding a profile of English in which displaced constituents bear long-distance dependencies to other remote constituents. However, restrictions on thematic-role assignment, feature distribution, and so forth, serve to restrict the limits of these dependencies, producing a more constrained system in the end.

In this section we investigate another constraint on long-distance dependencies falling under the category of *bounding*. As a point of departure, consider again the double indirect question *I know where Bill wrote what*. We have already seen one explanation for why *what* cannot appear along with *where* at the front of the subordinate clause *(*I know what where Bill wrote)*. However, there is no obvious reason why *what* cannot appear at the front of the whole construction, yielding **What do I know where Bill wrote?* in effect mixing a direct question and an indirect question in a single string. The putative long-distance dependencies involved in this construction look like this (ignoring the analysis of *do*):

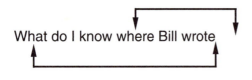

A structure with two long-distance dependencies.

Since each of these displacements is possible independently of the other (consider: *What do I know Bill wrote?* and *I know where Bill wrote*), why can't both displacements be maintained simultaneously? Linguists have addressed this question by developing an analysis of the bounding properties of long-distance dependencies. In general terms, displaced constituents must be linked to argument positions within the same clause. From the perspective of a movement analysis, this means that the top CompP is "out of bounds" as a landing site for the movement of *what*.

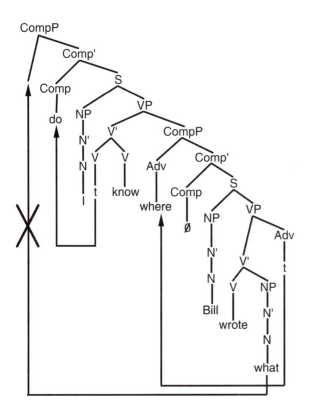

Representation of two long-distance dependencies.

We can formalize this analysis within the movement framework by imposing the following condition on movement:

Local Movement Constraint
Movement must take place within a local domain.

In English, an argument position (a subject or object position) and a potential landing site are local with respect to one another if no more than one clause boundary (or S node) intervenes between the argument position and the landing site. By restricting the landing site for a Wh-word to a local CompP, we insure that a moved Wh-word always lands in the closest CompP. Recent work has attempted to derive the Local Movement Constraint from deeper principles governing movement. Radford (1997) discusses a number of such principles falling under the category of *economy* considerations. One of these conditions, the principle of *Shortest*

Movement, gives preference to short movements over longer ones. Since the local CompP is closer to the underlying argument position of a Wh-word that is eligible for movement than is a CompP in a higher clause, this might explain why only the closest CompP is available as a legal landing site.

The general strategy for this approach is to construe movement as an essentially free process, but one subject to several independently motivated constraints that restrict the possible outcomes. In fact, it may appear that the current restrictions on movement are too strong, making it impossible to account for the unbounded character of A'-displacement. Notice for example, that the derivation of *What do I know that Bill wrote?* is blocked on the present analysis.

However, there is an alternative derivation for this example that relies on a sequence of two separate movements, each of which is consistent with the Local Movement Constraint.

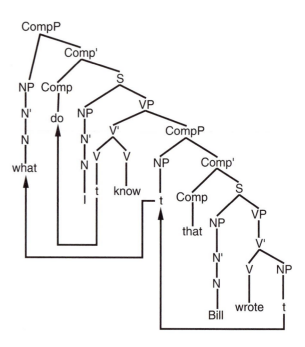

Derivation for *What do I know that Bill wrote?*

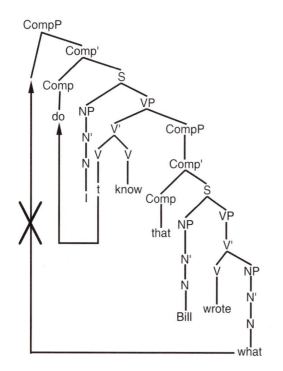

Blocked derivation for *What do I know that Bill wrote?*

Consider the contrast in following examples:

1. *Which guitarists do you think t envy which singers?*

2. **Which singers did you think which guitarists envy t?*

The t is the trace of movement left by the displaced Wh-word. Explain the difference in grammaticality in these data using the Shortest Movement principle.

Notice that a trace of movement has been left behind not only in the original argument position for *what,* but also in the intermediate CompP position that is the landing site for the first movement operation. In such circumstances, binding chains have intermediate links between the head and foot of the chain. In effect, movement through an unfilled CompP phrase is what confers its unbounded character on A'-displacement.

The Local Movement Constraint requires that each "leg" of a movement take place within a local domain. In English, the local domain seems to be the clause; more precisely, the simple phrase dominated by CompP (possibly including one embedded CompP slot) must contain the head and the foot of the local binding chain. There is also evidence that NP establishes a local domain, as the following evidence suggests:

1. Who do you believe that Bill saw *t?*
2. *Who do you believe the claim that Bill saw *t?*
3. Whose book did you read *t?*
4. *Whose did you read *t* book?

The ungrammaticality of (2) and (4) can be attributed to the fact that the Wh-word has moved out of a position (marked by the trace, *t*) within a NP, to a position outside the NP. We can illustrate this most easily by using a labeled bracketing to show the relevant aspects of the constituency, using (2) as an example:

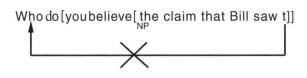

Partial labeled bracketing for *Who do you believe the claim that Bill saw?*

English-speakers often produce strings like It is something that a teacher is a person who already understands *that are not grammatical. (1) Explain why the string is ungrammatical. (2) Why do you think English-speakers might produce utterances like this?*

Observe that this observation allows us to account for the puzzling case of obligatory pied-piping discussed above, which (3) and (4) illustrate nicely. All things being equal, we would expect both (3) and (4) to both be grammatical because pied-piping is normally optional; and the ungrammaticality of (4) therefore requires an explanation. On the basis of the present discussion, we can argue that (4) is ruled out by the Local Movement Constraint, allowing us to maintain that pied-piping is in principle optional, explaining the data in question on the basis of an independently motivated constraint.

You may have noticed that we have been careful to identify the clause as a bounding node for English, anticipating a degree of variation across languages as regards the specification of what counts as a local domain for movement. Some languages, like Russian, are more conservative in their specification; others, like Italian, are more liberal. Russian Wh-questions in which both the head and the foot of the local movement chain are within a single CompP (not including any embedded CompP positions), resemble the parallel

English examples under discussion. In simple questions like *Chto on chityet?* ('what he reads', meaning *What does he read?* — *Chto* is the moved Wh-word), Wh-movement applies, and both the head and the foot of the movement chain are within a single CompP.

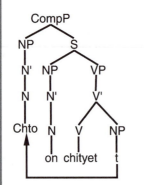

Representation for *Chto on chityet?*

However, "long-distance" movement of a Wh-word to a higher CompP is ruled out in Russian (in certain types of clauses), because the foot of the second link of the movement chain in the embedded CompP would be in a different CompP than the "landing site" see Radford 1981).

Although Russian does have other strategies available for asking this kind of question, the effect of incorporating a more restrictive definition of domain should be clear. And as a more general observation, we have seen an example of a syntactic constraint, the Local Movement Constraint, that applies somewhat differently depending on the language under analysis. ■

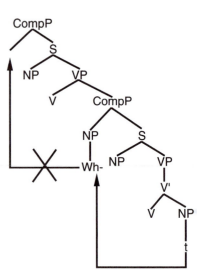

Schematic illustration of a blocked long-distance Wh-movement in Russian.

4.24 Binding Theory

In chapter 3 we argued that reflexive pronouns require linguistic antecedents that agree in number and gender. The following data bear on this claim about reflexive *binding*:

1. Ella surprised herself frequently.
2. *Ella surprised himself frequently.
3. *Ella surprised themselves frequently.
4. *Herself surprised Ella frequently.
5. Ella, herself, was surprised frequently.
6. *Herself, Ella was surprised frequently.
7. Herself, Ella surprised frequently.
8. *Ella's range surprised herself frequently.
9. *The picture of Ella surprised herself frequently.
10. I thought Ella surprised herself frequently.
11. *Ella thought I surprised herself frequently.

Draw an analysis tree for Billie surprised herself. *Draw a second tree in which you substitute* himself *for* herself, *and a third in which you substitute* dogs *for* Billie. *Discuss and explain the grammatical status of each example.*

The first three examples illustrate the basic paradigm: The third person singular reflexive pronoun *herself* agrees with *Ella* in the first example, but lacks an appropriate antecedent in the next two cases. The fourth example, however, presents a bit of a puzzle.

Although it is ungrammatical (in most English dialects), this string appears to satisfy the agreement requirements for *herself* in that it contains an occurrence of the third-person singular NP *Ella* that might be expected to serve as its antecedent.

We need to amend our view of reflexive binding by imposing an additional condition on the structural relationship that must obtain between a reflexive and its antecedent. On the basis of the first four examples, it seems that the extra consideration may be order, since the ungrammatical **Herself surprised Ella frequently* is unlike the other examples in that the antecedent follows the reflexive. The contrast between the fifth and sixth examples, *Ella, herself, was surprised frequently* and **Herself, Ella was surprised frequently* seems to support this conclusion. However, the next example, *Herself, Ella surprised frequently* is acceptable for many speakers (the following context may help: *Ella never surprised Billie, but herself, Ella surprised frequently*), but inconsistent with this analysis. Still, we can maintain the spirit of our current conjecture that antecedents must precede reflexives by noting that these examples involve A'-displacement of the reflexive pronoun. Apparently, displaced reflexives behave as if they were in their associated argument position for the purposes of binding.

Unfortunately, the next two examples, **Ella's range surprised herself frequently* and **The picture of Ella surprised herself frequently* are difficult to reconcile with our current hypothesis. Despite the fact that *herself* and *Ella* agree, and appear in the proper order, both of these strings are ungrammatical. It turns out that our proposed ordering relation between reflexives and antecedents is insufficient: some constituents that precede a reflexive are nevertheless unavailable to serve as its antecedent. In order to distinguish the cases under discussion from permissible cases of reflexive binding, we introduce the following constraint:

Binding Theory
A reflexive must be bound by a C-commanding constituent.

The *C-command relation* is defined as follows (with a branching node defined as one that dominates two daughters):

C-Command
A node *X* C-commands a node *Y* if and only if the first branching node that dominates *X* also dominates *Y*.

Let us see how these conditions work to explain the above cases of reflexive binding. First, we examine the analysis tree for *Ella surprised herself frequently*.

C-command and Reflexive Binding.

Draw analysis trees for Sarah amuses herself *and* Herself amuses Sarah. *Discuss and explain the grammatical status of both examples.*

Draw analysis trees for The drummer near Sarah amuses herself *and* The drummer near herself amuses Sarah. *Discuss and explain the grammatical status and interpretation of both examples.*

The NP *Ella* C-commands the reflexive *herself* by virtue of the fact that S, the first branching node that dominates the NP *Ella* also (indirectly) dominates the NP *herself*. One way to think of the C-command relation is that it defines for each constituent, a region of the sentence in which that constituent can function as an available antecedent. In the case of *Ella's range surprised her frequently* the only possible antecedent, *Ella*, fails to C-command *herself* because the reflexive is not dominated by the NP that branches above it:

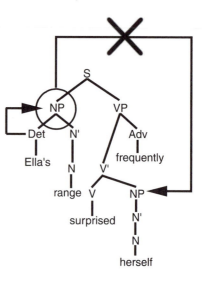

C-command and Reflexive Binding.

Next, we turn to the contrast between *I thought Ella surprised herself frequently* and **Ella thought I surprised herself frequently*. These are both cases in which a reflexive appears in a subordinate clause. The second example is the problematic one: it contains a potential antecedent for *herself* of the right flavor and that C-commands the reflexive, yet it is still ungrammatical.

The problem is that the antecedent *Ella* is too far from the reflexive to bind it. In English, an antecedent cannot be an argument of a separate clause from the one in which the reflexive it purports to bind appears. Since *Ella* is the subject of the main clause, and the reflexive is the object of the subordinate clause, a proper binding relation fails to obtain. We can revise the Binding Theory to capture this locality effect (where local means roughly, 'in the same clause'):

Binding Theory (revised)
A reflexive must be bound by a local C-commanding constituent.

We conclude our discussion with a brief consideration of the binding properties of nonreflexive, personal pronouns. With a few exceptions (see Sag and Wasow 1996), the binding properties of personal pronouns are the opposite of those of reflexive pronouns: reflexives must be bound, pronouns need not be (compare *He left* with **Himself left*); reflexives cannot be bound across a discourse, pronouns can (consider A: *John left.* B: *He/*Himself did?*); and reflexives can't tolerate antecedents that are too far away, whereas personal pronouns do not allow antecedents in their local domain (consider: *John told Bill to help him/himself* — the reflexive *himself* must be bound by *Bill,* and the personal pronoun *he* can only be bound by *John*). We can capture these binding properties of personal pronouns by incorporating a second clause in the Binding Theory as follows:

Binding Theory (revised)
A reflexive must be bound by a local C-commanding constituent.
A personal pronoun must not be bound by a local C-commanding constituent.

The way we have stated the second clause of the Binding Theory; we leave open two possibilities for the binding of pronouns: they must either be unbound (or "free"), leading to a discourse interpretation; or if they are bound, their antecedent must not be local.

Suppose we consider one last pair of examples to illustrate the predictions that this analysis makes. Here are the data we are interested in:

1. Ella surprised her.
2. Ella's range surprised her.

The first example is like one we discussed earlier *(Ella surprised herself),* but with a personal pronoun substituted for the reflexive in object position. Notice that *her* cannot be Ella — the pronoun must be provided with a discourse interpretation (the opposite of the state of affairs in the reflexive case). Our Binding Theory explains

Draw analysis trees for The drummer near Sarah surprised herself, The drummer near Paul surprised herself, The guitar near Sarah surprised herself, *and* The dogs near Sarah surprised herself. *Discuss and explain the grammatical status and interpretation of each example.*

Draw an analysis tree for Ringo said that Ella surprised herself. *Draw a second tree in which you substitute* George *for Ella. Discuss and explain the grammatical status of both examples.*

Draw analysis trees for Paul waited for herself *and* Ella amuses himself with Paul. *Suppose that these two sentences constitute a part of a larger discourse. Do these facts support the conclusion that reflexives cannot be bound across sentences in a discourse?*

Draw analysis trees for The dogs surprised themselves *and* The dogs surprised each other. *Draw two more trees in which you substitute* drummer *for dogs in both of the original sentences. Discuss the binding behavior of* each other *compared to that of* themselves. *Draw a tree for* Each other fell. *Explain the grammatical status of this example.*

IN DETAIL 4.24

Although the claim that personal pronouns display binding behavior opposite to that of reflexives carries us further toward a successful analysis of binding, there is a class of well-known counterexamples to this generalization that we should mention. The following data illustrate one of the problematic cases:

1. Sally tied the rope around herself.
2. Sally tied the rope around her.

Example (1) is unremarkable; the reflexive *herself* is bound by the antecedent *Sally,* in keeping with the first clause of the Binding Theory.

However, given our current analysis, (2) should be ungrammatical on a reading in which *her* is construed as referring to Sally. Unfortunately, (2) seems well formed in this interpretation; and along with (1), it illustrates a paradigm in which a personal pronoun can substitute for a reflexive pronoun with no change in interpretation.

Sag and Wasow (1996) argue that the unusual behavior exhibited by these examples can be attributed to special properties of prepositional phrases which, in certain circumstances, seem to alter the domain in which binding can take place. They

trace this effect to subtle differences in the argument structures of the examples under consideration, and they propose an alternative Binding Theory that is sensitive to these aspects of syntactic analysis (see Sag and Wasow 1996 for more details and further discussion). ■

this as follows: *Ella* is within the local domain of *her,* and is therefore disqualified as an antecedent, and there are no other linguistic antecedents available. The second example is even more interesting. *Ella's* is contained inside of the branching NP *Ella's range,* and therefore it does not C-command the pronoun *her.* As a consequence of the failure of C-command, *Ella* does not count as locally binding *her* (although it does bind *her* nonlocally). This explains why *her* can be bound by *Ella* in this case, in addition to the possibility of a discourse interpretation for the pronoun (see the analysis tree at right):

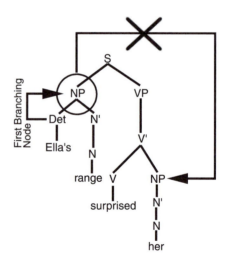

C-command and pronoun binding.

Draw analysis trees for Ella brought himself, The dogs with Paul surprised herself, *and* The dogs with Paul surprised her. *Explain the grammatical status of each example.*

4.25 Ellipsis

Very often in speech, sentences like *Mick sang the blues and Eric sang the blues* are substituted for by sentences like *Mick sang the blues and Eric did too*. The linguistic phenomenon exemplified in the second example is called *ellipsis*. In this section we present several different elliptical constructions and discuss the roles that they play in discourse.

Elliptical constructions can take several different forms in English. Here are three to consider:

1. Moe added some salt but Curly didn't.
2. Mac preferred the mackerel and Bill the brill.
3. Mick wrote some lyrics and George wrote some too.

In these examples there is a phrase that is understood but not overtly present. In (1), for example, a case of VP-ellipsis, what Curly is understood to have not done is *added salt*. (2) illustrates V-ellipsis (or "gapping"); in this example Bill is construed as having *preferred* the brill. Finally in the example of N'-ellipsis in (3), what George wrote was some *lyrics*. Notice that the interpretation of elliptical constructions is limited by what information is recoverable from the syntactic context. So, to take VP-ellipsis as an example, in a normal discourse, the elliptical predicate in *Moe added some salt but Curly didn't* is assigned the same interpretation as the parallel VP *added some salt* in the first conjunct. In particular, the elliptical sentence does not mean *Moe added some salt but Curly didn't add some pepper* or *Moe added some salt but Curly didn't swim*.

In this regard, some elliptical constituents are reminiscent of reflexive pronouns in that their interpretation must be fixed by an antecedent. Notice that **John did* is ungrammatical as a free-standing sentence in the same way that **Himself lost* is — in both cases it is impossible to assign an interpretation to a semantically dependent item. Because of this similarity, it is appropriate to think of ellipsis as a type of *anaphoric* (pronounlike) process, along with pronouns and reflexives. Indeed, the interpretation of some elliptical constituents resembles that of personal pronouns (and is unlike that of reflexives) in that an appropriate antecedent may be located in a separate sentence in a discourse. So, in a conversation like:

Speaker A: John died.
Speaker B: He did?

Not only can *he* be an antecedent for *John*, but *died* can (and must)

The following examples each involve elliptical interpretations. Explain what part of the interpretation is elliptical in each case:

1. *I wanted to leave but I never said so.*

2. *Sue had done an excellent job on the test, but not Bill.*

3. *John knows how to play sitar but Paul doesn't know how.*

be the antecedent for the elliptical VP. To complicate matters further, not all elliptical constructions share the same conditions on interpretation. For example, gapping does not allow the antecedent for the missing verb to appear in a separate sentence:

Speaker A: Mick played the guitar.
Speaker B: *Charlie the drums.

We are also faced with deciding what the proper syntactic representation of elliptical constructions looks like. One possibility, popular in early analyses of ellipsis, involves deriving elliptical sentences from the representations underlying the parallel, un-elliptical sentences by applying transformations that delete duplicate VPs. On this approach, the representation for *John can sing and Paul can too* would look like that for *John can sing and Paul can sing too;* and a transformation called VP-deletion would apply to delete the second VP. A second, more contemporary approach involves generating the elliptical phrases directly, leaving out missing constituents and marking the phrases for interpretation so that their meaning is made dependent on the appropriate antecedents. On this analysis of *John can sing and Paul can too, can* would be treated in effect as a "pro-VP" whose interpretation must be fixed by the VP in the first conjunct (see Sag and Wasow 1996 for further discussion). Obviously there remain many questions of substance and detail that must be addressed before settling on a general account of elliptical phenomena. Our purpose here has not been to provide a definitive analysis, but merely to introduce the topic and to present some of the interesting linguistic properties displayed by elliptical constructions.

4.26 Universal Grammar

According to much contemporary linguistic theory, many of the principles we have discussed in the preceding pages, C-Command and the Case Checking Principle, for two examples, are manifested in every natural language. Consequently, many of the properties we have described in our analysis of English are not best understood as having been accidentally written into English grammar. Instead, linguists, following in the tradition of Chomsky (1965) and Ross (1967) have located such principles in so-called *universal grammar* (UG). UG is not a grammar in the usual sense; rather, it comprises features that are instantiated in the grammars of every natural language (principles), and limited sets of options that allow a small degree of variation within the bounds established by the principles (parameters). The conditions expressed in UG are perfectly general; the grammars of individual languages need only to state the idiosyncratic properties of the languages they generate, along with the language-specific parameter settings (see below). The principles and parameters of UG have also been claimed to play a central role in language acquisition by children, and to constitute species-specific, domain-specific, innate properties of the human mind. Each of these claims is profound, and worthy of careful consideration.

In the early 1960s, Joseph Greenberg re-invigorated the study of language universals with his important work (1966), in which he proposed no less than forty-five candidate universals based on an analysis of approximately thirty languages drawn from around the world, and representative of several different language families and typological classifications. Greenberg was working in a nongenerative framework, and some of his "universals" have a decidedly probabilistic feel. For example, Universal 4 states "With overwhelmingly greater than chance frequency, languages with normal SOV order are postpositional" (that is, they put the preposition after its object). Other Greenberg universals are quite absolute: "Universal 3. Languages with dominant VSO order are always prepositional"; finally, some have an overtly implicational character, as Universal 29 illustrates: "If a language has inflection, it always has derivation." Greenberg's work has been quite influential in guiding the inquiries of generative linguists, who often strive to capture his generalizations in contemporary terms of analysis. ∎

HISTORY 4.26-A

A given organismic property is species-specific if it is displayed only by members of a single species (see Marler and Sherman 1985 for a classic discussion of variation in sparrow song). To establish such properties we must investigate at a sufficient level of detail — obviously, other animals maintain communication systems that are certainly effective and may even possess languagelike properties to some degree. But it is generally agreed that none of these systems rely on principles like C-command and the Case Checking Principle that make up UG and constitute the theory of natural language (see Premack 1986 for discussion). The more successfully we pin down the details of UG, the more confident we can be about the restriction of human language to Homo sapiens. Linguists have also reasoned that, lacking access to the principles of UG and without the advantages that these principles confer on the language learner, other organisms cannot convincingly acquire human language.

To say that the principles and parameters of UG are domain-specific is to claim that no other (human) cognitive ability relies on

PRO 4.26

Children are born with an innate capacity to learn language. While this obviously does not mean that the actual grammars of all of the world's languages are hard-wired into the mind of the infant, it does imply that there is domain-specific knowledge available to the child that supports the acquisition of these grammars.

A number of considerations motivate this conclusion. First, only humans learn natural language. Even the most cognitively advanced of other organisms do not acquire human grammars on the basis of exposure to primary linguistic data, a fact that can only be explained if we assume that human minds manifest an ability to learn language that other minds do not. Moreover, even human language learners only exhibit the full flower of their language-learning ability during a critical period for language acquisition. That is, like other biologically based abilities, language learning has an onset and an offset; and perhaps more interestingly, this ability seems to be the most active at a stage of development at which many other abstract abilities (like computing sums or to finding one's way home) are not acquirable at all. Language learning is also only loosely connected to other cognitive capacities and skills, suggesting that it has its own biological program. This explains why people who differ markedly in IQ, musical ability, resourcefulness, and sociability nonetheless tend to be linguistically equal; their dialects may differ, but their ability to acquire language and their resulting linguistic competence are functionally equivalent.

This equivalence is often achieved despite large and significant variation in linguistic experience from child to child, group to group, and culture to culture. We conclude that language learning is robust in the sense that it is substantially insulated from many effects of the environment — a position that only makes sense if we assume that this resilience is a design characteristic of the mind. Finally, despite the apparent complexity of linguistic information, and the relative paucity of evidence from which the child must extrapolate the linguistic pattern, children proceed efficiently, avoiding many kinds of errors, a fact that cannot be explained without assuming a language-learning system that works to restrict the available linguistic hypotheses, eliminating those that are logically possible but unfruitful. The latter tempting but misleading analyses are best regarded as going against the grain of the mind, and thus are safely ignored. ■

this information. While this claim is far from obvious, the conjecture is that, as a matter of fact, descriptions of other cognitive phenomena (such as the visual system) do not benefit from appealing to the theory of UG. This position forms a part of what is sometimes called the *modularity* thesis that ascribes different cognitive capacities to separate faculties of mind (Fodor 1983; Piatelli-Palmerini 1980; Garfield 1987). In this view, since language is a distinct cognitive capacity, the principles of the theory of language, UG, should not be expected to characterize other cognitive domains. This position also suggests that the way children learn language may be unrelated to the way they learn anything else.

Finally, the principles of UG have been claimed to be innate (Chomsky 1965, 1980). Innate principles are taken to be part of the organism's biological endowment, ultimately traceable to aspects of

The claim that the ability to learn language is an innate capacity of human beings can be understood in several ways. For example, there is undoubtedly something about human mental architecture that disposes us to learn language, given the right environmental stimuli and a normal course of development. But the claim that there is a body of linguistic knowledge that language learners innately possess and that aids in the acquisition of language (and language alone) is implausible. Ultimately, anything that is innate must be genetically representable and evolutionarily transmittable. There is reason to believe that the kind of innate knowledge posited by linguistic theory does not qualify on either of these grounds.

Well-known principles of Darwinian evolution can account for the gradual emergence of characteristics that increase an organism's fit with its environment. Since human language appears to have emerged relatively recently in phylogenetic time, it is questionable whether it is possible to explain the development of a "language organ" in evolutionary terms (but see also Pinker 1994). It is also unclear whether it makes sense to posit a selective advantage for the kinds of abstract rules and principles that linguists propose as aspects of UG. Since these principles seem to offer little functional advantage for an organism outside the context of a full-blown linguistic system, it is hard to see how they could emerge little by little under selective pressure. There are also difficulties presented by the idea that human brains are capable of representing (and more especially, innately representing) the kinds of information that are frequently assumed to be biologically fixed. Elman et al. (1996:26) argue that this sort of representational innateness "…is relatively rare in higher organisms, at least at the cortical level…Indeed, there are many reasons to think that the cortex, in higher vertebrates (especially humans) has evolved as an 'organ of plasticity' which is capable of encoding a vast array of representational types."

In short, in the absence of plausible biological and evolutionary models that can begin to explain how domain-specific knowledge can be represented and inherited, it is unreasonable to make strong claims about the innateness of the principles of UG (see Elman et al. 1996:27). ■

After you have read both sides of the debate in the text, write a brief essay defending one of the points of view.

CON 4.26

human genetics. A number of arguments have been taken to support this position (in addition to the above observation that language is species-specific). First, having examined candidate principles of UG, we can now fully appreciate the force of the argument from the poverty of the stimulus. Given the underspecification of grammars by the primary linguistic data available to the child, and the abstractness of the principles of UG, it seems reasonable to conclude that these principles must be available to guide the learning process, and are not themselves part of the child's learning task. Linguists also point to the fact that individual speakers experience quite diverse learning environments, including different kinds of information (arising in different situations), different schedules of reward, and varying amounts and types of feedback and monitoring. Nevertheless, the linguistic outcomes for such speakers are

Although the relative independence of the language learner from the ebb and flow of the linguistic environment is recognized as a feature of most contemporary linguistic theories, this was not always the case. Accounts of language learning as recently as the beginning of the twentieth century have assumed that the central learning mechanism during the process of linguistic development is the simple imitation of adult forms. For example, Jespersen, writing in 1922, claimed, "One thing which plays a great role in children's acquisition of language, and especially in their attempts to form sentences, is Echoism: the fact that children echo what is said to them." He goes on to argue that the act of repetition, even without the assignment of meaning, is what fixes early sentence patterns in the children's minds (Jespersen 1968).

Pointing out that other linguists of that day had undervalued the role of imitation, Jespersen suggests the following support for his position: Children's early linguistic errors, for example, saying *chine* for *machine* and *Why you smoke Father?* for *Tell me why you smoke,* cannot be explained except as echoes of the well formed adult equivalents. ∎

Do you find Jespersen's argument persuasive? Write a brief critical essay explaining whether you are persuaded by his evidence for imitation. Can you think of any other way to explain his data?

remarkably similar: each learns the native dialect perfectly and shares substantially the same grammar with other members of the same speech community (see, for example, Chomsky 1980:34). Moreover, successful language acquisition does not seem to require high intelligence or any other special abilities that distinguish one speaker from another. The principles of UG are taken to be part of every normal language learner's basic endowment (just like the design principles for the visual system or the digestive system), producing basically the same results in each case: the attainment of the adult system with relatively constrained variation and typically normal functionality.

As Chomsky has repeatedly pointed out: When one finds oneself in a learning domain in which there are impoverished data, limited feedback, and significant variation in the learning population, yet, remarkably, an essentially uniform learning result is produced, it is safe to conclude that significant properties of mind are working to constrain the course of development. The research program for generative linguistic theory during the last four decades has been directed toward supporting this argument by demonstrating that the linguistic structures of different languages, although superficially distinctive, are in fact fundamentally alike, and differ from one another only in the way that variations differ from a theme.

The claim that the principles of UG constitute an innate linguistic endowment has been one of the most controversial conclusions of work in generative grammar in the last four decades. In particular, the philosophical community was considerably skeptical of Chomsky's argument that grammatical analysis based on linguistic data could yield insight into the structure of genetically fixed aspects of a language organ. Quine argued that it is impossible in principle to be certain that any grammar proposed for a natural language is the actual grammar that guides the native speakers' linguistic behavior, a position sometimes called the indeterminacy thesis (Quine 1972). As a result of indeterminacy considerations he concludes that "[t]imely reflection on method and evidence should tend to stifle much of the talk of language universals…"

Other criticisms included the conviction that a general learning theory could be developed that accounted for language acquisition as just one more thing humans can learn on the basis of their general intelligence (see Chomsky 1975). Still others held that children learned language by repeated practice, relying on nothing more complicated than trial and error. In this view, it was unnecessary to posit a language-learning system to bootstrap the acquisition process, because the linguistic environment was assumed to be rich enough to support language development directly.

The status of language universals was also challenged by the allegation that common linguistic properties could be explained by the assumption that all languages evolved from a mutual linguistic ancestor, to which they bear a degree of structural similarity. Common to many of these criticisms is the worry that language does not deserve the special status accorded it by contemporary analysis, and that methodological problems will make it impossible for linguists to derive conclusions about the biological character of human nature. These are, of course, age-old debates that have been of continual interest for literally thousands of years of intellectual history. And many believe that recent work in cognitive science (including research in modern linguistics) is illuminating these traditional philosophical problems in important new ways, building a solid basis for a theory of the mind. ■

Write a brief essay in which you reply to each of the critical points made in the text. Be as specific as you can in providing evidence that supports your argument.

Although this inquiry is still in its infancy, impressive progress has been made in developing substantial models of UG that account for a significant number of properties of an ever-expanding range of languages (see Chomsky 1988 for a discussion of recent results). To the extent that it succeeds, there is evidence for a language faculty that provides the basis for the acquisition of any human language, given the right triggering experience — a universal cognitive capacity shared by all members of the species as an essential component of human nature. In the next section, we turn to some illustrations of how a principles- and parameters-based approach to UG provides an account of universal linguistic properties and constrained variation across languages.

4.27 Principles and Parameters

In the above approach to language acquisition and linguistic theory, we argued that the child derives a learning advantage from the principles of UG. When faced with deciphering the pattern illustrated by a set of linguistic data, there are a number of grammatical analyses consistent with the available facts, but ultimately inappropriate to describe the target language as a whole. The task for the language-learning child is to reject the locally correct but ungeneralizable hypotheses, and to adopt descriptively adequate, extensible hypotheses.

The principles of UG aid in this task by delimiting the live options. Only those grammars consistent with the UG principles are available to the child as candidate hypotheses to capture linguistic patterns. Without this restriction on the hypothesis space, the child's task seems daunting, perhaps impossible. Consider, for example, a young child presented with primary linguistic data that incorporate a significant number of indirect Wh-questions taking the following form:

1. I know what you want.
2. Daddy told you why you have to.
3. Show Mommy who you love.
4. You don't know when to go potty?

One reasonable hypothesis that a child might formulate on the basis of these data is that question words can appear in the middle of a sentence. (You can verify that this generalization fits all the data above.) As an alternative hypothesis, recall the analysis we advanced earlier in this chapter, according to which Wh-words can appear in CompP position at the front of any clause (all things being equal). The first hypothesis, call it the Linear Hypothesis, is *structure-independent* in the sense that it does not appeal to any considerations of linguistic structure; whereas the latter, *structure-dependent* hypothesis makes reference to the lin-

---

PRO 4.27

We may liken children learning language to "little linguists," devising hypotheses based on the consideration of linguistic data, and testing these hypotheses against future experiences (Valian et al. 1981). The acquisition process therefore resembles that of conscious, adult, scientific inquiry in the regard that it involves choosing the simplest hypothesis provided by the theory for successive sets of data. From this point of view, children play an active role in learning their native language, processing linguistic information according to principles of their cognitive architecture that support the language acquisition process. These information-processing principles restrict the range of hypotheses that the child must consider, but there remains the burden of hypothesis testing — choosing a grammar from the set of grammars made available by the theory that generates the primary linguistic data. ■

CON 4.27

Although the linguistic environment does provide an empirical base for the child's efforts to learn a native language,

It is clear that the primary linguistic data do not include much of what linguists use to choose between hypotheses. To this extent, children are not 'little linguists,' constructing their grammars in the way that linguists construct their hypotheses. For example, the primary data do not include well-organized paradigms or comparable data from other languages. Nor do the primary data contain rich information about what does not occur — that is, negative data [note omitted]. It is true that some zealous parents correct certain aspects of their child's speech and so provide negative data, but this is not the general basis for language development. (Lightfoot 1991:10) ■

guistic category CompP. To make matters more interesting, the Linear Hypothesis seems at least as simple as its structure-dependent competitor, and is certainly less abstract, suggesting that children should be disposed to consider it a large percentage of the time. Suppose, however, that following Chomsky (1975), we posit Structure Dependence as a principle of UG:

Structure Dependence
All linguistic rules must refer (only) to aspects of linguistic structure.

According to our account of how the principles of UG work to limit the range of available hypotheses, adopting Structure Dependence as a principle entails that the language learner will not access the Linear Hypothesis, despite the fact that it seems consistent with the previous indirect question data. We predict that our hypothetical language learner, armed with the theory of UG, will be constrained from considering this possibility in practice, since only structure-dependent hypotheses are permitted. Of course, ultimately, this is an empirical claim about how actual children learn language, which must be tested by examining relevant experimental studies of language learners.

To pursue the claim that children benefit from a restriction of their hypothesis space imposed by the principle of Structure Dependence, Crain and Nakayama (1986) investigated yes/no questions like *Can Suzie eat her supper?* hoping to discover whether children would seize on a linear solution to question formation (for example, placing the second word *can* at the front of the sentence) or a structural solution (for example, inverting the main clause auxiliary verb with the subject NP). Crain and Nakayama argue that subjects consistently chose a structural analysis, as the present theory of UG would predict.

The view of UG we are promoting does not suggest that the actual rules of the target language are included in the child's theory of language. Clearly, children are not born with fully articulated grammars for all of the world's languages (past, present, and future). Instead, we are arguing that children are preequipped with a mechanism that imbues them with an economical strategy for learning grammars that conform to universal principles.

The task of elucidating the properties of UG would be (relatively) straightforward if all languages embodied a fixed set of linguistic principles. However, recent research has shown that many UG principles admit a restricted range of alternative realizations in

What predictions does the linear approach to forming embedded questions discussed in the text make with respect to the following examples?

1. *The woman said Bill said to do what?*

2. *Bill knew Sue wanted which book?*

3. *You knew the singer lost which guitar?*

different languages, which may be accounted for by specifying a range of parametric variation in conjunction with the principles, where necessary. Let us consider an illustrative example. Our theory of phrase structure provides for canonical phrase-structure positions for *heads, modifiers, specifiers,* and *complements.* There are, however, even stronger generalizations about English phrase structure that we would like to express, one of which is the order relation between heads and their complements. Phrases like *on the table, eat the radish, angry at Bill, picture that you took,* and so forth, demonstrate that English is a head-initial language, meaning that the head precedes its complement. Indeed, other languages (French and Spanish, for example) that have SVO (subject-verb-object) word order are quite generally head-initial languages, suggesting that the generalization should not be considered a feature of English grammar. Unfortunately, still other languages use different basic word orders — SOV is the most frequently encountered alternative, Sinhala and Japanese being examples — and SOV languages typically feature head-final phrase structure, including post-positional phrases (with the order NP-P), relative clauses following head nouns, and so forth.

Although it is difficult to see how we can capture these facts in a strictly principle-based conception of UG, Chomsky (1986) has suggested a principles- and parameters-based approach to these data. First, as a basic principle of UG, we adopt the condition that languages must have uniform head-complement order — call this the Uniform Complement Order Principle. Next we posit a parameter called the Head Feature Parameter, which allows for two possible settings: "heads right," or "heads left," to account for the two possible head positions we have encountered. Taken together, the principle and the associated parameter constrain the range of variation possible in phrase structure, allowing a degree of freedom without losing significant generalizations. One way to visualize how parameters function is to imagine a bank of binary switches, each one of which may be set in one of three positions. Suppose that the switches are initially in a neutral default position, and must be set to a fixed position on the basis of exposure to a particular language's primary linguistic data. These parameter switches and their values facilitate the child's acquisition of language by establishing a set of important structural concerns and a range of permissible outcomes.

Let's examine this idea in more detail, starting first with the Head Feature Parameter. An English-learning child, upon repeatedly encountering examples like *read the book* or *on the table* eventually analyzes them into head-complement sequences. This motivates the

Some researchers are exploring the possibility that the default setting for some parameters might not be "neutral," like we are assuming in the text. Instead, they conjecture that one of the actual parameter settings may constitute the default setting for a given parameter. What kind of evidence would you expect to find that would motivate this alternative account of parameter settings?

HISTORY 4.27

Lightfoot (1991) argues that language change can lead children to reanalyze the grammar in the course of language acquisition, ultimately resulting in the parameters for that language being reset over time. In Lightfoot's view, "A grammar is not an object floating smoothly over time and space, but a contingent object that arises afresh in each individual." (Lightfoot 1991:172) Often as a consequence of a series of changes in the language, the adult grammar, with its particular parameter settings, no longer provides a simple account of the pattern for a language. In such cases, a child learning the language may have the opportunity to construct a less-opaque grammar by setting a parameter for the target language differently than it had been set by the previous generation. Lightfoot argues that such circumstances can result in extremely rapid changes, since the compatibility of a linguistic change in process with an alternative parameter value makes the emerging form of the language relatively easily for children to learn.

As an example, he contrasts changes in English like the slow loss of gender markers on determiners and nouns, with the much more rapid change in word order from SOV order in Old English to SVO order in Middle English. The former change does not correspond to any proposed parameter in the theory of UG. However, the word-order change can be analyzed as involving a resetting of a parameter that determines the position of heads in phrases, accounting for the relative speed of this type of change (see Lightfoot 1991 for further discussion). ■

---

child to set the Head Feature Parameter to the "left" position.

As a result, the child expects other types of phrases to also conform to head-complement order. In effect, a relatively small amount of data has been projected into a powerful hypothesis about the phrase structure of the language. By the same logic, a child learning Japanese, a SOV language, encounters phases like the VP *hon-o yonda* ('book read') that are analyzed as complement-head sequences, triggering the setting of the Head Feature Parameter to the value "right." This decision also establishes the correct expectation that other Japanese phrases conform to complement-head order.

The "Wh-Displacement Parameter" is intended to distinguish languages that allow displaced Wh-words from those that do not (which may ultimately be a part of a larger generalization). English, of course, allows displaced Wh-words in Wh-questions. An English-learning child might be induced to set the Wh-Displacement parameter to "yes" on the basis of examples like *Who do you love?* building the expectation that other construc-

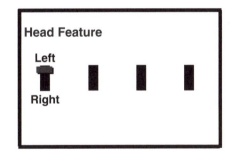

Setting the Head Feature Parameter to "left."

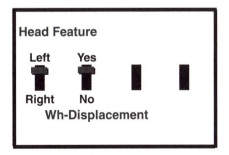

Setting the Head Feature and Wh-displacement Parameters for English.

IN DETAIL 4.27

We have already considered the possibility that the specification of the bounding domain might differ from language to language. It would be natural to incorporate this kind of variability into our principles and parameters framework by identifying a Bounding Domain Parameter, along with an appropriate array of settings that it can take. Suppose we set the Head Feature and Wh-Displacement switches to "left" and "yes," respectively (the settings for English), and introduce the Binding Domain Parameter, with the settings "clause" and "tensed clause." This parameter is responsible for establishing the domain in which reflexives must be bound (and, correspondingly, in which pronouns must be free).

In English, reflexives must be bound by a local, C-commanding antecedent, where local means roughly clause. In particular, in both tensed and tenseless subordinate clauses, reflexives must be bound within the clause (assuming a clausal analysis for tenseless subordinate clauses — the generalization must be expressed somewhat differently if we adopt the nonclausal analysis for tenseless subordinate clauses):

1. Paul prefers for John to write by himself.
2. Paul prefers that John writes by himself.

This explains why, in both examples, *himself* must be bound by *John* (and not by *Paul*), providing justification for setting the Binding Domain Parameter to the "clause" position to indicate that it is the clause that counts, irrespective of presence or absence of tense.

Icelandic reflexive binding facts are similar for tensed subordinate clauses; but, as the following example illustrates, tenseless subordinate clauses allow reflexive binding in a larger domain than is tolerated in English:

1. Jón skipaði Haraldi að raka sig.
   John ordered Harold to shave himself

In this case, the reflexive pronoun *sig* can be bound by either *Haraldi* or *Jón,* the latter interpretation being unavailable in English. We can account for this fact by

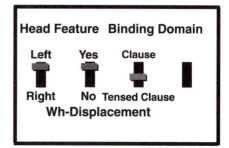

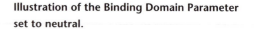

Illustration of the Binding Domain Parameter set to neutral.

setting the Binding Domain Parameter to the value "tensed clause" for Icelandic, with the effect that reflexives must be bound within smallest tensed clause. Although *Jón* is not within the same clause as the reflexive pronoun *sig,* both *Jón* and *Haraldi* are within the smallest tensed clause (namely, the entire sentence). We can account for the ambiguity of this example in Icelandic by providing for the option of an extended binding domain as a consequence of choosing the "tensed clause" setting of the Binding Domain Parameter.

Notice, finally, that the reflexive binding possibilities in English constitute a subset of the possibilities available in Icelandic: Any English reflexive binding pattern is possible in Icelandic, but not vice versa. In circumstances in which this type of subset relation obtains, Berwick (1985) has argued for the Subset Principle, which requires that language-learning children move successively from more conservative parameter settings to less conservative ones, stopping when they reach the appropriate setting. Wexler and Manzini (1987) apply the Subset Principle to explain how children fix the binding domain relative to their target language. They propose that there may be five or more progressively less-conservative characterizations of the binding domain available within linguistic theory.

IN DETAIL 4.27

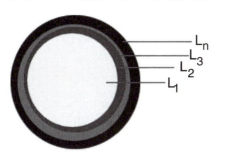

Illustration of the subset relation among different languages.

In their account, each of these competing definitions is represented by a parameter setting in a multivalued version of the Binding Domain Parameter. They suggest that language learners begin with the most conservative assumption about the domain of reflexive binding (which happens to correlate with the English parameter setting). Of course, if the children are learning English, their initial parameter setting will prove correct; but if they are learning Icelandic (or any other language requiring one of the less conservative parameter settings), they need to reset the Binding Domain Parameter, working through the increasing more liberal characterizations of the binding domain, step by step. Prior to resetting the Binding Domain Parameter, the grammars of Icelandic-speaking children undergenerate the target language, since only those reflexive binding patterns consistent with the English parameter setting are possible. Eventually, the child confronts Icelandic sentences that do not square with this initial grammar, and this triggers the resetting of the parameter (see Wexler and Manzini 1987).

One interesting learning-theoretic consequence of this approach to parameter setting is that it explains how language development might proceed largely on the basis of positive evidence (that is, actual examples of the target language). Linguists have long thought that negative evidence (like corrections, examples of ungrammatical strings, and other kinds of feedback) plays a less central role in the acquisition process (see Brown and Hanlon 1970; Pinker 1989, and the references cited there). Since the Subset Principle predicts that children's early grammars will reflect errors of omission more than they will exhibit errors of overgeneration, the relatively greater importance attributed to positive linguistic evidence is explained: Whereas negative information is in principle useful to the child who needs to filter out ungrammatical strings that have crept in, only positive evidence is needed to trigger the resetting of a parameter in accordance with the Subset Principle.

Although more experimental work is needed before we can be sure of the extent to which the Subset Principle guides the language acquisition process, and there are both critiques (Valian 1990) and alternative models of parameter setting being developed (Hyams 1987), this work constitutes some of the most important research in cognitive science seeking to illuminate language learning from a simultaneously linguistic and experimental point of view. ∎

tions involving displaced Wh-words (like relative clauses, for example, *the guitar which I busted*) also exist in English, as a consequence of this parameter setting.

In contrast, a Japanese-learning child sets the Wh-displacement parameter to "no" after having been exposed, for example, to Japanese questions (which do not involve displaced Wh-words). This, in turn, sets up the prediction that other Japanese constructions, such as the relative clause, also do not involve displaced Wh-items. This prediction makes the acquisition of relatives clauses like *Jon-ga yonda hon-wa* (literally *John read book,* meaning 'book that John read') easier. Notice also that Japanese relative clauses place the head *hon-wa* ('book') after the relative *Jon-ga yonda* ('John read'), since Japanese also sets the Head Feature Parameter to "right" (see discussion above).

In this view, a language displays properties that are fixed by UG principles combined with parameter settings particular to that language. Since there two binary features in play, we would expect to find heads-left, Wh-displaced languages like English as well as heads-right, non-Wh-displaced languages like Japanese. But there are two other possible combinations of parameter settings: heads-right, non-Wh-displaced and heads-left, Wh-displaced languages. And, in fact, there are languages like Chinese that incorporate verb-object, preposition-object, and other head-initial phrase structures (like English) along with the absence of Wh-movement in questions and relative clauses. The fourth possibility involves setting the Head Feature Parameter to "right" and the Wh-Displacement Parameter to "yes." Although word order in German is a complicated story, it is generally agreed that the basic order is object-verb, consistent with the "right" setting of the Head Feature Parameter. However, as in English, German employs Wh-displacement, for example to form questions.

We leave open spaces in our diagram to indicate other parameters that have been proposed as a part of the theory of UG. There is, furthermore, some controversy about the nature of default settings, the alleged binary nature of parameters, and the precise process by which children set and reset parameters, among other open questions (See Roeper and Williams 1987; Frazier and de Villiers 1990, for further discussion). But many linguists agree that the principles and parameters framework provides an excellent approach to integrating our analysis of universal grammar with an independently motivated account of child language acquisition.

5. Meaning

5.1 Language and Meaning

Approximately how many meanings can you identify in the sentence *Mary had a nice time on Thursday?* This may seem an odd question. How do we identify meanings? Can we determine the number of meanings in a single word, let alone in a whole sentence or a discourse? Indeed, are meanings something that we can count, at all and if not, what kind of thing is a meaning (or meaning), anyway? Philosophy is the traditional bailiwick of investigations into the nature of meaning. Although the history of this inquiry stretches back thousands of years, analytic philosophy in the early and middle decades of the twentieth century has been the most important recent influence on direction of current research in linguistics.

Philosophers investigated meaning for a number of reasons. Some believed philosophical problems in the domains of metaphysics, ethics, and other areas of study would be illuminated by studying the meanings of terms used to express arguments and analyses. Others were drawn to the study of logics — *formal languages* that provide models of reasoning, inspired by the goal of understanding what it is that makes humans rational animals; these philosophers also tended to discover an interest in natural language. Although some logicians contended that natural languages were too unruly to be profitably subjected to logical scrutiny, others applied logical tools of analysis to English and other languages with considerable success. In part, their work has provided insight into human reasoning; but in addition, as we discuss below, another by-product has been progress in understanding meaning. This line of research, in particular, has framed much of the analysis of meaning undertaken by linguists in the generative tradition (see, for example, Larson and Segal 1995). Finally, philosophers have been attracted to the study of meaning because of the status ascribed to meanings themselves — a point of analysis that differs considerably from theory to theory.

Meanings have been variously analyzed as concepts, behaviors, ideas, objects, dispositions, brain states, programs, and feature bundles, among other things. Obviously, we cannot do justice to this range of theorizing about meaning in the confines of a single chapter. Instead, we develop one promising approach to semantic

PRO 5.1

Just as syntax is devoted to the examination of sentence structure, and phonology investigates the sound system of natural languages, semantics explores meaning. Of course, no one underestimates the challenges in this fascinating domain; but it is clear that inquiry into the nature of meaning is among the most important parts of our mission as linguists. There are, furthermore, a variety of different approaches to semantics, many of which start with fundamentally different assumptions and strikingly different methodologies. As Dillon (1994) notes:

Most writers on semantics would agree that it is the study of meanings. This is probably the only statement about the subject that all would subscribe to, and disagreement starts with what is meant by meaning.

But Dillon continues on a more optimistic note:

Nonetheless, a number of linguists have in recent years come to an understanding of what they would like to explain…

Our goal, Dillon suggests, is to account for a native speaker's ability to make certain judgments about the words and sentences of the languages they speak, including the following:

- Many words are ambiguous — they can be understood in more than one way (like *pig,* meaning boorish person or farm animal).
- Some sentences are anomalous (like *My pet iguana is a prime number*).
- Some combinations of words are contradictory (like *married bachelor*).
- Other combinations are redundant (like *unmarried bachelor*).
- Some words are related in meaning (like *buy* and *sell*).

- Some are more specific than others (like *dog* and *animal*).
- Some sentences entail other sentences (*John left and Bill left* entails *John left*); others have the same truth value (like *2+2 = 4* and *You are reading* Theory of Language).
- Some elements of meaning are typically associated with certain word meanings (like *Fleas are small*).

Adapted from Dillon (1994). ■

Determine whether each of the following examples is ambiguous, anomalous, or contradictory:

1. *Did you break the record?*

2. *I did and I didn't.*

3. *He is the bomb.*

4. *This sentence is false.*

5. *2 + 2 = 5.*

6. *My dog thinks.*

theory in some detail, raising additional questions and mentioning alternative points of view along the way. We begin our survey by considering more carefully what we mean by "meaning." Next, we develop a system of interpretation that allows us to evaluate a small fragment of English. Finally, we investigate some of the ways in which meaning is connected to aspects of linguistic structure.

The grasping of meaning is one aspect of language use that is sometimes claimed to distinguish the human capacity for language from that of otherwise intelligent apes or high-speed computers. Does it seem plausible to you to claim that humans alone assign meaning to symbolic expressions? Why (or why not)?

Loose talk about the "meaning" of a word is the bane of semantic analysis, responsible more than anything else for setting our inquiry in the wrong direction. It makes no sense to posit a thing called a "meaning" that a word "has," any more than it does to admit the existence of "cores" or "roots" just because we talk about "the core of the matter" or the "root of the problem." It is improper (and hopelessly muddled) to conclude that words "have" "meanings" just because they are (as we willingly stipulate) meaningful. The philosopher J.L. Austin puts the point as follows:

Having asked in this way, and answered, 'What is the meaning (of the word) "rat"?', 'What is the meaning of (the word) "cat"?', 'What is the meaning of (the word) "mat"?', and so on, we try, being philosophers, to ask the further general question, 'What is the meaning of a word?' But there is something spurious about this question. We do not intend to mean by it a certain question that would be perfectly all right, namely, 'What is the meaning of the word "word"?' ... No: we want to ask rather, 'What is the meaning of a-word-in-general?' or 'of any word' ... Now if we pause even for a moment to reflect, this is a perfectly absurd question to be trying to ask. (Austin 1961) ∎

5.2 The Nature of Meaning

As we shall soon discover "meaning" means different things to different people; and, as a result, it should come as no surprise that different theories have emerged in the various disciples devoted to its study. We begin with a theory of meaning that counts simplicity among its virtues; and even though we are forced to modify this approach in the long run, it serves us well as a point of departure.

Let's start with a truism: Language is, at its core, a symbolic system. One way of explicating this categorization is to note that languages consist of forms of expression that stand for (or "refer to") things and relations in the world around us. Inherent in this relationship between the word and the world is the essential "aboutness" by virtue of which languages serve their function as communicative systems. They allow us to express our thoughts about external situations so that meaning may be shared with others, despite the manifestly personal and apparently subjective character of our individual mental states. We can better understand the public character of meaning by focusing on how language is used to refer. This function is perhaps most transparent in the case of names: It is plausible to say that *Clinton* refers to Clinton, and that this reference exhausts its meaning. We do, of course, acknowledge a potentially vast range of attitudes about Clinton — different amounts and types of knowledge about him, considerable variability in affective states produced in different speakers at the mention of his name, and so forth. But a use of *Clinton* to pick out Clinton still succeeds in anchoring our thoughts and discourse by providing a common *referent* for us to talk about.

HISTORY 5.2-A

The proposition that language is a symbolic system has been expressed by many authors, over thousands of years. For example, in the dialogue *Cratylus,* written over 400 years B.C., Plato discusses how words get invested with their symbolic value (see Bloomfield 1933 for discussion). In a more recent examination written in the beginning of the 20th century, de Saussure (1959) investigates the relationship between linguistic "signs" and what they represent, developing what has come to be known as semiotic theory.

Another important precedent for contemporary approaches to meaning is found in the work of Morris (1938) whose own theory of signs was quite systematic. One important class of signs he discusses is called "designators." These are expressions used with respect to a particular situation; when the situation satisfied the conditions of reference associated with a designator, it is said to "denote." Morris's particular interest was to use his theory of signs to explain the connection between language and behavior (see Weinreich 1963). ■

Ferdinand de Saussure, an eminent linguist of the turn of the twentieth century, pointed out that the symbolic nature of language was simultaneously rooted in an individual capacity and in a social system (de Saussure 1959). Discuss some of the motivations for thinking that language has this dualistic character.

HISTORY 5.2-B

The notion that a name refers to an object called a referent was proposed by Frege, who at the time was interested in devising a procedure that would establish beyond the possibility of error that a mathematician's proof was free of logical mistakes or inconsistencies. In the course of his work on this "proof-checker" (which incidentally, proved to be an impossible goal), Frege became concerned with matters of meaning. He conceived of language as a symbolic system that included what he called "signs" whose semantic role he described as follows:

It is clear from the context that by 'sign' and 'name' I have understood any designation representing a proper name, which thus has as its reference a definite object (this word taken in the widest range) but not a concept or relation… (Frege 1892) ■

We can explore this idea more formally by establishing a model in which the *semantic value* of English expressions can be evaluated. Here is a very simple model that evaluates identity sentences.

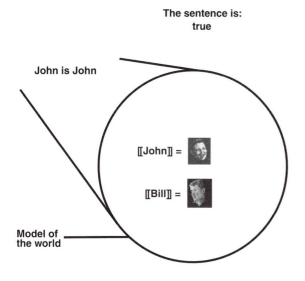

Proper names like John *stand for physical objects — in this case the individual, John. How would you have to extend your idea of what an object can be to account for the semantic values of the following names?*

a. Democracy
b. 7 (the number)
c. Pegasus
d. Satan

Evaluating identity sentences.

The double brackets can be read as 'the semantic value of' (see below); in our present analysis, the semantic value of a name is its referent; here, an individual represented by an icon. This model allows us to evaluate simple identity statements like *John is John* (which are, we confess, somewhat awkward out of context) based on the assignments of semantic values to names and the content of the sentence. The interpretation of the verb *is* is taken to be the identity relation, often expressed in arithmetic terms as = and requiring that the semantic value of the subject NP be identical to the semantic value of the object NP. In this simple model, this condition is only satisfied by placing the same name in both subject and object position. Otherwise the referents of the two arguments are different, and the sentence turns out false.

5.3 Extending the Model

The next step is to elaborate this approach so that it allows us to evaluate other kinds of linguistic expressions. For example, we need to work up a referent for intransitive verbs, like *sleeps*. Suddenly, we are on shaky ground. What kind of object does *sleep* refer to? We might consider abstract objects (like *sleepings*) or actions (like being *asleep*) as likely candidates; but with an eye toward our next consideration (namely, some way of combining meanings into larger meanings), let us consider a rather different proposal. Suppose we say that *sleep* refers to a collection of objects called a set, in particular, to the set of sleepers. Although this move may seem to contradict the intuition that verbs express actions, we may think of the set in question (that is, the sleepers) as containing precisely those individuals who engage in the act, in effect, imposing a criterion for admission to the set. More formally, we can introduce the notational convention of flanking an expression with double brackets when we want to talk about its semantic value (in this case, its referent). So,

⟦Clinton⟧ = Bill Clinton
and
⟦sleeps⟧ = {individuals who sleep}

(using the traditional braces to indicate a set). It is important to remember that *Clinton* and *sleeps* are linguistic expressions, but ⟦Clinton⟧ and ⟦sleeps⟧ are things (an individual and a set). Perhaps now you can more clearly see how this account of reference captures the way in which our language is directed at the external world. It remains to combine the referents of the expressions *Clinton* and *sleeps* to derive the referent of the sentence *Clinton sleeps*.

Since our approach to the theory of reference is grounded in formal objects like individuals and sets, we are naturally led to consider methods of combining referents that preserve this way of analyzing reference. You may remember from your studies of set theory that one type of well-defined relation between an individual and a set of individuals is that of set membership. We can exploit this relation in explicating the semantic relationship between *Clinton* and *sleeps* by allowing that the sentence *Clinton sleeps* asserts that:

⟦Clinton⟧ ε ⟦sleeps⟧

The ε symbol stands for set membership, and the resulting formula expresses the claim that the referent of *Clinton* (namely, Bill Clinton) is a member of the set of sleepers (the referent of *sleeps*). More generally, we can conclude that:

A sentence S is true if and only if the semantic value of the subject NP is an element of the semantic value of the predicate VP.

In this section we consider a slightly more complicated approach to interpreting intransitive verbs like *sleeps,* one that generalizes more easily to provide interpretations for other parts of speech. In this alternative view, the semantic value for *sleeps* will be a function that maps each individual in the domain to the truth value "true" or "false," depending on whether that individual sleeps. We begin by explaining what a function is.

The sense of function we have in mind may be familiar to you from your studies of mathematics. For example in the expression 5^2, the exponent ^{2} can be thought of as a function that takes 5 as its input and returns the square of 5 as its output. Of course, ^{2} operates on other inputs, as well; and so the square function could be thought of something like this (limiting the inputs to the counting numbers):

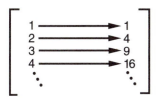

The square function.

The column on the left of the diagram represents the input to the function (called the *domain*), and the column on the right represents the output, or *range* of the function. The arrows are intended to symbolize that for each different member of the domain, the function returns a particular member of the range.

In an extremely thorough analysis of meaning in English, the logician Richard Montague (1973) proposes to extend this treatment to nonmathematical predicates as well. In the spirit of this important paper, we can analyze verbs like *sleeps* as functions whose domain is the set of individuals (here we limit ourselves to four) and whose range is the *truth values* 1 (for true) and 0 (for false). This function tells us that George and Paul sleep, but that John and Ringo do not.

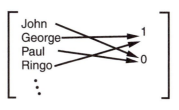

The *sleeps* function.

If we assign this function as the semantic value of *sleeps,* we can calculate the semantic value of a sentence like *Ringo sleeps* by evaluating the *sleeps* function for the input Ringo (that is, we apply the function constituting the predicate's semantic value to the argument that corresponds to the semantic value of the subject of the sentence — we use parentheses to indicate the application of a function to an argument):

⟦sleeps⟧ (⟦Ringo⟧)

which in this case, evaluates to "false." Although this method of assigning interpretations is a bit different that the one adopted in the main discussion, you can verify that it produces the same results. We return to consider the advantage of using the functional approach below. ■

In this way, we can describe the *truth conditions* for a sentence based on a relation between the referents of its constituents. We can express this generalization more formally as follows:

If a sentence has the structure:

```
       S
      / \
    NP   VP
```

then [[S]] = true iff [[NP]] ε [[VP]].

This generalization defines a systematic relationship between the semantic value of the sentence and semantic values of its constitutive parts. On our current view, sentences refer to the values "true" and "false," according to whether the subject's referent is a member of the predicate's referent set of. Approaches to semantic interpretation treating semantic values in this way are sometimes called *truth-conditional semantics*. Here is a model that incorporates these ideas about semantic interpretation. If you were to change the set of sleepers, the sentence's semantic value would change depending on its content:

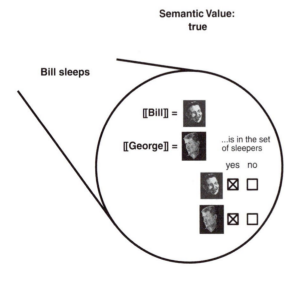

Evaluating simple sentences.

Discuss any difficulties you encounter assigning truth conditions to the following sentences using the rule in discussed in the text. How would you modify the approach to account for this data?

1. It rains.

2. Who left?

3. Leave!

4. Did John sleep?

Much of the ground-breaking work on the enterprise known as truth-conditional semantics was contributed by Alfred Tarski in the middle of twentieth century (see Tarski 1944). Tarski's aim was to devise a systematic procedure that would ultimately provide a theory of truth. His approach involved assigning truth conditions to the simple sentences of a formal language based on relations between predicates and their arguments, and then systematically assigning truth conditions to complex sentences (like conjunctions, for example) on the basis of the truth conditions assigned to the constituent simple sentences.

Tarski's theory of truth also provided a rigorous method for assigning truth conditions to formulas that contained quantifiers, negations, and other complex sentences.

Despite the fact that Tarski's theory was not intended as a theory of meaning (and hardly as a model for a theory of meaning for natural languages), it has been recruited by philosophers and linguists for these new purposes with great success (see for example Davidson 1967 for some early work of this kind). The insight that led to this application of Tarski's work to natural language semantics has been expressed by Quine, who writes:

A reasonable way of explaining an expression is by saying what conditions make its various contexts true.

(Quine 1970; see further in work for a critical discussion). ■

5.4 Conjunction and Disjunction

We can further develop this model to account for certain kinds of complex sentences. To begin, consider the following data:

1. George sleeps and Bill sleeps.
2. George sleeps or Bill sleeps.

The first example is a conjunction of two clauses joined by *and*. Intuitively, for this sentence to be true, both of its conjuncts must be true, a generalization we can capture as follows (assuming, for ease of exposition, a simplified syntactic structure for conjunctions):

If a sentence has the structure:

then $[\![S]\!]$ = true iff $[\![S^1 = \text{true}]\!]$ and $[\![S^2 = \text{true}]\!]$.

Write a semantic rule parallel to the one for conjunction to assign interpretations to disjunctions — sentences connected with or *like* John smiles or Sadie sleeps.

Logical words like *and* are sometimes called truth-functional connectives since the truth of sentences they appear in is a function of the *truth values* assigned to the sentences they connect. In the above cases, we already know how to interpret the conjuncts *George sleeps* and *Bill sleeps* using the semantic rule for interpreting

The simplified analysis in the main discussion treats the syntax of conjoined sentences in a way that is incompatible with binary branching. In this section we investigate how our semantic analysis of conjoined sentences would have to be adapted to fit with a binary-branching approach. We begin with the syntactic analysis. There is evidence that the conjunction (*and*, for instance) forms a constituent with the right conjunct in examples like the following:

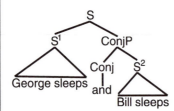

Representation for *George sleeps and Bill sleeps*.

For example, given the logic of the incredulity test, the grammaticality of *And Bill sleeps?* supports this proposed analysis (compare **George sleeps and?*). We can accommodate these results by positing a new type of syntactic phrase called a conjunction phrase (ConjP) that domi-

nates conjunctions (like *and* and *or*) followed by a conjunct, itself. ConjPs will then combine with a second conjunct to form the whole conjoined S structure. Assuming that an analysis along these lines can be worked out, it becomes clear that our semantics for conjoined structures needs to be revised as well. For as it stands, this analysis depends on having both of the conjoined Ss available for interpretation at the same level of syntactic tree — a condition not met in our current representations of conjunction.

Notice, furthermore, that *and* itself was not directly assigned a semantic value in the analysis in question — a decision that seems odd in the light of the reasonable assumption that all vocabulary words ought to receive an interpretation. We can rectify this omission by assigning a function as the semantic value for *and* that takes as its input the truth value of the conjunct with which *and* combines syntactically, and maps this input into the semantic value for the ConjP. With respect to the case at hand, the semantic value for *and* combines with that of *Bill sleeps* to determine the semantic value of *and Bill sleeps*.

It remains to establish what the latter semantic value (that is, the one for *and Bill sleeps*) looks like, and how

subject/predicate sentences. To evaluate the first conjunct, we determine if the semantic value of *George* is an element of the set of sleepers, that is, if the following is true:

$[\![George]\!] \ \varepsilon \ [\![sleep]\!]$

For the second conjunct to be true, the following must also be true:

$[\![Bill]\!] \ \varepsilon \ [\![sleep]\!]$

Finally, for the conjunction itself to be true, we require that that both of the conjuncts must be true; in other words:

$[\![George]\!] \ \varepsilon \ [\![sleep]\!] \ \ \text{and} \ \ [\![Bill]\!] \ \varepsilon \ [\![sleep]\!]$

it is composed to determine the semantic value for the whole sentence. We know, of course, that the final outcome must be a truth value, since the semantic value of *George sleeps and Bill sleeps* must be either true or false. We also know what the semantic value of *and Bill sleeps* must combine with, namely the semantic value of the left conjunct *George sleeps*. It follows that, the semantic value of *and Bill sleeps* is itself a function; in this case, mapping from the truth value of the left conjunct to the truth value of the whole sentence. Putting this all together, the semantic value for *and* looks like this:

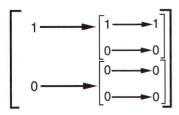

The *and* function.

Perhaps an informal characterization will help you to see what is going on here. Reading across the top line of the

illustration above, *and* requires that you first combine it with a true sentence; and then, if you combine the result with a second true sentence, the whole conjunction is true. The other lines in the diagram represent all other possible combinations of truth values for the two conjuncts, which culminate in the final semantic value false, consistent with our intuitions about the interpretation for *and*. Although we adopt a simpler analysis of conjoined sentences in the main discussion, this gives the flavor of how a functional theory of semantic interpretation can be applied to produce an analysis of conjunction that is consistent with binary branching (see Dowty, Wall, and Peters 1981). ■

IN DETAIL 5.4

Suppose someone proposed that near *was a conjunction in* I saw John near Bill *(on the basis of the fact that it means nearly the same thing as* I saw John and Bill*). Evaluate this claim using the constituency test for conjunction discussed in the text. Discuss.*

must both be true. We can approach sentences like *George sleeps or Bill sleeps* similarly. The rule for *disjunction* — sentences connected by *or* — is quite parallel to that for conjunctions, with one important difference:

If a sentence has the structure:

$$
\begin{array}{c}
S \\
\diagup \mid \diagdown \\
S^1 \quad or \quad S^2
\end{array}
$$

then $[\![S]\!]$ = true iff $[\![S^1$ = true$]\!]$ or $[\![S^2$ = true$]\!]$.

In this case we require that at least one of the two disjuncts must be true for the whole disjunction to

While or *normally only requires one disjunct to be true, in English, "inclusive"* or *allows both disjuncts to be true* (Students with higher than a 90 average or students who get an *A* on the final exam get an *A* for this course) *and "exclusive"* or *does not* (You live or you die). *Our rule captures the "inclusive"* or. *Write a new semantic rule to accommodate the other type of* or.

be true. This amounts to being able to show that either

⟦George⟧ ε ⟦sleep⟧   or   ⟦Bill⟧ ε ⟦sleep⟧

is true. Finally, let's examine a model that incorporates this analysis of conjunction:

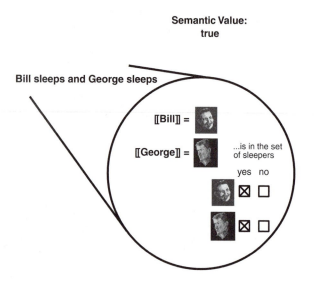

Evaluating conjoined sentences.

Notice that if the truth conditions for the *and* sentence are met, the corresponding *or* sentence is also true (but not vice versa). In other words, the conjunction of two sentences *entails* their disjunction.

5.5 Complex Sentences and Ambiguity

It is also possible to apply this analysis of the interpretation of conjunction and disjunction to more complicated examples of these constructions. Consider the following examples:

1. George sleeps and Bill sleeps and Al sleeps.
2. George sleeps and Bill sleeps or Al sleeps.

The first sentence involves three clauses all connected by the conjunction *and*. We can assign the following analysis tree (with many details omitted):

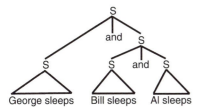

Representation for *George sleeps and Bill sleeps and Al sleeps.*

Notice that, even with sentences with multiple conjuncts, the conjuncts are always assembled two by two. So, if we work our way up from the bottom of the tree, we can use our existing semantic rules first to compose the interpretation of *Bill sleeps* and then of *Al sleeps*. Next, we use the conjunction rule to assign an interpretation to *Bill sleeps and Al sleeps*. This small conjunction will be true just in case

⟦Bill⟧ ε ⟦sleep⟧
and
⟦Al⟧ ε ⟦sleep⟧

are both true. Then, we can assign an interpretation to the leftmost conjunct, *George sleeps* in the usual way:

⟦George⟧ ε ⟦sleep⟧

Finally, it remains to combine the interpretation of the rightmost conjunct *George sleeps* with that of the complex right conjunct *Bill sleeps and Al sleeps*. This involves determining that

⟦George⟧ ε ⟦sleep⟧

is true, and that both

⟦Bill⟧ ε ⟦sleep⟧
and
⟦Al⟧ ε ⟦sleep⟧

are true, as well — ultimately, making sure that all three conjuncts are true, just as intuition demands. Furthermore, we have managed to interpret this rather complicated example without adding any new semantic rules to our system of interpretation. When we look at the second example incorporating complex patterns of conjunction and disjunction (repeated below), an even more impressive property of our semantic theory emerges.

George sleeps and Bill sleeps or Al sleeps.

Considered carefully, this example is ambiguous. On one reading, either both George and Bill sleep or else Al does; on the second interpretation, George sleeps and so does either Bill or Al. We can reflect this ambiguity structurally, as indicated in these two analysis trees.

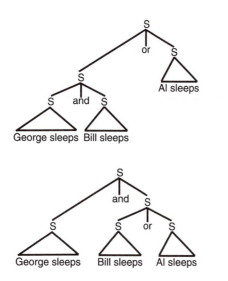

Two representations for *George sleeps and Bill sleeps or Al sleeps*.

The first structure is intended for the reading in which either George and Bill or else Al sleeps. In the second structure, George sleeps, and so does either Bill or Al.

How does our semantic theory establish the right interpretations for both readings? What is crucial, here, is to key the semantic interpretation to the constituency involved in each analysis tree. Starting with the top representation and skipping some steps that have by now become familiar, we first derive the truth conditions for the complex left conjunct *George sleeps and Bill sleeps* — both $[\![George]\!]$ ε $[\![sleep]\!]$ and $[\![Bill]\!]$ ε $[\![sleep]\!]$ need to be true for this conjunct to be true. This interpretation then combines with the interpretation of the

right disjunct *Al sleeps*, requiring, in the end the truth of either

$[\![George]\!]$ ε $[\![sleep]\!]$
and
$[\![Bill]\!]$ ε $[\![sleep]\!]$

or else of

$[\![Al]\!]$ ε $[\![sleep]\!]$

If we go through the parallel procedure for the second analysis tree, we end up first calculating the interpretation of the right disjunct, *Bill sleeps or Al sleeps* and then combining it with the interpretation of the left conjunct *George sleeps*. The result here is the rather different requirement that

$[\![George]\!]$ ε $[\![sleep]\!]$

must be true, plus either

$[\![Bill]\!]$ ε $[\![sleep]\!]$
or
$[\![Al]\!]$ ε $[\![sleep]\!]$

as well.

Explain why the previous example, George sleeps and Bill sleeps and Al sleeps *is not ambiguous in the same way that* George sleeps and Bill sleeps or Al sleeps *is. Be sure to consider all relevant syntactic analyses and to provide explicit semantic derivations to support your answer.*

5.6 Tense and Possible Worlds

Our approach to semantic interpretation proposes to develop a theory of reference as the basis of the theory of meaning. We have adopted an interpretation of sentences, proper names, and intransitive verbs that assigns formal objects like individuals, sets, and the truth values "true" and "false" as the semantic values of linguistic expressions, and have suggested a way to compose the interpretation of simple sentences like *Clinton sleeps* out of the semantic values of the subject *Clinton* and the predicate *sleeps* by appealing to the relation of set membership. In the next few sections we extend our analysis in an attempt to account for a wider range of linguistic data. We follow these discussions by discussing some challenges to our basic approach.

We begin by noting a feature of semantic interpretation that we have been conveniently ignoring — the matter of tense. *Clinton sleeps* is true, in our analysis, just in case the individual named by *Clinton* is among the sleepers. But we have been playing fast and loose with our temporal frame of reference, as becomes obvious when we consider the closely related sentence *Clinton slept*. We can bring out the problem in the following way: If Clinton is a member of the set of those who slept yesterday, that is enough to make today's utterance of *Clinton slept* true, but it is insufficient to guarantee the truth of today's utterance of *Clinton sleeps*. More generally, *Clinton sleeps* is true in its interpretation as a simple present-tense assertion if and only if the set of those who are sleeping at the moment of utterance includes Clinton. The past-tense utterance *Clinton slept* obviously has different truth-conditional requirements.

We can explain the interpretation of this type of sentence by appealing to the notion of a *possible world*. Suppose we think of the historical time line leading up to the present moment in terms of a series of states of the world, sequentially ordered from earlier moments to more recent prior moments, culminating with a world state corresponding to the moment of utterance. Suppose, further, we allow expressions like *sleeps* and *slept* to pick out their reference set in different possible worlds: the present-tense verb *sleeps* refers to the set of sleepers in the possible world that corresponds to the moment of utterance (the *actual world*), and *slept* refers to a different set of sleepers in each world ordered prior to the actual world. So, *Clinton sleeps* is evaluated relative to the actual world, whereas *Clinton slept* requires that there be at least one prior possible world in which *Clinton sleeps* is true. It is part and parcel of this approach to semantic interpretation that linguistic expressions may refer not only to objects in the actual world, but also to objects in other possible worlds. The ability to refer to things that are absent from the immediate frame of reference, sometimes called *semantic displacement,* is a property of human language that has been thought to be a characteristic that distinguishes it from many other types of animal communication systems.

IN DETAIL 5.6

Although English has only two tenses, past and present, there are other resources available in the language that modify the temporal frame of reference. For example, English uses various helping verbs including *will, shall,* and *must* indicating action taking place in the future. We can extend the possible-worlds approach to tense to interpret these kinds of cases by incorporating future states of the world into our timeline, as well as prior states of the world. In this view, not only do we model ways the world has been but also ways it will be in the future. The interpretation of sentences like *John will sleep* involves identifying a future world in which *John sleeps* is true. Of course, at any given moment, we do not know what the world of the future will be like, which might lead you to think that developing a model that includes future worlds would be problematic. However, despite our ignorance of the future, we do know what it must be like for *John will sleep* to be true — the individual named by *John* must be in the set of sleepers (assuming the set-theoretic approach to intransitive verbs). Our model

simply describes how the world must turn out in order for a given sentence to be true (see Dowty, Wall, and Peters 1981).

So far, so good; but when we examine more-complicated helping verb constructions, we find additional aspects of the tense system that must be accounted for. Consider, expressions like *John had been sleeping* and *John will have been sleeping*. In these cases, the temporal reference point cannot be simply placed before or after the moment of utterance. In an effort to provide interpretations for these and other related examples, Reichenbach (1947) proposes to fix the time frame of an utterance relative to three anchor points: the point of speech, the point of the event, and the point of reference.

The point of speech is what we would call the time of utterance; and by identifying moments before, at, and after this time point we have seen how to account for past, present, and future time reference.

The point of the event is the time at which the action expressed by a sentence takes place. In an example

like *John had slept,* the point of event is the moment prior to the point of speech at which the sleeping took place.

Reichenbach then observes that this example also involves a point of reference that is prior to the moment of speech, but after the point of the event — a prior moment that defines a reference point prior to which the sleeping occurred. Reichenbach also discusses additional cases like *I shall have been seeing John* that involve references to the duration of the events, as well as to the three points of reference described above. Taken together, these examples suggest that our approach to tense interpretation needs to be extended to account for the full range of expression possible in English (see Hornstein 1990). ■

5.7 Names and Descriptions

Our inquiry into meaning has yielded the outlines of a theory of reference that assigns interpretations to linguistic expressions with respect to a set of possible worlds. We now consider some additional complications, beginning with a class of expressions like *the solution to the problem* or *a revolutionary new product* called *descriptions*. Descriptions are NPs that contain a common noun, and may also include determiners, adjectives, PPs, and other complements and modifiers. Descriptions that begin with words like *the, this,* and *that* are called *definite descriptions,* and those beginning with *a, some,* and the like are called *indefinite descriptions*. Descriptions are of particular interest because they play a semantic role that goes beyond the simple ability to refer to objects in the world. Consider for example, the interpretation of *Clinton* compared to that of *the president*. Although the two linguistic expressions *Clinton* and *the president* are different, their referents are the same, namely Clinton, in both cases. (Terms that pick out the same referent are called *co-referential* expressions.) More formally, the following statement is true:

⟦Clinton⟧ = ⟦the president⟧

So far, so good; but this simple extension of our account of the reference of names to handle the interpretation of descriptions

---

HISTORY 5.7-A

The distinction between names and descriptions was discussed systematically by the great philosopher Bertrand Russell (1919). He begins by observing that devoting two chapters to an analysis of the word *the* might seem excessive to many readers, but that it is, as he puts it, "a word of very great importance...". He notes the following dialogue: "Who did you meet?" "I met a man." "That is a very indefinite description." He goes on to ask: "What do I assert when I assert "I met a man"? — not, he suggests, the same thing I assert when I say "I met Jones," even if Jones is the man I met.

Definite descriptions like *the man,* Russell suggests, also function differently from names, although in this case, it is more difficult to see that this is so. He characterizes the distinction as follows:

We have, then, two things to compare: (1) a name, which is a simple symbol directly designating and individual which is its meaning, and having this meaning in its own right, independently of the meanings of all other words; (2) a description, which consists of several words, whose meanings are already fixed, and from which results whatever is to be taken as the meaning of the description. ■

Which of the following descriptions are definite descriptions and which are indefinite?

1. *some man drinking a martini*

2. *this type of problem*

3. *that type of problem*

4. *two people over there*

raises a set of questions with extremely far-reaching implications. We can put the nub of the issue like this: Does the fact that the referents of *Clinton* and *the president* are the same imply that these two expressions mean the same thing? Co-referential though these terms may be, they do not seem to be *synonymous* in the way that *groundhog* and *woodchuck* are. The term *the president,* in particular, seems to identify Clinton via the expression of descriptive content (pertaining to the presidency) that does not seem to be involved in the interpretation of *Clinton.* We can bring the problem into sharper relief by considering the interpretation of a second description, say *the leader of the free world,* which also refers to Clinton. Using our formal semantic notation we can write:

⟦the president⟧ = ⟦the leader of the free world⟧

In this case, it is quite clear that these two expressions do not mean the same thing by virtue of being co-referential. Put another way, there seems to be more to the theory of meaning than just a theory of reference.

Which of the following pairs of expressions strike you as synonymous? Discuss.

1. submarine sandwich *and* hoagie

2. woodchuck *and* groundhog

3. bachelor *and* unmarried man

4. 2+4 *and* 4

5. Jo hit the ball *and* The ball was hit by Jo

6. and *and* but

HISTORY 5.7-B

Frege first discussed the fact that the meaning of a description was not the same thing as its reference in the context of an analysis of equality. Suppose, he reasoned, that we consider the identity statements,

a = a   and   a = b

where *a* and *b* represent two different expressions that refer to the same object (say, *the Morning Star* and *the Evening Star,* each of which refers to the planet Venus). Frege (1892) observes that "If we were to regard equality as a relation between that which the names 'a' and 'b' designate [(that is, their referents)], it would seem that a = b could not differ from a = a (i.e., provided a = a is true)." But, Frege, points out, many of the great discoveries of science take the form of statements like a = b (*The Morning Star is the Evening Star,* for example) whereas statements of the form a = a (*The Morning Star is the Morning Star.*) convey no new information at all.

He concludes that a theory of meaning must include more that just an account of reference to explain why the cognitive value of a statement of the form a = a is different from that of a corresponding statement of the form a = b. ■

Let's examine our progress to see how we arrived at our current difficulty. We began by asserting that a theory of reference might explain two important properties of linguistic meaning: that language manages to be "about" the world outside our minds and that meaning may be shared among a community of speakers. Unfortunately, this quite-plausible set of assumptions has saddled us with a theory of meaning that cannot explain the difference in interpretation between co-referential expressions like *the president* and *the leader of the free world* that do not to share the same meaning. We must now explore one possible conclusion: Meaning does not equal reference.

5.8 Meaning and Reference

We can further clarify the distinction between meaning and reference by considering an example discussed by Gottlob Frege, a great logician and philosopher of language whose work at the turn of the century forms a point of departure for much current research in semantic theory. Frege draws attention to a diagram that shows two line segments intersecting at a common midpoint.

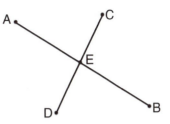

Two line segments intersecting at a common midpoint.

In this illustration, the midpoint of line segment *AB* is identical to the midpoint of line segment *CD*, namely, the point *E*. Put another way, the two expressions *the midpoint of line segment AB* and *the midpoint of line segment CD* are co-referential:

⟦the midpoint of line segment AB⟧ = ⟦the midpoint of line segment CD⟧

Nevertheless, these two expressions obviously do not bear the same meaning. In support of this claim, consider the following sentences:

The midpoint of line segment *AB* lies on line segment *AB*.
The midpoint of line segment *CD* lies on line segment *AB*.

We know that the examples are not synonymous because the first example is *analytic* (true on the basis of meaning alone); whereas the second sentence is *synthetic* (true depending on matters of fact). But if these sentences are not synonymous, Frege reasons, they must contain constituents that differ in meaning (assuming that the meaning of the whole is built out of the meanings of the parts, so-called *compositionality*).

Since the predicates of the two sentences are identical (namely, *lies on line segment AB*), the difference in meaning must lie in the interpretations of the subject NPs *the midpoint of line segment AB* and *the midpoint of line segment CD*. Finally, since the referents of these two subject NPs are the same (namely, the point *E*), it follows that the meaning of these expressions must not be identified with their referent. More generally, there must be more to interpreting descriptions than is provided by a theory of reference. This argument, a *reductio ad absurdum* (reduction to absurdity) may be summarized as follows:

Make a list of at least three other pairs of expressions that are co-referential. Can you think of any co-referential pairs that are intransitive verbs?

Make a list of three analytic and three synthetic sentences. Discuss whether the following sentences are analytic or synthetic:

1. *Everything that is green takes up space.*

2. *Either you are dead or you are alive.*

3. *Either it is raining or it isn't raining.*

4. *5 + 7 = 12*

Discuss the implications of these examples.

1. The meaning of an expression is its referent.

2. The referent of "The midpoint of line segment AB" = the referent of "The midpoint of line segment CD."

3. The meaning of the whole depends on the meanings of its parts.

4. "The midpoint of line segment AB lies on line segment AB" is analytic; "The midpoint of line segment CD lies on line segment AB" is synthetic.

5. Therefore, the meaning of "The midpoint of line segment AB" ≠ the meaning of "The midpoint of line segment AB."

6. Therefore, the referent of "The midpoint of line segment AB" ≠ the referent of "The midpoint of line segment CD."

A reductio-style argument begins with a premise (in this case, the assumption that meaning = reference) that is eventually shown to lead to a contradiction. To avoid the bane of contradiction, we must give up at least one of the premises, making the first premise look suspicious given the solid grounding of the others. We shall briefly consider two arguments that also point to the conclusion that meaning and reference are not the same. The first of these has to do with the nature of the relationship between names and their referents as compared to that between descriptions and their referents.

5.9 Names and Substitutivity

Frege's theory of reference treats names and descriptions in the same way: each type of expression takes as its referent an object in the world — for example, Clinton for *Clinton* and Yeltsin for *the last leader of the U.S.S.R.* There is evidence, however, that it is problematic to treat both kinds of NPs exactly the same way. Returning to *Clinton* as an example of a proper name, we note first that the connection between *Clinton* and Clinton is intimate and direct, and that the name does not seem to describe its bearer so much as it simply identifies him. In fact, as Kripke (1980) points out, once Clinton has been dubbed *Clinton,* the connection between the name and the referent seems to become a matter of necessity rather than a consequence of the properties that Clinton happens to have. It is easy to imagine that Clinton might have followed a different life history (had the world been different than it is); but we can still think about Clinton and refer to him as *Clinton,* even as we imagine him in an array of alternative circumstances.

In contrast, the relationship between the description *the leader of the free world* and its referent (again, Clinton) seems to be contingent on circumstances. Notice, for example, that this expression picks out different individuals in temporally distinct possible worlds, since the referent of the expression shifts over time. Once again, we are led to the conclusion that meaning may involve more than referring, since names and descriptions appear to connect to the object they name in somewhat different ways. One final consideration in support of this conclusion has come to be known as the principle of the *Substitutivity of Identicals*.

Substitutivity of Identicals
The substitution of one co-referential expression for another does not affect the truth value of a sentence.

To illustrate this principle, suppose we start with a by-now familiar example: *Clinton has some explaining to do.* Supposing that this sentence is true, we can substitute any other expression that is co-referential with *Clinton* into subject position, all the while preserving the truth of the sentence (and similarly, if the initial sentence is false, its falsity will be preserved). The sentence *The leader of the free world has some explaining to do* is an example of this type of substitution. Such an example seems to indicate that sameness of reference is sufficient to establish sameness of meaning. But the result is illusory, as we shall now see. Consider, in this regard, the sentence *Selma thinks Clinton has some explaining to do.*

To fully appreciate the problem, you have to know something about Selma. She knows perfectly well that Clinton is the president, but, being partial to conspiracy theory, she maintains that the head of the CIA is actually the leader of the free world. Furthermore, being a life-long Democrat, Selma finds Clinton beyond reproach. So, whereas

HISTORY 5.9

The principle of the Substitutivity of Identicals can be traced to the work of the late-nineteenth-century philosopher Leibniz, whose analysis is described by Frege (1892):

If our supposition that the reference of the sentence is its truth value is correct, the latter must remain unchanged when a part of the sentence is replaced by an expression having the same reference. And this is in fact the case. Leibniz gives the following definition: Eadem sunt, quae sibi mutuo substitui possunt, salva veritate. ■

Donnellan (1966) discusses descriptions like the man drinking a martini *which can be used to pick out an intended referent (say, Peters), even though Peters is in fact drinking water from a martini glass and the speaker is mistaken. And, even if Jones does fit the description (because he is drinking a martini), it is Peters who is picked out. Is this example a problem for the referential analysis of descriptions? Discuss.*

IN DETAIL 5.9

The failure of the substitutivity of co-referential expressions to preserve truth value is one of the interesting properties of *opaque contexts*. Such contexts may arise in various syntactic circumstances, such as in the complement position of subordinate-clause-taking verbs like *believe* and *know*. Montague (1973) discusses several other opaque contexts, noting that certain transitive verbs and prepositions can also introduce opacity. For example, the verb *want* and the preposition *about* seem not to tolerate the substitution of co-referential expressions while preserving the truth value:

1. John wants Jones.
2. Mary was talking about the president.

Suppose, for example, that John wants Jones, but does not know that Jones is the murderer of Smith. If we ask John, "Do you want Jones?" he says yes; but if we inquire, "Do you want the murderer of Smith?" he says no (indicating that substitutivity does not preserve truth). In a similar vein, if Mary carries on talking about the president, it does not necessarily follow that *Mary was talking about the owner of Buddy* or *Mary was talking about the ex-Governor of Arkansas,* at least if Mary (who

may not know these equivalences) is any judge of the matter.

Montague's analysis of these sorts of expressions departs from Frege's in one crucial regard: He treats these examples as systematically ambiguous between so-called "de re" and "de dicto" interpretations. Suppose we illustrate this ambiguity by considering the example *Maureen thinks that the richest man in town is a Republican*. In the de dicto interpretation, what Maureen thinks is that whoever the richest man in town is, he is also a Republican — she may have no clue who this individual is, and may be committed to this proposition only because of her general beliefs about the concentration of wealth and political identities. Notice, furthermore, that it will not do to describe her belief by freely substituting a co-referential description for *the richest man in town*. So if the richest man in town turns out to be the chairman of the chamber of commerce, it does not follow from the fact that Maureen thinks that the richest man in town is a Republican that she thinks that the chairman of the chamber of commerce is a Republican. Consequently, if we substitute *the chairman of the chamber of commerce* for *the richest man in town,* we turn a true sentence (*Maureen believes*

Selma thinks that Clinton has some explaining to do happens to be false, and *Selma thinks that the president has some explaining to do* is false as well, the third possible result of substitution, *Selma thinks that the leader of the free world has some explaining to do* is true. In short, the substitution of co-referential expressions for one another does not always preserve truth. Although this example may seem contrived, we can put the point more simply: there are some uses of descriptions in which it is the descriptive content of the description, rather than its referent, that the expression is "about." In particular, the interpretation of subordinate clauses introduced by verbs like *think, know,* and *hope,* among many others that express mental states,

places the subject's referent in a relation to a complement meaning that does not strictly depend on the referents of the sentence's constitutive parts.

In such cases, to properly understand the thoughts, knowledge, or hopes that are expressed, we must take seriously the descriptive content of the descriptions, for they are part of the meaning expressed by the subordinate clause as a whole. In the case at hand, this means that even if the expression *the leader of the free world* actually is Clinton, its use in the sentence *Selma thinks the leader of the free world has some explaining to do* implicates the head of the CIA.

that the richest man in town is a Republican) into a false one *(Maureen believes that the chairman of the chamber of commerce is a Republican).*

In contrast, by the de re interpretation, the description *the richest man in town* is taken to be about its referent; and Maureen's thought, in this case, is taken to be about whomever the description names. We can paraphrase this interpretation accurately, if somewhat awkwardly as 'The richest man in town is such that Maureen believes of him that he is a Republican.' Moreover, in this type of interpretation, we can substitute a co-referential description for *the richest man in town,* without affecting the truth value of the sentence, since it is the referent of the description rather than its sense that is involved in the interpretation of the sentence as a whole. Hence, even though Maureen might not put it this way, if *Maureen believes that the richest man in town is a Republican is true,* then so is *Maureen believes that the chairman of the chamber of commerce is a Republican,* as long as we interpret these sentences both de re.

There are two other characteristics that distinguish interpretation de re from interpretation de dicto, which have also proven to be important areas of research in semantic theory. Consider the sentence *Jill wants to marry a Norwegian.* Taken de re, it means that there is a Norwegian, say Sven, that Jill hopes to wed. But de dicto, it means that Jill hopes her husband will be Norwegian, and she may well have no particular individual in mind. Such an interpretation is sometimes labeled nonspecific, to point out that the described desire is not asserted to be about any specific individual.

The final aspect of interpretation we want to discuss may be brought out by considering a related example in which the description *a unicorn* appears, say *Smith thinks a unicorn is in the garden.* De re, the sentence cannot be true, since in order for there to be a unicorn that is such that Smith thinks it to be in the garden, there must be unicorns. However, it is an interesting feature of the de dicto interpretation of this sentence that its truth does not require the existence of unicorns. Indeed, if Smith has the relevant belief (mistaken as it may be), the sentence is true, the absence of unicorns notwithstanding (see Montague 1973 for an analysis; and Dowty, Wall, and Peters 1981; Stillings et al. 1995 for discussion and a critique). ■

IN DETAIL 5.9

5.10 Sense

In addition to the idea of compositionality and of the truth value as the referent of the sentence, Frege also introduced the distinction between *sense* and reference to account for the problems we have been considering. And even though Frege's approach to meaning remains controversial, it has served as a point of departure for much contemporary theorizing about meaning in the linguistic and philosophical traditions (see Chierchia and McConnell-Ginet 1990; Larson and Segal 1995). When Frege introduced the sense/reference distinction, one of his purposes was to challenge the popular view that meaning and reference were the same thing. He argued that the interpretation of linguistic expressions takes place on two levels, reference and a new level he called sense.

The sense of a sentence (sometimes called a *proposition*) is what it takes to make the sentence true, incorporating all of the ways that the world might be that are consistent with the truth of the sentence. In a similar vein, the sense of an intransitive verb like *sleeps* is not the set of sleepers (which is its referent), but the property of sleeping. In fact, the sense of a predicate is sometimes called a *property,* since this type of sense is the expression of the property that an individual must have to count as a member of the referent set.

We can appeal to the distinction between sense

and reference to explain the semantic difference between co-referential descriptions like *the president* and *the leader of the free world*. Both expressions pick out the same referent, but their senses are different. In this view, the sense of an expression determines its referent, but it is still possible for two expressions that share a single referent to have different senses. The different senses correspond to distinct modes of presentation. For example, *the leader of the free world* presents Clinton in terms of his role as a world leader, and *the president* presents him under a description that picks him out by

virtue of his being the chief executive officer of the US. By identifying sense as a second aspect of the meaning of descriptions, we can explain how co-referential descriptions can receive different interpretations (namely, because they express different senses). By acknowledging senses, we provide a role in our theory of interpretation for the content of a description to play.

Another motivation for positing sense as a second level of semantic interpretation concerns the interpretation of linguistic expressions that fail to refer, such as *the largest prime number* or *the*

HISTORY 5.10

Kripke's 1980 analysis of proper names captures the intuition that names identify individuals without describing them. This treatment of names (*Clinton,* for example) assigns them a different semantic role from that assigned to descriptions (like *the leader of the free world*), since only in the latter case does the content of the description serve to identify the referent. Kripke's approach to the interpretation of names differs markedly from Frege's; for Frege, names and descriptions function in the same way, each expressing a sense and denoting a referent. For example, Frege thought that the sense of a proper name like *Aristotle* might be something like *the pupil of Plato and teacher of Alexander the Great,* although he concedes that different speakers may associate different senses with the same proper name.

One of Kripke's arguments is that names succeed in picking out a referent even in circumstances in which the properties that a speaker

associates with the referent turn out (unbeknownst to the speaker) not to apply. For example, Larson and Segal (1995) discuss Galileo, who is commonly believed to have (1) dropped a cannon ball from the leaning tower of Pisa, (2) invented the telescope, and (3) first proven that light and heavy bodies fall at the same rate. It turns out that Galileo did none of these things; but speakers who use the name *Galileo* still succeed in referring to Galileo, even though the properties they ascribe to Galileo do not describe him. Under the circumstances, these false beliefs are better analyzed as such, rather than as senses that determine the referent of the name.

Kripke's analysis of proper names seems to work best for names like "John" and "Sue" that do not seem have any descriptive content. What kind of problems do names like "Mr. President" and "Miss America" pose for this theory of names?

There is also, however, evidence that cuts the other way. Consider, for example, two names like *Mark Twain* and *Samuel Clemens,* both of which refer to the same individual. In Kripke's view, it is difficult to see how we can make sense of a circumstance in which Jones (being unaware that Twain and Clemens are one and the same) believes that *Mark Twain is a great author,* but does not believe that *Samuel Clemens is a great author.* Since the two names are simply co-referential for Kripke, there is no difference in content on which to hang the different interpretations Jones assigns to them. Of course, Frege could argue that these two names express two different senses for Jones, accounting for the differences in interpretation on this basis (see Larson and Segal 1995 for a specific proposal for how to resolve this matter). ■

Frege's (1892) theory of meaning achieves generality by subsuming proper nouns, descriptions, and even sentences under the rubric of names:

Every declarative sentence concerned with the reference of its words is therefore regarded as a proper name, and its reference, if it has one, is either the True or the False.

What does Frege mean by "if it has one?" Apparently, in his view, some sentences lack a truth value:

In hearing an epic poem, for instance, apart from the euphony of the language we are interested only in the sense of the sentences and the images and feelings thereby aroused. The question of truth would cause us to abandon aesthetic delight for an attitude of scientific investigation. Hence, it is a matter of no concern to us whether the name 'Odysseus', for instance, has reference, so long as we accept the poem as a work of art [note omitted]. It is the striving for truth that drives us always to advance from the sense to the reference. (Frege 1892).

Frege argues that sentences incorporating names that lack a referent (like *Odysseus*), are themselves without a truth value, and are to be appreciated only for the thoughts they express. Frege extends his account to explain the meaningfulness of descriptions that fail to describe a referent as well. For example, the description *the celestial body most distant from Earth* has a sense, but no referent. As a consequence, a sentence like *The celestial body most distant from Earth is flat* is interpreted as a meaningful utterance, but one which is neither true nor false, owing to the gap in reference introduced by the non-referential description. ■

It is a mistake to conclude that sentences incorporating non-referential descriptions always lack a truth value. Indeed if this were the case, the status of examples like *Neptune is the celestial body most distant from Earth* and *Neptune is not the celestial body most distant from Earth* would be the same (and in Frege's view, both sentences would be neither true nor false!). Frege's conclusion that the meaningfulness of such expressions derives from their sense is incorrect; we need a more radical "therapy" for the semantics of descriptions. Russell (1919) remarks that our mistake is in assuming that descriptions are referring expressions:

"I met a unicorn" or "I met a sea-serpent" is a perfectly significant assertion…In the case of "unicorn," for example there is only the concept: there is not also, somewhere among the shades, something unreal which may be called "a unicorn." Therefore, since it is significant (though false) to say "I met a unicorn," it is clear that this proposition, rightly analyzed, does not contain a constituent "a unicorn"…

Russell also discusses the analysis of similar examples like *The King of France is bald,* arguing that the correct interpretation of this sentence would produce three assertions: (1) there is a King of France, (2) that individual is unique, and (3) that individual is bald. The truth of the sentence requires the truth of each of these three assertions. Consequently, since the first assertion is false, the whole sentence is false. ■

In Russell's view the sentence The King of France is not bald *comes out true on one interpretation. (1) Explain how Russell's analysis of definite descriptions manages to produce this result, and (2) indicate whether you think this is a plausible result (and why).*

current leader of the U.S.S.R. The theory of reference cannot provide a referent for these expressions, since there is no real-world object that these descriptions actually describe. At the same time, we do not want to conclude that a sentence that incorporates one of these descriptions is uninterpretable because of its lack of a referent. For example, the sentence *Yeltsin is the current leader of the U.S.S.R.* may not be true, but it surely is not meaningless. Frege concludes that even sentences containing constituents that lack referents express a sense (and are therefore meaningful). Furthermore, as with reference, the sense of a sentence is composed of those of its constitutive parts. This is possible even in cases involving nonreferring descriptions since, Frege proposes, though they lack referents, these descriptions still express a normal sense, which they contribute to the sense of the sentence.

Finally, let's examine how the composition of senses proceeds using the example *The president sleeps*. To determine the sense of the sentence, we combine the sense of the predicate (the property of sleeping) with the sense of the subject (which we may paraphrase as 'the chief executive officer of the US'). The result is a proposition relating these two senses, resulting in the expression of the thought that the president sleeps.

5.11 Sense and Substitutivity

We can employ the distinction between sense and reference to illuminate the substitutivity problems we faced earlier. Recall that although *the leader of the free world* and *the president* were interchangeable without affecting the truth value of:

The president has some explaining to do.

we cannot substitute one of these expressions for the other in examples like:

Selma thinks the president has some explaining to do.

without changing the truth value. It is the second example that is problematic in that it appears to violate the principle of the Substitutivity of Identicals.

Frege suggests that in special contexts like subordinate clauses introduced by verbs like *think*, occurrences of descriptions take their normal senses as their semantic values, rather their referents. By this view, the substitution fails in the above example because the two expressions *the leader of the free world* and *the president* do not have

---

Frege claims sentences containing nonreferential names are neither true nor false. Does this provide a reasonable account of the following examples?

1. Sherlock Holmes was a detective.

2. Sherlock Holmes was a fictional detective.

3. Sherlock Holmes was a prime number.

4. Sherlock Holmes was tall and Sherlock Holmes was not tall.

Discuss the implications of each example.

the same semantic value. In other words, the (real-world) referent of *the leader of the free world* is not relevant to the interpretation of the subordinate clause, accounting for why Selma's thoughts are not about the leader of the free world. This explains our observation that, in such uses, descriptions do not refer to individuals but rather contribute their content to the interpretation of the sentence. Frege's dual-level analysis of meaning provides a way of interpreting these fascinating examples without giving up the principle of Substitutivity of Identicals, while at the same time grounding our intuition that some occurrences of normally referential expressions can function more abstractly in certain contexts.

5.12 Sense and Possible Worlds

Although the notion of sense has proven quite useful in unpacking a range of semantic puzzles, there remain many questions about its nature and status. For Frege, senses were other-worldly concepts that stood outside of, but were graspable by, the human mind — a view that does not resonate with much of contemporary psychology and cognitive science. Indeed, many philosophers are skeptical of this aspect of Frege's theory (for example, Quine 1953:11). One approach to clarifying the admittedly abstract notion of sense exploits the notion of a possible world, presented earlier to account for the interpretation of tensed sentences. Recall that in this view, expressions pick out a referent in each temporally alternative world, to account for the role that tense plays in semantic interpretation. We can extend this analysis by expanding our conception of which worlds are possible to include logically possible worlds (in addition to the temporal alternatives). A logically possible world is nothing more than a way the world could have been, consistent with logic. So, another way of thinking about the claim made by *Clinton could be impeached* would be to imagine that there is a possible world in which Clinton is impeached.

We shall now see how we can use the device of (logically) possible worlds to explicate the notion of sense. Let's begin with predicate expressions like *sleeps*. Recall that the sense of a predicate is a property, a usage that accords fairly well with our informal use of the term; whereas the referent of *sleeps* is a set of sleepers, the corresponding property is what it is to be sleeping. Using the language of possible worlds, when we grasp the meaning of *sleeps,* we understand what it takes to qualify for membership in the set of sleeping things in any possible world. Thus, when we understand *sleeps,* if we were to go to another logically possible world (using our imagination), we would be able to identify the set of sleepers (that is, the referent of *sleeps*) in that world.

From the possible-worlds point of view, the property associated with a predicate turns out to be a set whose members are the referent sets of the predicate in each possible world. This mechanism allows us to reconstruct sense, which is concept-like in nature, as a set of referents. Moreover, we can generalize this insight to account for the senses of other linguistic expressions, as well. For example, the sense of a sentence (the proposition)

can be understood in possible-worlds terms as a set of worlds consistent with the truth of the sentence. Finally, names and descriptions can also be associated with senses that may be identified with sets of referents. For example, the sense of *the president* is the set whose member is the individual in each world (if any) who is the chief executive of the US.

Notice that this approach to sense preserves Frege's explanation for the apparent failure of substitutivity for co-referential expressions like *the president* and *the leader of the free world* in subordinate clauses like *thinks the president has some explaining to do*. In our current analysis, these two

---

IN DETAIL 5.12

Our appeal to possible-worlds semantics to account for the substitution properties of expressions inside and outside opaque contexts capitalizes on the ability of possible-worlds models to reconstruct Frege's distinction between sense and reference using numerous formal objects, including sets of worlds, various functions, and so forth. In the case of the failure of substitutivity in opaque contexts, our possible-worlds approach assigns semantic values to potentially intersubstitutable expressions that take into consideration the reference of these expressions in every possible world, allowing us to limit the substitutivity of co-referential expressions. So, for example, if we attempt to substitute *the president* for *the leader of the free world* in *Smith believes the leader of the free world is in trouble,* we do not expect to preserve truth because each description picks out different individuals in different worlds (hence the descriptions have different semantic values, and are thus not freely inter-substitutable).

Elegant though this analysis is, there turn out to be notable difficulties. The two problems we discuss are closely related, both deriving from the fact that the sense of a sentence has been identified with the set of worlds in which it is true. The first matter is the problem of the equivalence of *necessary truths*. Consider the following data:

1 a. Clinton is Clinton.
   b. Irene believes that Clinton is Clinton.

2 a. $5 + 7 = 12$
   b. Irene believes that $5 + 7 = 12$.

3 a. There are infinitely many prime numbers.
   b. Irene believes there are infinitely many prime numbers.

Each of the (a) sentences above expresses a necessary truth, meaning that each sentence is true in every possible world. However, given the account we have proposed of the sense of a sentence (the proposition), this means that all of the (a) sentences express the same proposition; and therefore, that they receive the same interpretation. But this seems clearly wrong: (1a) is about Clinton, (2a) is an elementary truth of arithmetic, and (3a) is a theorem requiring considerable mathematical sophistication to prove.

Worse, if our semantics is really compositional, then, because (1) the (a) sentences above express the same proposition, (2) the (b) sentences differ from one another only as to which of the (a) sentences constitute their subordinate clauses, and (3) the propositions expressed by the subordinate clauses constitute their contribution to the semantic value of the sentences in which

descriptions pick out different referents in many of the possible worlds available in our model (like one where the US lost the revolutionary war, one where Russia won the Cold War, and so forth). As a consequence, the sets of these referents that constitute the senses for each description will be different; and since expressions in semantic contexts like *think that…* take their sense as their semantic value, the principle of Substitutivity of Identicals correctly predicts the non-equivalence of the two linguistic items.

Because it explains a wide range of semantic data, the notion of sense (and its reconstruction in terms of possible worlds) has gained great favor in semantics. This approach to interpretation allows us to retain our intuition that the interpretation of complex expressions is compositional, that meanings are public, and that to know the meaning of a sentence is to know under what circumstances it would be true. Our approach to semantic interpretation provides a method for interpreting a sentence based on the interpretations of its constitutive parts. At the level of sense, we determine a set of possible worlds that covers the range of conditions consistent with the truth of the sentence. In each possible world, the sentence refers to one of

---

IN DETAIL 5.12

they appear, we predict that all the (b) sentences have the same interpretation, and that all the (b) sentences have the same truth value. Obviously, this is incorrect — Irene might well believe the identity statement about Clinton and the simple equality, while not even understanding (let alone believing) the proposition about primes. In short, it seems our semantic theory makes a false prediction, namely, that all necessary truths express the same proposition by virtue of the equivalence of the sets of worlds in which they are true.

The second problematic consideration is sometimes called the problem of logical omniscience. Consider a Sherlock Holmes story in which Holmes and Watson know all the clues to the case. Holmes performs his "elementary" deduction, and now knows who did it. Watson, however, is still in the dark, and remains so until Holmes leads him through the argument, step by step. The problem is that on the possible worlds model we have been considering, Watson's condition of believing the premises of Holmes' argument but not yet believing the conclusion is an impossible state. For consider: What makes Holmes's reasoning valid is that in every possible world in which the premises of his argument are true, the conclusion he deduces is also true. But if Watson, too, believes all the premises of the argument, and if what he believes by virtue of believing them is a proposi-

tion (a set of worlds), and if the butler did it in all those worlds, then it would seem that Watson must believe that the butler did it too. Clearly, our semantic model imputes too much — believing the premises of a valid argument does not necessarily mean that one believes the conclusion.

In consideration of these two problems, some philosophers have suggested that our semantic theory is too coarse grained; finer distinctions must be drawn among different propositions than those determined by noting the worlds in which each is true; and some provision must be made for the existence of less-than-perfect reasoners who nevertheless can still understand their native language (see Cresswell 1985; Barwise and Perry 1983, for example; see also Chierchia and McConnell-Ginet 1990). ∎

the two truth values ("true" or "false") according to whether the state of the world is consistent with the truth of the sentence. This truth value is also calculated compositionally, taking into consideration the referents of the sentence's parts.

PRO 5.12

Chierchia and McConnell-Ginet (1990) explain that a possible world is "a possible but nonactual state of affairs" that "…would be the case if some (many, most, or even all) events had different outcomes from those they in fact have." They also cite David Lewis's famous characterization:

It is uncontroversially true that things might have been otherwise than they are. I believe, and so do you, that things could have been different in countless ways. But what does this mean? Ordinary language permits the paraphrase: there are many ways they could have been besides the way they actually are. On the face of it, the sentence is an existential quantification. It says that there exist many entities of a certain description, to wit, "ways things could have been." I believe permissible paraphrases of what I believe; taking the paraphrase at its face value, I therefore believe in the existence of entities which might be called "ways things could have been." I prefer to call them "possible worlds." (Lewis 1973:84)

Although Chierchia and McConnell-Ginet (1990) acknowledge the considerable philosophical controversy surrounding the acceptance of possible worlds, they suggest that this device has proven to be "an extremely useful tool in understanding meaning." They urge that, even without fully resolving the metaphysical issues that possible worlds raise, it is reasonable to adopt possible worlds as a formal apparatus in the context of a systematic semantic theory. ∎

CON 5.12

The admission of possible worlds is an invitation to metaphysical confusion and methodological obfuscation. The virtue of explaining meaning in terms of individuals, sets of individuals, and so forth, was that we saw a way to reduce problems of meaning to more tractable (although certainly not simple) questions about individuals and their groupings and relations. By introducing possible worlds into our semantic theory, we replace one mystery — meaning — with another — possible worlds. As the philosopher W.V.O. Quine (1953) put it, possible worlds (and especially possible individuals) lead to

an overpopulated universe [that] is in many ways unlovely. It offends the aesthetic sense of us who have a taste for desert landscapes, but this is not the worst of it. [This] slum of possibles is a breeding ground for disorderly elements. Take, for instance, the possible fat man in that doorway; and, again, the possible bald man in that doorway. Are they the same possible man, or two possible men? How do we decide? How many possible men are there in that doorway? Are there more possible thin ones than fat ones? How many of them are alike? Or would their being alike make them one? Are no two possible things alike? Is this the same as saying that it is impossible for two things to be alike? Or, finally, is the concept of identity simply inapplicable to unactualized possibles? But what sense can be found in talking of entities which cannot meaningfully be said to be identical to themselves and distinct from one another? These elements are well-nigh incorrigible. (p. 4) ∎

5.13 Quantification

We turn now to a new class of linguistic expressions called *quantifiers* that raise additional challenges for our theory of interpretation. Quantifiers are expressions in certain logical languages that quantify the domain of discourse by establishing how many of its members must bear a relevant set of properties. For example, many versions of the *predicate calculus* contain the quantifiers ∀ and ∃, which may appear in the following expressions (where *S* is the predicate 'sleeps'):

1. $\forall x[S(x)]$
2. $\exists y[S(y)]$

(1) may be loosely paraphrased in English as 'For all individuals *x, x* sleeps.' Since this statement asserts that all of the members in the domain sleep, ∀ is called the *universal quantifier*. In (2), we confront the *existential quantifier,* ∃. This example may be rendered as 'There exists at least one individual *y* such that *y* smiles.' Notice that the choice of *x* or *y* makes no difference to the interpretation of these examples — such expressions are called *variables*, whose range of interpretation is fixed by the quantifier.

Logical languages like the predicate calculus include syntactic rules that define the class of well-formed expressions (including (1) and (2)) as well as a set of interpretation rules that assign the appropriate semantic values to the names and predicates in the language. Such languages also include rules for interpreting quantifiers. The rule of interpretation for (1), for example, requires us to consider each member of the domain as a case of the variable *x*, and to check to see whether *x* is in the set *S*, relative to this variable assignment.

5.14 Quantification in English

Natural languages also involve linguistic expressions that function similarly to logical quantifiers. For example, many English NPs that include determiners like *each, some, every, no,* and the like, manifest this resemblance. These English quantificational expressions have two properties in particular that merit our attention. First, these

---

IN DETAIL 5.14

Although the resemblance between the quantifiers of the predicate calculus and quantificational expressions in English is more than superficial, the English constructions involve certain complications that have led semanticists to consider alternative analyses of quantification in natural languages. As we shall see, our analysis of expressions like *all* runs into difficulties when we consider other types of quantificational expressions, and other theoretical implications. Consider, in this regard, the following sentence and its approximate translation into the predicate calculus:

1.   All dogs bark.
2. $\forall x[D(x) \rightarrow B(x)]$

The formula can be read as 'For all things *x,* if *x* is a dog then *x* barks' (the symbol $\rightarrow$ stands for 'if...then'). Notice that both the noun *dog* and the verb *bark* are treated as predicates in the logical translation, and that the quantifier binds a variable, *x,* that is the argument for each of these predicates.

This approach to quantification in

English has many virtues: It is precise, it allows us to assign reasonable interpretations to a wide range of expressions, and its formal foundations have been wellstudied. For these reasons, among others, many linguists and philosophers have thought it reasonable to translate English sentences into representations in the predicate calculus, assigning interpretations directly to the latter, thereby providing an indirect account of the semantics of natural-language expressions. There are numerous challenges that must be surmounted for this research program to succeed. First, granting that we have assigned a plausible representation to *All dogs bark,* it is difficult to see which part of the predicate calculus formula represents the interpretation of *all.*

$\forall \underline{x}[D(\underline{x}) \rightarrow B(\underline{x})]$

To the extent that we can identify symbols in the formula that correspond to *all,* the material (underlined above) is discontinuous and does not constitute a well-formed constituent of the whole. If we assume that every

expression in English must receive an interpretation (in addition to the phrases and sentences in which expressions occur), this is a problematic result.

A second difficulty concerns the generality of our analysis. Consider these examples:

1a.   Some dogs bark.
  b. $\exists x[D(x) \ \& \ B(x)]$
2a.   Most dogs bark.
  b. $\Delta x[D(x) \ \& \ B(x)]$

Example (1a) can be represented in the predicate calculus as (1b); the symbol & is the logical symbol for conjunction. (1b) says that there must exist an individual *x,* such that *x* is in the set of dogs and *x* is in the set of barkers (or alternatively, such that *x* is mapped to true by both predicates). So far, so good. Suppose we attempt to apply this style of analysis to (2a), as well, introducing the symbol Δ to represent the quantifier corresponding to *most.* Notice, that (2b) cannot be the representation of (2a), however, since (2b) requires most things to be dogs and barkers, whereas (2a) requires that

expressions can not be treated like names as expressions with *constant* interpretations, as the following example illustrates:

Nobody lives forever.

The problem is that there is no individual for *nobody* to refer to! If the interpretation of this sentence were based on the referent of *nobody,* the sentence would seem to count as meaningless — clearly the wrong result. A more reasonable way to interpret

---

most things that are dogs bark (and what is more, (2a) is true and (2b) is false — see Montague 1973; Barwise and Cooper 1981; Chierchia and McConnell-Ginet 1990; Larson and Segal 1995).

Suppose we represent Most dogs bark *as:*

$\Delta x[D(x) \rightarrow B(x)]$

Do you see any problems with this approach?

The final problem for a predicate-calculus-based theory of quantification for natural language concerns the disparity we have introduced between the semantics of names and the semantics of quantificational expressions. Recall that names, in our current view, stand for individuals, whereas quantificational expressions are represented by chains of quantifiers and variables. We may wonder if this asymmetry is reasonable given that both names and quantificational expressions are instances of the same syntactic category, NP. Furthermore, adopting this approach greatly complicates

our analysis of the interpretation of expressions like transitive verbs, since transitive verbs occur freely with both names and quantificational NPs.

For all these reasons and more, many semanticists have doubted that the predicate calculus-based analysis of quantification is suitable for natural languages. There are a variety of alternatives that have been proposed (Montague 1973; Barwise and Cooper 1981; Larson and Segal 1995, for example) many of which share a common insight. Put informally, if we treat NPs as standing for sets of properties (*John* for the set of John's properties, *every dog* for the set of properties possessed by all dogs, and so forth), we can regain parallelism between the semantic values assigned to names and those assigned to quantificational expressions. Next, we must change the method of composition for the semantic value of sentences. Suppose, then, we reverse the usual relation of set membership (which, you will recall, asks whether the individual named by the subject is

an element of the referent set picked out by the predicate), so that the truth of a sentence like *John sleeps* requires that the property of sleeping be among the set of properties that John has. If we construe properties as sets, this means that the set of sleepers must be an element of the set of sets picked out by *John.*

The same analysis can be extended to *Everybody sleeps.* In this case, the subject NP *everybody* will pick out the set of properties that everybody has; and if the property of sleeping is among that the properties in that set, the sentence will be true. Of course, there are many further details that must be resolved before this generalized analysis of quantification can be adopted (including a satisfactory account of transitive verbs, quantifier scope and opaque contexts), but there has been much work suggesting that this alternative analysis of quantificational expressions in natural language holds great promise (Chierchia and McConnell-Ginet 1990; Larson and Segal 1995). ■

IN DETAIL 5.14

quantificational expressions involves treating them as operators on a domain of individuals. In this simplified example, there are only three individuals in the domain.

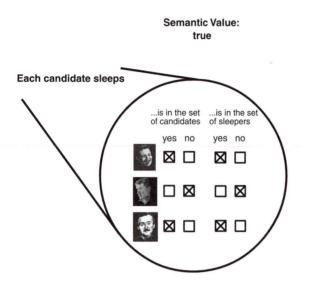

Semantic Value:
true

Each candidate sleeps

Evaluating quantificational expressions.

Describe what the model in the text needs to look like to establish the truth of the following examples:

1. *Most candidates sleep.*

2. *Many candidates sleep.*

3. *Few candidates sleep.*

4. *A few candidates sleep.*

5. *No sleepers are candidates.*

If we change the reference sets for *sleeps* and *candidate* we are effectively changing the description of the state of the world (or at least the state of this model of the world). Different property assignments will affect the semantic value of the sentence, in turn (and different quantificational expressions enforce different requirements on the state of the world required for the truth of a given sentence).

5.15 Quantifier Scope

The second interesting property exhibited by quantificational expressions is a phenomenon known as *scope ambiguity*. As background for this discussion, recall that we have previously considered the analysis of ambiguous sentences in which each different interpretation was assigned a different syntactic representation. For example, the alternative constituency for *over* correlates with the two different meanings expressed by the sentence *The people talked over the noise*. There are also well-known cases of ambiguity in which the cause of the multiple interpretations can be traced to ambiguities in word meaning. Examples like *Harry bought a CD* (investment or music?) is a case in point. Consider, now some examples that involve quantifier scope ambiguities:

1. Blik is not available in all areas.
2. Somebody bought everything.

The first sentence can be used to assert that the item *Blik* is available only in some areas or to assert that it is available in none. The second example entails either that a single individual has been on a spree, or alternatively, that all goods were sold (but not necessarily to the same purchaser).

5.16 Analyzing Scope

Part of the interest in these sentences lies in the fact that their ambiguity is not traceable to either structural or lexical causes. Note, for example, that there are no ambiguous words in either of the sentences above. The surprising conclusion is that quantificational expressions introduce ambiguity only in combination with certain other linguistic items. As you can see from the examples below, the generalization capturing the range of expressions that interact with quantificational expressions to introduce ambiguity is quite complex.

1. Everybody loves somebody sometime.
2. Pat loved Mary forever.
3. Somebody voted for every candidate.
4. Somebody voted for some candidate.
5. Everybody voted for some candidate.
6. Everybody voted for all the candidates.
7. Mary liked all the ducks.
8. All the ducks liked Mary.
9. Mary didn't like all the ducks.
10. All the ducks didn't like Mary.

For example, quantificational expressions like *all* and *every* often lead to ambiguity in the context of negation (*Mary didn't like all the ducks*) or in the context of other quantificational expressions that act like existential quantifiers (*Everybody voted for some candidate*), but not in combination with each other (*Everybody voted for all the candidates*). Existential-style quantificational expressions like *some* and *a* produce ambiguity in consort with universal quantifierlike expressions (*Somebody voted for every candidate*), but not with negation, or with each other.

List three other words that are ambiguous in the way that CD is. Can you think of any words that are three-ways ambiguous? (We can think of record — music, Guinness, or stenography.) How about one that is four-ways ambiguous? How many distinct meanings can you assign to bug? Does it surprise you that languages reuse vocabulary in this way? Discuss.

You have probably heard sentences like Blik is not available in all areas many times on television, following advertisements for a new product that is being test-marketed. If you have, did the ironic ambiguity occur to you? (It does not, to most people.) Can you explain why a sentence like this might seem unambiguous even though it is in fact ambiguous?

How can we explain this puzzling array of facts while maintaining the principle of compositionality to which we are committed? One analysis, based on the theory of quantification incorporated in the predicate calculus, allows two different ways to combine the interpretations of the parts of quantificationally ambiguous sentences to compose the interpretation of the whole sentence. Simplifying the notation somewhat, on this approach, *Blik is not available in all areas* can be represented in roughly the two following ways:

1. ¬∀x[Blik is available in x]
2. ∀x[¬Blik is available in x]

"¬" is the logical symbol for negation ('it is not the case that'). Assuming that the quantifier ranges over areas in this case, the representation in (1) can be roughly paraphrased as 'It is not the case that for all areas *x*, Blik is available in *x*.' This captures the reading of the English sentence *Blik is not available in all areas* in which Blik is missing from some sales markets. The second representation, (2), paraphrased roughly as 'For all areas *x*, it is not the case that Blik is available in x,' captures the other reading of the English sentence. For this formula to be true, it must be true of all areas that Blik is unavailable in them.

We can refer to these two different interpretations as the NOT/ALL and the ALL/NOT readings, respectively, since in the first case, the interpretation of the negation takes precedence over the interpretation of the quantifier, whereas these roles are reversed in the second representation. Alternatively, we can say that in (1) (repeated below), the negation is outside the scope of the quantifier (marked by the brackets), whereas in (2), the negation is within its scope.

1. ¬∀x[Blik is available in x]
2. ∀x[¬Blik is available in x]

When we interpret (1) with respect to a possible world, in effect we check to see that the assertion ∀x[*Blik is available in* x] is false in that world. Correspondingly, the proposition expressed by (1) is the set of all worlds in which ∀x[*Blik is available in* x] is false. (2), however, is a different story. To determine its referent we must evaluate each relevant member of the domain to establish that it is not the case that Blik is available in it. The corresponding proposition is the set of worlds in which each area satisfies this requirement.

A similar scope contest operates in multiply quantified examples like *Somebody bought everything*. In this case, the two predicate calculus representations are as follows:

1. ∃x[∀y[x bought y]]
2. ∀y[∃x[x bought y]]

(1) is read 'there is an *x* such that for each *y*, *x* bought *y*.' This is the SOME/EVERY interpretation in which the universal quantifier falls inside the scope of the existential quantifier. In (2), the scopes are reversed, yielding, in paraphrase, 'For each *y* there is an *x* such that *x* bought *y*.' This is the representation for the EVERY/SOME interpretation. Once again, the rules of interpretation for these formulas guarantee the assignment of the correct interpretation based on the form of the logical expressions (their *logical form*).

How many different interpretations can you assign to Everybody loves somebody sometime? *Describe each distinct reading unambiguously.*

Unlike the distributional properties of quantifiers in the predicate calculus, quantificational expressions in English exhibit many complications and idiosyncrasies that must be explained before we can claim to fully understand this aspect of semantic theory. Consider, for instance, the class of *negative polarity items* — expressions (including quantificational expressions) that must appear in tandem with negation (or in a small number of other licensing constructions). The following examples involve the quantificational expression (and negative polarity item) *any*.

1. I didn't eat any beans.
2. *I ate any beans.
3. John left without eating any beans.
4. *John left after eating any beans.

The first two examples illustrate the typical restriction displayed by negative polarity items: This class of items can appear in negative sentences but not in the corresponding positive sentences. The next two examples show that the characterization of an appropriate negative item is complicated — *without* seems to count, but *after* does not (see Chierchia and McConnell-Ginet 1990; Larson and Segal 1995 for further discussion).

You have probably heard the old saying two negatives make a positive. *If this were true as far as the grammar were concerned, we might expect that* It is not the case that I don't eat beans anymore *would be ungrammatical (since the double-negative context would equal a positive context. Does this sentence seem acceptable to you? Discuss.*

Another complexity displayed by the English quantificational system concerns the proper analysis of descriptions like *a foreign language* or a *friend of Bill's*. To some extent, these constructions behave like the quantificational expressions *every* and *no*. For example, it is easy to produce cases in which these descriptions seem to enter into scope ambiguities with other quantificational expressions:

1. Everybody admires a friend of Bill's.
2. Every student speaks a foreign language.

In these two cases, for example, both the *EVERY/A* and the *A/EVERY* readings are available. These facts suggest that Russell's analysis of indefinite determiners as quantificational expressions is preferable to Frege's analysis of indefinites as referring expressions. However, there are other considerations that point in the opposite direction. For example, quantificational expressions cannot normally serve as antecedents for pronouns across conjuncts or across sentences in a discourse:

1. Every boy thought he passed.
2. Every boy passed and he was lucky.
3. Speaker A: Every boy passed.
   Speaker B: Was he lucky!
4. John thought he passed.
5. John passed and he was lucky he did.
6. Speaker A: John passed.
   Speaker B: Was he lucky!

In (1), *every boy* can bind *he,* but not in (2) or (3) (in which *he* must receive a discourse interpretation). Examples (4) through (6) show that names are not subject to the same restriction, and so *he* may be bound by *John* in all three cases. The following data show that indefinite descriptions pattern like names, in this regard:

1. A boy thought he passed.
2. A boy passed and he was lucky.
3. Speaker A: A boy passed.
   Speaker B: Was he lucky!

Note that in each case, *a boy* can serve as the antecedent for *he.*

As a result of evidence like this, some semanticists have considered the possibility that indefinite descriptions may be capable of supporting both quantifierlike and namelike interpretations, an interesting wrinkle in our analysis of quantificational expressions in English that we return to below. ▪

HISTORY 5.16

One of the most important historical antecedents for the level of interpretation known has *logical form* is found in the work of Bertrand Russell (1919). Russell became convinced that the analysis of meaning was handicapped by the inappropriate assumption that the grammatical form of an utterance dictated the nature of its semantic composition.

Misled by grammar, the great majority of those logicians who have dealt with this question [concerning the interpretation of descriptions] have dealt with it on mistaken lines. They have regarded grammatical analysis as a surer guide in analysis than, in fact, it is. And they have not known what differences in grammatical form are important.

Russell's more specific claim was that the subject/predicate grammatical structure of sentences like *The King of France is bald* leads to the unwarranted assumption that the subject NP *the King of France* is a logical constituent of the meaning of the sentence, and the false conclusion that this description is a referring expression. Russell determined that the logical form of an utterance must be analyzed separately from its gram-

matical form. The influence of Russell's position can be seen in the quantifier-variable style analysis of quantificational expressions in English. In this approach, although a grammatical analysis of a quantified sentence posits an NP and a VP, the quantificational structure is quite different. Here, by way of example, is the syntactic structure for *Everybody loves somebody*:

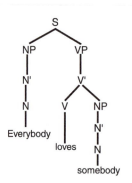

Representation for *Everybody loves somebody*.

The representations for the each of the two interpretations of (the scopally ambiguous) *Everybody loves somebody* are shown below:

1. $\forall x[\exists y[x \text{ loves } y]]$
2. $\exists y[\forall x[x \text{ loves } y]]$

In addition to the lack of isomorphism between these syntactic and logical forms, we should also note that there is little motivation for assigning different syntactic structures to *Everybody loves somebody* to correspond to its two different interpretations. In short, this Russell-style analysis of quantification treats semantic interpretation as independent of syntactic analysis.

When the 1970s and 1980s found generative linguists becoming more and more interested in quantification, several analyses were developed that attempted to provide a more systematic analysis of the relationship between syntactic structure and interpretation. It was proposed that logical form, or as these linguists called it, LF, constituted a new level of syntactic representation derived by applying movement transformations to quantified NPs. This new type of transformation, called Quantifier Raising was a way of assigning scope to quantificational expressions in the framework of a syntactic analysis. Since these moved constituents were still pronounced in their pre-movement positions, it was assumed that Quantifier Raising applied after the pronunciation of the sentence was calculated. Here is the LF for the

SOME/EVERY interpretation of *Everybody loves somebody* (we present the *EVERY/SOME* interpretation below):

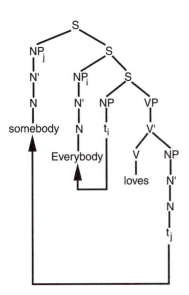

Representation for the *SOME/EVERY* interpretation of *Everybody loves somebody*.

The traces (indicated by the special terminal symbol *t*) are each indexed to a particular quantifier, creating movement chains with properties similar to those created by other movement rules. Notice also that Quantifier Raising moves quantificational expressions to the left

periphery of *S,* and that this adjunction rule can apply iteratively to append more than one quantificational expression to this position. The derivational approach to LF assigns representations to quantified sentences that look in many ways like the predicate-calculus formulas that were traditionally used to interpret quantification. In particular, Quantifier Raising allows us to assign scope to moved expressions, and the traces of movement function similarly to the variables in the predicate-calculus notation. Finally, by allowing Quantifier Raising to apply in either order in multiply quantified examples like *Everybody loves somebody,* we can derive alternative scope assignments. The LF representation for the *EVERY/SOME* interpretation is shown at right.

This analysis of quantification at LF has had profound implications for work on semantic theory in the generative tradition (see Larson and Segal 1995). Still, there are several rival analyses (for example, Chierchia and McConnell-Ginet 1990), and much continued debate. In particular, as interest has developed in nontransformational grammars, new approaches have been developed that attempt to account for the

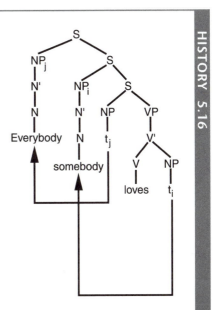

Representation for the *EVERY/SOME* interpretation of *Everybody loves somebody*.

interpretation of quantificational expressions without appealing to Quantifier Raising (see Brody 1995 and the references cited there). Indeed, the question of how to best interpret quantificational expressions in natural languages continues to be an engaging research question to this very day (see Heim and Kratzer 1998). ■

5.17 English Scope Ambiguity

Let us try to exploit these insights to develop an account of scope ambiguity for English quantificational expressions. Suppose we treat the transitive verb *bought* as picking out a reference set whose members are the pairs of things that are in a buyer/purchase relation to one another, in each possible world. So, in a world in which the sales transactions were limited to Joe's purchase of the Batmobile and the White House and Sally's acquisition of the Taj Mahal, the semantic value for *buy* would be as follows (postponing a discussion of how we evaluate the semantic contribution of the past-tense marker on the verb):

$[\![buy]\!]$ = {<Joe,the Batmobile>, <Joe,the White House>, <Sally,the Taj Mahal>}

The angle brackets indicate that the members of this set are "ordered pairs." As you might guess, order is crucially important in such pairs. In particular, note that the ordered pair <Joe,the Batmobile> is not equivalent to the ordered pair <the Batmobile,Joe>; in order to treat the semantic value of *buy* as a set of pairs, we must keep straight which member is the buyer and which the purchase. It is important to remember that the ordered pair <Joe,the Batmobile> is a pair of objects, not a pair of names. We dwell on this point to establish that ordered pairs are just like individuals and reference sets in that they are formalized representations of part of the furniture of the world and not parts of the language.

Next, let's consider the evaluation of the scope-ambiguous sentences beginning with *Somebody bought everything*. The linear scope SOME/EVERY reading asks us to choose a buyer who has purchased everything. The crossed-scope interpretation (EVERY/SOME) places weaker requirements on the world. On this reading, we must check that with respect to each thing available for purchase, somebody purchased it. Similarly, *Everybody bought*

HISTORY 5.17

The ordered pair is a construct drawn from elementary set theory. Quine (1970) introduces ordered pairs in the following passage:

I have taken to speaking in pairs. the pairs wanted are ORDERED pairs; that is, we must distinguish the pairs <x,y> and <y,x> so long as x ≠ y. For we have to say that the pair <3,5> satisfies 'x < y' while <5,3> does not. The law of ordered pairs is that if <x,y> = <z,w> then x = z and y = w.

Since our proposed use of ordered pairs treats them as the semantic values of transitive verbs, we might inquire as to what kind of object they are (as a way of ensuring that we are on safe ground when using them as part of our semantic theory). Quine goes on to suggest that we do not need to recognize pairs are primitive objects in our theory; it is enough to recognize the objects that constitute the members of the pairs:

When I say the pair <3,5> satisfies the sentence 'x < y', I am assuming for the time being that the sentence 'x < y' belongs to the object language [that is, the language we are studying, in this case, elementary arithmetic] and that the domain of objects of the object language includes the numbers 3 and 5; but I do not need to assume that this domain include their pair <3,5>. The pair belong to the apparatus of my study [the "metalanguage"], and this is enough. (Quine 1970) ■

In addition to transitive and intransitive verbs, English also has a smaller number of "di-transitive" verbs like show *that take two NP objects — for example* Mary showed Bill Harry. *How could we extend our analysis of transitive verbs to handle these new cases?*

something allows for two different scopal interpretations. The linear EVERY/SOME reading of this sentence requires each purchaser to have bought at least one thing. The crossed-scope SOME/EVERY reading is stronger in this case, requiring that some one thing be purchased by all the buyers.

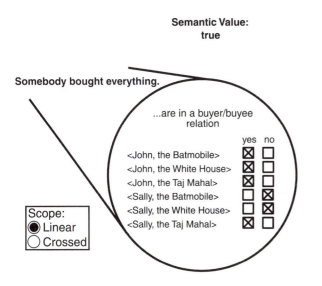

Somebody bought everything.

Semantic Value:
true

...are in a buyer/buyee
relation

Scope:
● Linear
○ Crossed

Evaluating quantificationally ambiguous sentences.

Describe what the model in the text must be like to establish the truth of the following sentences (beware of ambiguities!):

1. Nobody buys everything.

2. Most people buy something.

3. Nobody buys anything.

Finally, we return to the matter of tense, which we postponed at the beginning of this discussion. The sentences we are evaluating contain the word *bought,* the past-tense form of the verb *buy.* We have provided a semantic value for *buy* directly in our model, but it remains to take account of the meaning of the past tense morpheme. In the possible-worlds approach to the interpretation of tense, the meaning of X *bought* Y can be captured by evaluating the corresponding present-tense sentence X *buys* Y with the further requirement that there be a possible world in which the present-tense sentence is true that describes a state of the world prior to the moment of utterance. In effect, we treat X *bought* Y as requiring that there is a possible prior world in which X *buys* Y is true.

5.18 Restrictions on Scope

Our approach to the interpretation of quantificational expressions draws much of its motivation from the traditional analysis of quantifiers in the predicate calculus. The emphasis in this tradition is to provide a systematic general procedure capable of assigning interpretations to quantified sentences of arbitrary complexity. Indeed, the solution of this problem constitutes one of the major accomplishments in semantic theory (Tarski 1944). Research in the last few decades has emphasized a second, more structurally motivated interest in quantification that concerns itself primarily with the ways in which syntactic principles restrict the range of interpretation of quantificational expressions. Although we do not explore this interesting topic in much detail, a survey of some of the relevant phenomena is perhaps in order. We begin with a consideration of locality conditions.

We have established that universal and existential quantificational expressions can participate in quantifier scope ambiguities, accounting for the multiple interpretations available for (1) and (2), below:

1. Somebody stole all the guitars.
2. Everybody speaks two languages.
3. Everybody fell and somebody laughed.
4. Somebody thinks that Bill likes everybody.

However, it comes as something of a surprise that (3) and (4) are unambiguous, despite that each of these examples contains a pair of the kinds of quantificational expressions that usually induce scope ambiguities. In the case of (3), it is the fact that each of these expressions lies in a separate conjunct that limits their interaction. We can capture this restriction by formulating the following principle:

IN DETAIL 5.18

In the previous "In Detail" section, we discussed some complications in the analysis of indefinite descriptions suggesting that these expressions share properties with quantificational expressions and with names. Here, we consider one additional piece of evidence that bears on this question. It is because indefinite descriptions can take scope with respect to other quantificational expressions that we are inclined to treat them as such. So, the ambiguity of *Everybody speaks a foreign language* (implying on one reading, a single universal tongue; and on the other, merely broad bilingualism) supports this analysis. The Scope Principle allows us to test the analysis further. If indefinite descriptions are true quantificational expressions, their scopes should be limited by this principle in the same way that the scopes of other quantificational expressions are. Here are some data that bear on this question:

1 a. Everybody spoke few languages.
  b. Everybody thought Mary spoke few languages.
2 a. Everybody spoke an exotic language.
  b. Everybody thought Mary spoke an exotic language.

(1a) incorporates two quantificational expressions (*everybody* and *few languages*) and is ambiguous in the usual way: by the *EVERY/FEW* reading it means that everyone was such that they spoke a small number of languages (that is, no polyglots); by the *FEW/MANY* reading, it means that a small number of languages were such that everybody spoke them (say, English and Spanish). Turning now to (1b), notice that there is only one possible scope interpretation: It means only that everyone is such that they thought that Mary spoke a small number of languages. In particular, (1b) cannot mean that there are few languages (say, only English and Spanish) that everyone thought Mary spoke. Note that it is not that this isn't a perfectly good thing to mean — it is just that (1b) does not express this proposi-

Scope Principle
Crossed-scope interpretations are only possible between quantifiers in the same local domain.

Although it is complicated to define the relevant local domain precisely, for our purposes we can take it to be "clause" (see May 1985; Larson and Segal 1995). In this view, there is no ambiguity in *Everybody fell and somebody laughed* because there is only one quantificational expression in each of the conjoined clauses. Notice that this analysis automatically predicts the univocality (lack of ambiguity) of *Somebody thinks that Bill likes everybody.* For in this case, as well, the two quantificational expressions *Somebody* and *everybody* occur in separate clauses, the former in the main clause and the latter in the subordinate clause. In such circumstances, the Scope Principle limits the possible interpretations to those consistent with linear scope. In this case, a SOME/EVERY interpretation

The Scope Principle predicts that quantificational expressions in the same clause should be able to participate in scope contests, potentially introducing scope ambiguities. Given this analysis, how many readings for Somebody's picture of everybody was over-exposed *would you expect? Are any of these readings missing? Discuss.*

IN DETAIL 5.18

tion; a fact explained by the Scope Principle.

Turning now to (2a), once again we find a familiar scope contest at work between *everybody* and an *exotic language.* On the *EVERY/AN* reading, different people may speak a different exotic language, so long as everyone speaks one; the *AN/EVERY* reading requires that there be a particular exotic language that is such that it is spoken by everybody. We begin by noting that (2b) does support the expected *EVERY/AN* interpretation, according to which everybody is such that they think that Mary speaks an exotic language (with possibly different languages for each different thinker). The surprise

is that the *AN/EVERY* interpretation also seems available for the current example. By this reading, there is a particular exotic language that is such that everybody thought Mary spoke it. For this interpretation to be assigned, it seems to be necessary for the description in the subordinate clause, *an exotic language* to take wider scope than the NP *everybody.* Since the latter is in main-clause subject position, this appears to contravene the Scope Principle.

Of course, the other possibility is that the indefinite description *an exotic language* should not be treated as a quantificational expression in this case, and should therefore not be expected to conform to

the Scope Principle. This conclusion is consistent with our previous observations about the polymorphous character of indefinite descriptions. Although we shall not resolve this debate about the proper treatment of quantification in English, our discussion may serve as a detailed example of the character of the data and the subtlety of analysis involved in investigations of meaning. We also hope you can see why questions about quantification remain some of the most interesting topics in current research. ■

requiring that a single individual thinks that Bill likes everyone is all that is available. In particular, the putative crossed-scope interpretation in which, for example, Seymour believes that Bill likes Joe, Sally believes that Bill likes Hugh, and so forth (that is, different believers correlating with different "lovees"), is not supported by the example in question.

5.19 Wh-quantifiers

Finally, we want to acknowledge another class of quantificational expressions that we have confronted before, but perhaps not considered from the semantic point of view. All the Wh-words in English, *which, who,* and so forth, are not only of interest for their syntactic behavior but also because of their quantifierlike behavior. Consider, in this regard, the following examples:

1. Who do you like?
2. Tell me who likes everyone.
3. Who thinks Bill likes everyone.

We note that the first of these examples can be straightforwardly paraphrased as Who is a person, *x,* such that you like *x.* with a manifestly quantifier-variablelike interpretation. More evidence for this analysis comes from (2), an embedded question that displays a scopal ambiguity. In one interpretation, a responsive answer would indicate which person has the property of liking everyone ("Bill — Bill likes everyone."). But in a second interpretation, the question may be answered as follows:

Hansel likes Gretel, Harry likes Sally, Romeo likes Juliet, and I like you.

The former interpretation seems to treat *who* as taking scope over *everyone,* and the latter construes *everyone* as taking scope over *who.*

Finally, we note that the possibilities of scopal interactions between Wh-words and other quantificational expressions seem to observe the Scope Principle. Sentence (3), for example, allows for just one interpretation despite containing the same two quantificational expressions (*who* and *everyone*) that we have seen introduce an ambiguity in (2).

The explanation is once again that the two quantificational expressions are in separate clauses, forcing *everyone* to be interpreted as falling within the scope of *who,* with the interpretation 'Who is a person, *x,* such that *x* thinks that for all persons, *y, x* likes *y?*'.

Does the interrogative quantificational expression who *seem more like an existential quantifier or a universal quantifier in the following examples (that is, would you answer with a single name or a list)?*

1. Who died and left you boss?

2. Who has passed the physics test?

3. Who did you marry?

What seems to account for the shifts in meaning?

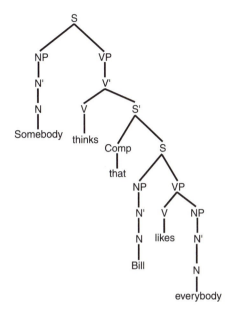

Representation for *Somebody thinks that Bill likes everybody.*

5.20 Summary

Our brief survey of meaning has concentrated on how interpretations can be systematically assigned to English sentences of several different types, with the interpretations of phrases and sentences dependent on the interpretations of their constitutive parts. At the heart of our approach is a model-based truth-conditional semantics that assigns semantic values to expressions based on their referents in a possible world. We also argued, following Frege, that a second level of interpretation called sense must be added to our semantic framework.

We employed senses to explain certain puzzles with substitutivity and with the interpretation of referentless linguistic expressions that nevertheless bear meaning. We also discussed a more contemporary reconstruction of the idea of sense in terms of possible-worlds semantics. Next, we explored the fascinating world of conjunctions and quantificational expressions, stopping along the way to consider a theory of quantification developed as a part of the predicate calculus that is the historical antecedent for much contemporary work on natural-language semantics. We then developed our model of evaluation to incorporate English quantificational expressions and conjunctions into the semantic system, and followed this up with analysis of scope ambiguities. In a pair of final sections, we considered some recent work in syntactic theory that has lead to a better understanding of some of the interactions between syntactic structure and semantic interpretation.

6. Brain and Language

6.1 What Is Neurolinguistics?

Neurolinguistics is a relatively young branch of science investigating the relationship between language and the brain. While it is generally accepted that language ability is supported by brain structures, the relationship is far from clear.

Up to now, even the use of modern research tools like Positron Emission Tomography *(PET)* scans or Nuclear Magnetic Resonance Imaging *(NMRI)* did not definitively answer exactly how, and precisely which, brain structures are involved in language production and comprehension. However, these techniques did provide us with important insights into the language/brain relationship.

Theoretically, obstacles to a better understanding of the brain/language relationship can result from the following conditions:

- There is a lack of fundamental insights into the physiology and biochemistry of neuronal structures;

- Our theory of language is incomplete;

- In spite of recent advances, our technology is not sophisticated enough.

Each of the above mentioned bears on the modern science of neurolinguistics.

One goal of this science may be defined as an attempt to answer the seemingly simple question, is linguistics reducible to neurology? That is, is it possible to describe our language ability using only the vocabulary of neurology — terms like *neurons, synaptic connections,* and *cerebral cortex?* At this point, there is no definitive answer to this question; and it is the subject of lively debate. While there are no decisive proofs, the proponents of the opposing views have collected convincing arguments for their respective cases. Welcome to the discussion!

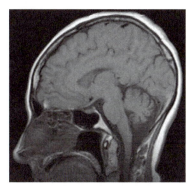

This MRI image illustrates the level of detail that can be obtained with this technique. One can easily distinguish major anatomical structures like the corpus callosum and the cerebellum.

PRO 6.1

If we accept the premise that brain structures are necessary and sufficient for language, then it is just one more step to the claim that language can be explained using terms from neurology. To achieve this goal, we would need only to relate linguistic phenomena (like understanding of the meaning of words) to the corresponding brain states.

For example, let us say that we can demonstrate that whenever one hears a simple sentence like *Sit on that chair!*, certain groups of neurons in the brain are activated in a particular fashion. If this is the case, the process of understanding the meanings of the words and their relationship in this sentence could be described solely in terms of neuronal activity. Furthermore, if it were possible to demonstrate that for every known linguistic phenomenon there exists a corresponding brain state, then linguistics as a branch of science would become superfluous and obsolete. ■

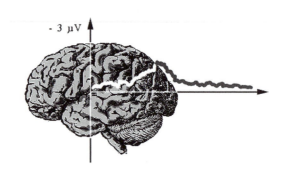

Sit on that chair! =

CON 6.1

Linguistics can never be reduced to neurology for the simple reason that there is no direct and consistent correspondence between linguistic and neurological phenomena. While it is true that brain structures are necessary for language production and comprehension, language cannot be explained by describing the activity of these structures.

By way of an analogy, Fodor (1975) discusses the relationship between the science of the economy, and economic transactions. While the trade and market value of goods follow certain economic laws, these laws cannot be reduced to the description of actual trade transactions. There is an infinite number of possible forms that economic transactions can take. One may trade labor for land, and land for a house, a house for money and money for a horse; but even a very detailed description of all these activities cannot explain the laws of economy. If this is the kind of relationship that exists between the rules of language production and comprehension and brain structures, then it will never be possible to explain language by describing brain activity. ■

Most linguists agree that language can be represented by a set of principles and parameters plus a set of language-specific rules (a grammar). From this point of view, one way to examine the language/brain relationship is to look for neurological structures that embody the rules of grammar.

Is it possible to explain your thoughts and intentions by a description of the activity of neurons? Write an essay discussing the position you disagree with.

HISTORY 6.1

During the history of humankind, there have been many speculations about the purpose of the brain and its function. The ancient Greeks (e.g., Aristotle, 384–322 BC) believed that the major function of the brain is to cool the blood, in a manner similar to the way radiators cool automobiles. For a while, actual brain tissue was even considered to be only an inert supporting structure, while the real function was localized in the spaces of the brain filled with fluid — the brain ventricles.

Galen (129–200 AD), depicted here, was one of the greatest physicians of his time. Although some of his hypotheses were blatantly

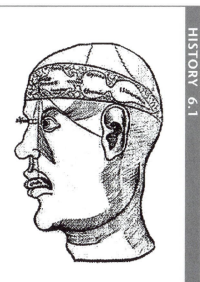

wrong, his enormous authority helped maintain them over the centuries. ■

A sixteenth-century drawing of the brain parts involved in major cognitive functions.

IN DETAIL 6.1

According to Fodor (1975), there are two general relationships that may exist between psychological and neurological terms. One of them, which he calls type reductionism, is a relationship of principled correspondence between the phenomena, the laws of psychology, and brain states. Specific psychological states and laws would exist just because they are embodied in corresponding brain structures or their states. In this case it would be theoretically possible to replace psychological laws with a description of specific brain states. However, even if brain structures are necessary for the existence of psychological phenomena, these structures and their activity do not have to be related to each other in a lawful manner. This view, which Fodor terms token physicalism, is illustrated by the relationship between computer programs ("software") and their physical embodiment ("hardware"). While it is not possible to run computer programs without computers, the individual physical states of a computer chip are on their own not lawfully related to each other.

The physical states of a computer chip are only temporarily organized by instructions provided by the program. A different program would impose a different sequence of states of the same chip. If our brains function in this way, then the description of language ability using neurological terms would not be possible. ■

6.2 Neural Structures Supporting Language Functions

The main coordinator of the body is the nervous system. It is made up of billions of special cells called neurons. The nervous system is responsible for synchronizing the events within the body in order to regain and maintain fine inner balance (*homeostasis*). It is also responsible for regulating interactions with the outside world across all levels of our existence. A part of the nervous system called the *central nervous system (CNS)* hosts all of the so-called higher cognitive functions, including our ability to comprehend and produce grammatical utterances.

The CNS is contained and protected by the bony casing of the skull and spinal vertebrae. Anatomically, it is divided into two major structures, the brain and the spinal cord (see illustration).

The main part of the brain, called the *cerebrum*, consists of approximately 54 ounces of wrinkled, jellylike tissue, divided in two symmetrical parts — the left and the right cerebral hemispheres. The hemispheres are connected by the *corpus callosum,* a white band of tissue made up of an estimated 150–200 million nerve fibers.

The corpus callosum allows for the almost instantaneous transfer of information between the hemispheres. However, the hemispheres are not symmetrical in function — the capacity for language is localized almost exclusively in one hemisphere, most often the left.

You should familiarize yourself with the basic anatomical landmarks of the brain. Note the wrinkled surface with an abundance of *convolutions*. The hilly parts of these convolutions are called *gyri* (singular, gyrus), and the crevices between them are called *sulci* (singular, sulcus) or fissures.

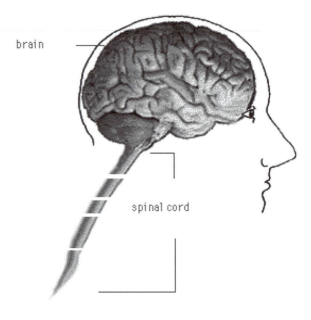

brain

spinal cord

If you have already studied the section describing the anatomy of the brain, you should be able to identify some of the major anatomical landmarks, like the *sylvian fissure,* frontal lobe, or central sulcus. Although there are significant differences in the topography of individual brains, the basic pattern and number of convolutions are fairly consistent.

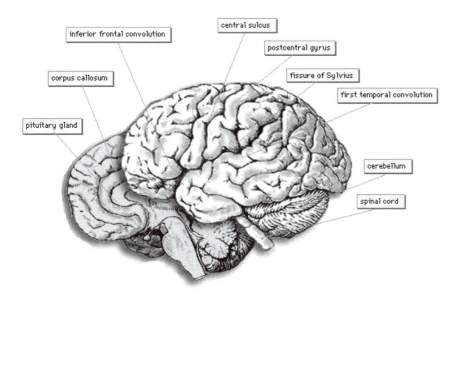

inferior frontal convolution

central sulcus

postcentral gyrus

corpus callosum

fissure of Sylvius

first temporal convolution

pituitary gland

cerebellum

spinal cord

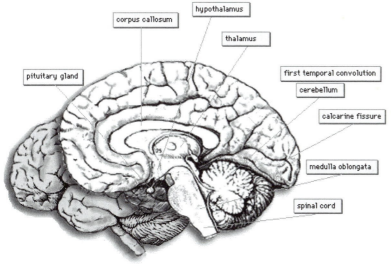

corpus callosum

hypothalamus

thalamus

pituitary gland

first temporal convolution

cerebellum

calcarine fissure

medulla oblongata

spinal cord

Distinguishable anatomical landmarks of the brain.

The properties of the nervous system are derived from the properties of a specialized type of cell that is its basic building block — the neuron. The neuron's structure is consistent with its specialized role in collecting and transferring information. Neurons are the only cells that actively communicate and are connected with many more cells than those that physically surround them.

This communication is achieved through branchlike extensions called dendrites that connect to other neurons, as well as through connections of other neurons to the cell body. These sites, which under the microscope resemble buttonlike structures adjacent to the cellular membrane, are called *synapses*. It has been estimated that the cell body of a single motor neuron may receive up to 15,000 connecting synapses from other neurons.

The information is not only collected — a single neuron is capable of transferring the information (which is the net product of all "messages" it has received) across incredible distances.

This is achieved through a filament-like cellular appendage called the axon. The axons of some motor neurons can span distances of several feet, placing them among the largest living cells (even though the cell body and its axon still remain invisible to the naked eye).

The supporting structure for these delicate cells is provided by specialized connective tissue cells called glial cells. Glial cells surround, protect and provide a nourishing environment for neurons. Specialized types of glial cells (oligodendrocytes and Schwann cells) produce myelin. This fatty, white substance makes the bulk of what is known as "white matter" (in contrast to "gray matter" which consists mainly of cell bodies and unmyelinated fibers).

Neurons of the human cortex, as seen through the microscope. The cells appear scattered because only some of them are pigmented.

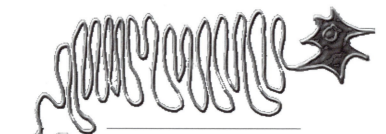

length up to several feet

A typical neuron. The axon of this neuron is depicted in a unnatural "folded" fashion only to indicate its length.

Myelin not only physically protects neural fibers but insulates them, preventing the spillover of the conducted impulses to the other fibers. It also makes the conduction of bio-electric impulses along the neural fibers more economical and quicker by providing special notches in the insulation. These notches are known as the nodes of Ranvier, and the impulse literally jumps from notch to notch. ■

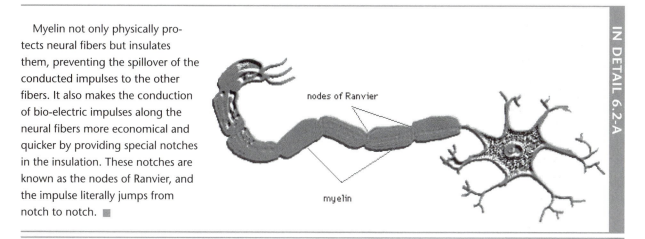

nodes of Ranvier

myelin

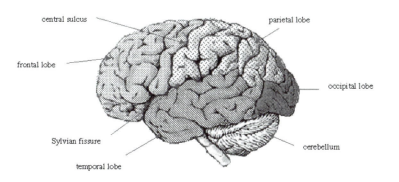

central sulcus

frontal lobe

Sylvian fissure

temporal lobe

parietal lobe

occipital lobe

cerebellum

The frontal lobe plays a major role in integrating complex cognitive functions like planning, abstract reasoning, language expression, and emotions. Although damage to the frontal lobe may spare the majority of communicative functions it often leads to dramatic changes in personality.

The part of the parietal lobe closest to the central sulcus, the postcentral gyrus, is involved in the reception of sensory information. The receptors for touch, pressure, hot and cold, and body position (kinesthesia) provide information to this region. Other parts of the parietal lobe play a major role in the integration of auditory, visual, and somatic information.

The temporal lobe contains structures involved in a number of language-related functions, such as auditory processing, language comprehension, memory, and emotions. Wernicke's area is localized in the superior temporal gyrus of the left hemisphere.

The occipital lobe is specialized for the processing of primary visual information.

In spite of major technological breakthroughs the approximate number of cells that compose the brain is still not known. Conservative estimates for the cortex alone (the uppermost layer of the brain) are of around 20 billion neurons. Keeping in mind that a single neuron has on average more than one thousand connections, the number of possible different physical states this system can assume is virtually unimaginable.

This fact alone illustrates well the complexity of the phenomena that are the subject matter of neuro-linguistics. This is also why some eminent scientists disregard the possibility of our ever understanding the mechanism of mental processes. ■

6.3 Neurolinguistic Methods of Study

In the field of neurolinguistics, one can make inferences about brain and language structures either from linguistic and psychological theories or by generalizing from the knowledge of neurological structures to language structure.

If the word is the basic unit of the language, what are the implications (if any) for our theories of the level of neural structure?

For example, one can start with the linguistic explanation of parsing for certain types of sentences and examine the ability of brain-damaged individuals to understand them. Or, one may look at the differences in activity of specific brain regions during certain linguistic tasks. However, the oldest (and the most common) approach is carefully observing the consequences of naturally occurring brain diseases. Before plunging into modern neurolinguistic theories, we briefly examine the developments in the field since its inception in the mid-nineteenth century.

6.4 Brain and Language

The localization of the higher cognitive functions in the brain was one of the hotly debated topics during the nineteenth century. The first half of that century was dominated by phrenological theories based on the ideas of Franc Josef Gall. The main postulate of *phrenology* (mockingly called "the science of the bumps on the head" later in the century) was that moral, intellectual, and spiritual functions were supported by specific regions of the brain.

Using an analogy with muscles and other organs, phrenologists argued that the size of a particular region of the brain reflected the degree of development of that region's function. Thus, by careful *palpation* of the head, and registering the parts of the skull corresponding to over- or underdeveloped parts of the brain, they claimed it possible to assess different individual capacities.

However deformed and grotesque his ideas became, Gall's initial intuition was perfectly correct. In the history of cognitive science, Gall undoubtedly deserves credit for laying down the following key concepts:

1. the mind depends on the structure of the brain;

2. the cerebral cortex is the site of mind; and (an idea that is particularly important for the present study),

3. language is localized in the frontal lobes of the brain.

It was in relation to these proposals that the orientations of thought on the functionality of the brain would be defined in the nineteenth century (Bouton 1991). And so, in spite of all the ridicule it received, one of the basic premises of phrenology — that psychological functions are localized in particular regions of the brain — is, for the most part, still accepted by modern theorists.

Although the phrenological doctrine was mostly abandoned by the scientific community of the late nineteenth century, its popularized and sometimes grotesque versions survived well into the twentieth century. This old Victorian drawing mockingly depicts a phrenologist delivering a lecture.

The idea that various mental functions are localized in different parts of the brain occurred to Franc Josef Gall after observing that a number of his friends who had very good memories also had large, bulging eyes. Gall devoted himself to collecting the actual skulls (or their measurements) of individuals who exhibited particular mental characteristics.

Gall's ideas had a mixed reception. Although most of the scientific community was very skeptical about the supposed correlation between the shape of the skull and mental faculties, Victorian society enthusiastically embraced phrenol-ogy. The number of faculties which could be detected by feeling one's skull was growing on a daily basis. The described faculties were also becoming more specific and up to date. In 1894, J. W. Redfield, a physician from New York published a chart of 160 characteristics that could be assessed by the shape of one's face and skull. Feature No. 149 was "Republicanism."

Phrenological societies lasted well into this century. The Ohio State Phrenological Society published its own journal until 1938, and the British Phrenological Society was not officially disbanded until 1967. ■

HISTORY 6.4

6.5 Broca's Discovery

In 1861, French physician and anthropologist Pierre Paul Broca published what is considered the first scientific paper advocating the idea of localization of function in the analysis of the relationship between brain and language. After dissecting the brain of a patient who had suffered from a severe expressive-language disorder, Broca concluded that this individual's problems were related to damage to a small part of the front end of the left hemisphere. This area, at the bottom of the left third frontal convolution, is still referred to as *Broca's area.*

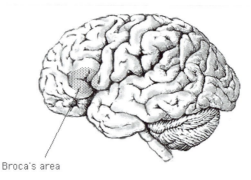

Broca's area

Broca's analysis was original in many respects. Observing that his patient apparently had been capable of understanding simple spoken directions, Broca distinguished between receptive and expressive linguistic abilities. As a result, his diagnosis became very specific: A lesion of the bottom part of the left frontal convolution caused an isolated loss of what Broca called the "faculty of articulate language."

Broca's other contribution was choosing the convolutions of the brain as the basic unit for the localization of function. This was in contrast to the absolute measurements from arbitrarily chosen landmarks of the brain and skull used by the phrenological school. After examining several additional cases with similar clinical symptoms, Broca made another important discoveryby drawing attention to the fact that disorders of expressive-language ability most often resulted from damage to the left hemisphere.

HISTORY 6.5-A

Pierre Paul Broca (1824–1880) may be considered the founder of modern day neurolinguistics. His clinical findings and autopsy report for a patient who had lost his ability to speak are considered even today to be the examples of the neurolinguistic method of inquiry. Broca attributed the patient's problem to a lesion of the left prefrontal region of the cortex. He thought this region to be where the speech center is localized in the brain.

Broca's hypothesis was based on the autopsy he performed following the death of his patient. Broca was one of the first to formulate the idea that *lateralization* of the language function was predominately to the left hemisphere. He was also among the first to relate language lateralization and handedness. His main conclusions are still generally accepted interpretations. Besides his contributions to what is now the field of neurolinguistics, Broca was an active surgeon and the founder of the French Anthropological Society. ■

HISTORY 6.5-B

The name of Broca's patient was Leborgne, but he was known as Tan; "Tan" being the only syllable he could pronounce (the sudden loss of the ability to speak was the initial reason that brought him to the hospital). Tan spent the following 21 years at Bicetre hospital in Paris. He seemed to understand everything said to him, but was known as an impulsive character. When agitated he would regain his ability to speak to the extent of being able to articulate swear words.

Initially, Broca's examination of Tan had nothing to do with Tan's language ability. At the time Broca saw him, Tan has already lost the use of his right arm and, more recently, developed a paralysis of the right leg.

Soon thereafter Tan died as a consequence of an infection. Immediately after the autopsy, Broca examined his brain. He found a cyst and pathological softening of the brain tissue in left frontal region at the base of third convolution. These findings were the basis for Broca's hypothesis, which is considered to be the first scientific approach to an analysis of an aphasic syndrome. ■

6.6 Wernicke's Model

Broca's discovery of the localization of the center for expressive language gave rise to the frantic search for the localization of other psychological and intellectual functions. However, the major focus of interest remained the confirmation or rejection of Broca's claim. Numerous case studies were described. In some, patients had language disorders associated with lesions of parts of the brain other than the one Broca had described. Others apparently had no language problems, but autopsy revealed the presence of a lesion in

Broca's area. In 1874, an attempt to bring order to the chaos in the field was made by another great thinker of that time, Carl Wernicke.

Wernicke proposed a theory of language representation in the brain that not only accounted for numerous described case studies, but could also predict yet-unrecognized types of language disorders. His basic assumption was that different aspects of language function were supported by different areas of the brain.

Wernicke described individuals with expressive-language disorder who, unlike Broca's virtually mute patient, were able to speak but often did not make sense. They produced words pronounced similarly to those one would expect them to say (for example, *rattle* instead of *battle*); at other times the words were apparently semantically related, sometimes even completely invented. These patients, again in contrast to Broca's case, also had problems understanding what was said to them. Although their deficit gave them the appearance of having a hearing problem, they were perfectly able to hear and discriminate individual sounds.

Following the death of one of these individuals, an examination of the brain revealed the presence of a lesion in the area around the first temporal gyrus. Wernicke postulated that lesions of this area (which came to be known as *Wernicke's area*) were responsible for deficits in receptive-language function. Since there were no detectable lesions in Broca's area of these patients, Wernicke argued that the same lesion is also responsible for the deficit in expressive language. He explained the deficit by proposing that the area around the first temporal gyrus contained auditory memories for words. These word memories were necessary not only for auditory comprehension (hence the deficit in understanding) but also for word articulation carried out in Broca's area.

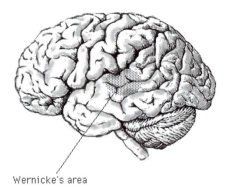

Wernicke's area

In this view, the expressive-language deficit of Wernicke's patients was not caused by impairment of Broca's area but rather by inadequate input from Wernicke's area. This explanation encompassed all of the major ideas of Wernicke's theory:

- Different areas of the brain (centers) support different language functions;

- These centers are connected by neural pathways;

- Linguistic information is transmitted across these pathways.

A logical consequence of Wernicke's theoretical framework was that impairments of the language function could be caused not only by lesions of different centers but also by the disruption of the connection between them.

It also followed that, by analyzing the possible disruptions of the information flow in the model, one should be able not only to account for already-described aphasic disorders but also to <u>predict</u> the new, as-yet-unencountered possible variations in language disorders.

Based on Wernicke's model, Lichtheim produced a diagram (original illustration on the right) that captured the relationship among seven major aphasic disorders.

Besides Broca's and Wernicke's areas, Lichtheim's diagram also included the hypothetical "concept center" (top of diagram). Broca's area was described as a center containing motor representations of words, and Wernicke's area contained auditory "pictures" of words. The concept center contained meanings that could be associated with either type of representation. The attractiveness of a diagram model lies in the fact that even a hypothetical model with only two centers (A and B) can account for at least three "simple" conditions or two "complex" ones with larger lesions. Allowing bidirectional information flow (c) could further complicate the situation.

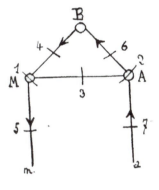

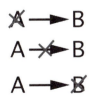

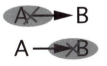

a. A hypothetical model accounting for three simple conditions.

b. A hypothetical model accounting for two complex conditions.

c. A hypothetical model with bi-directional information flow.

Below is an illustration of the Wernicke-Lichtheim model of aphasias. Before reading the descriptions of the different aphasic syndromes, try for yourself to predict the consequences of a lesion to a center or a connection. For example, one question could be: Would an interruption of connection between the concept center (B) and the motor center (M) interfere with one's ability to repeat words?

Add a "writing center" to Lichtheim-Wernicke's model presented in the text, draw it, and explain how it would connect to other centers. Could your model support a clinical picture of a person who could write but would quickly lose the ability to read what has been written?

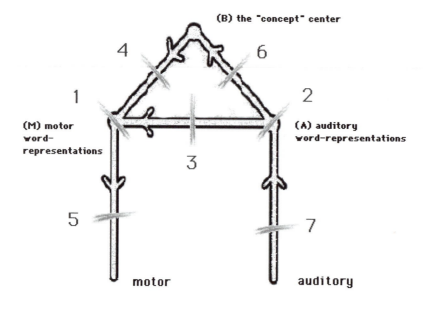

1. A lesion to the center where motor word-representations are stored would cause classical *Broca's aphasia,* with disturbances in spontaneous speech and repetition but with preserved auditory comprehension.

2. A lesion to the auditory word-representation center would lead to *Wernicke's aphasia* — severe deficit of comprehension with preserved expressive-language abilities. However, repetition also would be impaired because of the inability to match the incoming sounds with the stored representations.

3. Interruption of the connection between Wernicke's and Broca's area leads to *conduction aphasia* with preserved comprehension but severe impairment of repetition.

4. Interruption of the B-M connection leads to *transcortical motor aphasia,* which is similar to Broca's aphasia but with excellent preservation of repeating ability.

5. Disruption of motor output leads to severe articulation impairment, known as *dysarthria.*

6. Interruption of the A-B connection leads to *transcortical sensory aphasia* with severe comprehension deficit, but preserved repetition and fluent (although inappropriate) production.

7. Disruption of auditory input leads to impairment of comprehension known as *pure word deafness.*

Note that although (A) corresponds to Wernicke's area and (M) to Broca's area, other connections and centers were not anatomically defined in the Wernicke-Lichtheim model.

6.7 Learning from Brain Damage

One of the most accessible ways to learn about the brain/language relationship is careful observation, recording, and measurement of language-related changes following damage to the brain tissues. A number of disorders may lead to brain damage and consequent impairment of the ability to communicate.

Some of these disorders, like *atherosclerosis* (clogged and narrowed blood vessels) affect the brain in a diffuse fashion that makes the isolation of specific language-related symptoms difficult. The disorders that cause more localized damage to brain structures can be interpreted more straightforwardly. These include brain hemorrhage *(stroke),* tumors, and the congenital malformation of blood vessels *(aneurism).* Another important source of information is provided by a variety of externally inflicted brain injuries, most of them resulting from human violence and technological advances.

It is important to note that valuable insights do not have to be connected to observing the presence of a specific language disorder. In some cases, it is the <u>absence</u> of observable deficit after brain injury that provides significant information.

6.8 Modern Techniques

Besides the data from neuropathology, questions regarding the brain/language relationship can be addressed in a more controlled and active fashion. Within neurolinguistics there are several techniques used for this purpose. Broadly speaking, they can be divided

The skull of Phineas Gage, with an iron bar that went through his brain in a mining accident. Although it led to personality changes, the case is famous for the absence of speech and language impairments.

into two groups: techniques that rely on interference with brain function and careful observation of its effects, and those based on recording normal brain activity in a controlled context. There is also a third group, which could be considered the combination of the two above. The techniques in this group, an example of which is lateralized presentation of the stimulus, probe brain function in a non-invasive fashion by using often ingenious ways to construct and present stimuli.

An example of a technique that interferes with brain function is direct electrical stimulation of the exposed cortex. The fact that the brain has no pain receptors makes it possible to use this technique on fully conscious subjects prior to brain surgery. Contrary to one's expectations, stimulating of the areas involved in language functions never leads to articulate speech production (Penfield and Roberts 1959). In experiments where subjects were asked to name objects, Penfield and Roberts found that the most common outcome of stimulation is interference with speech. The observed effects ranged from complete blockage to slurring or repetition of words. The stimulation of the areas indicated by stars on the illustration produced naming errors (after Penfield and Roberts 1959:130).

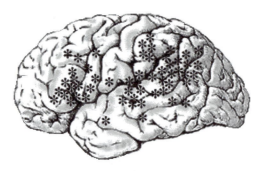

Another technique of dramatic interference with brain function was first introduced by the Japanese neurosurgeon Juhn Wada in 1949. The technique involves literally putting one hemisphere to sleep by injecting a potent anesthetic (sodium amytal) into the blood stream. The method is still in use for determining the *lateralization* of language function before performing brain surgery. It also revealed that in early brain lesions (before age 5) it is possible for language lateralization to shift to the undamaged hemisphere (Rasmussen and Milner 1977).

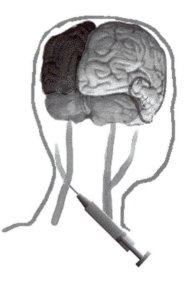

An overview of findings using electrical stimulation mapping of the brain (Ojemann 1983) provides interesting data regarding localization of different language functions. First, language functions seem to be organized discretely — often, stimulation of a small area produces an effect, whereas stimulation of adjacent areas, even under the same conditions, has no effect. The same function may be affected by stimulation of different sites, and often it is an isolated function that is affected. However, a large number of sites where stimulation produced errors in phoneme identification <u>simultaneously</u> produced impairments of oral and facial movements. The fact that the same regions of the brain play a part in speech

perception and production provides supporting evidence for the so-called motor theory of speech perception (Liberman et al. 1967).

In this realm, it is interesting to observe electrical stimulation of the brain in patients who speak more than one language: Stimulating sites that impaired their ability to name an object in one language did not affect their ability to do so in another. ■

IN DETAIL 6.8-A

stolica

Stuhl

ch~~air~~

The ability of the nondominant hemisphere to take over language functions is most vividly demonstrated in cases where, because of a tumor or some other clinical condition, it was necessary to remove an entire hemisphere (*hemispherectomy*). In adults this leads to severe reduction of verbal output with somewhat better-preserved comprehension. However, if surgery is performed at an early age, recovery of language functions may be almost complete (Smith 1966).

The *dichotic listening task* is a noninvasive technique that can be used to assess the lateralization of different aspects of language function. Pioneered by Doreen Kimura (Kimura 1961), the technique relies on simultaneous presentation of different auditory stimuli to both ears. Because of the way the brain processes auditory information, the stimulus that is detected better with one ear indicates the dominance of the opposite hemisphere for this kind of stimulus.

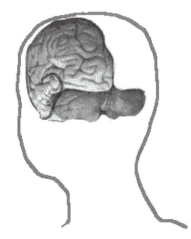

Kimura proposed the following model: During monoaural (to 'one ear' only) presentation, auditory pathways leading to both hemispheres are active and the subject accurately identifies the stimulus.

During simultaneous presentation to both ears, the auditory pathways leading to the hemisphere on the same side are suppressed, with the stimulus from each ear going predominantly to the opposite hemisphere. Thus, the syllable *ga*, presented to the right ear, is directly accessible to the left hemisphere; while the syllable *ba* is available only through the connections (commisures) between the hemispheres. The subject is capable of more accurately identifying *ga*. In a subject with a split corpus callosum, where the exchange of stimuli is not possible between the hemispheres, there is an absolute right-ear advantage. These results are valid only for individuals with left-hemisphere language dominance (the majority of normal population). ▓

A technique called *lateralized presentation,* where a visual stimulus is presented to only one hemisphere, is possible because of the anatomy of visual pathways. If the subject is looking straight ahead and a stimulus is presented on the left side, its picture is projected onto the right half of each eye.

Neural connections for each inner half cross the midline of the brain (optic chiasm) and send fibers to the opposite hemisphere. In a patient who has had the corpus callosum cut (see *commissurotomy*) for medical reasons, it is possible to present visual stimuli to a single hemisphere. Since each hemisphere controls the opposite arm, by asking subjects to indicate their responses by arm movements, it is possible to find out how the stimuli are processed.

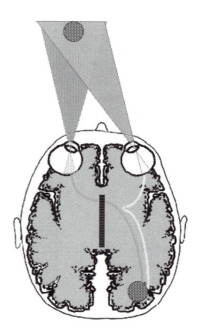

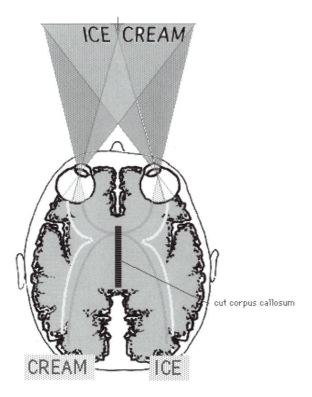

In an experiment depicted above, while the subject is looking at the fixation point (a little cross in the middle), two words (ICE and CREAM) are flashed briefly on either side of the fixation point. If the subject is then asked to say which word was flashed on the screen, the answer would be CREAM. However, when asked to show the corresponding object with the left hand, the subject would choose a bowl of ice! A person with an intact corpus callosum would report seeing ICE CREAM.

Using a computer to determine precisely what a person is looking at is called *eye-tracking*. This technique allows researchers to formulate hypotheses about linguistic processes that occur during reading. As you may notice while observing others, the eyes do not move continuously during reading. Rather, they make short jumps called *saccades*, with periods of brief *fixations* in between. Although eye movements in general follow the flow of text, isolated jumps backwards are quite common, especially while reading complex content.

After a split-brain patient chooses an object with the left hand corresponding to a stimulus flashed on the screen, what would the subject say to justify the choice? Explain.

The basic assumption underlying this methodology is that eye-fixation times are related to the times different brain regions need to process information arriving through visual channel.

```
221        268 292 197 204    177      156
 1          6   2   3   7      4        5
```

The horse raced past the barn fell.

The figure above presents a simulation of an eye-tracker recording. The fixation points are sequentially marked with their duration (in milliseconds). The sentence used is a well-known example (Bever 1970) of a "garden-path" sentence that (as you probably have experienced) leads the reader to an initial wrong interpretation. This often results in an increased number of *regressive saccades* (number 6 and 7 in the above example). In the past two decades, a variety of such ingenious experiments and techniques have been developed using reading as a "window" to the analysis of linguistic processes (see Rayner and Pollatsek 1989; Henderson et al. 1995).

IN DETAIL 6.8-C

Many eye-trackers use the reflection from the shiny surface of the eye (known as Purkinje's image) as a reference point to calculate the position of the fixation point on a computer screen. An alternative method is to beam (invisible) infra-red light towards the eye and then register eye movements by picking up changes in reflected light. The position of the fixation point can be determined with precision corresponding to one-third of a printed character. Manipulating the text in the proximity of the area of clear vision (approximately 7 characters around the fixation point) allows many ingenious experiments that probe the mechanisms of written language comprehension. ∎

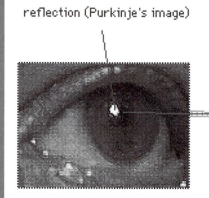
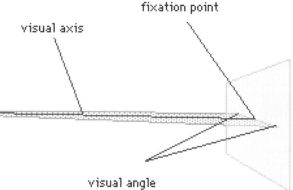

reflection (Purkinje's image)

fixation point

visual axis

visual angle

One problem with metabolic scanning techniques is that they are relatively slow. As a result, another technique has become increasingly popular for measuring rapid changes in brain activity. It is based on registering "event-related" changes in electrical activity of the brain (event-related potentials, *[ERP]*) using externally placed electrodes. Since it is very hard to trace the source of electrical changes, the interpretation of recorded activity is notoriously complex (right).

However, the combination of the increased computing power of modern computers and advances in psycholinguistic theory have already produced significant results in the analysis of fast, unconscious aspects of language processing.

Technological breakthroughs play a major role in shaping current neurolinguistic theory. This is most evident in the case of modern neuroimaging techniques. The first technique to allow precise visualization of soft tissues was X-ray computed tomography *(CT)* or computed axial tomography *(CAT)* scan.

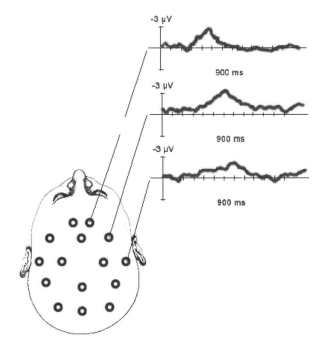

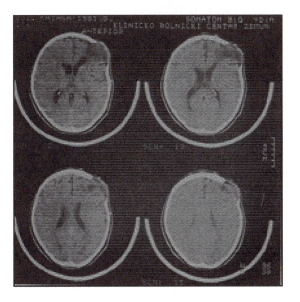

X-ray CT scans (left) deliver sharp detail of soft tissues. However, this technique does not provide clues about the metabolic activity of different parts of the brain.

Another step forward in neuroimaging techniques was the introduction of *PET* and *MRI*. Both techniques can record changes in brain metabolism over time, which made possible the correlation of specific activities with brain events. The kind of information available from PET studies is demonstrated with the simulated depiction of brain activity in subjects presented with words on a computer screen. The illustration below, representing numerous experimental findings, shows that the brain activity, as measured through blood flow, is markedly localized in the occipital left regions of the brain during analysis of linguistic stimuli.

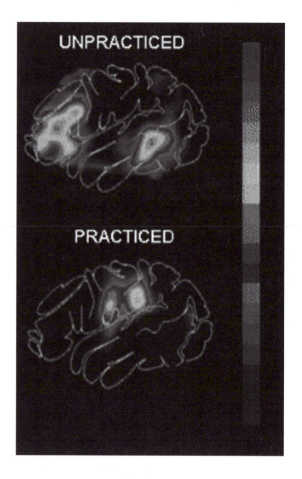

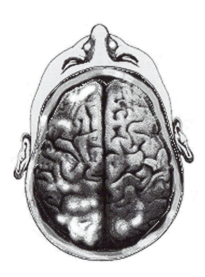

The PET images above, taken by Dr. Marcus Raichle at the Neuroimaging Lab of the Washington University School of Medicine, illustrate the real-time activity of the brain of a single individual while learning a novel language task and performing the same activity after the task was well rehearsed. Computer-assigned colors indicate different levels of activity, with "warmer" colors corresponding to increasing levels. Note that, during the first task, most of the activity occurred in the prefrontal and temporal areas, while during the second task it was localized in and around Broca's area.

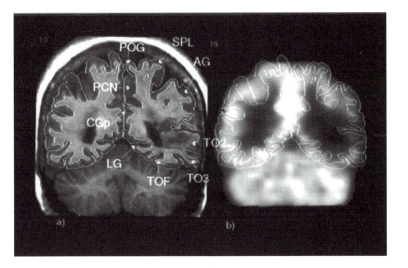

Metabolic scanning of brain activity in brain damaged individuals provides different kinds of data for linking language deficits with brain lesions. In the original scans above, the image on the left (MR) shows both the cortex (yellow) and the area of the lesion (red). A PET scan on the right shows glucose metabolism in the same patient, with darkening of the injured area.

6.9 Lateralization of Function

Regardless of the technique used to study the brain/language relationship, a consistent finding emerges. In the vast majority of individuals, it is the left hemisphere that is specialized for language. The right hemisphere, although contributing to the processing of some language-related phenomena like *prosody,* is essentially mute (see the experiment on lateralized presentation).

Since lateralization of function is predominantly genetically determined, there are a number of studies focused on other genetic factors that might further influence the localization of lateralized functions. Kimura (1992) presented evidence indicating different localization of language functions in males and females. According to these data, women are more likely than men to experience language problems after injury to frontal parts of the brain. However, since strokes occur more in the posterior parts of the brain, most aphasics are men.

Kimura's data can be also interpreted as indicating the difference in the degree of specialization between male and female brains. The analysis of electrical stimulation mapping data (Ojemann et al. 1989) during naming tasks indicated gender-related differences, particularly in the parietal (Wernicke's) region. More recent studies (Shaywitz et al. 1995), using online monitoring of brain function during language tasks, suggest different patterns of linguistic processing in male and female brains. Although some of the results from the above studies have been replicated, their interpretation is still far from clear and is the subject of ongoing discussion.

6.10 Unit of Localization

Investigating the localization of functions raises yet another question that has not been answered in a satisfactory fashion for neurology as a whole: What is the proper unit for the localization of function?

Is the proper unit a gyrus? Or a part thereof, such as Broca's area? Or is it a group of adjacent gyri? Or should one use regions of different cellular organization (above) to define mental functions (after Brodmann 1909)? Alternatively, one could look for neurons that share the same *neurotransmitter*…or are metabolically active at the same time…or are connected through synaptic circuits.

The problem is that every new technology that has been used to study the brain has provided us with yet another map; however none of these divisions alone is sufficient to explain functional localization. If one adds to this the existence of individual variations observable even at the level of visible anatomical features, it is clear that neurolinguistics, in spite of the enormous progress it has made in the past decades, is a young science with an exciting future.

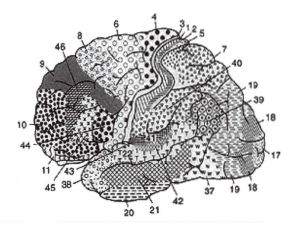

6.11 Early Classifications

Early classifications of aphasic syndromes were made on an anatomical basis, dividing them into anterior and posterior groups. Anterior lesions were thought to be associated with expressive language disorders such as Broca's aphasia. Lesions of the posterior regions were exemplified by Wernicke's aphasia and were associated with receptive disorders. It is worth mentioning here that today we know that all aphasic disorders are associated with some degree of linguistic deficit.

Broca's aphasia (now more commonly referred to as cortical motor aphasia) is characterized by slow, halting and effortful speech. Omission of small grammatical words in the utterances of Broca's aphasics earned this style of speaking the label "telegraphic." In contrast to their problems with expressive language, Broca's aphasics' ability to understand language in an everyday context seems preserved to a surprising degree.

Wernicke's aphasia (now known as cortical sensory aphasia) may be described as the mirror image of Broca's aphasia. The major symptoms of this disorder are difficulties in understanding language. The ability to produce grammatically correct utterances is often unaffected, although these utterances may be completely meaningless.

6.12 Clinical Classifications

In spite of recent advances in neurolinguistic and psycholinguistic techniques, most data still come from clinical studies of the effect brain injury has on language ability. This is reflected in classification schemes of aphasic syndromes that are most often based on clinical observations.

Many current clinical classifications of aphasic syndromes still closely resemble the classical Wernicke-Lichtheim model. They are based on the notion that language-related activity is carried out in a linear fashion in the brain. The revival of the connectionist model was promoted by the influential work of Norman Geschwind (1965) and was followed by a proposal for clinical classification (Benson and Geschwind 1971).

Geschwind suggested a new categorical distinction for the classification of aphasias: fluent vs. non-fluent disorders. Fluent aphasics are capable of effortlessly producing well-articulated sentences at a striking rate (usually faster than normal). However, their statements are devoid of real content. Linguistic analysis of their production reveals an abundance of circumlocutions *(The thing, you know, you use to unlock the door with)* and the use of nonreferential words *(stuff, thing)*. Production errors known as paraphasias are also common. They consist of substituting either similar sounding words *(tame* for *lame)* or words related in meaning *(chair* for *table)*.

Since fluent aphasics preserve the normal rhythm and melody of speech, listening to their production from a distance might give one an illusion of normal discourse. This just emphasizes the strange sense of emptiness one feels when coming closer and trying to understand what they are saying.

Goodglass (1976) provides a transcript of a fluent aphasic's response when asked how he is feeling:

> I feel very well. My hearing, writing been doing well, things that couldn't hear from. In other words, I used to be able to work cigarettes I didn't know how…This year, the last three years, or perhaps a little more, I didn't know how to do me any able to…

In contrast, even when heard from a distance, the speech of non-fluent aphasics is recognizably impaired. Their production is slow, labored, and halting. The effort during speaking is so manifest that the disorder was initially interpreted as an articulation problem. However, on isolated tests, non-fluent aphasics were found capable of articulating all of the necessary speech sounds and even singing correctly a known melody (suggesting that language and music are subserved by different areas of the brain). Another typical feature of non-fluent speech is the absence of small function words, with typical utterances consisting of one or several content words joined together in a telegraphic fashion *(Dinner...table).*

The table on the following page presents the characteristics of different aphasic syndromes using both the anatomical and fluency distinctions. Descriptions appear below.

Broca's aphasia is a representative of non-fluent aphasic disorders. Its hallmark characteristics are slow, effortful, and halting speech with omission of small function words and grammatical morphemes. Although it is traditionally associated with the lesions of the lower parts of the left frontal lobe, the diagnosis is most often based on clinical observation of typical symptoms.

Wernicke's aphasia is a classical counterpart to Broca's aphasia. It is characterized by fluent and copious production with preserved melodic and rhythmic patterns but marked loss of content. Comprehension is often severely impaired. Lesion sites are often found in the middle upper portions of the temporal lobe, sometimes extending to the parietal lobe.

Conduction aphasia is thought to be caused by a lesion of the subcortical pathway, the arcuate fasciculus, which connects Wernicke's with Broca's area. The result is fluent speech output with relatively good comprehension but impaired repetition.

Global aphasia, as the name implies, indicates impairment of all testable language functions. Most often the degree of impairment is very severe. It is associated with broad lesions spread over the adjoining areas of the frontal, parietal and temporal lobes. Global aphasia is frequently found in the beginning stages of brain damage and, with recovery of some functions, may shift to another type.

Anomic aphasia is often the mildest form of aphasia, manifested only by word-finding difficulties in absence of other aphasic syndromes. During the recovery from other types of aphasia, the anomic phase is frequently the last and the mildest. Anomia as a symptom is also frequently associated with other aphasic disorders. Lesions are often localized at the junction of the temporal and parietal lobes.

Transcortical motor aphasia resembles Broca's aphasia and is characterized by impaired ability to initiate propositional speech. It is thought to be caused by a lesion of the connections between Broca's area and adjacent frontal lobe areas. The preservation of the connections with Wernicke's area leads to better repetition ability than in Broca's aphasia.

Transcortical sensory aphasia resembles Wernicke's aphasia in fluent verbal output with abundance of paraphasias. The difference is in ability to repeat verbal stimuli — in contrast to Wernicke's aphasics, the patients with transcortical sensory aphasia suffer from compulsive repetition, known as echolalia. Lesions associated with this syndrome involve the connections between the auditory cortex and the surrounding association areas and is clinically known as the isolation of Wernicke's area.

Mixed transcortical aphasia, also known as the isolation syndrome, refers to the state resembling fluent aphasia with severe impairment of comprehension. Affected individuals are often speechless until spoken to, but then they are able to repeat with ease even lengthy sentences with perfect articulation and prosody. The lesions that cause this syndrome tend to spare all traditional speech areas (Broca's and Wernicke's) and their connections, while cutting them off from other parts of the brain.

Aphasia type	Spontaneous speech	Repetition	Paraphasia	Comprehension	Naming
Broca's aphasia	non-fluent	poor	rare	good	fair, cues help
Wernicke's aphasia	fluent	poor	semantic	poor	poor, cues do not help
Conduction	fluent	poor	phonemic	good	poor, paraphasias
Global	non-fluent	poor	variable	poor	poor
Anomic	fluent	good	never	good	poor
Transcortical motor	non-fluent	echolalia	rare	good	poor
Transcortical sensory	fluent	echolalia	common	poor	poor
Mixed transcortical	non-fluent	echolalia	rare	poor	poor

Characteristics of different aphasic syndromes. The table uses both anatomical and fluency distinctions (after Cytovic 1996).

6.13 Luria's Model

One of the first detailed neurolinguistic accounts was proposed by
Alexandr Romanovich Luria. Although his work arose as a critique
of classical connectionist models (Wernicke, Lichtheim), Luria's
account is also, to some extent, an elaboration of these traditional
models. The main distinction in Luria's model is that general linguistic functions (like language comprehension) are divided into a
number of subcomponents (see illustration at right). These components have a definite localization and are shared by multiple functions.

   Thus, damage to one of subcomponents would tend to produce
qualitatively similar deficits across several functions. Affected
functions may belong to different domains (linguistic, behavioral,
cognitive). For example, individuals with a medial frontal-lobe
lesion have difficulty initiating spontaneous activity. Even if they
manage to engage in an activity, it quickly deteriorates into repetition of movements that can last for hours (this condition is known
as *akinetic mutism*). Language production in these individuals is
affected in a strikingly similar fashion — the patients have problems
spontaneously initiating conversation, and when they do, their
speech is full of *perseverations*.

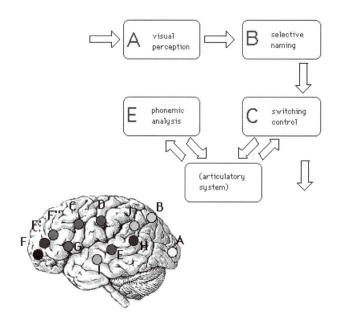

**Luria's decomposition of the
naming function. Note the
sub-components (A–J). Although
depicted in a sequential fashion,
some of the components may be
active in parallel (after Arbib and
Caplan 1979).**

Luria's greatest contribution to modern neurolinguistics was to shift the focus from quantitative (how much) to qualitative (in what fashion) aspects of language deficits.

6.14 Neurology and Linguistics

Although clinical classifications of aphasias were good enough to offer practical diagnostic and rehabilitation guidelines, they failed to explain how the brain supports language. The advancement in linguistic and psycholinguistic theory (Chomsky 1965; Fodor 1975) provided additional tools for clinicians. Language impairments specific to different aphasic syndromes could be described qualitatively using linguistic terms of analysis. However, this practice introduced another problem: Clinical description of a symptom, for example, reduced phrase length, could be linguistically explained in a variety of ways (see illustration below).

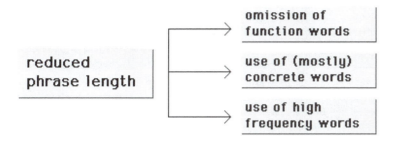

Thus, diagnosing a patient as Broca's aphasic indicates only that this individual has a problem with speech and a lesion in Broca's area, but does not tell us anything about the linguistic (and psycholinguistic) characteristics of the problem. That any two individuals who satisfy the clinical criteria for the diagnosis of Broca's aphasia may have different linguistic impairments makes it impossible to correlate their brain lesions with language impairment.

The mixing of clinical and linguistic descriptions can also create an opposite problem: Many different clinical syndromes may not differ significantly when compared by linguistic criteria (Caplan 1987:151).

A good example of the relationship between modern linguistic theory and neurology is illustrated through the study of *agrammatism*, a syntactic deficit common in non-fluent aphasias. Although grammar impairments in Broca's aphasics' production were described early in the century (Pick 1913), it was only after the development of the Token Test (DeRenzi and Vignolo 1962) that it became evident that non-fluent aphasics also have comprehension problems. The outcome of experimental studies of agrammatism will have a significant impact on modern theories of normal language production and comprehension. Currently there are several competing interpretations of agrammatism.

IN DETAIL 6.14

The Token Test was one of the first tests to provide an assessment of aphasics' ability to perform syntactic operations. It uses abstract geometric figures (thus real-world knowledge is of little help) and the commands are of increased length and complexity. In the final section, in order to correctly carry out the verbal request, a subject has to perform a variety of syntactic analyses. An example of such a statement would be: *After you have touched the little red rectangle point to the big green triangle.* Although of great historical and clinical significance, Token Test results were never systematically analyzed due to the heterogeneity of tested operations. ▦

PRO 6.14

One of the hypotheses attempting to explain impairment of comprehension in agrammatic aphasics is the mapping hypothesis (Linebarger et al. 1983; Linebarger 1995). The basic claim made by this hypothesis is that impairment is due to the aphasics' inability to map grammatical functions (such as subject or object) onto thematic roles (such as agent or patient). The exact cause of the mapping deficit is still under investigation.

The mapping hypothesis is currently the only approach that offers practical guidelines in terms of rehabilitation of agrammatic aphasics (Schwartz et al. 1994; Marshall 1995; Schwartz et al. 1995). ▦

CON 6.14

Competing accounts of agrammatism can be grouped in two general categories: chain disruption and trade-off accounts. An example of the first account is the Trace-Deletion Hypothesis (Grodzinsky 1995a, 1995b), which explains the comprehension deficit by the impairment (deletion) of traces that allow the transmission of theta roles from D-structure to S-structure (for more on D- and S-structure, see Chomsky 1981). The trade-off accounts claim that the deficit is the consequence of the reduction of shared cognitive resources such as short-term memory (Myake et al. 1995). One of the experimental approaches used by the proponents of this account has been the creation of circumstances that make normal subjects perform in aphasic-like fashion (Myake et al. 1994). ▦

6.15 Summary

In view of the brain's complexity, along with individual differences among different brains, it seems that a simple explanation of how the brain supports language is impossible. However, in a mosaiclike fashion we have assembled an array of valuable insights. For example, we can claim that certain discrete areas of the brain do play a major role in linguistic functions such as word finding and grammatical formulation.

We are also certain that, for the majority of individuals, most language-related functions are supported by the left hemisphere. Although relatively fixed in adults, this lateralization of function seems to be modifiable in children at an early age. Studies of signed languages also have established that linguistic function is not constrained to the vocal-auditory channel. Left-sided lesions involving Broca's and Wernicke's areas disrupt the production and comprehension of signed words and sentences.

Today, the field of neurolinguistics is undergoing exciting changes. With the advancement of noninvasive techniques for monitoring brain activity, the focus of study has shifted from the observation of pathological processes to the recording of normal function. Developments in linguistic theory are continuously opening new areas of research. Collaborations among different areas of study are creating new disciplines (like linguistic aphasiology) that focus on specific aspects of the brain/language relationship.

Since the answers to our questions are nowhere near, further exploration of this field seems to be bound only by our creativity.

Glossary

abstract case

A circumstance in which a linguistic item is bears a case feature (for example, *[NOMINATIVE]*) but nevertheless is not overtly marked for case. Nonpronominal nouns in English exemplify this phenomenon in that the nominative form of the noun is identical to the accusative form.

accusative

A case that normally marks the object of an English sentence. *Me, her, he, us,* and *them* are accusative pronouns in English (compare *I, she, he, we,* and *they*).

adjective phrases

Syntactic constituents with adjective heads that may be specified and modified by other phrases. Examples include *old,* and *much happier than Bill.*

affix

Prefixes, suffixes, or infixes.

affricate

A sound that begins like a stop sound followed by a fricative release.

African-American English

A variety of English spoken primarily by some American Black speakers. Although often not carefully defined, it is typically taken to involve certain distinguishing phonological, syntactic, and semantic features.

agent

A thematic role that may be borne by a noun phrase in a sentence. It is the agent that is construed as undertaking the action of the sentence.

agrammatism

The impairment of comprehension often associated with agrammatic production in non-fluent aphasics. Although the term was earlier equated with Broca's aphasia, the current view is that Broca's aphasia is not always associated with agrammatism.

akinetic mutism

A severe clinical syndrome produced by a lesion of deep areas of the frontal lobes. It is characterized by the almost total absence of language and a general lack of motor activity, although the individual is not paralyzed.

allomorph

The different phonetic manifestations of a morpheme; for example, [d] and [t] are two allomorphs of the English past-tense morpheme /d/.

allophone

The different phonetic manifestations of a phoneme; for example, [pʰ] and [p] are two allophones of the English phoneme /p/.

alveo-palatal

A place of articulation between the alveolar ridge and the hard palate. [š] and [ž] are examples of English alveo-palatal sounds.

alveolar ridge

The bony ridge just behind the top teeth. English sounds articulated in this region include [t] and [s].

ambiguity

A linguistic item with more than one interpretation. For example, *Everybody saw a bank* is four ways ambiguous (same bank or different bank, river or financial institution). (Note that this sentence cannot mean that some people saw a financial institution and the rest saw a riverside!)

analytic

An analytic sentence is true on the basis of meaning alone (e.g., *A bachelor is an unmarried man*). The philosopher Quine disputes whether this is a clear linguistic category (see Quine 1961:40). Usually contrasted with *synthetic* sentences.

anaphora

Pronouns, or, more generally, "proforms" whose interpretation is dependent either on another linguistic item or on elements of the discourse. Reflexives and cases of ellipsis are two examples of anaphora.

aneurism

A congenital malformation of the wall of a blood vessel. Often leads to rupture of the vessel.

antecedent

A linguistic expression that fixes the interpretation of a pronoun or other semantically dependent item. In the sentence *Mary admires herself, Mary* is the antecedent of the reflexive pronoun *herself.*

argument

A subject or object.

aspiration

An extra build-up of air pressure released during the articulation of a consonant resulting in a period of breathiness (that can be seen in a spectrogram).

assimilation

Phonological or morpho-phonemic rules that enforce agreement between some feature of the elements involved in the rule. In "progressive" assimilation, a preceding element determines the agreement value; in "anticipatory" assimilation, a following element determines the value. For example, English inflectional rules like the plural rule involve progressive assimilation of the feature of voicing (c.f. *dogs* vs. *cats*).

atherosclerosis

A condition in which the diameter of the blood vessels is narrowed by the accumulation of fatty deposits.

automaticity

Processes are those over which an individual has no control. The input processes involved in sensory modalities like hearing and seeing are good examples — once visual or auditory stimuli are received they are automatically processed.

autosegment(al)

A level of representation parallel to the segmental level at which aspects of phonetic information (e.g., tone) may be represented.

auxiliary

"Helping" verb; in English, including tenses, modals, and *have* and *be.*

back vowel

A vowel that involves moving the tongue back from its rest position. Opposite of *front vowels.* [u] and [o] are examples in English.

backformation

A process of linguistic change whereby a previously existing lexical item is creatively analyzed into root+affix, and then the root enters into new derivations, yielding novel lexical items.

bilabial

Sounds produced with the place of articulation located at the lips. Constriction is produced by bringing the lips together, to different degrees depending on the nature of the bilabial sound. [b] is an English bilabial sound.

binary branching

A structure in which a mother node dominates exactly two daughter nodes.

binding

An abstract link between two or more linguistic items that typically makes the interpretation of the "bindee" dependent on that of the "binder" in some way. For example, reflexive pronouns must be bound by an appropriate antecedent (*We/*I like ourselves*) that assigns an interpretation to the reflexive.

Binding Theory

A statement of the binding conditions for pronominal elements (including reflexive pronouns).

bound morpheme

A morpheme that can only appear as a lexical item in a given language in tandem with an affix or in a compound construction. Opposite of *free* morpheme.

bounding

The structural relationship (and, especially, the limits thereof) between a displaced item and its corresponding gap.

branch

Notated by a line in a tree diagram, a representation of a hierarchical relationship between two nodes (a mother-daughter relationship).

Broca, Pierre Paul

Pierre Paul Broca (1824–1880), French surgeon and physician mostly known for his interpretation of the role in language and production played by the left third frontal convolution of the brain. This area of the brain is often referred to as "Broca's area."

Broca's aphasia

A disorder characterized by slow, halting, and effortful speech. In contrast to their problems with expressive language, Broca's aphasics' ability to understand language in an everyday context seems preserved to a surprising degree.

Broca's area

The region of the brain localized at the base of the third frontal convolution in the left hemisphere. It was named after Pierre Paul Broca, who pronounced it "the seat of articulate language."

C-command

A node *X* C-commands a node *Y* if and only if the first branching node that dominates *X* also dominates *Y*. A node branches if it has more than one daughter. See also *binary branching*.

case

A property of linguistic elements, typically of nouns and their corresponding phrases, that allows a language to mark the grammatical role that the element plays (for example, subject, object, and so forth). One standard scheme involves assigning nominative elements to subject position and accusative elements to object position (in English *I* is a nominative form and *me* is an accusative form).

Case Checking Principle

A principle requiring that every NP be in a phrase-structure position in which its case can be licensed ("checked"), for example, by a verb or a preposition.

CAT

The acronym for computerized axial tomography, a neuroimaging technique based on detection of beams of X-rays passing through the brain from multiple angles.

categorical perception

A circumstance in which a range of stimuli that vary continuously along a certain dimension is perceived as falling into a number of discrete categories. The categorical perception of sounds with varying degrees of voicing as either voiced or unvoiced is an example.

central vowel

A vowel that is neither a front vowel nor a back vowel, articulated in the center of the oral tract. [ß] is an English central vowel.

cerebellum

The most prominent part of the hindbrain. Its major function is in coordinating movement. However, more recent studies indicate that the cerebellum may be also involved in carrying out higher cognitive processes.

cerebral cortex

See *cortex*.

cerebrum

The Latin name for *forebrain*, consisting of the two hemispheres and their connections.

chain

Abstract linkages between a moved constituent (the "head" of the chain) and its trace (the "foot" of the chain).

closed syllable

A syllable ending in a coda (rather than with a vowel nucleus). Opposite of *open syllable*. [not] is an example of an English closed syllable.

CNS

An acronym for the central nervous system. It includes the parts of the nervous system encased within the skull and the spinal column. Its major function is to organize, collate, and store information. The CNS is anatomically divided into the brain and the spinal cord. The human brain is further divided into the *hindbrain, midbrain,* and *forebrain*.

co-referential

Two expressions that refer to the same object.

coarticulation

The tendency for the articulation of a sound to overlap the articulation of a neighboring sound. This produces an overlaying of acoustic information that complicates the parsing of the speech stream into phonetic and morphological units.

coda

The portion of a syllable that follows the nucleus. Together, the nucleus and coda make up the rhyme.

commissurotomy

A surgical procedure with the goal of cutting connecting fibers between the left and right hemispheres — see *corpus callosum*.

communication system

Broadly defined, any symbolic system that represents meaning. Consequently, whereas all natural languages are communication systems, communication systems include other, nonlinguistic systems (for example, gestural systems).

complement

Complex phrasal categories can be analyzed as a head that may be preceded by a specifier and followed by a complement. For example, in *John believes that the earth is flat*, the *subordinate clause that the earth is flat* is the complement to the verb *believe* in the verb phrase *believe that the earth is flat*.

complementary distribution

If a set of linguistic items is distributed in such a way that only one member of the set can occur in a certain position (in, say, a word or a sentence), then the members of the set are said to be in complementary distribution. See *contrasting distribution*.

complementizer

A function word like *that* or *if* that introduces a subordinate clause. Sometimes also refers to the position at the front of a subordinate clause (complementizer position). Often abbreviated *Comp*.

compositionality

The principle that the meaning of the whole is composed out of the meanings of the parts. For example, the meaning of the phrase *hit the ball* is composed out of the meanings of *hit, the,* and *ball*. Compare to *idioms*.

compounds

Words formed by combining two or more root morphemes. Typical examples are noun-noun compounds like *dog catcher* and adjective-noun compounds like *hot dog*.

compound stress

A special stress pattern often assigned to compounds in which stronger stress is assigned to the left element of the compound; for example, the compound *blackboard* (i.e., a board that is black), as distinguished from the non-compound "black board" (i.e., the thing you write on with chalk).

Compound Stress Rule

The rule that assigns compound stress.

conjunction

Function words (e.g., *and* and *or*) that combine with two categories of a certain type to form a complex category of that type (like *John and George*). Also used to refer to the conjoined expression that results. Sometimes the technical terms "disjunct" and "disjunction" are used when *or* is involved.

consonant

A sound made with a constriction in the vocal tract. Consonants that involve air flow in the nasal tract are called nasal consonants. Includes stops, fricatives, and affricates.

constant

A linguistic expression (for example, a proper name) that receives a semantic value independent of context. Compare to *variable*.

constituent

A sequence of one or more items that function as a single unit in a linguistic analysis. For example, the sequence *the man* (but not *man is*) is a constituent in *The man is old*.

content words

Lexical items that bear rich semantic content. Compare with *function words*.

continuant

Sounds that involve incomplete constriction in the vocal tract, consequently maintaining greater duration than noncontinuants (such as stops).

contraction

The omission of a part of a morpheme, typically marked in the English spelling system with an apostrophe; e.g., *I'd* for *I would* and *Bill's* for *Bill is.*

contrasting distribution

If a set of linguistic elements is distributed in such a way that the members of the set overlap in their distribution, they are said to be in contrasting distribution. Opposite of *complementary distribution.* [t] and [d] are in contrasting distribution in English, since it is possible to substitute one for the other, as in the frame [_il] (e.g., *teal* and *deal*)

convolution

Readily observable parts of the anatomy of the brain. See also *gyrus* and *sulcus.*

corpus callosum

Meaning 'callous body,' the Latin name for the dense band of neural fibers that connects the two hemispheres of the brain.

cortex

Meaning 'bark,' refers to the outer wrinkled surface layer of the brain. In evolutionary terms, the cortex is the youngest structure to develop within the central nervous system. The cortex plays essential role in the support of so-called higher cognitive functions.

count

Nouns that inflect for plural, and require a determiner when they appear in their singular form. Compare to *mass.*

creativity

The ability to produce and understand novel utterances. In virtue of this characteristic,

knowledge of language is not limited by previous experience.

critical period

The hypothesis that there is a stage of ontogeny during which the growth of a particular structure or competence is facilitated. More specifically, proponents of the critical-period hypothesis for language acquisition contend that there is a particular period of development during which the organism is biologically disposed to learn language.

cross-linguistic

A property that holds in all natural languages. Taken collectively, these properties constitute universal grammar.

dative

A case that normally marks the indirect object, or the object of a preposition. This case was marked in Old English, but is not in Modern English.

daughter

A node dominated by another node in a linguistic representation. See also *mother.*

deep structure

A level of syntactic analysis to which transformations applied in the so-called "standard" theory of transformational grammar developed in the mid-sixties (see Chomsky 1965). See also: *surface structure.*

definite description

A description that begins with an definite determiner like *the* or *this.* See also *indefinite description.*

derivation

The application of a set of linguistic rules to an input form to produce ("derive") an output form.

derivational morphology

A process of attaching affixes to lexical items to derive other lexical items. The application of a rule of derivational morphology modifies the meaning of the input item in a systematic way, and may change its syntactic category; the attachment of the suffix *-ly* to an adjective like *sad* to derive the adverb *sadly* is an example. To be contrasted with *inflectional morphology* (for example, the attachment of the plural marker in English), which adds purely grammatical markers and never introduces a change in syntactic category.

derived root

A root in combination with one or more other morphemes, to which yet another morpheme is attached.

description

The class of NPs that describe (or purport to describe) a referent. *The last time I saw Richard* is an example. See *indefinite description* and *definite description*.

descriptive (linguistics)

A scientific analysis of the human language capacity. Descriptive linguists are not interested in changing linguistic behavior, but rather, in understanding its nature and the method of its acquisition. See also *prescriptive linguistics*.

determiner

Function words (like *the, some,* or *three*) that are specifiers in the noun phrase.

diachronic (linguistics)

The investigation of language change. Also known as "historical linguistics." Opposite of *synchronic linguistics*.

dialect

Very similar versions of a language spoken by a group of speakers; a collection of closely related idiolects.

dichotic listening test

An experimental procedure in which different stimuli are presented to each ear.

diphthong

Sequence of a vowel and either a glide or a second vowel, constituting a complex single sound. [ɔi], the vowel in *boy,* is an English diphthong.

disjunction

See *conjunction*.

displacement

A circumstance in which a syntactic dependency between two constituents that normally obtains in some local domain (within a phrase, for example) is extended so as to relate constituents that are not within the expected syntactic domain.

domain

The input to a function.

dominate

If two nodes X and Y in a linguistic representation are in a hierarchical relationship, and X exhaustively contains Y (as well as all of the constitutive parts of Y), then X is said to dominate Y.

economy

A set of considerations that favor simpler derivations over more complicated ones, all things being equal. See the principle of *shortest movement*.

ellipsis

Elliptical constructions are ones in which a constituent that is present in the interpretation is missing from the string of words.

entailment

If it is impossible for a sentence S^1 to be true in a model without a second sentence S^2 also being true, then S^1 semantically entails S^2.

ERP

Acronym for event-related potentials. Recorded electrical changes in brain activity in response to presented stimuli.

existential quantifier

A quantifier that corresponds most closely to English expressions like *some* and *every*.

experiencer

A thematic role that may be borne by a noun phrase in a sentence. It is the experiencer that is construed as manifesting some psychological state.

eye-tracking

An experimental technique for monitoring eye movements usually during the observation of stimuli presented on a computer screen.

fixations

The periods during which the eyes do not move while reading. The average duration of a fixation is 150-500 milliseconds. See also *saccades*.

forebrain

Consists of the cerebral cortex, the thalamus, the hypothalamus, the basal ganglia, and the limbic system. The cortex and the thalamus are involved in perception, thinking, and learning. The hypothalamus and limbic system play an essential role in the control of emotions and motivation. The basal ganglia also play a role in the control of emotions, as well as in motor control.

formal language

An invented language, including logical and computer languages. They are to be distinguished from natural languages — those acquired and used by people in the normal course of development.

free morpheme

A morpheme that can appear alone (i.e., without affixation or compounding) as a lexical item in a given language. Opposite of *bound morpheme*.

fricative

A speech sound involving partial obstruction of the airstream. [s] and [f] are examples of fricatives.

front vowel

A vowel that involves moving the tongue forward from its rest position. [i], [e], and [æ] are examples of English front vowels.

function word

Lexical items that primarily play a grammatical role in a construction, and typically carry little content of their own. Complementizers (like *that*) are good examples of function words. Compare with *content words*.

Gall, Franc Joseph

Franc J. Gall (1758–1828), Viennese physician. The founder of cranioscopy, or as it is known today, phrenology. His ideas still serve as the foundation of localizationists' approaches to the interpretation of the brain/language relationship.

geminate

A sequence of two identical sounds.

gender

A feature of agreement that may be borne by a member of a lexical category. In English the contrast between *he* and *she* illustrates the genders 'masculine' and 'feminine.'

generative

A fully explicit rule or grammar that provides a precise analysis of the data it aims to account for. Refers to the contemporary style of grammatical analysis we are investigating in this book.

genitive

A case that normally marks possessive nouns. English often marks this case with *'s*.

glide

A vowellike sound (i.e., a sonorant) that cannot serve as a syllable nucleus. The English glides are [y], [w], and [h]. In English, [y] and [w] combine with certain vowels to form diphthongs (e.g., [ay]).

glottal

Pertaining to the glottis or larynx.

grammar

A formal, descriptive theory of linguistic competence. Although in traditional usage, *grammar* often to refers specifically to accounts of syntactic knowledge, in contemporary usage we understand a grammar to include a phonological, lexical, and semantic component. See also *universal grammar*.

grammatical

With respect to a particular dialect, an utterance that is consistent with the rules of that dialect.

gyrus

The Latin name (pl. gyri) for the hilly parts of brain convolutions. The gyri that play an important role in language functions are the third frontal gyrus (at the base of which is Broca's area) and the first temporal gyrus (the middle of which is known as "Wernicke's area"), both in the left hemisphere.

hard palate

The hard dome at the roof of the mouth. It is bounded by the alveo-palatal region in front and the velum at the rear. [y] is an English sound articulated in this region.

head

The syntactic category that forms the core of its eponymous phrase — the constituent that the determiners and modifiers in the phrase specify and modify. For example, a noun phrase has a noun head, and a verb phrase has a verb as its head.

hemispherectomy

A surgical procedure in which one of the brain's hemispheres is removed.

hi

See *high*.

high
Vowels that involve moving the tongue up from its rest position. Also spelled *hi*. [i] and [ɪ] are examples in English.

hindbrain
The hindbrain is located at the base of the brain and consists of three parts: the cerebellum, the pons, and the medulla.

homeostasis
The state of balance or equilibrium. Often used to refer to the ideal internal state of an organism.

homonym
Two words that sound the same but mean different things. *Bank* is an example.

homophonous
'Having the same sound as.' See *homonym*.

homorganic
Sounds that share the same place of articulation.

idiolect
The way a single individual speaks. Closely related idiolects make up a dialect, and closely related dialects compose a language.

idiom
An phrase with a conventional meaning that is not entirely compositional. For example, the expression *stuffed to the gills* can be aptly applied to people who are neither stuffed nor in possession of gills.

iff
An abbreviation for *if and only if*.

incredulity test
Evidence that a sequence of items can be used to form a phrasal constituent when it can be used as an incredulous response. For example, in response to the claim *Sue weighed fifty thousand pounds!* one might say: *Fifty thousand pounds?* but not **weighed fifty?* suggesting that *fifty thousand pounds* is a constituent but *weighed fifty* is not.

indefinite description
A description that begins with an indefinite determiner like *a* or *some*. See also *definite description*.

indirect object
The first object of verbs like *give*. *Bill* is the indirect object in *John gave Bill a CD*.

Indo-European
The name of the language family to which English (and French, German, Italian, Sanskrit, Latin, and many others) belong.

infinitive
The basic forms of verbs that may be conjugated into a variety of other forms marked for number, gender, person, and so on. English infinitives can also appear on their own, typically introduced by the infinitival marker *to* as in *to be or not to be*.

infix
A morpheme that can occur within a root morpheme. For example, the intensifying morpheme *frigging* functions as an infix as in *That wasn't very diplo-frigging-matic, was it now?*

inflectional morphology
English inflectional morphology involves the addition of one of a number of suffixes to a lexical item that records certain grammatical

information like number (e.g., singular/plural) or person (cf., *The women swim/Mary swim(s).* The *-s* on *swims* is the third-person singular marker). Compare to *derivational morphology.*

inter-dental

Sounds involving a place of articulation formed by bringing the upper and lower teeth in close proximity and then placing the tip of the tongue into the space in between. Relatively rare across the languages of the world, English has two inter-dental sounds, [ð] and [θ].

interrogation test

One of the main ways to determine syntactic constituency. If a sequence of items can be used as the answer to a question, we have evidence that it is a constituent.

intransitive

A member of a grammatical category that forbids an object, for example, a verb that may not take a noun-phrase complement. As the following examples illustrate, *elapse* is an example of a intransitive verb.

a. The time elapsed.
b. *The time elapsed an hour.

Opposite of *transitive.*

inversion

A type of movement transformation that permutes two adjacent constituents. For example, the rule that derives *Can you?* from *You can* is an instance of inversion (the helping verb *can* is inverted around the subject).

IPA

Acronym for the International Phonetic Alphabet, one of the frequently encountered phonetic alphabets.

isomorphic

X is isomorphic to *y* if *x* has the same structure as *y*. The opposite of *non-isomorphic.*

labial

Pertaining to the lips.

labio-dental

Sounds involving a place of articulation formed by bring the lower lip in close proximity to the upper teeth. [f] is an example of an English labio-dental.

labio-velar

Sounds involving two places of articulation — a labial constriction made by rounding the lips and bringing them together, and a velar constriction. [w] is an English labio-velar.

larynx

A cartilaginous structure (also called the "voice box") that houses the vocal folds (more commonly known as the vocal cords). Voiced sounds are produced in this region by bringing the vocal cords close enough together so that the air passing through causes them to vibrate.

lateral

Sounds involving the release of air over the side of the tongue. English [l] is an example of a lateral sound.

lateralization

A term used to indicate the dominance of a single hemisphere in controlling a certain function.

lateralized presentation (of a stimulus)

A technique pioneered by Ronald Myers. In patients who had their corpus callosum cut ("split-brain" patients), projecting a stimulus to one-half of the visual field makes it available only to one hemisphere.

lax

Vowels that involve a relatively lower and less front tongue position than their tense counterparts. [ɪ] and [i] are a lax/tense pair in English.

Lax Vowel Constraint

A phonological principle that prohibits lax vowels from appearing in open syllables.

lengthening

See *vowel lengthening*.

lexical access

The process of locating a lexical item and placing it into working memory.

lexical decision

An experimental condition in which subjects are asked to make a decision about a lexical item. The task of discriminating words from nonwords is an example of lexical decision.

lexical insertion

The process of inserting items from the lexicon into a syntactic representation.

lexical item

Words and other items that are included in the mental dictionary of a speaker. Taken together, they make up the lexicon.

lexical redundancy rule

A rule that adds certain lexical features to an entry based on other lexical features. For example, since every count noun in English must either be singular or plural, we rely on a lexical redundancy rule to associate either the feature value *[SINGULAR]* or *[PLURAL]* with every lexical noun bearing the feature value

[COUNT]. In other words, redundancy rules add features that are predictable, and hence need not be written into each and every lexical entry.

lexicon

The mental dictionary.

Lichtheim, L.

Lichtheim, L. A 19th-century Austrian physician who provided the first comprehensive model of aphasias in his paper "On aphasia" (1885 *Brain* 4, 433–484). The Wernicke-Lichtheim classification is still the basis for most current clinical classifications.

linguistic competence

A speaker's knowledge of a language (i.e., your knowledge of English). Of course, you continue to possess this competence even when it is not displayed in linguistic performance.

linguistic determinism

The position that linguistic structure determines, to some extent, the nature of thought. Usually put forth in combination with *linguistic relativity*.

linguistic performance

The act of using the language to perform a task (such as speaking or listening). Takes place in real time, and is often contrasted with *linguistic competence*.

linguistic relativity

The position that there are important structural differences that distinguish the world's languages, and that these differences correspond to differences in the way in which speakers of different languages think about the world. Usually put forth in tandem with the *linguistic determinism* hypothesis. See also *universal grammar*.

liquid

A Consonant made with relatively little obstruction in the vocal tract (a type of sonorant). Liquids may occupy the syllable nucleus in some languages.

lo

See *low*.

Local Movement Constraint

A restriction on requiring that movement take place within a local domain (roughly, within the same clause).

locative

A word with the function 'location' or 'place.' In English, locative prepositions include *on* and *in* (but not *for*).

logical form

A level of semantic analysis in which the interpretation of a sentence is represented in the form of a logical expression or other semantic structure.

low

Vowels that involve moving the tongue down from its rest position. Also spelled *lo*.

Luria, Aleksandr Romanovich

Luria, Aleksandr Romanovich (1902–1977). Russian neuropsychologist who contributed greatly to the development of "process" models of the brain/mind relationship. He was highly productive and left behind dozens of books and hundreds of articles.

manner of articulation

The type of sound (e.g., stop, fricative, vowel) being produced.

mass noun

A noun that does not inflect for plurality and may appear without a determiner, even in its singular form. Picks out an amount of material (rather than an individuated entity — see *count*).

Maximal Onset Principle

A principle that guarantees that, all things being equal, a consonant will be syllabified along with the onset of a following syllable rather than with the coda of a preceding syllable. For example, *reveal* is syllabified into *re-* and *-veal* rather than *rev-* and *-eal*.

medulla

The part of *hindbrain* that contains centers for the control of vital functions, like breathing and heart rate.

merge

A syntactic operation that incorporates two constituents into a single, larger constituent.

metathesis

The switching of two adjacent elements in a linguistic representation.

metrical structure

A level of analysis at which the relative prominence of the syllables (and other constituents) that compose a word or phrase is marked. For example, in a metrical representation, syllables with relatively higher stress are marked *S* and those with relatively less stress are marked *W*.

midbrain

A part of the brain that lies on top of the hindbrain and is involved in visual and auditory functions, as well as in sleep and the arousal mechanism. Its upper part is called the "tectum," and the lower part the "tegmentum."

minimal pair

Two items identical in every regard at a relevant level of analysis, save one, constitute a minimal pair. For example, *pit* and *bit* form a minimal pair because they comprise the same segments, except for the single distinction between [b] and [p] in initial position.

minimalism

An approach to syntactic theory that strives to develop a minimal theoretical apparatus.

modal

Part of the auxiliary verb system in English. They are : *can, could, shall, should, will, would, may, might,* and *must.*

modifier

An optional constituent in a phrase that limits the interpretation of the head (and complement, if any). Adjectival modifiers like *old* in *this old man* are cases in point.

modularity

A theory of the architecture of the mind that posits a central processing system, as well as independent cognitive modules responsible for processing in individual cognitive domains.

morpheme

The smallest unit of meaning. For example, the lexical item *reestablishes* consists of three morphemes: *re-* ('again'), *establish,* and the third-person singular morpheme *-es.*

morpho-phonemics

Interactions between phonology and morphology. More specifically, morpho-phonemic rules apply to change the segmental representation of a morpheme as a consequence of a morphological derivation. The transformation of the final /k/ sound of *electric* (/ilɛktrɪk/)into an [s] when *-ity* is added to form *electricity* ([ilɛktrɪsəti]) is an example of a morpho-phonemic rule.

Morpho-syntax

The study of rules that operate at the morphology-syntax border. Contraction is an example of a word-level phenomenon that illustrates a morpho-syntactic interaction, because certain kinds of contraction are blocked in certain syntactic positions, e.g., at the end of a sentence:

Q: Who is going?
A: John is going.
   = John's going.
   = John is.
   = *John's.

morphology

The study of morphemes.

mother

A node that dominates another node in a linguistic representation. The dominated node is the daughter.

motherese

The name given to the special way parents and other caregivers often speak to young children. Marked by exaggerated intonation, frequent repetitions, simplified syntactic structures, and a limited vocabulary.

move

A syntactic operation that changes constituency by relocating a constituent from one phrase-structure position to another.

myelin

See *myelinization.*

myelinization

The process of laying down a fatty sheath around a nerve. In the case of the auditory nerve, this insulation improves high-frequency hearing.

nasal

A sound articulated with air flowing through the nasal tract.

nasal tract

A secondary acoustic chamber through which air flows during the articulation of nasal sounds. Air passes into the nasal passages if the *velum* is lowered.

natural class

A set of linguistic items that can be expected to pattern in the same way. For example, all things being equal, we would expect all members of the class of determiners or the class of voiced sounds to behave similarly, each therefore constituting a natural class.

natural language

A language that is (was, or could be) acquired in the normal course of development and used by human beings. Distinguished from a formal language, which includes invented languages such as logical languages (like the predicate calculus) and computer languages.

nature

The aspects of an organism's development due to its biological character. Often juxtaposed with nurture in the terms of the nature-nurture debate.

necessary truth

A statement that is true in every possible world consistent with the laws of logic.

negative evidence

Evidence that illustrates cases that may not occur. For example, a list of ungrammatical sentences would constitute negative evidence. Opposite of *positive evidence*.

negative polarity item

A constituent that is grammatical in negative environments, if-clauses, and yes-no questions, but not in simple unnegated sentences:

1. *John had a prayer of a chance.
2. John didn't have a prayer of a chance.
3. Did John have a prayer of a chance?
4. If John had a prayer of a chance then I would have voted for him.

neurons

Specialized cells that make up the nervous system. Unlike less-specialized cells (skin cells, for example), neurons cannot replicate.

neurotransmitter

A chemical that plays an essential role in transmitting information from one neuron to another. Acetylcholine and norepinephrine are among the best-known neurotransmitters.

NMRI

Acronym for nuclear magnetic resonance imaging, a neuroimaging technique based on measuring electromagnetic energy received from protons placed in a magnetic field.

node

An instance of a labeled category in a linguistic representation.

nominative

A case that normally marks the subject of an English sentence. *I, she, he, we,* and *they* are nominative pronouns in English (compare *me, her, he, us,* and *them*).

non-isomorphic

Different in structure. Not isomorphic.

non-terminal

All the nodes in a linguistic representation except the terminals.

noun phrase

A syntactic constituent that includes a noun and may also include specifiers (like determiners) and modifiers (like prepositional phrases or adjective phrases), for example, *the old solution to the problem.*

novel utterances

Speech that has never been heard or produced before. Of course, all of the words and phrases in a novel utterance need not be novel; but particular combinations of words and phrases are. We can also consider novelty from the point of view of a given speaker or language learner. Obviously, novel utterances cannot be learned, produced, or understood by looking them up in a list of sentences that has been memorized by the speaker.

nucleus

One of the constituents of a syllable that must be filled, typically by a vowel (or sequence of vowels) but in some cases occupied by a sonorant such as a liquid or a nasal.

Nucleus Constraint

A condition that requires every syllable to have a syllable nucleus. In English, this nucleus is normally a vowel or a diphthong, but may also be a syllabic consonant like *r* (cf., [bʌtr]).

number

A feature of morphological agreement that may be marked on a lexical item. English marks the distinction between singular and plural (*dog* vs. *dogs*).

nurture

Environmental influences that shape the course of an organism's development. Often contrasted with *nature,* as in the nature-nurture debate.

object

A noun phrase that serves as an argument; for example, to a verb or preposition (e.g., *hit the ball* or *near the end*). We can further distinguish between two kinds of verbal objects, direct and indirect, which differ in the roles they play in the action structure of the verb phrase. In *gave the teacher a headache* the first noun phrase, *the teacher,* is the indirect object (playing the role of recipient in the action structure), and *a headache* is the direct object.

obstruent

A sound made with a relatively large amount of constriction in the vocal tract. Stops are good examples of obstruent sounds. Opposite of *sonorant.*

onomatopoeia

The case of a word said to sound like what it means. Animal sounds (e.g., *bow-wow*) are frequently mentioned examples.

onset

The cluster of sounds that precedes the nucleus (which is typically a vowel). So, [pr] is the onset in [pro].

ontogeny

The course of an organism's growth and development over time. See also *phylogeny.*

opaque contexts

Sentential contexts in which expressions are not assigned their normal reference; such contexts are described as (referentially) opaque.

open syllable

A syllable that ends with a vowel nucleus; that is, a syllable without a coda. [no] is an English example of an open syllable. See *closed syllable*.

optimality theory

Refers to the tendency of languages to build representations that incorporate preferred ("optimal") structures and avoid less desirable ones. Allows analyses that are more highly ranked within a language to block less-highly ranked analyses.

oral

See *oral tract*.

oral tract

The chamber running from the larynx to the lips in which all oral sounds are articulated.

orthographic

A representation in a spelling system.

overgeneration

The result of a grammar that generates strings not in the language — an adequate grammar must generate all and only the sentences of the language.

palpation

The clinical method of obtaining information by using the sense of touch.

parser

The online system responsible for assigning linguistic representations to linguistic stimuli.

participle

A form of the verb. For example, the past participle is introduced by a form of the auxiliary verb *have*. In *I have hung an innocent man, hung* is the past participle.

particle

A function word that can be incorporated into a complex verb; for example, *up* in *Mary coughed up the secret*.

performance errors

Mistakes made in the heat of linguistic performance, contravening linguistic rules or principles that are part of a speaker's linguistic competence. Such errors may be caused by loss of attention, problems with recall, or other limitations of the language processing system.

perseverations

Involuntary repetitions of isolated words or whole phrases associated with certain aphasic syndromes.

person

An agreement feature that may be marked on a lexical item. In English, a distinction may be drawn among first-, second- and third-person forms (e.g., *I am/you are/she was*).

PET

The acronym for positron emission tomography, a neuroimaging technique that provides a three-dimensional representation of brain activity based on the changes in blood flow.

phoneme

A representation of the unpredictable aspects of the pronunciation of a speech segment — those aspects that must be listed as a part of a lexical entry. The remainder of the phonetic features associated with a particular instance of a segment are provided by the application of phonological rules and/or principles. See also *phonemic form*.

phonemic form

A level of phonological representation at which the unpredictable aspects of the pronunciation of a lexical entry are listed. The predictable aspects of a pronunciation are provided by the application of phonological rules and/or principles. See also *phonetic form*.

phonetic

Pertaining to the acoustic or articulatory nature of speech sounds. See also *phonetic form*.

phonetic alphabet

An alphabet (for example, the IPA) in which each symbol stands for a distinctive speech sound, and each speech sound correlates with a different symbol. Phonetic characters are written in brackets, for example, [p].

phonetic form

A representation of the pronunciation of a linguistic item (i.e., after the application of the phonological rules and principles to the phonemic form).

phonetics

The study of how speech sounds are made ("articulatory phonetics") and what their acoustic character is ("acoustic phonetics").

phonology

The study of the principles, rules, and representations involved in a speaker's knowledge of the sound system of a language.

phonotactic

The study of the permissible sequences of speech sounds within a language. The restriction against [ŋ] appearing in initial position in an English word is an example of a phonotactic constraint.

phrase-structure grammar

A set of rules with certain formal properties, useful in characterizing the well formedness of the phrases and sentences of a language. Although there are a variety of notations in use by different contemporary linguistic theories, rewriting rules of the form A → B C (meaning 'an expression of category *A* can consist of category *B* followed by category *C*') — S → NP V being an example — are common to many of these approaches.

phrenology

A theory put forward by Franc Josef Gall. The basic postulate was that the different brain regions are organs in which specific mental functions are localized.

phylogeny

The evolutionary history of an organism. See also *ontogeny*.

pied-piping

Observed in constructions like *Near whom did she stand?* in which a constituent (here, the PP *near whom*) appears in a displaced position containing a smaller constituent (here, *whom*) that is capable of standing in the displaced position by itself (compare *Whom did she stand near*).

place of articulation

The point in the vocal tract at which there is greatest constriction.

pons

The part of hindbrain that connects the two halves of the cerebellum.

possessor

A thematic role that may be borne by a noun phrase in a sentence. Construed as possessing some entity.

possible word

A word that may not (currently) be a part of a language, but which nevertheless follows the phonotactic constraints of the language.

possible world

A description of a state of the world. The actual world is a possible world that describes the actual state of affairs at a moment of utterance. Some semantic theories also refer to past worlds, future worlds, and logically possible (but unactualized) worlds.

poverty of the stimulus

The arguments from poverty of the stimulus develop the position that there is not enough information provided in the child's primary linguistic data to directly account for the possibility of language acquisition on the basis of imitation or training.

precede

If two nodes X and Y in a linguistic representation are in a linear relationship, and X is to the left of Y, then X is said to precede Y.

predicate calculus

A logical language that contains expressions for predicates (and typically, names and quantifiers), as well as certain logical expressions that do the work of *and, or, not,* and *if...then*. See *formal language*.

prefix

A morpheme that is attached to the beginning of a lexical item at a given point in a lexical derivation.

preposition

A function word (like *up, to,* or *near*) that typically introduces a noun phrase in a prepositional phrase.

prepositional phrase

A syntactic constituent that, in its simplest manifestation, includes a preposition followed by a noun phrase, e.g., *up the creek*.

prescriptive linguistics

Approaches to grammar that purport to establish a linguistic norm. Prescriptive linguists usually intend to modify speech behavior. See also *descriptive grammar*.

primary linguistic data

The aspects of the environment available as input to the child that are relevant to language development. These include linguistic and nonlinguistic data.

pro-drop language

A language in which the subject of the sentence is optional. Italian and Spanish are examples of pro-drop languages.

progressive

The form of the verb (in English) ending in the suffix *-ing* with the meaning 'in the process of.' Also known as the *-ing* form of the verb.

pronoun

Linguistic items that depend on another linguistic expression (or sometimes on the context) for their interpretation. In some cases they should more properly be called "proforms," because they stand in for items that are not nouns. *He, she,* and *it* are examples.

property

The sense of a predicate.

proposition

The sense of a sentence.

prosody

A general term used to indicate the melodic pattern and tempo of an utterance.

quantifier

Expressions in logical languages (like the predicate calculus) that are approximated by English expressions like *each goat* and *some guitar*. The interpretation of these expressions requires inspecting the domain of discourse to determine how many of its members bear the properties that are predicated in the sentence in which the expression occurs.

range

The outputs of a function.

reaction time

In experiments, the amount of time it takes to complete a task.

recursive

A rule that applies to its own output. For example, the rule that a noun can be substituted for by a conjunction of nouns (e.g., *John and Paul* in place of *George*) is recursive. A rule system may be said to be (indirectly) recursive if it contains rules that expand in such a way that a constituent *X* dominates second constituent *Y* that in turn dominates another occurrence of *X*. Note that recursive rules give rise to the infinite

capacity of language: *John played the guitar; John and Paul played the guitar; John and Paul and George played the guitar,* and so on.

reduction

See *vowel reduction.*

referent

The object to which a term refers.

reflexive

A type of pronoun that ends (in English) in *-self* or *-selves* (e.g., *ourselves*). Requires a local linguistic antecedent; that is, in *John thought Bill liked himself, himself* must be Bill, not John (compare *John thought Bill liked him*).

regressive saccades

Eye movements that, in contrast to regular saccades, have a direction that is opposite to the flow of text.

relative clause

A construction in which a subordinate clause modifies a noun. *The book that/which I read is boring* is an example.

Resyllabification Principle

A principle of English phonology that guarantees that consonants in unstressed syllables are resyllabified into the coda position of a preceding stressed syllable (superseding the Maximal Onset Principle).

retroflex

Said of a sound whose articulation involves curling the tip of the tongue back toward the hard palate. In many dialects of English, [r] is a retroflex sound. (The *r* in *rabbit* is an example).

rhyme

The nucleus and coda of a syllable. As you may expect, this is the part of the syllable that must match for two words to form a rhyme.

root

A basic lexical entry to which other morphemes may be added in a lexical derivation.

rounding

A feature of speech sounds involving a rounding and a bringing together of the lips. English [u] is an example of a round vowel, as opposed to [i], an unround vowel.

saccades

Rapid eye movements that occur between two fixations during reading. They span an average of 7–9 characters and last only 20–35 milliseconds. The word comes from the French word for "jump."

schwa

The name of [ə], the English lax central vowel.

scope

The scope of a quantifier corresponds to the part of a logical expression in which an occurrence of a variable has its interpretation fixed by that quantifier. For example, in the predicate calculus expression

$\forall x[S(x)]$

the variable x is within the scope of the quantifier $\forall x$, as marked by brackets.

semantic displacement

The ability to refer to objects that are not present in the physical frame of reference.

semantic value

In a formal semantic theory, the interpretation of a word or phrase. For example, on the "referential" theory of meaning, the semantic value of *John* would be its referent — that is, the individual John.

semantics

The study of meaning.

semi-productive

A morphological process that may be recruited sporadically to create new lexical items. Some of the outputs of a semi-productive rule qualify as conventionalized lexical items, and others may not.

semi-vowel

Sounds that share properties of both consonants and vowels. For example, [h], [j], and [w], the English semi-vowels, are like consonants in that they cannot occupy the nucleus slot of a syllable; but, like vowels, they involve very little constriction in the vocal tract.

sense

An aspect of semantic interpretation. According to some semantic theories, linguistic expressions express a sense, which determines the referent and may be grasped by all who speak the language.

Shortest Movement

An economy condition that gives preference to short movements over long movements in a derivation.

sister

Nodes that are dominated by the same mother.

slips of the tongue

Unintended speech errors, often involving substituting the wrong word or transposing certain sounds in a word or across words.

Spoonerisms (such as using *tons of soil* instead of *sons of toil*) are one kind of well-known slip of the tongue.

soft palate

See *velum.*

sonorant

Sounds made with relatively little closure in the oral tract. They include vowels, glides, and nasals. See also *obstruent.*

sonority hierarchy

A ranking of speech sounds according to the increasing degree of constriction in the vocal tract involved in the articulation of these sounds (sonority). Vowels are the most sonorous, and stops the least.

specifier

A category that (in English) precedes and forms a constituent with another syntactic category. In the case of the noun phrase, for example, determiners serve as specifiers for the head noun, as in *the book* (in which *the* is the specifier).

spectrogram

An illustration of acoustic energy distribution produced when a sound is recorded by a spectrograph. Time is represented on the horizontal axis, and frequency is represented on the vertical axis. The degree of darkness at a particular point indicates how much energy is present at a frequency at a particular point in time.

speech community

The group of speakers who provide the primary linguistic data for a group of language learners.

spoonerism

A sound substitution across words that results in a comical utterance indirectly related in meaning to the intended utterance. Named after a Bishop Spooner, who was prone to such utterances.

stative

A verb expressing a state; for example, a mental state (rather than, say, indicating an action). The English verb *know* is an example.

stop

A consonant during the pronunciation of which the airstream is completely blocked.

strident

Consonants that are acoustically noisy and have two distinct sound sources. [s] is an example of an English strident that involves a friction noise produced by the passage of air between the tongue and mouth, and additional noise produced by the airstream as it passes the teeth.

string

An ordered sequence of words that, if grammatical in a dialect of a language, counts as a sentence.

stroke

The lay term for a sudden obstruction or rupture of a blood vessel in the brain, often followed by language impairments and/or paralysis of the limbs on one side.

Structure Dependence

A principle of universal grammar according to which all linguistic rules must dependent solely on aspects of linguistic structure. In particular, linguistic rules may not reference nonlinguistic considerations, for example, the number of words in a sentence.

subject

In a simple English sentence, the leftmost noun phrase dominated by S. In many cases, the subject plays the role of the agent of the sentence — it is interpreted as undertaking the action expressed by the sentence.

subordinate clause

Roughly, a sentence within a sentence. A grammatical unit that has all or most of the properties of a sentence, but which appears as a part of a larger sentence. In *I know Mary hit the ball, Mary hit the ball* is a subordinate clause.

Subset Principle

An approach to language learning according to which the learner advances a series of linguistic hypotheses that progress from relatively more conservative (in the sense of generating a relatively smaller language) to relatively less conservative, until the child's grammar is appropriate for the target language.

Substitutivity of Identicals

A semantic principle according to which the substitution of one synonymous expression for another will not affect the truth value of a sentence.

substitution test

Used to establish constituency. If a syntactic category *X* substitutes for a second category *Y* (preserving grammaticality and thematic roles), *X* and *Y* are constituents of the same type.

suffix

A morpheme that attaches to the end of a lexical item in a lexical derivation. *-ly* and the plural are examples of two English suffixes.

sulcus

The Latin name (pl. sulci) for the fissures between brain convolutions. The most prominent fissures are the deep *sylvian fissure,* which cuts obliquely from the frontal to the posterior parts of the brain, and the "sulcus centralis" which separates the frontal from the parietal lobe.

suppletive

A form of a lexical item in which the phonetic form is unrelated to those of its morphologically alternative forms. For example, *went* is a suppletive past-tense form of *go.*

surface structure

A level of syntactic analysis. Provides the input to the semantic and phonological components of the grammar, and closely represents the structure of expressions in the form in which they may be uttered (i.e., the form in which they surface). See also: *deep structure.*

sylvian fissure

One of the largest fissures of the brain. Most of the neural structures that play a role in the language function are localized around this fissure, in the area often referred to as the "perisylvian" region.

synapse

(From Greek 'connection'), a structure that enables transmission of an impulse from one neuron to another. Most synapses are of a chemical type where the microscopic synaptic cleft is bridged through a release of a chemical neurotransmitter.

synaptic connections

See *synapse.*

synchronic

Analysis that concerns itself with a snapshot of the language at an instant of time. More generally, we idealize away from temporal factors, concentrating on the nature of linguistic knowledge as it is represented in the mind of an individual. Compare with *diachronic*.

synonymous

Expressions that have the same meaning. Although an apparently unproblematic notion, some philosophers have disputed whether this is as clear a concept as it seems (see, for example, Quine 1961:40).

syntax

The study of the structure of sentences.

synthetic

Sentences that depend for their truth on matters of fact (e.g., *The cat is on the mat*). Quine has argued that the distinction between synthetic sentences and analytic sentences is less than clear (see Quine 1961:40).

tacit knowledge

Knowledge of which the subject is unaware. Linguistic competence is considered tacit because speakers are generally not aware of the character of their grammars.

tense

Vowels that involve a relatively higher and more advanced tongue position than their lax counterparts. [i] and [ɪ] are a tense/lax pair in English.

terminal

The last level of expansion in a linguistic representation. In a typical tree diagram, terminals appear along the bottom line of the tree.

thematic role

Aspects of interpretation assigned to noun phrases and other parts of linguistic constituents that indicate, for example, who is doing what to whom. The assignment of thematic roles is also an important feature of syntactic analysis. *Agent* is an example of a thematic role — the agent of the sentence is who/what undertakes action. *John* bears the thematic role of agent in the sentence *John sat on Bill*.

theme

A thematic role that may be borne by a noun phrase in a sentence. It is the theme that is construed as having undergone the action of the sentence.

topicalization

A construction in which an NP called the "topic" appears in a position to the left of the subject. *That kind of car, I would never drive* is an example.

trace

A silent terminal element left behind in a phrase marker as the result of movement.

transformation

An operation on phrase-structure representations that modifies syntactic constituency by moving an item from one position to another (a "movement transformation") or deleting an item from a representation (a "deletion transformation").

transitive

A member of a grammatical category that requires an object; for example, a verb that must take a noun-phrase complement. As the following examples illustrate, *touch* is an example of a transitive verb.

a. John touched the wall.
b. *John touched.

Opposite of *intransitive*.

truth conditions

The conditions under which an assertion would be true.

truth value

According to some semantic theories, the referent of a declarative sentence, namely, true or false.

truth-conditional semantics

An approach to semantic interpretation by which the truth conditions for a class of sentences is systematically determined.

underlying form

See *phonemic form*.

ungrammatical

Not grammatical.

uninflected

A root form with no suffixes, prefixes, or infixes.

universal

Common to all languages. See *universal grammar*.

universal grammar

Those linguistic principles that apply to every natural language. Linguists are fundamentally interested in the study of Universal Grammar, with the goal of discovering the defining characteristics of language.

universal quantifier

A quantifier that corresponds most closely to English expressions like *every, each,* and *all.*

unvoiced

Speech sounds whose articulation is not accompanied by vibration of the vocal cords. The opposite of *voiced.*

uvula

Pendulous flap of skin that hangs off the end of the velum. Although the uvula does not constitute a place of articulation in English, it is involved in production of trilled sounds in some other languages.

valence

A term borrowed from chemistry that characterizes the range of elements that a given element can combine with. In its linguistic usage, refers to dependencies between, say, a transitive verb and its object. The valence of such a verb is transitive, indicating that it combines with an NP object.

variable

A logical expression whose interpretation is fixed by a quantifier.

velum

Also called soft palate; behind the hard palate. The location for velar sounds (like [k] and [g] in English). If the velum is lowered, air passes into the nasal tract.

verb phrase

A constituent headed by a verb, which may incorporate other constituents, including modifiers and objects.

vocal cords

Movable folds located in the larynx that may be brought close together or spread tautly apart. When the folds are in close proximity to one another, air rushing past causes them to vibrate, producing the feature of voicing.

vocal tract

Combines the oral tract and nasal tract. All speech sounds are produced in these two chambers.

voice onset time (VOT)

Refers to the period of time after the release of a consonant leading up to the onset of voicing. In English, the voice onset time is approximately 20-30 milliseconds after the consonantal release.

voiced

Speech sounds are said to be voiced if their articulation is accompanied by vibration of the vocal cords. The opposite of *unvoiced*.

vowel

A speech sound made with relatively little closure in the oral tract (all vowels are sonorants). Distinguished from one another by the position of the tongue, the shape of the lips, the chamber through which air flows, and so forth. Typically constitutes the nucleus of the syllable.

Vowel Lengthening

A rule of English phonology that adds extra duration to certain vowels preceding voiced sounds.

Vowel Reduction

An English phonological rule that reduces certain vowels in unstressed syllables to schwa.

well-formedness condition

A condition imposing a requirement on a linguistic representation that must be met. Any representation that fails to meet a well-formedness condition gives rise to ungrammaticality.

Wernicke's aphasia

A disorder that may be described as the mirror image of Broca's aphasia. The major symptoms involve difficulties in understanding language. The ability to produce grammatically correct utterances is often unaffected, although utterances may be completely meaningless.

wh-question

A construction in which a question word appears, (typically spelled in English with an initial *wh*, but *how* also counts), and to which an interrogative interpretation is assigned. *Where did that crazy rabbit go?* is an example.

X-bar syntax

A theory of phrase structure in which syntactic categories have a unified phrase structure involving a progressive expansion from a phrase of type XP (sometimes written X″) to an X′ constituent to a head of type X, for each syntactic category X, where X ranges over basic syntactic categories like N, Adj, Adv, P, V, and Det.

Bibliography

Akmajian A., R.A. Demers, A.K. Framer, and R.M. Harnish. (1995). *Linguistics: An introduction to language and communication*. Cambridge, Mass.: MIT Press.

Arbib, M.A. and D. Caplan (1979). Neurolinguistics must be computational. *Behavioral and Brain Sciences* 2, 449-83.

Austin, J.L. (1961). The meaning of a word. In J. Urmson and G. Warnock, eds. *Philosophical papers*. Oxford: Oxford University Press.

Baker, M. (1988). *Incorporation*. Chicago: University of Chicago Press.

Barwise, J. and Cooper, R. (1981). Generalized quantifiers and natural language. *Linguistics and Philosophy* 4, 159-219.

Barwise, J. and J. Perry (1983). *Situations and attitudes*. Cambridge, Mass.: MIT Press.

Benson, D.F. and N. Geschwind (1971). Aphasia and related cortical disturbances. In A.B. Baker and L.H. Baker, eds., *Clinical neurology*. New York: Harper & Row.

Bereiter, C. et al. (1966). An academically oriented pre-school for culturally deprived children. In F.M. Hechinger, ed. *Pre-school education today*. New York: Doubleday.

Berko, J. (1958). The child's learning of English morphology. *Word* 14, 150-177.

Berwick, R. (1985). *The acquisition of syntactic knowledge*. Cambridge, Mass.: MIT Press.

Bever, T.G. (1970). The cognitive basis for linguistic structure. In J.R. Hayes, ed. *Cognitive development of language*. New York: Wiley.

Bloom, A. H. (1981). *The linguistic shaping of thought: A study in the impact of language on thinking in China and the West*. Hillsdale, N.J.: Erlbaum.

Bloomfield, L. (1933). *Language*. New York: Holt, Rinehart, and Winston.

Bouton, P.C. (1991). *Neurolinguistics: Historical and theoretical perspectives*. New York: Plenum Press.

Brodmann, K. (1909). *Vergleichende Lokalisationslehre der Grosshirnrinde in ihren Prinzipien dargestellt auf Grund des Zellenbaues*. Leipzig: J.A. Barth.

Brody, M. (1995). *Lexico-logical form: A radically mimimalist theory*. Cambridge, Mass.: MIT Press.

Brown, R. and C. Hanlon (1970). Derivational complexity and the order of acquisition in child speech. In R. Brown, ed. *Psycholinguistics*. New York: Free Press.

Chierchia, G. and S. McConnell-Ginet (1990). *Meaning and grammar: An introduction to semantics*. Cambridge, Mass.: MIT Press.

Caplan, D. (1987). *Neurolinguistics and linguistic aphasiology*. Cambridge: Cambridge University Press.

Caroll, J. B. (1955). *The study of language*. Cambridge, Mass.: Harvard University Press.

Caroll, J. (1956). *Language, thought, and reality: Selected readings of Benjamin Lee Whorf*. New York: Wiley.

Chase, S. (1974). Gobbleygook. In P. Eschhloz et al. eds. *Language Awareness*. 1st ed. New York: St. Martin's Press.

Chickering, H. D. (1989). *Beowulf: A dual-language edition*. New York: Anchor Books.

Chomsky, N. (1957). *Syntactic Structures*. The Hague: Mouton and Co.

Chomsky, N. (1965). *Aspects of the theory of syntax*. Cambridge, Mass.: MIT Press.

Chomsky, N. (1968). *Language and Mind*. New York: Hartcourt Brace Jovanovich.

Chomsky, N. (1975). *Reflections on language*. New York: Pantheon.

Chomsky, N. (1980). *Rules and representations*. New York: Columbia University Press.

Chomsky N. (1981). *Lectures on government and binding*. Dordrecht: Foris Publications.

Chomsky, N. (1986). *Knowledge of language: Its nature, origin, and use*. New York: Praeger.

Chomsky, N. (1988). *Language and problems of knowledge: The Managua lectures*. Cambridge, Mass.: MIT Press.

Chomsky, N. (1995). *The minimalist program*. Cambridge, Mass.: MIT Press.

Chomsky, N. (1998). Some observations on economy in generative grammar. In Barbosa, P., D. Fox, P. Hagstrom, M. McGinnis, and D. Pesetsky, eds. *Is the best good enough? Optimality and competition in syntax*. Cambridge, Mass.: MIT Press and MIT Working Papers in Linguistics.

Crain, S. and M. Nakayama (1986). Structure dependence in children's language. *Language* 63, 522-543.

Cresswell, M. (1985). *The semantics of propositional attitudes*. Cambridge, Mass.: MIT Press.

Crosby F., and L. Nyquist (1977). The female register: An empirical study of Lakoff's hypotheses. *Language and Society* 6:3, 313-322.

Cytovic, R. (1996). *The neurological side of neuropsychology*. Cambridge, Mass.: MIT Press.

Davidson, D. (1967). Truth and meaning. *Synthese* 17, 304-323.

de Saussure, F. (1959). *Course in General Linguistics*. New York: McGraw-Hill Book Company.

DeRenzi, E. and L.A. Vignolo (1962). The token test: A sensitive test to detect receptive disturbances in aphasia. *Brain* 85, 665-678.

Dillon, G.L. (1994). The meaning of a word. In Clark, V.P., P.A. Escholz, and A. F. Rosa, eds. *Language: Introductory readings*. New York: St. Martin's Press.

Donnellan, K. (1966). Reference and definite descriptions. In Martinich, A.P. (1996). *The philosophy of language*. 3rd ed. New York and Oxford: Oxford University Press.

Dowty, D., R. Wall, and S. Peters (1981). *Introduction to Montague semantics*. Dordrecht: Riedel.

Eimas, P.D., E.R. Siqueland, P. Juscyzk, and J. Vigorito (1971). Speech perception in infants. *Science* 171, 303-306.

Elman J.L., E.A. Bates, M.H. Johnson, A. Karmiloff-Smith, D. Parisi, and K. Plunkett (1996). *Rethinking innateness: A connectionist perspective on development*. Cambridge, Mass.: MIT Press.

Fillmore, G., G. Lakoff, and R. Lakoff (1974). *Berkeley studies in syntax and semantics*. Vol. 1. Berkeley, Calif.: Department of Linguistics and Institute of Human Learning, University of California.

Fodor, J.A. (1975). *The language of thought*. Cambridge, Mass.: Harvard University Press.

Fodor, J. A. (1983). *The Modularity of Mind*. Cambridge, Mass.: MIT Press.

Fodor, J. A., and T.G. Bever (1965). The psycholinguistic reality of linguistic segments. *Journal of Verbal Leaning and Verbal Behavior* 4, 414-420.

Fodor, J. A., T. G. Bever, and M.F. Garrett (1975). *The psychology of language*. New York: McGraw-Hill.

Francis, W. N. (1958). *The structure of American English*. New York: The Ronald Press Co.

Frege, G. (1892). On sense and reference. In P. Geach and M. Black, eds. *Translations from the philosophical writings of Gottlob Frege*. Oxford: Basil Blackwell.

Fromkin, V. and R. Rodman (1988). *Introduction to language*. 4th ed. Fort Worth, Tex.: Holt, Rinehart and Winston, Inc.

Garfield, J.L. (1987). *Modularity in knowledge representation and natural language understanding*. Cambridge, Mass.: MIT Press.

Gazdar, G., E.Klein, , G.K.Pullum, and I.A. Sag (1985). *Generalized phrase structure grammar*. Cambridge, Mass.: Harvard University Press.

Gee, J.P. (1993). *An introduction to human language: Fundemental concepts in linguistics*. Englewood Cliffs, N.J.: Prentice Hall.

Geschwind, N. (1965). Disconnection syndromes in animals and man. *Brain* 88, 237-94, 585-644.

Giglioli, P. P. (1972). *Language and social context*. Harmondsworth, Middlesex, England: Penguin Books Ltd.

Gleitman, L. R., H. Gleitman, B. Landau, and E. Wanner (1988). Where learning begins: Initial representations for language learning. In F. J. Newmeyer, ed., *Linguistics: The Cambridge survey*. Vol . 3, *Language: Psychological and biological aspects*. Cambridge: Cambridge University Press.

Goldsmith, J. (1976). An overview of autosegmental phonology. *Linguistic Analysis* 2, 23-68.

Goodglass, H. (1976). Agrammatism, in H. Whitaker and A.H. Whitaker eds., *Studies in neurolinguistics*. Vol. 1. New York: Academic Press.

Goodluck, H. (1991). *Language acquisition: A linguistic introduction*. Cambridge, Mass.: Blackwell.

Greenberg, J. (1966). *Some universals of grammar*. In J. Greenberg, ed. *Universals of language*. 2nd ed. Cambridge, Mass.: MIT Press.

Grodzinsky, Y. (1995). A restrictive theory of agrammatic comprehension. *Brain and Language* 50, 27-51.

Grodzinsky, Y. (1995). Trace deletion, theta-roles and cognitive strategies. *Brain and Language* 51, 469-497.

Gumperz, J. and S. Levinson (1996). *Rethinking linguistic relativity*. Cambridge: Cambridge University Press.

Harris, Z. (1970). Introduction to transformations. In *Papers in structural and transformational linguistics*. Doredrecht: Riedel.

Harris, Z. (1970). Immediate-constituent formulation of English syntax. In *Papers in structural and transformational linguistics*. Doredrecht: Riedel.

Hayes, B. (1980). A metrical theory of stress rules. Ph.D. diss. MIT, Cambridge, Mass.

Hayes, B. (1982). Extrametricality and English stress. *Linguistic Inquiry* 13, 227-276.

Heim, I and A. Kratzer (1998). *Semantics in generative grammar*. Malden, Mass.: Blackwell.

Henderson, J.M., M. Singer, and F. Ferreira (1995). *Reading and language processing*. Princeton, New Jersey: LEA.

Hornstein, N. (1990). *As time goes by: Tense and universal grammar*. Cambridge, Mass.: MIT Press.

Hyams, N. (1987). The theory of parameters and syntactic developement. In T. Roeper and E. Williams, eds. *Parameter setting*. Dordrecht: Reidel.

Hymes, D. H. (1964). *Language in culture and society*. New York: Harper and Row.

International Phonetic Association (IPA) (1949). *The principles of the international phonetic association: Being a description of the international phonetic alphabet and the manner of using it, illustrated by texts in 51 languages*. London: University College, Gower Street.

Jackendoff, R. (1977). *X' syntax: A study of phrase structure*. Cambridge, Mass.: MIT Press.

Jakobson, R. 1968. *Child language aphasia and phonological universals*. A.R. Keiler, Trans. The Hague: Mouton. Originally published as *Kindersprache, aphasie und allgemeine Lautgesetze* (1941).

Jespersen, O. (1968). *Language: Its nature, development and origin*. London: Photolithography.

Jespersen, O. (1969). *Analytic Syntax*. New York: Holt, Rinehart & Winston.

Kimura, D. (1961). Cerebral dominance and the perception of verbal stimuli. *Canadian Journal of Psychology* 15, 166-171.

Kimura, D. (1992). Sex differences in the brain. *Scientific American* 267(3), 118-125.

Kripke, S. (1980). *Naming and necessity*. Cambridge, Mass.: Harvard University Press.

Labov, W. (1972). The Logic of Non-Standard English. In P. P. Giglioli ed., *Language and Social Context*. Harmondsworth, Middlesex, England: Penguin Books Ltd.

Lakoff, R. (1974). Why women are ladies. In G. Fillmore et al. eds., *Berkeley studies in syntax and semantics*. Vol. 1. Berkeley, Calif.: Department of Linguistics and Institute of Human Learning, University of California.

Lakoff, R. (1975). *Language and women's place*. New York: Harper Colophon Books.

Langacker, R. (1973). *Language and its structure: Some fundamental linguistic concepts*. New York: Hartcourt, Brace, Jovanovich, Inc.

Larson, R. (1988). On the double object construction. *Linguistic Inquiry* 19, 335-391.

Larson, R. and G. Segal (1995). *Knowledge of meaning*. Cambridge, Mass.: MIT Press.

Lasky, R.E., A. Syrdal-Lasky, and R.E. Klein (1975). VOT discrimination by four- to six-and-a-half-month-old infants from Spanish environments. *Journal of Experimental Child Psychology* 20, 215-225.

Lehman, Winifred, P. (1962). *Historical linguistics*. New York: Holt, Rinehart, and Winston.

Levelt, W.J.M. (1970). A scaling approach to the study of syntactic relations. In F.B. Flores-D'Arcais and W.J.M. Levelt, eds, *Advances in psycholinguistics*. New York: American Elsevier.

Lewis, D. (1973). *Counterfactuals*. Oxford: Blackwell.

Liberman, M. and A. Prince (1976). On stress and linguistic rhythm. *Linguistic Inquiry* 8, 249-336.

Liberman, A. M., F.S. Cooper, D.P. Shankweiler, and M. Studdert-Kennedy (1967). Perception of the speech code. *Psychological Review* 74, 431-61.

Lightfoot, D. (1979). *Principles of diachronic syntax*. Cambridge: Cambridge University Press.

Lightfoot, D. (1991). *How to set parameters*. Cambridge, Mass.: MIT Press.

Linebarger, M. C. (1995). Agrammatism as evidence about grammar. *Brain and Language* 50, 52-91.

Linebarger, M. C., M. Schwartz, and E. Saffran (1983). Sensitivity to grammatical structure in so-called agrammatic aphasics. *Cognition* 13, 361-392.

Marcus, G.F., S. Pinker, M. Ullman, M. Hollander, J. Rosen, and F. Xu (1992). *Overregularization in language acquisition*. Monographs of the Society for Research in Child Development 57:6.

Marler, P. and V. Sherman (1985). Innate differences in the singing of behaviour of sparrows reared in isolation from adult conspecific song. *Animal Behaviour* 33, 57-71.

Marshall J. (1995). The mapping hypothesis and aphasia therapy. *Aphasiology* 9: 517-539.

Martinet A. (1960). *Elements of General Linguistics*. Chicago: University of Chicago Press.

Matthews, P.H. (1974). *Morphology: An introduction to the theory of word structure*. Cambridge: Cambridge University Press.

May, R. (1985). *Logical form*. Cambridge, Mass.: MIT Press.

Mellinkoff, D. (1974). The language of the law. In P. Eschhloz, et al., eds. *Language awareness*. 1st ed. New York: St. Martin's Press.

Montague, R. (1973). The proper treatment of quantification in ordinary English. In R. Thomason, ed. *Formal philosophy*. New Haven, Conn.: Yale University Press.

Morris, C.W. (1938). *Foundations of a theory of signs*. Chicago: University of Chicago Press.

Myake, A., P.A. Carpenter and M.A. Just (1994a). A capacity approach to syntactic comprehension disorders: Making normal adults perform like aphasic patients. *Cognitive Neuropsychology* 11, 671-717.

Myake, A., P.A. Carpenter and M.A. Just (1994b). Reduced resources and specific impairments in normal and aphasic sentence comprehension. *Cognitive Neuropsychology* 12, 651-679.

Newport, E., H. Gleitman, and L, Gleitman (1977). Mother, I'd rather do it myself: Some effects and non-effects of maternal speech style. In Snow, C., and C. Ferguson, eds. *Talking to children: Language input and acquisition. Papers from a conference sponsored by the Committee on Socio-linguistics of the Social Science Research Council.* Cambridge: Cambridge University Press.

Nida, E.A. (1966). *A synopsis of English syntax.* The Hague: Mouton & Co.

Ojemann, G.A. (1983). Brain organization for language from the perspective of electrical stimulation mapping. *Behavioral and Brain Sciences* 6, 189-230.

Ojemann, G., J. Ojemann, E. Lettich, and M. Berger (1989). Cortical language localization in the left, dominant hemisphere. *Journal of Neurosurgery* 71, 316-326.

Osborn, H.A. (1967). Warao III: Verbs and Suffixes. *International Journal of American Linguistics* 33:1.

Penfield, W. and L. Roberts (1959). *Speech and brain mechanisms.* Princeton, NJ: Princeton Univeristy Press.

Pesetsky, D. (1998). Some optimality principles of sentence pronunciation. In Barbosa, P., D. Fox, P. Hagstrom, M. McGinnis, and D. Pesetsky, eds. *Is the best good enough? Optimality and competition in syntax.* Cambridge, Mass.: MIT Press and MIT Working Papers in Linguistics.

Pfeiffer, J. (1994). Girl talk–boy talk. In Clark, V.P., P.A. Escholz, and A. F. Rosa, eds. *Language: Introductory readings.* New York: St. Martin's Press.

Piatelli-Palmerini, M. (1980). *Language and learning.* Cambridge, Mass.: Harvard University Press.

Pick, A. (1913). *Die agrammatische Sprachstoerungen.* Berlin: Springer-Ferlag.

Pinker, S. (1989). Language acquisition. In M. Posner, ed. *Foundations of cognitive science.* Cambridge, Mass.: MIT Press.

Pinker, S. (1994). *The language instinct: How the mind creates language.* New York: William Morrow.

Pinker S., and A. Prince (1988). On language and connectionism: Analysis of a parallel distributed model of language acquisition. *Cognition* 28, 73-193.

Premack D. (1986). *Gavagi!* Cambridge, Mass.: MIT Press.

Prince, A. (1983). Relating to the grid. *Linguistic Inquiry* 14, 19-100.

Prince, A. and P. Smolensky (1995). *Optimality theory.* Cambridge, Mass.: MIT Press.

Pullum, G. (1991). *The great Eskimo vocabulary hoax and other irreverent essays on the study of language*. Chicago: University of Chicago Press.

Quine, W.V.O. (1953). On what there is. In W.V.O. Quine, ed. *From a logical point of view*. Cambridge, Mass.: Havard University Press.

Quine, W.V.O. (1961). Two dogmas of empiricism. In Martinich, A.P. (1996). *The philosophy of language*. 3rd ed. New York and Oxford: Oxford University Press.

Quine, W.V.O. (1970). *Philosophy of logic*. Englewood, N.J.: Prentice-Hall.

Quine, W.V.O. (1972). Methodological reflections on current linguistic theory. In G. Harman and D, Davidson, eds. *Semantics of natural language*. Dordrecht: Reidel.

Radford, A. (1981). *Transformational Syntax: A student's guide to Chomsky's Extended Standard Theory*. Cambridge, Cambridge University Press.

Radford, A. (1997). *Syntax: A minimalist introduction*. Cambridge: Cambridge University Press.

Rasmussen,T., and B. Milner (1977). The role of early left-brain injury in determining lateralization of cerebral speech functions. *Annals of the New York Academy of Sciences* 299, 355-369.

Rayner, K. and A. Pollatsek (1989). *The psychology of reading*. Englewood, New Jersey: Prentice Hall.

Reich, P.E. (1986). *Language development*. Englewood Cliffs, N.J.: Prentice Hall.

Reichenbach, H. (1947). *Elements of symbolic logic*. New York: McMillan.

Roberts, P. (1994). Speech communities. In Clark, V.P., P.A. Escholz, and A. F. Rosa, eds. *Language: Introductory readings*. New York: St. Martin's Press.

Ross, J.R. (1967). Constraints on variables in syntax. Doctoral Dissertation, MIT, Cambridge, Mass.

Rumelhart, D.E. and J.L. McClelland (1986). PDP models and general issues in cognitive science. In D.E. Rumelhart, J.L. McClelland, and the PDP Research Group. *Parallel distributed processing: Explorations in the microstructure of cognition*. Vol. 2. *Psychological and biological models*. Cambridge, Mass.: MIT Press.

Russell B. (1919). *Introduction to mathematical philosophy*. London: George Allen and Unwin Ltd.

Sag, I. and T. Wasow (1996). Syntactic theory: A formal introduction. Stanford, Calif.: CSLI Publications (Draft in progress). Published as: I. Sag and T. Wasow (1999).

Sag, I.A. and T. Wasow (1999). *Syntactic theory: A formal introduction*. Stanford, Calif.: CSLI Publications.

Sapir, E. (1921) *Language*. New York: Harcourt, Brace & World, Inc.

Schwartz, M. F., E.M. Saffran, R.B. Fink, J.L. Myers, and N. Martin (1994). Mapping therapy: A treatment programme for agrammatism. *Aphasiology* 8, 19-54.

Schwartz, M. F., R.B. Fink, and E.M. Saffran (1995). The modular treatment of agrammatism. *Neuropsychological Rehabilitation* 5, 93-127.

Selkirk, E. (1980). The role of prosodic categories in English word stress. *Linguistic Inquiry* 11, 563-605.

Selkirk, E. (1984). *Phonology and syntax: The relation between sound and structure*. Cambridge, Mass.: MIT Press.

Sells, P. (1985). *Lectures on contemporary syntactic theories*. Palo Alto, Calif.: Center for the Study of Language and Information.

Shaywitz, B., S. Shaywitz, K.R. Pugh, T. Constable, P. Skudlarski, R.T. Bronen, R. Fulbright, J. Fletcher, D. Shankweiler, L. Katz, and J. Gore (1995). Sex differences in the functional organizaton of the brain for language. *Nature* 373, 607-609.

Simon, J. I. (1976). *Paradigms lost*. New York: Clarkson N. Potter Publishers.

Smith, A. (1966). Speech and other functions after left (dominant) hemispherectomy. *Journal of Neurology, Neurosurgery and Psychiatry* 29,467-471.

Staal, F. (1988). *Universals: Studies in Indian logic and linguistics*. Chicago: The University of Chicago Press.

Steele, S. (1977). On being possessed. In Whistler, K., R.Van Valian Jr., C.Chiarello, J.Jaeger, M. Petruck, H.Thompson, R.Javin, and A.Woodbury, eds. *Proceedings of the third annual meeting of the Berkeley Linguistics Society*. Berkeley, CA: The University of California.

Stich, S. (1975). *Innate Ideas*. University of California Press. Berkeley, CA.

Stillings, N., S. Weisler, C. Chase, M. Feinstein, J. Garfield, and E. Rissland (1995). *Cognitive science: An introduction*. Cambridge, Mass.: MIT Press.

Tarski, A. (1944). The semantic conception of truth and the foundation of semantics. *Philosophy and Phenomenological Research* 4, 342.

Traugott, E.C. (1972). *A history of English syntax*. New York: Holt, Rinehart, and Winston.

Valian, V. (1990). Logical and psychological constraints on the acquisition of syntax. In Frazier, L., and J. de Villiers, eds. *Language processing and language acquisition*. Dordrecht: Kluwer.

Valian, V., J. Winzemer, and A. Errich (1981). A "little linguist" model of syntax learning. In S. Tavakolian, ed., *Language acquisition and linguistic theory*. Cambridge, Mass.: MIT Press.

Vygotsky, L. (1962). *Thought and Language*. Cambridge, Mass.: The MIT Press.

Weinreich, U. (1963). On the semantic structure of language. In J. Greenberg, ed. *Universals of language*. 2nd ed. Cambridge, Mass.: MIT Press.

Wexler, K. and R. Manzini (1987). Parameter and learnability in language acquisition. In Roeper, T. and E. Williams, eds. *Parameter setting*. Dordrecht: Reidel.

Index

affix 61, 64, 70–73, 79, 80, 81, 84–86, 89, 104, 106, 107, 111, 113, 114, 117, 305–307, 311
affricate 29, 305
African-American English 7, 39, 67, 305
agent 95, 96, 175, 185, 190, 194, 198, 302, 305, 327, 328
allomorph 108, 113, 116, 137, 138, 305
allophone 42, 305
ambiguity 55, 106, 156–159, 188, 197, 224, 228, 238–240, 248, 260–272, 305
analytic 245, 306, 328
anaphora 306
antecedent 119–123, 156, 158, 171, 179, 196, 208–214, 224, 263, 264, 272, 306, 307, 324
aphasia 286, 287, 296–299, 301, 305, 307, 316, 330
aspiration 19, 20, 37, 39, 40–61, 98, 306
assimilation 44, 102, 113, 114, 306
autosegment 78, 306, 333
auxiliary 8, 202, 221, 306, 318, 321

backformation 71, 306
binary branching 86, 153, 154, 157, 158, 164, 168, 236, 237, 307
binding 194, 196, 197, 207–212, 224, 225, 307
Binding Theory 208, 209, 211, 212, 307
bound 64, 72, 73, 75, 77–82, 89, 307, 312

C-command 209–215, 307
case 116–118, 180–184, 193, 196, 200–202, 305, 307, 310, 313, 319
Case Checking Principle 181–184, 214, 215, 307
CAT 293, 308
categorical perception 23, 308
co-referential 243–245, 247, 250, 254, 308
coarticulation 63, 308
coda 47–50, 54, 58, 59, 106, 111, 308, 317, 321, 324, 325

complement 114–116, 123, 138, 139, 144, 148, 149, 151, 154, 156, 159, 160, 162, 163–170, 172, 173, 175, 177–184, 186–188, 190, 191, 193, 194, 197, 200, 222, 223, 226, 243, 248, 309, 315, 318, 329
complementary distribution 41, 42, 309, 310
complementizer 131–133, 160, 162, 164, 201, 309, 312
compositionality 245, 249, 262, 309
compound 68, 69, 73, 89–92, 94, 111, 307, 309, 312
conjunction 14, 134–136, 139, 140, 196, 235–239, 258, 271, 272, 309, 311, 324
consonant 20–31, 34–38, 40, 46, 47, 48, 51–55, 306, 309, 317, 320, 324, 325, 326, 330
constituent 64, 84, 142–146, 148, 149, 155, 156, 158–160, 164, 169, 170, 171, 182, 187, 188, 189, 191–198, 200, 202, 204, 209–211, 213, 214, 234–236, 245, 251, 252, 258, 264, 305, 308, 309, 311–315, 317–320, 322–324, 326–328, 330
contraction 8, 39, 73, 74, 79, 112, 310, 318
contrasting distribution 42, 309, 310
count 87, 88, 96, 108, 116, 175, 310, 316, 317
creativity 10, 16, 72, 81, 86, 87, 134, 152, 303, 310
critical period 16, 68, 69, 216, 310

daughter 167, 197, 198, 307, 310, 318
deep structure 195, 310, 327
definite description 243, 251, 232, 310, 311, 314
derivation 41, 43, 51, 52, 55, 62, 70, 79, 81, 85, 86, 88, 89, 97, 104–107, 109, 110, 138, 152, 195, 200, 201, 206, 215, 240, 306, 311, 312, 318, 323, 325, 327
derivational morphology 79–82, 86, 311, 315
derived root 85, 89, 100, 311
determiner 88, 99, 118, 137–139, 141, 172, 174, 175, 177, 178, 183, 187, 199, 223, 243, 258, 263, 310, 311, 313, 314, 317, 319, 320, 326
diachronic 71, 311, 328
dialect 2, 5–8, 14, 17, 29, 31–34, 36, 39, 48, 69, 100, 119, 133, 178, 199, 200, 202, 209, 216, 218, 311, 313, 314, 324, 326

diphthong 33, 36, 48, 311, 313, 320
displacement 189–194, 196, 197, 200, 202, 204, 206, 207, 209, 223, 224, 226, 242, 311, 325
domain 233, 311
dominate 143, 146, 148, 152, 156, 160, 162, 163, 165, 170, 182, 194, 197, 201, 210, 236, 307, 311, 318, 324

economy 140, 205, 274, 312, 325
ellipsis 213, 214, 306, 312
elliptical 213, 214, 312
entailment 312
ERP 293, 312
existential quantifier 257, 261, 262, 270, 312

fixations 291, 312, 325
formal language 152, 235, 312, 319, 323
fricative 27–29, 48, 78, 305, 309, 312, 317

geminate 111, 313
gender 118–122, 131, 178, 208, 223, 296, 313, 314
generative 43, 44, 45, 61, 86, 195, 215, 218, 219, 227, 264, 265, 313, 332
genetive 117
glide 29, 30, 48, 311, 313, 326
grammar 6, 14, 61, 62, 99, 105, 112, 125–127, 129–133, 140, 142, 143, 146, 150, 152, 157, 161, 162, 164, 165, 170, 172, 174–176, 178, 179, 187–190, 192, 194, 197, 199, 202, 204, 214–226, 263–265, 274, 302, 310, 313, 316, 321–323, 326–329
grammatical 14, 44, 47, 72–74, 83, 86, 88, 119, 126, 128, 130–133, 136–143, 157, 159, 168, 173, 175, 177, 179, 180, 183, 184, 186, 190, 207–212, 219, 220, 264, 276, 296, 298, 302, 303, 307, 311–315, 319, 326, 327, 329
grammaticality 128, 130, 131, 140, 206, 236, 327

homonym 33, 314
homorganic 27, 314

idiolect 314
idiom 309, 314
iff 234, 235, 237, 314
incredulity test 148–151, 159, 161, 236, 314
indefinite description 243, 263, 268, 269, 310, 311, 314
indirect object 117, 139, 310, 314, 320
Indo-European 192, 314
infinitive 74, 94, 138, 162–164, 314
infix 61, 72, 73, 79, 84, 305, 314, 329
inflectional morphology 79, 86, 88, 311, 314
interrogation test 149, 151, 315
intransitive 83, 97, 157, 165–167, 169, 172, 180, 181, 183, 195, 231, 233, 241, 242, 245, 249, 266, 315, 329
inversion 201, 315
IPA 26, 27, 36, 315, 322
isomorphic 315, 320

larynx 24, 30, 313, 315, 321, 330
lateralization 283, 288, 289, 295, 303, 315
lax 32, 33, 48, 316, 325, 328
lengthening 51–55, 316, 330
lexical access 65, 316
lexical decision 65, 66, 316
lexical insertion 153, 165–167, 185, 188, 316
lexical item 40, 55, 67, 70–72, 81, 85, 92, 93, 98, 112, 115, 117, 137, 138, 153, 165, 166, 193, 306, 307, 312, 314, 316, 318, 320, 321, 323, 327
lexical redundancy rule 96, 98, 99, 316
lexicon 30, 61, 65, 66, 68–72, 75, 93, 94, 96–98, 101, 108, 112, 117, 128, 129, 151, 164, 165, 187, 193, 316
linguistic competence 4, 12, 15, 30, 38, 61, 79, 86, 126, 129, 130, 136, 162, 170, 176, 216, 313, 316, 321, 328
linguistic determinism 4, 316
linguistic performance 12, 38, 51, 316, 321
linguistic relativity 4, 316, 334
liquid 22, 30, 317, 320
Local Movement Constraint 205–208, 317

locative 168, 185, 186, 317
logical form 262, 264, 317

manner of articulation 24, 317
mass 87, 88, 94, 96, 116, 175, 177, 310, 317
Maximal Onset Principle 47, 49, 50, 58, 59, 317, 324
merge 187, 200, 317
metathesis 67, 317
metrical 56–59, 92, 317
minimal pair 22, 24, 25, 28, 42, 77, 90, 318
minimalism 187, 318
modal 202, 306, 318
modification 71, 90, 91, 139, 144, 158, 169, 188–190
modifier 144, 156, 158, 166–173, 183, 188, 190, 222, 243, 313, 318, 320, 330
modularity 216, 318
morpheme 22, 45, 53, 54, 56, 61, 64, 69–73, 78–82, 86, 89–91, 94, 100, 102–106, 108–114, 117, 267, 298, 305, 307, 309–312, 314, 318, 323, 325, 327
morpho-phonemic 62, 98, 99, 102, 106, 109–112, 114, 306, 318
morpho-syntax 62, 111, 112, 318
morphology 45, 61–63, 68, 71, 72, 75, 77, 79–82, 86, 88, 89, 97, 112, 114, 128, 195, 311, 314, 315, 318
mother 143, 153, 197, 307, 310, 318, 325
motherese 30, 318
move 196, 197, 200, 201, 202, 203, 318
myelin 28, 278, 279, 318
myelinization 28, 318, 319

nasal 24–27, 33, 48, 94, 102, 309, 319, 320, 329, 330
natural class 37, 41, 101, 136, 196, 319
natural language 2, 3, 5, 13, 16, 18, 35, 126–128, 134, 152, 187, 214–216, 219, 227, 228, 235, 258, 259, 265, 308, 310, 312, 319, 329

nature 1, 4, 11, 12, 15, 17, 19, 20, 32, 35, 44, 67, 72, 75, 79, 97, 108, 125, 126, 128–130, 170, 173, 176, 219, 226–230, 246, 253, 254, 264, 307, 311, 316, 319, 320, 322, 328
necessary truth 254, 319
negative evidence 82, 225, 319
negative polarity item 14, 263, 319
neuron 176, 273, 274, 276, 278, 279, 292, 319, 327
neurotransmitter 319, 327
NMRI 273, 319
node 56, 143, 146, 148, 151, 153, 163, 165, 168, 176, 182, 201, 205, 207, 210, 279, 307, 310, 311, 318–320, 323, 325
nominative 117, 118, 178, 180–182, 201, 305, 307, 319
nonisomorphic 1
noun phrase 130, 148, 154, 156, 174, 305, 311–313, 320, 323, 326–328
novel utterance 10, 13, 134, 310, 320
nucleus 46–48, 106, 107, 308, 313, 317, 320, 321, 325, 330
number 113–116, 119, 121–123,137–139, 175, 177–179, 189, 208, 314, 315, 320, 326
nurture 11, 319, 320

obstruent 47, 320, 326
onomatopoeia 22, 320
onset 2, 23, 25, 47–50, 58, 59, 69, 106, 216, 317, 320, 324, 330
ontogeny 2, 3, 68, 69, 125, 310, 320, 322
opaque contexts 248, 254, 259, 321
optimality theory 107, 321
oral 21, 24, 27, 29, 31, 32, 47, 289, 308, 321, 326, 330

parse 132, 133, 321
participle 77, 321
particle 14, 137, 159, 321
performance errors 12, 130, 321
perseverations 300, 321

person 8, 86, 113, 114, 118, 119, 121–123, 132, 137, 162, 175, 182, 209, 314, 315, 318, 321
PET 273, 294, 295, 321
phoneme 42–44, 55, 136, 289, 305, 321
phonemic form 42, 43, 51, 98, 102, 103, 322, 329
phonetic 16, 23, 26–28, 33–40, 42–46, 51, 52, 55, 61, 63–65, 67, 69, 76, 77–81, 86, 98–103, 105, 106, 108–111, 113–115, 117, 132, 136, 181, 195, 305, 306, 308, 315, 321, 322, 327
phonetic alphabet 26, 27, 35, 36, 315, 322, 334
phonetic form 38–40, 42, 45, 46, 51, 52, 55, 78–80, 99, 100, 101, 105, 106, 109, 111, 113, 115, 117, 136, 322, 327
phonology 50, 51, 55, 59, 62, 77, 128, 136, 228, 318, 322, 324, 330
phonotactic 25, 27, 111, 322, 323
phrase-structure grammar 129, 152, 157, 165, 174, 176, 187–189, 202, 322
phrenology 280, 281, 313, 322
phylogeny 3, 217, 320, 322
pied-piping 192, 207, 322
place of articulation 20, 21, 24, 27, 28, 31, 47, 305, 307, 314, 315, 322, 329
possible word 48, 72, 89, 323
possible world 241–243, 247, 253–256, 262, 266, 267, 271, 319, 323
poverty of the stimulus 11, 13, 15, 16, 217
precede 47, 52, 53, 103, 105, 109, 140, 143, 158, 209, 222, 309, 320, 323, 326
predicate calculus 257–259, 262, 263, 268, 272, 319, 323, 324, 325
prefix 45, 46, 53, 61, 70, 73, 79–84, 86, 89, 96, 100, 102, 305, 323, 329
preposition 74, 96, 138, 139, 149, 156, 168, 180–183, 186–188, 192, 197, 215, 226, 248, 308, 310, 317, 320, 323
prepositional phrase 14, 149, 167, 173, 212, 320, 323
prescriptive 5, 7, 43, 74, 131, 192, 311, 323
primary linguistic data 10–16, 30, 31, 65, 126, 135, 157, 178, 216, 217, 220, 222, 323, 326
pro-drop 5, 126, 323

proform 158, 171
progressive 70, 74, 88, 96, 98, 114–116, 137, 163, 170, 306, 323, 330
pronoun 14, 116–123, 129, 130, 132, 154–156, 163, 179–181, 184, 185, 191, 196, 208, 209, 211–213, 224, 263, 305–307, 319, 323, 324
property 249, 252, 253, 254, 259, 260, 324
proposition 113, 230, 248, 249, 251, 252, 254, 255, 262, 268, 324
prosody 295, 299, 324

quantifier 235, 257–265, 268, 269, 270, 312, 323–325, 329

range 233, 324
reaction time 324
recursion 70, 152, 158, 162, 324
reduction 55–58, 245, 289, 302, 324, 330
referent 185, 229, 230–232, 234, 243–256, 259, 262, 271, 308, 311, 324, 325, 329
reflexive 119, 122, 123, 132, 196, 208, 209–213, 224, 225, 306, 307, 324
relative clause 191, 222, 226, 324
Resyllabification Principle 50, 58, 324
retroflex 29, 324
rhyme 66, 308, 325
root 44–46, 56, 62, 70–74, 79–82, 84–86, 89, 90, 96–104, 106–110, 113, 114, 117, 138, 162, 175, 193, 306, 309, 311, 314, 325, 329
rounding 30, 32, 33, 315, 325

saccade 291, 292, 312, 324, 325
schwa 33, 55–57, 103, 105, 325, 330
scope 259–270, 272, 325
semantic displacement 242, 325
semantic value 231–237, 253–255, 259, 260, 266, 267, 309, 325
semantics 228, 234–236, 251, 254, 255, 258, 259, 271, 272, 325, 329
semi-productive 81, 86, 325
semi-vowel 30, 325
sense 249–256, 271, 324, 325

Shortest Movement 205, 206, 312, 325

sister 156, 158, 169, 171, 188, 189, 201, 325

slip of the tongue 12, 325, 326

sonorant 313, 317, 320, 326, 330

Sonority Hierarchy 47, 48, 326

specifier 116, 123, 138, 144, 148, 151, 160, 166, 170, 173–188, 193, 196, 222, 309, 311, 320, 326

spectrogram 18, 40, 41, 53, 62, 100, 306, 326

spoonerism 326

stative 88, 96, 326

stop 21, 24–29, 37, 39, 40–52, 58, 98, 104, 110, 111, 305, 309, 317, 326

strident 110, 111, 326

string 9, 15, 48, 63–65, 70, 89, 128, 130–133, 135, 141, 152, 154, 159, 160, 165, 175, 185, 204, 207, 209, 225, 312, 321, 326

Structure Dependence 221, 326

subordinate clause 131, 160–164, 166, 183, 191, 199, 200, 203, 204, 210, 211, 224, 248, 252–254, 269, 309, 324, 327

Subset Principle 224, 225, 327

Substitutivity of Identicals 247, 252, 255, 327

suffix 44, 56, 61, 70, 73, 76, 77, 79, 80, 83, 84, 86, 88, 89, 94, 96, 98–100, 106, 108, 115, 116, 120, 138, 163, 305, 311, 314, 323, 327, 329

suppletive 77, 327

surface structure 180, 195, 310, 327

synapse 327

synchronic 71, 311, 328

synonymous 14, 244, 245, 327, 328

syntax 62, 72, 111, 112, 127, 129, 152, 170, 188, 228, 236, 318, 328, 330

synthetic 23, 245, 306, 328

tacit 15, 18, 19, 61, 72, 131, 328

tense 5, 75, 77, 78, 86, 98, 99, 100, 101, 102, 103, 104, 105, 106, 108, 109, 110, 111, 112, 113, 114, 115, 122, 123, 137, 139, 146, 176, 193, 202, 224, 241, 242, 253, 266, 267, 305, 327

tense vowels 32, 33, 316, 327, 328

terminal 143, 146, 153, 265, 320, 328

thematic role 94–96, 112, 129, 175, 183–186, 188, 190, 191, 193, 194, 197, 200–202, 302, 305, 312, 323, 327, 328

topicalization 191, 198, 199, 328

trace 194, 196, 201, 206, 207, 302, 308, 328

transformation 140, 194–197, 200, 201, 214, 264, 265, 310, 315, 318, 328

transitive 83, 88, 95–99, 157, 159, 165–167, 169, 180, 181, 187, 190, 191, 193, 195, 197, 200, 248, 259, 266, 315, 329

truth conditions 188, 234, 235, 329

truth value 228, 233, 235–237, 241, 247–249, 251, 252, 255, 256, 327, 329

truth-conditional semantics 234, 235, 271, 329

underlying form 42, 44, 51, 56, 103, 104, 105, 107, 108, 109, 111, 114, 117, 329

ungrammatical 15, 79, 82, 83, 85, 99, 103, 114, 128, 130, 131, 133, 135, 152, 154, 165, 175, 183, 184, 185, 186, 207, 209, 210, 212, 213, 225, 263, 319, 329

universal grammar 214, 226, 310, 313, 316, 326, 329

universal quantifier 257, 262, 270, 329

valence 165, 166, 183, 329

variable 16, 20, 68, 131, 135, 257, 258, 259, 264, 265, 298, 309, 325, 329

verb phrase 151, 172, 173, 309, 313, 320, 330

vocal cords 24, 25, 315, 329, 330

vocal tract 20, 21, 29, 30, 31, 33, 47, 64, 65, 309, 317, 320, 322, 325, 326, 330

voice onset time 23, 25, 330

voiced 22–29, 37, 42, 51–54, 78, 100, 102–105, 108–110, 113, 114, 137, 306, 308, 315, 319, 329, 330

VOT see Voice Onset Time

vowel 17–20, 25, 28–37, 44, 46, 48, 51–58, 73, 77, 86, 94, 104–107, 306, 308, 311–314, 316, 317, 320, 321, 324, 325, 328, 330

Vowel Lengthening 51, 54, 316, 330

Vowel Reduction 55–58, 324, 330

well-formedness condition 116, 184, 330
Wh-question 191, 192, 200, 207, 220, 223, 330

X-bar theory 170, 330